Property of
do not remove.

P9-APG-003

HISTORY OF AMERICAN JOURNALISM

Exam

1. Trace development
2. Comparison
3. Explain briefly following

THURLOW WEED   HORACE GREELEY   CHARLES A. DANA

JAMES GORDON BENNETT   JESSE BUEL   ZACHARIAH POULSON

EPES SARGENT   BENJAMIN RUSSELL   PHILIP FRENEAU

HISTORY OF
AMERICAN JOURNALISM

BY

JAMES MELVIN LEE

Director of the Department of Journalism
New York University

WITH ILLUSTRATIONS

New Edition, Revised

BOSTON AND NEW YORK
HOUGHTON MIFFLIN COMPANY
The Riverside Press Cambridge

COPYRIGHT, 1917 AND 1923, BY JAMES MELVIN LEE

ALL RIGHTS RESERVED

The Riverside Press
CAMBRIDGE · MASSACHUSETTS
PRINTED IN THE U.S.A.

TO

MY FIRST JOURNALISM CLASS

NEW YORK UNIVERSITY SCHOOL

OF COMMERCE, ACCOUNTS

AND FINANCE

PREFACE TO NEW EDITION

ANOTHER printing of this volume affords the author the opportunity to make several changes and additions. New matter in the concluding chapter records recent changes. The first chapter has been revised in the light of recent discoveries of news-sheets published in English but printed in Holland. Additional matter has been inserted here and there throughout the book to supplement and in a few instances to supplant topics treated in the first edition.

Before the book was published American journalism had been a rich field that had long lain fallow. Recently the literary plowshares have been going through the field and turning up many interesting things of which the results may be seen in the books relating to the press in this country. The author reviewed a shelf of such books under the caption "The World's Diary" in *The Yale Review* for January, 1923.

With the passing of the years the author has become convinced that all any history of journalism can hope to do is — in newspaper language — to "hit the high spots." Such a history needs to be supplemented with a bibliography of those books which take up different phases of journalism more in detail. Consequently this new preface may well contain brief mention of such books.

Among the histories of individual papers attention should be called to five books relating to the press in New York. *A Story of a Page* by John L. Heaton is a record of thirty years of the public service and the public discussion in the editorial columns of *The New York World*. In brief, it is a history of that newspaper while under the control of Joseph Pulitzer. *The Evening Post — A Century of Journalism* by Allan Nevins is just what its title implies. One of its chief contributions is the record of the growth and development of literary and dramatic criticism in the daily press, with the columns of *The Post* taken by way of illustration. *The Story of The Sun* by Frank M. O'Brien is a history not only of that newspaper in particular but also of New York journalism in general. It gives a colorful picture of the penny press in its "cradle days," and is especially valuable for its comment about the treatment of the news. Naturally it pays a distinct tribute to Charles Anderson Dana and his influence on American journalism. *The History of The New York Times* by Elmer Davis is divided into two parts: Part I gives the history of the paper under Raymond, Jennings, and Foord; Part II records the achievements with Adolph S. Ochs as publisher and Charles R. Miller as editor. *America's Oldest Daily Newspaper — The New York Globe* by James Melvin Lee, published in the 125th anniversary issue of that newspaper, has since been reprinted in book form.

Public Opinion by Walter Lippmann blazes a new trail. The gist of the book is his assertion, "My conclusion is that public opinions must be organized for the press if they are to be sound, not by the press as is the case to-day." In his chapter on "News, Truth, and Conclusion," the conclusion is reached that the press "is like the beam of a searchlight that moves restlessly about, bringing one episode and then another out of darkness into vision," and hence "men cannot do the work of the world by this light alone." Public opinion regarding the immigrant press and its control has been most vague. Consequently *The Immigrant Press and Its Control* by Robert E. Park fills a long-felt want. *Fifty Years a Journalist* is a potpourri of historical data, notes of human interest, letters, documents, and bits of autobiography by Melville E. Stone, known affectionately throughout the newspaper world as the dean of newspaper men.

In the field of biography, *The Life of Whitelaw Reid* in two volumes by Royal Cortissoz is not only the history of *The New York Tribune* in recent years but also a valuable textbook on many phases of newspaper editing and making. *Marse Henry* by Henry Watterson contains numerous glimpses of editorial friends and their papers, especially those who have died and left no "copy." *Joseph Pulitzer* (new edition is entitled *An Adventure with a Genius*) by Alleyne Ireland gives a glimpse of that great editor as seen by his secretary. The authoritative life of Pulitzer will doubtless come from the pen of his lifelong friend and associate, Don C. Seitz, who now holds the position of publisher of *The Evening World*. *William Rockhill Nelson* by members of the staff of *The Kansas City Star* is the story of a great editor and of the paper he founded. *Editors I Have Known* by R. H. Henry is an interesting chat about many Southern newspapers and their editors. *From McKinley to Harding* by H. H. Kohlsaat, for many years publisher of *The Chicago Record Herald*, portrays present relations between politics and the press. The reader is referred for biographies of earlier editors to the two pamphlets, *Some Great American Newspaper Editors* and *Masters of American Journalism*, published by H. W. Wilson and Co., of New York City.

Possibly *The History of the Arkansas Press* by F. W. Alsopp, business manager of *The Arkansas Gazette*, should be mentioned in this connection. *Journalism in California* by John P. Young covers in an authoritative way the history of journalism on the Pacific Coast. It is especially rich in its data about *The San Francisco Chronicle*, published by M. H. de Young. Walter Williams, Dean of the School of Journalism of the University of Missouri, has compiled what amounts to an encyclopædia of journalism, in his volume *The Press Congress of the World in Hawaii*. This volume is about the only book in English on comparative journalism. In it will be found an account of the modern press in Korea, China, Australia, Switzerland, India, New Zealand, Greece, Norway, Philippine Islands, Russia, etc. The author is glad to welcome since his first edition *History of Journalism in the United States* by George Henry Payne. In this volume considerable stress is put upon the background of politics.

Four recent books in the field of vocational studies should be noted, as they relate to journalism. They are: *Training for the Newspaper Trade* by Don C. Seitz; *Opportunities in the Newspaper Business* by James Melvin Lee; *The Newspaper Man* by Talcott Williams, the first Director of the Pulitzer School of Journalism at Columbia University; and *The Young Man in Journalism* by Chester S. Lord, who was for many years the managing editor of *The New York Sun*. The author's book, *Opportunities in the Newspaper Business*, contains a bibliography of practical books relating to newspaper practice, news writing, newspaper ethics, etc.

The story of schools of journalism, from the time the movement was started at Washington College by General Robert E. Lee down to the present time, will be found in *Instruction in Journalism in Institutions of Higher Education* by James Melvin Lee. It is published by the Bureau of Education at Washington, D.C.

In the field of fiction, two books may be noted. *Success* by Samuel Hopkins Adams is a story dealing with the journalism of New York. *Deadlines* by Henry Justin Smith, news editor of *The Chicago Daily News*, contains the quaint, amusing, and tragic memoirs of the news room.

Journalism in America, in a technical sense, dates from 1619, when John Pory sent from "James Citty" (Jamestown) to his "goode and most gracious Lorde" letters of news about the Virginia Colony. Pory later returned to England and became possibly the foremost writer of news-letters, for which he received a remuneration from the Crown. He is the author's authority for the part played by Archer in the distribution of news-letters and for the important position given to Nathaniel Butter as the father of English journalism. Satirical glimpses of Archer, Butter, Pory, *The Weekly Newes*, *Mercurius Britannicus* — mentioned in the introductory chapter of this book — will be found in the works of Ben Jonson — especially in his play "The Staple of Newes."

J. M. L.

NEW YORK UNIVERSITY
January 1, 1923

PREFACE

THE first printed account dealing in any way with American journalism was undoubtedly a letter addressed to the president of the Massachusetts Historical Society and published for that society in 1798 as a part of its *Proceedings*. This letter, entitled "A Narrative of the Newspapers Printed in New England," was, though signed "A. Z.," written by the Rev. John Elliott, D.D., Pastor of the North Church of Boston. Full of errors, it is interesting only in a sense that it marked the beginning of printed literature on American journalism. A continuation of the narrative by the same author was published in the *Collections* of the Massachusetts Historical Society for 1800. Included in this second narrative was a shorter letter, sketching the newspapers of Connecticut from 1755 to 1800, from the pen of Noah Webster, who had already achieved fame as a distinguished lexicographer.

In 1810 Isaiah Thomas of Worcester, Massachusetts, published his *History of Printing in America*, in two volumes. But for these volumes little would be known about many of the early American printers and their papers. The second edition, revised and enlarged in 1878 by the American Antiquarian Society which had been founded by Mr. Thomas, will always be the standard work for the period which it covers.

Joseph Tinker Buckingham brought out in Boston in 1850 *Specimens of Newspaper Literature*, in two small volumes. With one or two exceptions, its contents were limited to the newspapers of New England. Though based upon the history by Thomas, it enlarged much of the biography and reprinted many extracts from the newspapers discussed. Two years later, Buckingham published two volumes, of about the same size as those already mentioned, entitled *Personal Memoirs and Recollections of Editorial Life*. The latter work was practically a biography of its author, who was closely associated with the journalism of Boston.

Frederic Hudson, for many years the managing director of *The New York Herald*, issued in 1873 his *Journalism in the United States*. This book, which aimed to cover the period from 1690 to 1872, contains many interesting sketches of editors and their papers, but is so full of errors, and is so biased in its point of view, that it cannot be accepted as an authority even for the period with which Mr. Hudson was most familiar.

The United States Government in 1880 issued, in connection with its publications of the census for that year, a *History and Present Conditions of the Newspaper and Periodical Press of the United States*. For the historical part, the book was based upon the works already mentioned and perpetuated their errors. Its statistical matter, being compiled from data furnished to the census, makes it a valuable contribution to journalism history.

In 1881 Charles Dudley Warner, a member of the editorial staff of *The Courant*, of Hartford, Connecticut, published an essay, *The American Newspaper*, which he had read before the Social Science Association at Saratoga Springs, New York, on September 6 of that year. Brief as was this booklet, it was a most comprehensive summary of journalism as it then existed.

Nothing else of general scope, except scattering magazine articles and biographies of individual editors, has appeared to record the developments of American journalism.

The author of this book, while acknowledging his indebtedness to the works already enumerated, has sought in every instance to verify facts at original sources: in his attempt to do so he has been greatly assisted by secretaries of state historical societies to whom acknowledgment for courtesies rendered must first be made.

To acknowledge in print others who have helped in the preparation of the manuscript is obviously impossible, except in a few cases. For information and data about papers of the Colonial Period the author is indebted to Albert Matthews, of Boston, Massachusetts, who has always been ready to answer questions about the early papers of New England, and to Clarence S. Brigham, of Worcester, Massachusetts, who, as secretary of the American Antiquarian Society, has furnished many dates as to the beginnings of early papers in several of the States. To these gentlemen, more than to any other two individuals, he is indebted for help and coöperation.

A partial statement of some indebtedness may be given as follows: Willis J. Abbot, journalism in Chicago; N. A. Baker, first paper in Wyoming; W. W. Ball, journalism in South Carolina; Edmund Booth, activities of *The Grand Rapids Press;* Hilton U. Brown, story of *The Indianapolis News;* John S. Butler, first newspaper in Idaho; William Conant Church, attempt to make *The New York Sun* a religious newspaper; Clyde Augustus Duniway, freedom of press in Massachusetts; Samuel E. Forman, newspaper activities of Philip Freneau; Frederick K. Freeman, history of *The Frontier Index;* Robert L. Fulton, early Nevada papers; C. B. Galbreath, early Ohio papers; H. J. Haskell, data about *The Kansas City Star;* Grace Raymond Hebard, pioneer papers of the West; George H. Himes, early Oregon newspapers; John W. Jordan, first papers in Philadelphia; Daniel S. B. Johnston, journalism in Minnesota Territory; Robert Lathan, early papers of Charleston, South Carolina; Virgil A. Lewis, early West Virginia newspapers; Colonel Clement A. Lounsberry, first paper in North Dakota; Charles R. Miller, Tweed's exposure by *The New York Times;* C. P. J. Mooney, peripatetic career of *The Memphis Appeal;* D. D. Moore, journalism of New Orleans; Albert H. Nelson, early papers of Oklahoma; William Nelson, early New Jersey papers; John R. Rathom, story of *The Providence Journal;* Don C. Seitz, Sunday journalism; Joanna H. Sprague, early papers of Utah; Melville E. Stone, news-gathering associations; Reuben Gold Thwaites, pioneer papers of the West; Rev. Richard H. Tierney, S. J., bulls against news-letters; Lyman Horace Weeks, early American news-letters; Richard H. Waldo, advertising ethics; Louis Wiley, modern tendencies; Stephen B. Weeks, early North Carolina papers; Horace G. Whitney, history of *The Deseret News;* John P. Young, California newspapers.

For many courtesies in checking up dates of newspapers the author is indebted to William A. Slade, Chief of the Periodical Literature, Library of Congress; Horace G. Wadlin, Librarian of Boston Public Library; Wilberforce Eames and John B. Elliott, of the New York Public Library. For information from unpublished manuscripts he is indebted to Victor Hugo Palsits, of the Manuscript Department of the New York Public Library.

The sins of omission are doubtless many owing to the difficulty, in spite of the coöperation received, to get information desired. Suggestions and additional information will be welcomed from any source.

The last chapter, dealing as it does with many points about which there is a difference of opinion, might very properly be considered a sort of appendix for the expression of personal views. In all other chapters a sincere attempt has been made to keep strictly to facts and to documents quoted. No history, however, would be complete without some discussion of the charges brought by critics against the newspapers of to-day. The evidence has been presented and readers may draw their own conclusions about the so-called weakness of the present press.

JAMES MELVIN LEE.

NEW YORK UNIVERSITY,
October, 1917.

CONTENTS

ILLUSTRATIONS

HISTORY OF
AMERICAN JOURNALISM

CHAPTER I

INTRODUCTORY

THE desire to hear or to know the new thing is as old as man. It was an instinct even of the most primitive people. Before the men of the Stone Age traded in the products of the soil or of the hand, they exchanged news. But the historian of journalism is interested primarily not in the news which is spoken, but in that which is written. He finds little to attract his attention until he reaches the invention of the written language. Triangular figures chiseled in stone and strange characters pricked on goatskin may give history, but not news. When the first written newspaper — for letters giving the news were sold and circulated long before the invention of the printing-press — appeared is not known. Some say it was in Rome; others assert it was in Venice. Recent investigators of the question have given the honor to China.

On one matter there has been no difference of opinion: in every country the printed has grown out of the written newspaper. Even after the invention of printing it was a comparatively long time before the printing-press was called upon to aid in the dissemination of news. A little thought on the subject will give the reason. Not until printed sheets could be produced cheaper or quicker — in actual practice both — than the written ones did the gatherer and seller of news forsake the latter for the former. Even then, the complete change was not made suddenly. Libraries and museums have in their archives combination sheets, half printed and half written. It was the custom at one time to leave one page free from printing in order that the latest news or freshest advices might be written in by hand.

Politics and finance have always been the two most important topics in Newspaperdom. There was no systematic collection or distribution of news until men had a political interest in the state, or were involved in financial transactions covering a fairly wide area of trade and transportation. In most countries both conditions were present before regular trade in news arose. The walled city required no newspaper: the tower watchman and the king's herald did the reporting. When, however, officials left the city to govern undefended towns, there must be devised some new method of publishing the official proclamations and of giving the gossip of the capital. When commercial houses began to import and export goods, maritime news had a cash value and might be sold.

ROMAN NEWS-LETTERS

By way of illustration, the Republic of Rome may be mentioned. As early as 449 B.C. official protocols of the transaction of the Senate were kept and deposited in the Temple of Ceres, in charge of the police commissioners (*ædiles*). It was permissible to take notes or to have them taken and then to communicate these memoranda to others. When sent to the provincial governors, or tax-farmers, these notes, with their additions of local gossip, became news-letters. Their writers, in the early days of the Republic, were intelligent slaves: later, bonded freemen took up the work and sold their letters to any one who would pay the price. Signs of "courtesy to the press" began to appear about this time, for these news-writers could, upon the presentation of proper credentials, obtain admission to the meetings of the Senate. Wealthy Romans in the provinces continued to supplement these regular news-letters by special reports from their own correspondents, just as the modern newspaper may, in addition to the service of the Associated Press, have its own correspondents at strategic points to send in special items — or "stories" as they are called in the language of the newspaper office.

Antony, for example, was one of these men who kept in touch with the political situation and the financial condition in Rome by means of such news-epistles. In a way, he owned his own newspaper of a single edition, for the man who wrote these news-letters was not allowed to write to other officials. There were in the city, however, men who sent out two or more news-letters to patrons.

In the year 51 B.C., when Cicero left for Cilicia, his friend Cælius promised "to write a full and careful account" of all that went on in Rome. The latter, being "the laziest man in the world at writing letters," shifted the burden of his correspondence to the shoulders of one of these professional writers of news. Later, Cælius did find time to send this line: "If the news-letters do not give you what you want, let me know, for I do not want to spend my money only to bore you." Cicero's reply was, in modern phraseology, "Stop my paper!" He did not care for the sporting news of gladiatorial matches; he did not want the court news, chronicling the adjournment of trials; he did not read with interest, so he asserted, the news that was n't fit to write — "such things as nobody ventured to tell" him when he was in Rome. What he desired was the political news of the city, and reports of occurrences where there was something especially affecting himself. In the last suggestion he gave to the professional journalist at Rome a tip which the modern school of journalism follows when it instructs its students to put names into the newspaper.

CÆSARS AS JOURNALISTS

First place in Roman journalism, however, belongs to Julius Cæsar, another friend of high-school days. One of his first acts after he became Consul in 60 B.C. was to issue a decree that the reports of the doings of the Senate should be daily written and published. Knowing the value of publicity, he hoped in this way to change the crooked politics of the time; at least, he was determined that no secret acts of the Senate should interfere with his plans. The result of Cæsar's decree was the establishment of that precursor of the modern daily newspaper, *Acta Diurna*, or *The Daily Acts*. At first, this daily compilation was published on a whitened wooden board, called *album* (white). In other words, the Romans got their news in the Forum, much as we often get an epitome of the latest events by standing and watching the bulletin-boards of the modern newspaper.

The Daily Acts had a special department in which were
recorded all the births and deaths of the city. It did not neglect
financial news, for it recorded the receipt by the treasury of
taxes from the provinces. Like the modern newspaper, it paid
special attention to both civil and criminal courts and made a
special feature of election news. Everything done by the Imperial
family was chronicled faithfully. One other fact must be noticed
in passing — both Julius and Augustus Cæsar knew how to work
the press. The former secured good display in *The Daily Acts*
when he declined the title of king; and the latter promoted his
attack on race suicide by inserting items about Romans who had
large families. In addition to the bulletin-board edition of *The
Daily Acts* there was a written one for circulation in the home.
One Latin author mentioned a Roman lady reading her morning
paper, and another said that he would wait at Thessalonica for
The Daily Acts. Seneca once boasted that his liberality was not
"written up" in *The Daily Acts*. Based upon this edition was
a still larger written newspaper sent to subscribers outside of
Rome. The professional journalist took the items of *The Daily
Acts*, gathered others of his own, and then, mounting a little
platform in his shop, dictated the news to a dozen slaves who
produced a written newspaper of twelve copies. The size of such
an edition was limited only by the number of slaves employed.

ORIGIN OF SENSATIONAL JOURNALISM

The Daily Acts probably continued even after the capital had
been moved from Rome to Constantinople. For fifteen centuries
little advance was made in the written newspaper — unless the
ability to manufacture news might in some way be considered a
development. The ability to invent news and to mix truth and
falsehood became almost a profession (*ars*) in Rome, and was
carried to such an extent that the church was forced to take
drastic action. Papal bulls were issued against the writing of
such news-letters, under penalties recorded in both temporal
and ecclesiastical laws. In 1572 the saintly Pope Pius V threatened "death and confiscation of property," according to "the
degree of the offense and the rank of the offender." His successor,
Gregory XIII, a great educationist, issued another bull which,

while leaving all former laws about the news-letters in full force, declared that writers of *lettere d' avvisi* should be sent "to the galleys, either for life or for a term, without hope of pardon."

THE WRITTEN NEWSPAPER

The written newspaper spread, chiefly by way of Venice, to other countries. Many fanciful tales are told about the contribution of Venice to journalism. The assertion has been made that that city also had its *Daily Acts*, for the privilege of seeing which a subscription price of a *gazetta* was asked, and that from this custom came the name so often applied to newspapers, *The Gazette*. But these rumors are doubtless highly colored, for this term did not come into general use until a much later date. Venice did have, however, the first press bureau, an organization which gathered and retailed news in a wholesale way. Its news-letters were far more timely in contents than those which had previously gone out from Rome.

By 1600, what might be called epistolary newspapers were appearing in Italy, in France, in Germany, and in England. It was in Germany that such sheets reached their highest development. France, however, led in the spoken newspaper. In Paris there were men who stood at street corners and told the gossip of the city. When they had finished, they passed around the hat. At night they met at a tavern where they swapped news-items gathered during the day.

THE SPOKEN NEWSPAPER

In the Swiss village of Champery the spoken newspaper still survives. Curiously enough, it is a Sunday edition. On that day, immediately after church, the villagers hear *The Town Crier*. Its editor, literally the publishing bailiff, appears on a balcony overhanging the street and announces the news to those on the village green. First of all, he gives the information about the decisions of the courts and announces the decrees both federal and cantonal. He speaks of the fines and penalties incurred by the citizens of the community and brings to public attention all the official decisions of the civil authorities. All citizens are expected to listen to this spoken newspaper, and no one can fall back, if he transgresses one of the published decrees, on the assertion that he was not present when *The Town Crier* announced the official decree.

The Town Crier of Champery has its spoken advertising department. Its publisher gives notice, by spoken word, of the public auctions of household goods, cattle, etc., as announced by the Office of Law and Bankruptcy. *The Town Crier* gives the news of mercantile houses, with the prices of the goods they are offering. It gives notice of lost and found articles and quotes the price paid by local establishments for farm products. In other words, it takes the place of a local printed newspaper, which, up to the present time, has never existed in Champery.

BIRTH OF ENGLISH JOURNALISM

In some respects the evolution of journalism in London was the same as that found in Rome. Men of wealth lived only four or five months in London and spent the rest of the year in the country. While away from the city, they wanted to know the doings of the court and the gossip of the coffee-houses. To keep themselves informed, they hired professional letter-writers who gathered the items and then forwarded the most important by special post. One of the best and hence busiest writers of such letters was one Thomas Archer. So excellent was his service that demand for his letters became larger than he could supply by his pen. To meet this demand he called the printing-press to his aid, and instead of posting items on irregular days of the week, he put them all in one letter, printed it, and mailed it by a certain post. Nathaniel Butter was the first regular publisher of this printed news-letter, *The Weekly Newes*, and posterity has called him rather than Archer the founder of the English newspaper press. There had been an occasional printed news-sheet or news-book before the appearance of *The Weekly Newes*, but to Nathaniel Butter belongs the honor of "printing all the news of the day upon a single sheet and publishing it regularly week by week upon fixed days and of giving it a distinctive title at a time when there was nothing that could with strictness be called a newspaper." Papers with dates prior to 1622, when *The Weekly*

THE
CONTINVATION
OF OVR WEEKLY
Newes, from the 30 of *Decem-*
ber, to the 5 of *Ianuary.*

From Rome, Venice, Naples, Millan, Sauoy,
Germany, France, Denmarke, the Low-Coun-
tries, and diuers other places of
Chriftendome.

Faithfully Colle&ed and Tranflated out
of the Originalls.

LONDON,
Printed for MERCVRIVS
BRITANNICVS, 1625.

Newes first appeared, have come to light from time to time. Some of these have been shown to be forgeries, but as early as 1620 news-sheets were printed in English at Amsterdam — "the staple of news" at that time — and shipped over to England for distribution. The earliest of these, dated December 2, 1620, bore the imprint George Veseler. The fact that it had no title of any sort suggests that it marks the beginning of the English press. The name commonly applied by contemporary writers to the news-sheets printed first in Holland and later in England was "corontos." Their publishers were called "coronto-coiners," and they were sold in the book stalls of St. Paul's and at the Exchange. Later these "corontos," instead of being printed on a single sheet, appeared in pamphlet form. Typical of such was *Mercurius Britannicus*. Technically this name was that of the publisher and not that of the paper. Ben Jonson in his "Staple of Newes" makes no end of fun of these early attempts to print the news.

CONDITIONS IN CHINA

In the case of China, however, the change from the written to the printed sheet was abrupt. Chinese publishers wasted no time by printing from movable type, but jumped at once from the hand-written production to the impression from a wooden block. The news was written on a transparent sheet, pasted face downward on a wooden block, and then, save where the Chinese characters showed, the wood was chiseled away. The block was then inked, pressed upon a sheet of white paper, and lo, a printed newspaper!

By way of conclusion, it may be noted that the English term "newspaper" was first used, according to the best information obtainable, in the year 1670, when it appeared in a letter addressed to Charles Perrot, the second editor of *The Oxford Gazette*. The expression was found in the request, "I wanted your newes paper Monday last past."

CHAPTER II

PRECURSORS OF AMERICAN NEWSPAPERS

AMONG the broadsides published in New England during the early colonial days, to correct false reports, may be found certain printed sheets so closely resembling a newspaper that such a term has been applied to them. While they did give some domestic news of the colonies and while they were printed to sell as news sheets, they had no regularity in publication, being issued only once. Consequently, they are to be regarded as the precursors of the newspaper press and not as real newspapers.

GREEN'S BROADSIDE

One of the earliest of these broadsides — in some ways the most important — was *The Present State of the New-English Affairs* (1689). It was a single sheet, 8 x 14½ inches, printed on only one side. Its printer and publisher was Samuel Green. The first part consisted of an extract from a letter of the Reverend Increase Mather, dated at Deal in Kent, to Simon Baldwin, Governor of the Massachusetts colony in New England. The most important item in the sheet was a "passage extracted from the publick *News-Letter*" (of London) for July 6, 1689. Because the extract has historical value and at the same time shows, to a certain extent, the kind of news found in *The London News-Letter*, it is worth quotation: —

The people of New England having made a thorow Revolution, and secured the publick Criminals. On Thursday last, the Reverend and Learned Mr. Mather, President of the Colledge, and Minister of Boston, waited on the King; and in a most Excellent Speech laid before His Majesty, the State of that People; saying, That they were sober, and Industrious, and fit for Martial Service; and all with their Lives and Interests were at His Majesties Command, to tender the same unto His Majesty: That they desired nothing but His Majesties Acceptance of what they had done, and His Protection; and that if His Majesty pleased to encourage and Commission them, He might easily be Emperour of America. His Majesty assured him, that He was pleased with what was done for Him, and for themselves in the Revolution, and that their Priviledges and Religion should be secured unto them.

The Present State of the New-English Affairs was published "to prevent false reports." Other news-handbills must have circulated rather extensively about this time, for, toward the close of 1689, the Massachusetts authorities passed a resolution that "whereas many papers have been lately printed and dispersed, tending to the disturbance of the peace," any person guilty of printing or even concealing "such like papers" should be "accounted enemies" of the Government and "be proceeded against as such with the uttermost severity." Nothing did more to hinder the development of American journalism than the requirement, "Published by Authority." Freedom of the press came only after a hard-fought struggle.

A NEAR-NEWSPAPER

An attempt, however, was made in 1690 to establish what would have been a newspaper had there been more than one issue. On September 25 of that year, Benjamin Harris brought out, in Boston, *Publick Occurrences*. It was to have been published once a month or oftener "if any glut of occurrences happen." As it was not published by authority, the Governor and Council promptly found that the pamphlet, as it was called, contained "reflections of a very high nature" and ordered its suppression. They also, in the same resolution, forbade "any person or persons for the future to set forth anything in print without license first obtained from those that are, or shall be appointed by the Government to grant the same." Because of this drastic action, it was almost fifteen years before another attempt was made to give Boston a newspaper.

Publick Occurrences, Both Forreign and Domestick, was a small, four-page sheet, $7\frac{1}{2}$ x $11\frac{1}{2}$ inches, and had two columns to the page, except on the fourth, which was free from any printing. The only known copy of this sheet is preserved in the London Public Record Office, where it was found in 1845 by the Reverend Joseph B. Felt, of Salem. Frederic Hudson, in his "Journalism in the United States," published an expurgated copy of its contents which has since been reprinted in many American publications, and in 1901 Samuel Abbott Green, of the Massachusetts Historical Society, reproduced the original in facsimile.

An unexpurgated version of *Publick Occurrences* is here given for the sake of historical accuracy. The purpose for which the sheet was printed, as well as the way in which the items were told, will surely attract the attention of the reader of to-day. Harris had a keener sense of news value than most of the other men who started Colonial newspapers.

PUBLICK OCCURRENCES

Both Forreign and Domestick.

Boston, Thursday, Sept. 25th. 1690.

It is designed, that the Countrey shall be furnished once a moneth (or if any Glut of Occurrences happen, oftener,) with an account of such considerable things as have arrived unto our Notice.

In order hereunto, the Publisher will take what pains he can to obtain a Faithful Relation of all such things; and will particularly make himself beholden to such Persons in Boston whom he knows to have been for their own use the diligent Observers of such matters.

The which is herein proposed, is, First, That Memorable Occurrents of Divine Providence may not be neglected or forgotten, as they too often are. Secondly, That people every where may better understand the Circumstances of Publique Affairs, both abroad and at home; which may not only direct their Thoughts at all times, but at some times also to assist their Businesses and Negotiations.

Thirdly, That something may be done toward the Curing, or at least the Charming of that Spirit of Lying, which prevails amongst us, wherefore nothing shall be entered, but what we have reason to believe is true, repairing to the best fountains for our Information. And when there appears any material mistake in any thing that is collected, it shall be corrected in the next.

Moreover, the Publisher of these Occurrences is willing to engage, that whereas, there are many False Reports, maliciously made, and spread among us, if any well-minded person will be at the pains to trace any such false Report, so far as to find out and Convict the First Raiser of it, he will in this Paper (unless just Advice be given to to the contrary) expose the Name of such person, as A malicious Raiser of a false Report. It is suppos'd that none will dislike this Proposal, but such as intend to be guilty of so villanous a Crime.

That Christianized Indians in some parts of Plimouth, have newly appointed a day of Thanksgiving to God for his Mercy in supplying their extream and pinching Necessities under their late want of Corn, & for His giving them now a prospect of a very Comfortable Harvest. Their Example may be worth Mentioning.

Tis observed by the Husbandmen that altho' the With-draw of so great a strength of them, as what is in the Forces lately gone for Canada, made them think it almost impossible for them to get well through the Affairs of their Husbandry at this time of the year, yet the Season has been so unusually favourable that they scarce find any want of the many hundreds of hands, that are gone from them; which is looked upon as a Merciful Providence.

While the barbarous Indians were lurking about Chelmsford, there were missing about the beginning of this month a couple of Children belonging to a man of that Town, one of them aged about eleven, the other aged about nine years, both of them supposed to be fallen into the hands of the Indians.

A very Tragical Accident happened at Water-Town, the beginning of this Month, an Old man, that was of somewhat a Silent and Morose Temper, but one that had long Enjoyed the reputation of a Sober and Pious Man, having newly buried his Wife, The Devil took advantage of the Melancholy which he thereupon fell into, his Wives discretion and industry had long been the support of his Family, and he seemed hurried with an impertinent fear that he should now come to want before he dyed, though he had very careful friends to look after him who kept a strict eye upon him, least he should do himself any harm. But one evening escaping from them into the Cowhouse, they there quickly followed him found him hanging by a Rope, which they had used to tye their Calves withal, he was dead with his feet near touching the Ground.

Epidemical Fevers and Agues grow very common, in some parts of the Country, whereof, tho' many dye not, yet they are sorely unfitted for their imployments; but in some parts a more malignant Fever seems to prevail in such sort that it usually gores thro' a Family where it comes, and proves Mortal unto many.

The Small-pox which has been raging in Boston, after a manner very Extraordinary, is now very much abated. It is thought that far more have been sick of it then were visited with it, when it raged so much twelve years ago, nevertheless it has not been so Mortal. The number of them that have dyed in Boston by this last Visitation is about three hundred and twenty, which is not perhaps half so many as fell by the former. The Time of its being most General, was in the Months June, July, and August, then 'twas that sometimes in some one Congregation on a Lords-day there would be Bills desiring prayers for above an hundred Sick. It seized upon all sorts of people that came in the way of it, it infected even Children in the bellies of Mothers that had themselves undergone the Disease many years ago for some such were now born full of the Distemper. 'Tis not easy to relate the Trouble and Sorrow that poor Boston has felt by this Epidemical Contagion. But we hope it will be pretty nigh Extinguished, by that time twelve month when it first began to Spread. It now unhappily spreads in several other places, among which our Garrisons in the East are to be reckoned some of the greatest Sufferers.

Altho' Boston did a few weeks ago, meet with a Disaster by Fire, which consumed about twenty Houses near the Mill-Creek, yet about midnight, between the sixteenth and seventeenth of this Instant, another Fire broke forth near the South-Meeting-House, which consumed about five or six houses, and had almost carried the Meeting house it self, one of the fairest Edifices in the Country, if God had not remarkably assisted the Endeavours of the People to put out the Fire. There were two more considerable Circumstances in the Calamities of this Fire, one was that a young man belonging to the House where the Fire began, unhappily perished in the Flames; it seems that tho' he might sooner awake than some others who did escape, yet he some way lost those Wits that should have taught him to help himself. Another was that the best furnished PRINTING–PRESS, of those few that we know of in *America* was lost; a loss not presently to be repaired.

There lately arrived at Piscataqua, one Papoon from Penobscot, in a small Shallop, wherein he had used to attend upon the pleasure of Casteen, but took his opportunity to run away, and reports: That a Vessel of small Bulk bound from Bristol to Virginia, having been so long at Sea, till they were prest with want, put in at Penobscot instead of Piscataqua, where the Indians and French seized her, and Butchered the Master, and several of the men: but that himself who belonged unto the Ships Crew, being a Jersey-man, was more favourably used, & found at length an advantage to make his Escape.

The chief discourse of this month has been about the affairs of the Western Expedition against Canada. The Albanians, New-Yorkers and the five Nations of Indians, in the West, had long been pressing of the Massachusetts to make an Expedition by Sea, into Canada, and still made us believe that they stayed for us, and that while we assaulted Quebeck, they would pass the Lake, and by Land make a Descent upon Mount Real. Accordingly this Colony with some assistance from our kind Neighbours of Plimouth; fitted an Army of near five and twenty hundred men, and a Navy of two and thirty sail; which went from hence the beginning of the last August, under the Command of the Honourable Sir William Phips.

In the mean time the English Colonies & Provinces in the West raised Forces, the Numbers whereof have been reported five or six hundred. The Honourable General Winthrop was in the Head of these, and advanced within a few miles of the Lake; He there had some good number of Maqua's to joyn his Forces, but contrary to his Expectation, it was found that the Canoo's to have been ready for the Transportation of the Army over the Lake, were not prepared, and the other Nations of Indians, that should have come to this Campaign, sent their Excuses, pretending that the Small-pox was among them, and some other Trifles. The General Meeting with such vexing disappointments, called a Councel of War, wherein 'twas agreed, That it was impossible for them to Prosecute their Intended Expedition. However he dispatched away the Maqua's to the French Territories, who returned with some Success, having slain several of the French, and brought home several Prisoners, whom they used in a manner too barbarous for any English to approve. The General coming back to Albany, there happened a misunderstanding, between him and the Lieutenant Governour of New-york which occasioned much discourse, but produced not those effects which were feared of it. Where lay the bottom of these miscarriages is variously conjectured, if any people further West than Albany, have been Tampering with the Indians, to desert the business of Canada, we hope time will discover it. And if Almighty God will have Canada to be subdu'd without the assistance of those miserable Salvages, in whom we have too much confided, we shall be glad, that there will be no Sacrifice offered up to the Devil, upon this occasion; God alone will have all the Glory.

'Tis possible, we have not so exactly related the Circumstances of this business, but this Account, is as near exactness, as any that could be had, in the midst of many various reports about it.

Another late matter of discourse, has been an unaccountable destruction befalling a body of Indians, that were our Enemies. This body of French Indians had a Fort somewhere far up the River, and a party of Maqua's returning from the East Country, where they have at a great rate pursued and terrified those Indians which have been invading of our North-East Plantations, and Killed their General Hope Hood among the rest; resolved to visit this Fort; but they found the Fort ruined, the Canno's cut to pieces, and the people all either Butchered or Captived. This gave them no little surprise, and they gave the English this account of it. That a body of Maqua's lately returning from the Spoil of Canada brought several French Prisoners with them That calling at this Fort in their way, the Indians there seeing themselves unable to resist them did pass divers Complements with them and partake of their Booties, That a French Captive after this, escaping from the Maqua's informed the French that these Indians had revolted unto the Maqua's, and hereupon the French or their Indians made a sudden Sally forth upon them, and utterly destroyed them, tho' they were in reality of their own party still.

Two English Captives escaped from the hands of Indians and French at Pascadamoquady, came into Portsmouth on the sixteenth Instant & say, That when Capt. Mason was at Fort Real, he cut the faces, and ript the bellies of two Indians, and threw a third Over board in the sight of the French, who informing the other Indians of it, they have in revenge barbarously Butcher'd forty Captives of our that were in their hands.

These two Captives escaped in a Shallop, which our Enemies intended to have set out with all the Circumstances of a Fishing Shallop but to have indeed fill'd it with Indians that should have Clap^td on board any English Vessel that came in their way; They say that about three or four weeks ago, some Indians were coming this way to War, but crossing a path which they supposed to be of the Maqua's, they followed it until they discovered a place where some Canoo's were making, whereupon twenty Kennebeck Indian-Warriors went to look further after the business, who never yet returned. Which gives hope that they may come short home, but upon this the Squaws are sent to Penobscot, and the men stand on their Defence.

Portsmouth Sept. 20th. Two days since arrived here a small Vessel from Barbaboes, in which is a Letter to Captain H. K. of 19th August that speaks thus,

Christophers is wholly taken from the French as also a small Island called Stacia; we are very strong in Shipping, and our Ships of War are now gone for Tobago, a very good place to shelter from any Storms, after the suspicious months are over, they will attack the rest of the French places. We have News here that K. William is safe arrived in Ireland, and is marched with one hundred and forty thousand Foot and Horse. Himself leads the Body, Duke Scomburgh the right Wing, and the Earl of Oxford the left Wing, Duke Hamilton of Scotland leads the forlorn Hope with ten thousand men under him. Great victory they dayly have, and much people dayly come in to him, with submission: He has 200 Shipping with him of one sort or other, above one hundred Sail dayly run between Ireland and England, with meat for Man and Beast; His Majesty being unwilling to trust false Ireland for it. France is in much trouble (and fear) not only with us but also with his Son, who has revolted against him lately, and has great reason if reports be true, that the Father used to lie with the Sons Wife. He has got all the Hugonots, and all the dissatisfied Papists, with the great force of the D. of Lorraign, and are now against him, resolving to depose him of his life and Kingdom.

It's Reported the City of Cork in Ireland, has proclaimed K. William, and turned their French Landlords out of Doors; of this there wants further confirmation.

From Plimouth Sept. 22. We have an Account that on Friday the 12th Instant, in the night, our Forces Landing privately, forthwith surrounded Pegypscot Fort; but finding no Indians there, they March'd to Amonoscoggin. There on the Lords-day, they kill'd and took 15 or 16 of the Enemy, and recovered five English Captives mostly belonging to Oyster-River; who advised, that the men had been gone about ten days down to a River, to meet with the French, and the French Indians; where they expected to make up a Body of 300 men, and design first against Wells or Piscataqua.

On Tuesday, the Army came to our Vessels at Macquot, but one of the Vessels touching a Ground stopt a Tide; by which means, young Bracket, who was a considerable distance up the River, above Amonoscoggin Fort, being advised by an Indian that ran away from Amonoscoggin, that an English Army was there attempted his Escape, and came down to the Sloop, just as they came on their Sail.

On Thursday, they landed at Saco; a Scout of 60 men of ours discover a party of the Enemy, and had the Advantage of killing three of them, and taking nine Canoos, and an English captive named, Thomas Baker, who informed, that the Enemy had left a considerable Plunder at Pegypscut-Plains, which he supposed the Enemy was gone to secure. Whereupon the Army immediately embark'd, and arriving there that night, the next morning found the Bever-Plunder accordingly.

While our Vessels where at Anchor in Cascoe-Bay, our Auxiliary Indians lodging on shore, and being too careless in their Watch, the Enemy made an Attaque upon them. The English forth with repair'd to their Relief; but were sorely galled, by an Embuscado of Indians, The Enemy soon quitted the Field, escaping with their Canoo's, whereof ours took several. In the Surprise, we lost 9 men, and had about 20 wounded; the blow chiefly fell on our dead Friends, the Plimouth Forces; 15 being kill'd and wounded of Captain Southworth's Company.

In spite of the fact that *Publick Occurrences* was ordered suspended, Benjamin Harris later met with public favor. In December, 1692, the official records show that he was ordered "to print the acts and laws made by the Great and General Court, or Assembly of their Majesties of Massachusetts-Bay in New England." Along about 1695 he returned to England where he became the publisher of *The London Post*.

WRITTEN AND SPOKEN NEWSPAPERS

Substitutes for the newspaper were found in two rather striking places — the public tavern and the local church. In the former, items of community interest were freely passed along over pipes and ale. The walls of the tavern were frequently decorated with notices of what to-day appear in the newspaper; some in the advertising columns, others in the text. Foreign news was found in the different gazettes for which the tavern subscribed. In order that such papers might be available for the perusal of news, a notice was frequently posted to the effect that persons learning to read would please use old copies of the gazettes. In some sections the news feature in the tavern was an attraction. At Bridgeton, New Jersey, a written newspaper called *The Plain-Dealer* was publicly posted at "Matthew Potter's Bar." A notice informed the public that those interested might read the paper by calling at the tavern every Tuesday morning. Frequently, however, the contents of *The Plain-Dealer* were more like essays than news-items. Issues, however, were not without human interest. One number, for example, discussed "bundling with the girls"; another made a special plea for more patriotism on the part of the Jersey colonies. Whenever a colonial farmer visited a tavern, he always carried the news away — possibly along with other things which he ought not to have had.

America has not been without its spoken newspaper. The clergy of New England frequently related or referred to items of news. The bellman, as he made his rounds, sometimes told other things besides giving the hour and informing the public that all was well. The spoken newspaper probably reached its highest development in the United States in Detroit, Michigan. The Reverend Father Gabriel Richard, a priest of the Order of Sulpice, who first came to that place as resident pastor of the Roman Catholic Church of St. Anne, was its conductor. To arouse the public and awaken an interest in the affairs of the Government, he appointed a town crier who every Sunday at the doors of his church told the public in general and the congregation in particular all the news that was fit to speak. In addition, this public crier mentioned the auction sales and related other advertising announcements. Later, to supplement the spoken newspaper, a written edition was posted at a convenient place near the church. Father Richard was assisted in his news enterprise by Theopolis Meetz, the sacristan of St. Anne's Church, but later, a printer and publisher.

The evolution of journalism in America has been much the same as that in other countries. There have been spoken newspapers, written newspapers, and later printed newspapers. In other words, journalism history has again repeated itself.

CHAPTER III

THE FIRST AMERICAN NEWSPAPER — THE BOSTON NEWS–LETTER

THE action of the Governor of Massachusetts in suppressing *Publick Occurrences* and the continued opposition of the Boston clergy in guarding its influence prevented any attempt to found another paper until 1704. The chief way that news was circulated, except for an occasional broadside, was through pulpit announcements and semi-public letters.

CAMPBELL'S WRITTEN NEWS-LETTERS

Foremost among these writers of news-letters was one, John Campbell, the postmaster at Boston. He made a practice of sending rather regularly letters to the various governors of the New England colonies. These letters, after being read, were passed along to others so that they had a comparatively wide circulation. Sometimes they were publicly posted so that their contents might be read after the manner news was communicated in ancient Rome. An examination of the Campbell letters show that they were what might be termed written newspapers. By way of illustration, the following one is reproduced from "The Proceedings of the Massachusetts Historical Society": —

BOSTON June 14th 1703

On the 8th Instant the Assembly was adjourned unto the Last Wednesday of this month.

On the 9th His Excell. being Accompanyed with Severall Gentlemen, went to his Govermt of New hampshire.

On the 10th a Sloop from the Bay of Campeachy brings no News.

On the 11 Esqr. Bromfield mett wth a Sore Mischance, coming out of his Warehouse door a Sloop Lying before his Warehouse door the mr of the Sloop hoising up his boom, the Sail being Loose to Dry it, gave Such a Swing that it struct him upon his Shouldier, Brock his Collar bone, put his Shouldier out of joynt, was for sometime speechless with the Stroak but its hoped He'l Recover and do well —

On the 12th Arrived a Sloop from the Bay of Vandovas, one Lamson m[r]., who sayes that Cap[t]. Wheeler that went hence for Jamaica is Dead his men all prest on board men of warr and his Ship Hal'd up.

Cap[t]. Blew from R[d]. Island is arrived here this Day.

The Gosport and Gally is this Day sailed for Piscataqua.

Philad. May 28: Arrived a Sloop in 22 Dayes from Antegua in whom Came Cap[t]. Roach an Inhabitant of that Island wth his family to Setle here, brings the bad news of our forces Leaving Guardilup untaken wth. the Loss of about 1000 by Enemy and Sickness. The Day (?he) Sailed the Gener[ll]. Arrived who has lost his Eye Sight wth Some Distemper, the rest of the fleett and forces were Exspected from Guardiloop, the Gene[ll]. Layes the Miscarridge so to heart that it's thought he'l hardly Recover upon it.

It's said that the men of warr that were at Guardiloop were all ordered home, and were to Sail the 29th may.

Some prisoners that made their Escape from Martinico to Antegua Says that the french were fitting out abundance of privateers from that place many of them Stout Vessels.

It's reported in the West Indies that mons[r]. Ponti was daylie Exspected there wth a Squadron of men of warr of 22 Sail besydes other Vessells.

The 31 Arrived here a Sloop from Jamaica 28 Dayes passage, Admir[ll]. Whetstone wth his Squadron was at Jamaica, he's done nothing only burnt a Ship the french took from us and two privateer Sloops at Pettiquavis.

A fleet of merchantmen between 40 & 50 Sail und[r] Convoy a 2 or 3 men of warr was to sail in May from Jamaica to England.

N Yorke June 7: Last Week Arrived here a Sloop from Coraso, 21 Dayes passage sayes the Dutch have an open Trade wth New Spain and that the Governour of Coraso has stopt Cap[t]. Wrightington & his Comp[a] who Sailed from R Island on what pretence knows not.

Cap[t]. Bond & Cap[t]. Sinclair Sails in a fourth Night or 3 Week's for London.

Boston Cap[t]. Travise sails to Day or Too morrow for London —
    (Superscribed)

To The Hon[ble]
John Winthrop Esq[r]
Gov[r] of Connecticut
N London

ffranke

CAMPBELL'S PRINTED NEWS-LETTERS

So numerous were the requests to John Campbell for extra news advices that neither he nor his brother, Duncan Campbell, was able to make the supply equal to the demand simply by the pen. He was forced to employ the printing-press. His first

N. E.   Numb. 1.

The Boston News-Letter.

Publiſhed by Authority.

From **Monday** April 17. to **Monday** April 24. 1704.

London Flying-Poſt from Decemb 2d to 4th. 1703.

Etters from *Scotland* bring us the Copy of a Sheet lately Printed there, Intituled, *A reaſonable Alarm for Scotland. In a Letter from a Gentleman in the City, to his Friend in the Country, concerning the preſent Danger of the Kingdom and of the Proteſtant Religion.*

This Letter takes Notice, That Papiſts ſwarm in that Nation, that they traffick more avowedly than formerly, & that of late many Scores of Prieſts and Jeſuites are come thither from *France*, and gone to the North, to the Highlands & other places of the Country. That the Miniſters of the Highlands and North gave in large Liſts of them to the Committee of the General Aſſembly, to be laid before the Privy-Council.

It likewiſe obſerves, that a great Number of other ill-affected perſons are come over from *France*, under pretence of accepting her Majeſty's Gracious Indemnity ; but, in reality, to increaſe Diviſions in the Nation, and to entertain a Correſpondence with *France*. That their ill Intentions are evident from their talking big, their owning the Intereſt of the pretended King *James* VIII. their ſecret Cabals, and their buying up of Arms and Ammunition, whereever they can find them.

To this he adds the late Writings and Actings of ſome diſaffected perſons, many of whom are for that Pretender, that ſeveral of them have declar'd they had rather embrace Popery than conform to the preſent Government, that they refuſe to pray for the Queen, but uſe the ambiguous word Sovereign, and ſome of them pray in expreſs Words for the King and Royal Family ; and the charitable and generous Prince who has ſhew'd them ſo much Kindneſs. He likewiſe takes notice of Letters not long ago found in Cypher, and directed to a Perſon lately come thither from St. *Germains*.

He ſays that the greateſt Jacobites, who will not qualifie themſelves by taking the Oaths to Her Majeſty, do now with the Papiſts and their Companions from St. *Germains* ſet up for the Liberty of the Subject, contrary to their own Principles, but meerly to keep up a Diviſion in the Nation. He adds, that they aggravate thoſe things which the People complain of, as to *England's* refuſing to allow them a freedom of Trade, &c. and do all they can to foment Diviſions betwixt the Nations, and to obſtruct a Redreſs of thoſe things complain'd of

The Jacobites, he ſays, do all they can to perſwade the Nation that their pretended King is a Proteſtant in his Heart, tho' he dares not declare it while under the Power of *France* , that he is acquainted with the Miſtakes of his Father's Government, will govern us more according to Law and endear himſelf to his Subjects.

They magnifie the Strength of their own Party, and the Weakneſs and Diviſions of the other, in order to facilitate and haſten their Undertaking ; they argue themſelves out of their Fears, and into the higheſt aſſurance of accompliſhing their purpoſe.

From all this he infers, That they have hopes of Aſſiſtance from *France*, otherwiſe they would never be ſo impudent , and he gives Reaſons for his Apprehenſions that the *French* King may ſend Troops thither this Winter, 1. Becauſe the *Engliſh* & *Dutch* will not then be at Sea to oppoſe them. 2. He can then beſt ſpare them, the Seaſon of Action beyond Sea being over. 3. The Expectation given him of a conſiderable number to joyn them, may incourage him to the undertaking with fewer Men if he can but ſend over a ſufficient number of Officers with Arms and Ammunition.

He endeavours in the reſt of his Letters to anſwer the fooliſh Pretences of the Pretender's being a Proteſtant, and that he will govern us according to Law. He ſays, that being bred up in the Religion and Politicks of *France*, he is by Education a ſtated Enemy to our Liberty and Religion. That the Obligations which he and his Family owe to the *French* King, muſt neceſſarily make him to be wholly at his Devotion, and to follow his Example ; that if he ſit upon the Throne, the three Nations muſt be oblig'd to pay the Debt which he owes the *French* King for the Education of himſelf, and for Entertaining his ſuppoſed Father and his Family. And ſince the King muſt reſtore him by his Troops, if ever he be reſtored, he will ſee to ſecure his own Debt before thoſe Troops leave *Britain*. The Pretender being a good Proficient in the *French* and *Romiſh* Schools, he will never think himſelf ſufficiently aveng'd ; but by the utter Ruine of his Proteſtant Subjects, both as Hereticks and Traitors. The late Queen, his pretended Mother, who in cold Blood when ſhe was Queen of *Britain*, adviſed to turn the Weſt of *Scotland* into a hunting Field will be then for doing ſo by the greateſt part of the Nation , and, no doubt, is at Pains to have her pretended Son educated to her own Mind: Therefore, he ſays, it were a great Madneſs in the Nation to take a Prince bred up in the horrid School of Ingratitude, Perſecution and Cruelty, and filled with Rage and Envy The *Jacobites*, he ſays, both in *Scotland* and at St. *Germains*, are ſo impatient under their preſent Straits, and knowing their Circumſtances cannot be much worſe than they are at preſent, are the more inclinable to the Undertaking. He adds, That the *French* King knows there cannot be a more effectual way for himſelf to arrive at Univerſal Monarchy, and to ruine the Proteſtant Intereſt, than by ſetting up the Pretender upon the Throne of *Great Britain*, he will in all probability attempt it , and tho' he ſhould be perſwaded that the Deſign would miſcarry in the cloſe, yet he cannot but reap ſome Advantage by imbroiling the three Nations.

From all this he Author concludes it to be the Intereſt of the Nation, to provide for Self defence; and ſays, that as many have already taken the Alarm, and are furniſhing themſelves with Arms and Ammunition, he hopes the Government will not only allow it, but encourage it, ſince the Nation ought all to appear as one Man in the Defence

ot

printed news-letter appeared Monday April 24, 1704, and was called *The Boston News-Letter*. It was printed on both sides of a half-sheet folio, 7 x 11½ inches. Because it was dated "From Monday April 17 to Monday April 24, 1704," several writers on colonial journalism have erroneously set down the first date as that on which number one of volume one of the first American newspaper was published. There were two editions of this first issue, for a typographical difference is found in the three copies that have been preserved. The copy of the New York Historical Society and that of the American Antiquarian Society are alike, while the third, that of the Massachusetts Historical Society, is clearly a second edition. (Harvard University has a piece torn from the first issue.)

The publisher's announcement was in the nature of an advertisement. It read as follows: —

This News-Letter is to be continued Weekly; and all Persons who have any Houses, Lands, Tenements, Farmes, Ships, Vessels, Goods, Wares or Merchandizes, Ec. to be Sold, or Lett; or Servants Runaway; or Goods Stoll or Lost, may have the same Inserted at a Reasonable Rate; from Twelve Pence to Five Shillings, and not to exceed: Who may agree with Nicholas Boone for the same at his Shop, next door to Major Davis's, Apothecary in Boston, near the Old Meeting-House.

All Persons in Town and Country may have said News-Letter Weekly upon reasonable terms, agreeing with John Campbell Post-Master for the same.

The early issues of this printed newspaper differed little from its written predecessors save that they had extracts from English papers. That of Number 1, for example, had an extract from *The London Flying Post* (December 2 to 4, 1703) about "a pretender, called King James VIII of Scotland, sending Popish missioners from France to Scotland," and another from *The London Gazette* (December 16 to 20, 1703) about "a most gracious speech made by Her Majesty to both Houses."

CONTENTS OF FIRST ISSUE 1690

For the sake of comparison with *Publick Occurrences* all the American items of the first issue are reproduced: —

Boston, April, 18 Arrived Capt. Sill from Jamacia about 4 Weeks Passage, says they continue there very Sickly. Mr. Nathaniel Oliver

Boston News Letter 1704 — Campbell

a principal Merchant of this place died April 15 & was decently inter'd April, 18. Ætatis 53.

The Honourable Col. Nathanael Byfield Esq. is Commissioned Judge of the Admiralty for the Provinces of Massachusetts-Bay, New-Hampshire and Rhod-Island. And Thomas Newton Esq. Judge-Deputy for the Colony of Massachusetts-Bay.

The 20. the Rd. Mr. Pemberton Preach'd an Excellent Sermon on 1 Thes. 4. 11. And do your own business: Exhorting all Ranks & Degrees of Persons to do their own work, in order to a REFORMATION: which His Excellency has ordered to be Printed.

The 21. His Excellency Dissolved the Gen. Assembly.

Rhode-Island 22. The Rd. Mr. Lockyer dyed on Thurs. last

Capt. Toungrello has taken Five Prizes off of Curraso, one of which is come in to Rhode-Island mostly Loaden with Cocco, Tobacco, Liquors &c. She is a Curraso Trader, as all the rest were. One of the Five was one Larew a French-man, a Sloop of 8 Guns & 8 Patteraro's 76 Men, Fought him Board and Board three Glasses; Capt. Larew was kill'd, and 20 of his Men kill'd & wounded: Capt. Toungrello wounded thro' the Body; and five of his men, but none kill'd, he had but 40 Fighting Men, when he took Larew.

The 18 Currant, came in a Sloop to this Port from Virginia, the Master informed Governour Cranston Esq. he was Chased by a Top-sail Shallop off of Block-Island, which he judged to be a French Privateer, and that there was two other Vessels in her Company, which he judged to be her Prizes. Whereupon his Honour being concerning for the Publick Weal and Safety of Her Majesties good Subjects, immediately caused the Drum to beat for Voluntiers, under the Command of Capt. Wanton, and in 3 or four hours time, Fitted and Man'd a Brigantine, with 70 brisk young men well Arm'd, who Sail'd the following Night, returning last Evening, and gave his Honour an Account, that they found the aforesaid Shallop, with one other, and a Ketch at Tarpolian Cove, who were all Fishing Vessels belonging to Marblehead or Salem, who were Fishing off of Block-Island, one of them was a French built Shallop with a Topsail, which gave the great suspician that they were Enemies.

New-York, April, 17. By a Barque from Jamacia, (last from Barmuda, 7 Weeks Passage,) says, there was an Imbargo in that Island several Months, occasioned by News they had of a design the French & Spaniards had, to make a descent upon them: She came out with the Homeward bound London Fleet, who are gone home without Convoy.

Capt. Davison in the Eagle Gally, Sailes for London, in a Month, if the Virginia Fleet stays so long; he intends to keep them Company Home, if not, to run for it, being Built for that Service.

Philadelphia, April, 14. An Account that the Dreadnaught Man of War was Arrived in Marryland.

N. London, April, 20. The Adventure, A Vessell 60 Tuns, will Sail from thence to London, in three Weeks or a Months time.

The issue on March 7, 1728, published the following item about Campbell's death: —

On Monday Evening last the 4th Currant at 8 a-Clock, died, John Campbell, Esq; Aged 75 years, former Post Master in the Place, Publisher of the Boston News-Letter, for many years, and One of His Majesties Justices of the Peace for the County of Suffolk.

Such a notice does scant justice to the man who founded the first regular newspaper in the British colonies of North America. Because so little has been written about the service he rendered American journalism something more should be said than that he was simply editor "for many years" of *The Boston News-Letter*.

CAMPBELL AND HIS PAPER

John Campbell was of Scotch ancestry, coming to Boston about the year 1692. He was a son of Duncan Campbell. His brother, also Duncan, was a bookseller and was at one time postmaster of Boston. In fact, John Campbell succeeded his brother in that office.

It is seen from the material between the lines of his *News-Letter* that John Campbell was practical and purposeful. No useless words appeared in his announcement of the first issue — no promises of what the publisher intended to do. No advertisement costing over five shillings was to be inserted. That he did not enlarge on matter is proved in the copy of March 18 to 25, 1706, "On Thursday night last, Sampson Waters, a Young man went well to Bed, and was found dead next morning." Nothing more!

Campbell was a man who could wax indignant over dishonesty. This fact is shown in his editorial in *The News-Letter* of July 24 to 31, 1704, in regard to the arrest of a band of counterfeiters and the seizure of their plate and press. He also made many telling comments on immorality and profaneness (October 30 to November 6, 1704). In the issue of August 6 to 13, 1705, he concludes an obituary notice of a suicide with, "She was esteemed to be a Person of a Pious and Sober Conversation: And we hope the Inserting of such an awful Providence here may not be offensive, but rather a Warning to all others to watch against the wiles of our Grand Adversary."

His subtle sense of humor is proven in *The News-Letter* of November 5 to 12, 1705, in regard to one Henry Burch, a Quaker: "Only, that he may have his NAME a little stick to him (and because he told us, you know, that he had been at AMSTERDAM) we will Humbly move, that if the Authority see meet, it may be LAID ON after the DUTCH-fashion; that is with good BURCHEN RODS, Tho' such dealing may be too easy for such a SKEELUM to meet withal."

Sarcasm came easily from his pen. To quote from his account of some French and Indian, and English encounters, "And that notwithstanding the negligence of our People, they do acknowledge to have lost Two of their principal French Officers, and 50 French & Indians in the action." Or to quote Campbell's words after his removal from the postmastership of Boston in regard to the establishment of *The Boston Gazette*, by William Brooker, the new postmaster, "I pity the readers of the new paper; its sheets smell stronger of beer than of midnight oil. It is not reading fit for people!"

On the other hand, he was public-spirited and appreciative of good work. In *The News-Letter* of June 3 to 10, 1706, Campbell wrote: "There are two things therefore which I shall chiefly recommend to your care, one is the providing a Fund for the Fortifying this City; the other is, the providing a Fund for the Repairing this Her Majesties Fort, which is extreamly out of Order, and for mounting the Guns, most of the Carriages being rotten and unserviceable. And you may be sure, that whatso ever you shall think fit to give, shall be applied to the Uses for which you give it, and to no other." In another place he said: "I cannot conclude without putting you in mind of the necessity of making provision for Out-scouts this next Winter, to be sent from ALBANY." He spoke with appreciation of the inhabitants of the Town of Milton freely offering their services, at a time of the year when laborers were very difficult to be got even for wages, "to their Reverend Minister, Mr. Peter Thacher, to cut down his Grass, to make his Hay, and to carry it into his Barn, and to their praise and commendation be it spoken: On

Monday last there was no less in his Field than 26 men Mowers in a Breast, and on Wednesday there was 14 others that were Rakers; and on Thursday 16 more, and no doubt there was a competent number on Friday and Satturday (though not come to our knowledge) to carry it into the Barn."

John Campbell had a very decided belief in the continuity of foreign news. At one time he announced, with as much regret as simplicity, that he was "thirteen months behind in giving the news from Europe." The number for November 25 to December 2, 1706, opens with an editorial note, introducing the foreign news: "According to our usual manner (on the Arrival of Ships from England, Portugal, or by the West-India Pacquets) we gave you in our Last, a Summary of the most Remarkable Occurrences of Europe for six weeks time, viz from the 1st of August, to the 15th of September last; And now we must proceed to the more particular Account of the Foreign Occurrences where we left off; So that any one having this Print for the year, will be furnished not only with the Occurrences of Europe, the West-Indies, but also those of this and the Neighbouring Provinces."

If Campbell did not show enterprise in his treatment of foreign news, his domestic news service in later issues may be considered a little more up-to-date. For the most part it consisted of "ship news, the governor's proclamations, reports of the elections of representatives to the General Court, accounts of engagements with the Indians or with the French privateers, news from the West Indies, Nova Scotia, Newfoundland, Maine, New Hampshire, Rhode Island, Connecticut, and New York and occasionally from far-away Philadelphia, or farther away South Carolina." Remarkable incidents in neighboring towns were occasionally printed. Skippers sailing between Boston and the West Indies or ports of the other colonies were his reporters of adventure stories.

He obtained news by letter; the accounts of Indian operations in the Connecticut Valley, and "to the Eastward," came in letters from Colonel Church who was commander of the colonial forces; by adventurers returning from the South, as in September 4 to 11, 1704, "By some gentlemen arrived here last Week from MARYLAND, we have the following Account"; or, in November 20 to 27, 1704, "In the domestic news is a report by an express from Albany to New York, as brought by an Indian from Canada, of preparations in Canada for a French and Indian winter attack upon some point in the colonies not named." Later, packet-boats helped in gathering both foreign and domestic news: "Her Majesty Hath Settled Packet-Boats for the West-Indies, who are to go from Plimouth at the beginning of every Month throughout the Year, no accident preventing the same; who are to touch and stay at each of the English Island-Plantations in the following manner — And thence to Return to England, and not to be stayed on any pretence whatsoever." In the issue of February 3 to 10, 1706, there is a statement of three definite post-routes; "All the Three Posts are now in, the Eastern and Southern to go out on Monday night the 10th Currant, in order to return on Satturday next; and the Western Post to set out then also in order to return on Saturday the 22d Instant and then to set out on the Monday following the 24th Currant, to go and come once a week as the other Posts do."

FIRST EXTRA

Campbell showed great enterprise in his handling of an execution on the Charles River. Six pirates were executed on Friday, June 30, 1704. The description of the scene, the "exhortations to the malefactors," and the prayer made by one of the ministers after the pirates were on the scaffold, "as near as it could be taken in writing in the great crowd," filled nearly one-half of the paper.

LATER PUBLISHERS

Incidentally, it may be remarked that *The Boston News-Letter* was first printed by Bartholomew Green in a small wooden building on Newberry Street. Eighteen years later Green himself became the owner and publisher of the paper. To quote from the issue for December 31, 1722: —

These are to give Notice, That Mr. Campbell, Designing not to Publish any more News-Letters, after this Monday the 31st Currant, Bartholomew Green the Printer thereof for these 18 Years past, having had Experience of his Practice therein; intends (Life permitted) to carry on the same, (using his Method on the Arrival of Vessels from Great Britain, &c., to give a Summary of the most Remarkable Occurrences of Europe, and afterwards the Thread of the News,) provided he can have due Encouragement by competent Numbers taking it by the Year, so as to enable him to defray the necessary Charges. And all those who have a Mind (either in Town or Country) to Promote and Encourage the Continuation of the abovesaid Intelligence, are hereby desired to Agree with the said Green, either by Word or Writing; who may have it on reasonable Terms, left at any House in Town, Sealed or Unsealed.

In the meantime, another room had been added to the printing-house for the use of the son, Bartholomew Green, Jr. January 30, 1734, the building burned, being occupied at the time by the son and his brother-in-law, John Draper, each of whom had his own plant. Draper put up a new structure which on his death, December 6, 1762, passed to his son, Richard Draper. It was used as a printing-house until the British evacuated Boston in 1776 and *The News-Letter* was discontinued. For almost threescore and ten years, *The Boston News-Letter* was printed at this same spot on Newberry Street. Four years during the editorship or authorship of Campbell, 1707–1711, the paper was printed elsewhere by John Allen.

When *The News-Letter* passed into the hands of Bartholomew Green, he tried to give its readers what they wanted by making the paper semi-religious in character. In an announcement from the publisher he says on January 21, 1723: —

¹ It being my Desire to make this as profitable and entertaining to the good people of this country as I can, I propose to give not only the most material articles of intelligence, both foreign and domestic, which concern the political state of the world; but also because this is a country, that has yet, through the mercy of God, many people in it, that have the State of religion in the world very much at heart, and would be glad, if they knew how to order their prayers and praises to the Great God thereupon, I shall endeavour, now and then, to insert an article upon the state of religion. I shall, therefore, from time to time, wait upon such as I may know to cultivate a correspondence with the most eminent persons in several nations, who may please to communicate with me, and thereby to the public, such things as all good men cannot but receive with satisfaction.

Whenever Green printed any special news item he was pretty sure to add some reflection of a religious character. By way of illustration, Buckingham gave the following: —

Yesterday, being the Lord's-Day, the Water flowed over our Wharffs and into our streets to a very surprizing height. They say the Tide rose 20 Inches higher than ever was known before. The Storm was very strong at North-East. The many great Wharffs, which since the last overflowing Tydes have been run out into the Harbour, and fill'd so great a part of the Bason, have methinks contributed something not inconsiderable to the rise of the Water upon us. But if it be found that in other Places distant from us, and where no such reason as this here given can have place, the waters have now risen in like proportion as they did with us; then we must attribute very little to the reason above suggested. The loss and damage sustained is very great, and the little Image of an Inundation which we had, look'd very dreadful. It had been a great favour to the town, if upon the first Rising of the Waters in the Streets, which hapn'd in the time of the Fore-noon Service, some discreet Persons had in a grave and prudent manner inform'd some or other of the Congregations of it; that such whose Houses & Stores lay most exposed might have repair'd timely to them. The reason in this case seems the same as if there had been a Fire in the Town. Let us fear the GOD of heaven, who made the sea and the dry land, who commandeth & raiseth the stormy wind, which lifteth up the waves; who ruleth the raging of the sea, and when the waves thereof arise, He stilleth them.

SIAMESE TWINS OF JOURNALISM

John Draper, to whom the management of the paper fell in 1733, tried to follow in the footsteps of his father-in-law by continuing this semi-religious editorial policy. On Draper's death in 1762, his son Richard became the publisher. One of his acts was to change the name to that of *The Boston Weekly News-Letter and New-England Chronicle*. Not satisfied with this, he tried *The Massachusetts Gazette and Boston News-Letter*. When he acquired *The Boston Post-Boy* in 1768 he ran what has been called the Siamese Twins in journalism. The union was called *The Massachusetts Gazette*, but each paper continued separate publication: the twin papers came out on Monday and on Thursday; the first half of the paper on each day was *The Gazette* and was the official organ of the Government to publish the laws, etc.; the second half was *The Post-Boy* on Monday and *The*

News-Letter on Thursday. This singular arrangement lasted from May 23, 1768, till September 25, 1769. Draper, separating the twin sheets, kept alive only *The News-Letter*. On his death, June 6, 1774, his widow and his partner, John Boyle, conducted the paper. A little later, John Howe purchased Boyle's interest and together with Mrs. Draper ran the paper until some time between September 7 and October 13, 1775, when Howe conducted it alone until its suspension in 1776. The last known issue was on February 22 of that year.

END OF NEWS-LETTER

In this way *The Boston News-Letter* had a continuous existence for practically seventy-two years. Loyal to the Home Government, it had the distinction of being the only paper published in Boston while Washington was besieging the city. That it did not survive longer was doubtless due to its malicious attacks upon Washington and other generals of the Revolution: the Boston patriots, aroused by their desire for independence at any cost, refused to tolerate a Tory paper which they had long dubbed *The Court Gazette*.

Newspapers to follow *The News-Letter* in Massachusetts may be listed briefly, even though some of them are mentioned more in detail in other chapters:

The Gazette, 1719; *The Courant*, 1721; *The Weekly Journal*, 1727; *The Rehearsal*, 1731; *The Post-Boy*, 1734; *The Evening Post*, 1735; *The Independent Advertiser*, 1748; *The Boston Chronicle*, 1767; *The Essex Gazette* (Salem), 1768; *The Massachusetts Spy*, 1770; *The Essex Journal* (Newburyport), 1773; *The Continental Journal*, 1776; *The Independent Ledger*, 1778; *The Springfield Advertiser* (Springfield), 1782; *The Massachusetts Herald* (Worcester), 1783.

From *The Essex Gazette*, in Salem, came several newspapers to bear the name of *Chronicle* as part of the title. The paper was moved to Cambridge in 1775, and still later moved to Boston, where it was known as *The Chronicle*. Papers were published in Boston unless otherwise noted.

CHAPTER IV

BEGINNINGS IN COLONIES

MASSACHUSETTS, PENNSYLVANIA, AND NEW YORK

BOTH for historical and for sentimental reasons, the beginnings of anything have unusual interest. This fact will explain why so much space is given to the first two or three newspapers in each of the original thirteen colonies. Some of these papers were most unpretentious and were born to bloom unseen save by a comparatively few subscribers who were usually so delinquent in the payment of their subscriptions that many of the papers continually faced the possibility of suspension. The newspaper must be properly nourished and must have a fairly good circulation or it cannot withstand those diseases which thrive best when the circulation is poor and the newspaper is struggling for existence. Though the high death-rate among these papers tells its own story, nowhere will be found a more practical demonstration of following the advice, "If at first you don't succeed, try again." Whatever else may have been his qualifications, the early American printer as a usual thing was persistent in his efforts to enlighten his neighbors through the press, and in his attempts to found papers may be found that distinguishing characteristic of American journalism which knows no such thing as defeat. The fact must not be lost sight of that during the early history of this country newspaper censors were ever present who, clothed by the law with authority, never hesitated to annoy the poor printer whenever he put anything interesting in his paper. A jail sentence rather than a libel suit was the sword of Damocles which hung in every newspaper office should something be printed which reflected in any way upon the Government. Feeble as were some of these pioneer papers, they were the foundations upon which rests the journalism of to-day.

POSTAL ORGAN OF MASSACHUSETTS

When John Campbell, the founder of American journalism and the publisher of *The News-Letter*, was, in 1719, removed from his office as postmaster at Boston, his successor was William Brooker. The latter for several reasons evidently felt the need of a special organ, for on December 21, 1719, he started *The Boston Gazette*. Campbell, said to have been so indignant over his removal from office that he would not let his paper be distributed through the mails, intimated that his *News-Letter* was "held up" in the post-office so that "people remote have been prevented from having the News-Paper." Whatever his reason he kept his paper out of the mails, a fact which is said to have helped Brooker's decision to bring out *The Gazette*. The latter paper became practically the organ of the Boston postmaster and was accordingly passed along one to the other until it became a part of *The England Weekly Journal* in 1741. From 1719 to 1754 every postmaster had his own paper, and five out of the six who held the office during this time were connected with *The Boston Gazette*.

So long as Brooker was postmaster, the printer of *The Gazette* was James Franklin. When the paper changed hands, the printing went to Samuel Kneeland. Peeved at the loss of this business, Franklin retaliated by starting *The New-England Courant* on August 7, 1721.

FIRST NEWSPAPER WAR

Of the newspaper war which arose after the starting of *The New-England Courant* between — or among — the three Boston papers, only the briefest mention is necessary. Campbell doubtless felt the competition, for his appeals for support of *The News-Letter* became more urgent. If, in the end, he had to yield, he at least "died with his boots on."

The conflict, however, that Franklin had, not only with the authorities, but also with the clergy, deserves more than passing mention. The controversy with the latter started over vaccination for smallpox. Franklin was bitterly opposed to such a practice, and the way he lampooned the Reverend Increase

Mather for upholding such a doctrine has never been equaled even by the yellow press. The distinguished clergyman was something of a fighter, as may be seen from his "Advice to the Publick" published in *The Gazette:*

Whereas a wicked Libel called the *New-England Courant*, has represented me as one among the Supporters of it; I do hereby declare, that altho' I paid for two or three of them, I then, (before the last *Courant* was published) sent him word I was extreamly offended with it ! In special, because in one of his Vile *Courants* he insinuates, that if the Ministers of God approve of a thing, it is a Sign it is of the Devil; which is a horrid thing to be related ! And altho' in one of the *Courants* it is declared, that *The London Mercury* Sept. 16, 1721, affirs that Great Numbers of Persons in the City and suburbs are under the Inoculation of the Small Pox; in his next *Courant* he asserts, that it was some Busy Inoculator, that imposed on the Publick in saying so; Whereas I myself saw and read those words in *The London Mercury:* And he doth frequently abuse the Ministers of Religion, and many other worthy Persons in a manner, which is intolerable. For these and such like Reasons I signified to the Printer, that I would have no more of their Wicked *Courants.* I that have known what New-England was from the Beginning, cannot but be troubled to see the Degeneracy of this Place. I can well remember when the Civil Government would have taken an effectual Course to suppress such a Cursed Libel! which if it be not done I am afraid that some Awful Judgment will come upon this Land, and the Wrath of God will arise, and there will be no Remedy. I cannot but pity poor Franklin, who tho' but a Young Man it may be Speedily he must appear before the Judgment Seat of God, and what answer will he give for printing things so vile and abominable? And I cannot but Advise the Supporters of this *Courant* to consider the Consequences of being Partakers in other Mens Sins, and no more Countenance such a Wicked Paper.

The Reverend Mr. Mather was reported to have said that *The New-England Courant* was "carried on by a Hell-Fire Club, with a Non-Juror at the head of them." Not content with picking a quarrel with the clergy Franklin began to criticize the acts of civil magistrates. But let Benjamin Franklin tell the tale how he broke into journalism as the result of his brother's troubles with the Assembly, even though he is in error about dates and numerical rank of *The New-England Courant* which was the third paper in Boston and the fourth in the colonies: —

My brother had, in 1720, begun to print a newspaper. It was the second that appeared in America, and was called the *New England Cou-*

rant. The only one before it was the *Boston News-Letter.* I remember his being dissuaded by some of his friends from the undertaking, as not likely to succeed, one newspaper being in their judgment enough for America. At this time, 1771, there are not less than five-and-twenty. He went on, however, with the undertaking. I was employed to carry the papers to the customers, after having worked in composing the types and printing off the sheets. . . .

My brother's discharge was accompanied with an order, and a very odd one, that "James Franklin no longer print the newspaper called *The New England Courant.*" On consultation held in our printing-office amongst his friends, what he should do in this conjuncture, it was proposed to elude the order by changing the name of the paper. But my brother, seeing inconvenience in this, came to a conclusion, as a better way, to let the paper in future be printed in the name of Benjamin Franklin; and in order to avoid the censure of the Assembly, that might fall on him, as still printing it by his apprentice, he contrived and consented that my old indenture should be returned to me with a discharge on the back of it, to show in case of necessity; and, in order to secure to him the benefit of my service, I should sign new indentures for the remainder of my time, which were to be kept private. A very flimsy scheme it was; however, it was immediately executed, and the paper was printed accordingly, under my name, for several months.

The fact not to be lost sight of is that every such conflict with the civil authorities brought the freedom of the press a little nearer its realization. Another fact, almost equally as important, was that liberty of the press not only in England, but also in America has been intimately associated with liberty of religious worship and that freedom in both was simultaneous in New England. *The Courant* was probably discontinued in 1727.

FIRST PENNSYLVANIA PAPER

On December 22, 1719, the Tuesday following the Monday on which *The Boston Gazette* was established, *The American Weekly Mercury*, the first newspaper in the middle colonies and the third paper in America, appeared in Philadelphia from the press of Andrew Bradford, the local postmaster and a son of William Bradford, who was to be the publisher of the first newspaper in New York. At first, the paper was sold by "Andrew Bradford at The Bible in the Second Street and John Copson in the High Street," but on May 25, 1721, Copson's name was withdrawn from the imprint and that of "William Bradford in New York" was substituted. When the elder Bradford started *The New York Gazette* November 8, 1725, his name, as the seller of *The American Weekly Mercury* in New York, was removed. On December 13, 1739, *The Mercury* was "printed by Andrew and William Bradford," — a partnership, however, which lasted only about eleven months, when *The Mercury* was again printed by Andrew Bradford. After his death on November 23, 1742, the next issue, December 2, was put in mourning with the inverted column rules. His widow, Cornelia Bradford, suspended the paper for one week on account of the death of her husband and then continued the black borders for the next six weeks. Later, with Isaiah Warner as a partner, she published *The Mercury* until October 18, 1744, when she again became the sole proprietor. The paper bore her name in the imprint so far as can be learned until its suspension early in 1747.

Andrew Bradford, like other colonial editors, had his troubles with the civic authorities, for on January 2, 1721, he printed an item which read, "our General Assembly are now sitting and we have great expectation from them at this juncture that they will find some effectual remedy to revive the dying credit of this Province and restore us to our former happy circumstances." The Provincial Council saw a criticism of its actions in this paragraph and summoned its publisher on February 21 to explain why such an item was inserted in his paper. In its defense Bradford said the notice was written and inserted by a German printer without authority and that he regretted exceedingly its publication. With the usual reprimand and with a warning never to publish anything in the future about the affairs of any of the colonies, he was discharged.

This punishment was mild compared with the one that he received for printing some communications from Benjamin Franklin signed "Busy Body." These communications by Franklin, while simply insisting that those in authority should be inspired with a public spirit and with a love of their country, so offended the Governor and his Council that they arrested Bradford, sent him to jail, and later bound him over to the court. In colonial days editors did not seem to mind being locked up in jail: editing a paper from prison was always sure to increase the circulation. Certainly, Bradford's *Mercury* never occupied a very important place in Philadelphia until after he had been in prison.

During much of the time that Bradford conducted *The American Weekly Mercury* he was postmaster of Philadelphia. This office was of great help to him, if the words of Franklin can be accepted at their face value. To quote from his "Autobiography": —

As he (Bradford) held the post office, it was imagined that he had better opportunities for obtaining the news, and his paper was thought a better distributor of advertisements than mine, and therefore had many more; which was a profitable thing for him and a disadvantage to me, for tho' I did receive and send papers by the post, yet the public opinion was otherwise; for what I did send was by bribing the riders, who took them privately, Bradford being unkind enough to forbid it, which occasioned some resentment on my part; and I thought so meanly of the practice that when I afterwards came into the position, I took care never to imitate it.

SECOND PAPER IN PHILADELPHIA

With the issue of Number 80 of *The New-England Courant* on February 11, 1723 (Old Style), Benjamin Franklin had become a Boston newspaper publisher in name, if not in fact. After a quarrel with his brother, James, he had gone to New York: not finding employment with William Bradford, the only printer there at that time, he had gone on to Philadelphia where he worked at his trade in the office of Samuel Keimer, one of the two printers of the place. Of his trip to England and of his partnership, upon his return to Philadelphia, with Hugh Meredith, nothing needs to be said here until that time when they had decided to publish a newspaper. Unfortunately for them, their decision reached Keimer through a former fellow-workman, George Webb, before they were prepared to bring out the paper.

Keimer, on the other hand, lost no time in publishing a prospectus of one he would speedily print. His announcement reminds one of modern magazine braggadocio: —

Whereas many have encouraged me to publish a Paper of Intelligence: and whereas the late *Mercury* has been so wretchedly performed as to be a Scandal to the Name of Printing, and to be truly styled Nonsense in Folio, This is therefore to notify that I shall begin in November next a most useful Paper, to be entitled, *The Pennsylvania Gazette or Universal Instructor*. The Proposer having dwelt at the Fountain of Intelligence in Europe, will be able to give a Paper to please all and to offend none, at the reasonable Expense of Ten Shillings per annum, Proclamation Money.

The paper, with the longer title of *The Universal Instructor in all Arts and Sciences; and Pennsylvania Gazette*, appeared on December 24, 1728. The next week Keimer, adopting the style of the Quakers, dated his paper, "The 2d of the 11th mo. 1728." In spite of the fact that the first two pages were given up to extracts from Chambers' "Dictionary of the Arts and Sciences," a book just imported from London, Keimer boasted that with the thirteenth issue the paper had a circulation of two hundred and fifty copies. Then the subscribers began to drop off: not even selected tales of English life or extracts from Defoe's "Religious Courtship" prevented the diminution. One reason for the decline may have been the ridicule hurled at the paper by Franklin, under the *nom-de-plume* of "Busy Body," in the columns of *The Mercury*. After nine months the paper had less than one hundred subscribers, and Keimer was glad to sell at any price to Franklin and Meredith, who assumed control with Number 40 on October 2, 1729.

FRANKLIN A REAL NEWSPAPER PUBLISHER

The new firm shortened the title to *The Pennsylvania Gazette*, cut short the "Religious Courtship," and referred its readers to Chambers' "Dictionary" for further information which it would take them fifty years to give if they followed Keimer's example of printing. In the place of these features, Franklin put good news-items mixed with a little comment of his own. With the fourth issue he announced a "Half Sheet twice a Week" and gave America its first semi-weekly. But he was too progressive a journalist for the time, and after a few numbers he returned to weekly publication.

On July 14, 1730, the partnership of Franklin and Meredith was dissolved: the former continued the sole publisher of the paper until 1748 when he admitted David Hall who had started to work on the paper five years before. Hall, to quote Franklin's words, "took off my hands all care of the printing-office, paying me punctually my share of the profits." This second partnership lasted eighteen years, during which time the paper became possibly the most influential and certainly the most successful financially of any of the colonial newspapers. By way of illustration of the latter, the profits from 1748 to 1766, when Hall became the sole proprietor, amounted to over twelve thousand pounds for subscriptions and over four thousand for advertising.

When the Stamp Act went into effect on November 1, 1765, *The Pennsylvania Gazette* appeared not only without a title, but also without an imprint so that the publisher might not be known to the authorities. When the paper resumed its old title, Franklin's name was omitted in the imprint. He doubt-less sold out to Hall at that time, but he did not dissolve the partnership formally until February 1, 1766. In May of that year Hall took in William Sellers as partner and together they continued *The Pennsylvania Gazette.*

After Franklin ceased to be connected actively with *The Pennsylvania Gazette,* he achieved fame in so many lines that he has often been spoken of as the many-sided Franklin. To the last, however, the diplomat and scientist thought of himself first as a printer. This epitaph, composed by and for himself, before his death on April 19, 1790, showed this fact: —

The Body of
Benjamin Franklin, Printer,
(Like the cover of an old Book,
Its contents worn out,
And stript of its lettering and gilding)
Lies here, food for worms!
Yet the work itself shall not be lost,
For it will, as he believed, appear once more
In a new
And more beautiful edition,
Corrected and amended
By its Author.

The demise of *The Pennsylvania Gazette* occurred on October 11, 1815. An advertisement on that date reprinted a notice dated September 20, 1815, in which an announcement was made that owing to the death of both proprietors, Hall and Pierie, *The Pennsylvania Gazette* would discontinue on October 11, 1815. The notice asserted that if enough subscribers could be obtained by a certain date the paper would be revived. New papers which had appeared in Philadelphia seemed to have the popular favor, for the required number of subscribers was not secured and *The Pennsylvania Gazette*, which had held a foremost place in two different eras of American journalism, was no more. The plant of the paper was sold and the equipment became scattered among the various printing-offices of the city.

FIRST PAPER IN NEW YORK

Because William Bradford was the founder of the first paper in New York, and because he trained in his shop many of the printer-editors of colonial New York, he should receive special attention. After learning his trade in the office of his father-in-law, Andrew Sowle, he accompanied William Penn to America in 1682. Upon his return to England in 1685 he procured a press and type and again set sail for Philadelphia where he opened a bookshop and did a general printing business — a work which needs only passing mention, as he did not at that time think of starting a newspaper.

Invited to come to New York by Governor Benjamin Fletcher, Bradford was appointed "Royal Printer" in 1693. In 1696 Bradford evidently reprinted an English newspaper, — probably *The London Gazette*, — for a letter dated May 30, 1696, from Governor Fletcher to the Lords of Trade says: "A Ship belonging to this Place from Madera happily mett at Sea that Vessell which had your Lord's Packet for Virginia & brought me a *Gazett* which gave me an Account of that horrid Conspiracy against His Majesty's Sacred Person. I caused it to be reprinted here." Possibly Bradford was mindful of the fate of the venture attempted by Benjamin Harris in Boston and did not care to start a paper when the censorship was so severe.

Thomas, in his "History of Printing," reproduced a heading of a second number of *The New-York Gazette* in which it showed the date of from Monday, October 16, to October 23, 1725:

this would make the first issue on October 16, 1725 — a date which has been commonly accepted as that on which New York's first newspaper appeared. While Thomas undoubtedly knew at first hand about the early journalism of New England, he was evidently mistaken about the date of the first issue of *The New-York Gazette*. Unfortunately, no copy of the first issue of the paper has survived, but there are, however, copies of the paper published the first half of 1726. Taking any one of these as a starting-point and working backwards, one finds that Volume I, Number 1, should be dated November 1 to November 8, 1725: in other words, *The New-York Gazette* was first published on November 8, 1725, if there was regularity of publication.

To support the correctness of this date, the following facts may be cited: Bradford's day of publication was on Monday, and any almanac for 1725 shows that October 16 fell not on Monday, but on Saturday.

The New-York Gazette, Number 26, May 2, 1726, contained this item: —

N.B. This Numb. 26 of our *Gazette*, concludes the first half year and is the Time the first Payment should be made by the Gentlemen who encourage the same. And altho' the Number subscribed for does not defray the Charge, yet we intend to Continue it the next half year, in the hopes of further Encouragement.

The most positive proof of November 8 as the date on which Bradford first brought out his *Gazette* will be found in an item published after the paper had been in existence two and one-half years: —

By the Advice and encouragement of some Gentlemen, for the Information of the Publick, We began to Publish this *Gazette* the first of November, 1725 (not doubting but we should have Subscribers to take off such a Number as might defray the Charge), and the first of May last it was Two Years & a half that we have continued its Publication; but having calculated the Charge of Printing and Paper for the same, as also how much will arise to defray that Charge (when all those that take this *Gazette* have paid in what is due to the first of May last) do find that we shall lose Thirty-Five Pounds in the two years and a half by Publishing this Paper, besides the trouble and Charge of Correspondents, collecting the News, making up Pacquets and conveying the same to those in the Country who take them, And therefore if some further Encouragement be not given by a larger Number of Subscribers for said *Gazette* we must let it fall, and cease publishing the same. Many Persons that take this *Gazette* being above a year behind in their Payments, and some not having paid since the first publishing of the same, They are now desired to pay in what is due, in order to enable the further Publication, if it be continued.

This advertisement, or appeal, in Bradford's own paper settles, beyond the permissibility of a doubt, the month in which his *Gazette* first appeared. It should be noticed that Bradford did not say the first day of November, but "the first of November 1725," and consequently, because of the other proofs just given, his assertion may be taken as a common way about speaking of the first week of the month. In view of these facts, the date of New York's first newspaper may be set down as November 8, 1725.

From 1725 to 1730 *The New-York Gazette* consisted of a single sheet of four pages. From 1730 on, the number of pages was irregular, sometimes, two, other times, three, and occasionally, six. The paper was invariably poorly printed — doubtless due to the fact that Bradford had used the type for a long time before he began to print this newspaper. Advertisements were few in number and the subscribers were not numerous enough to afford much encouragement to the printer — a fact brought out by the two quotations already printed from Bradford's *Gazette*.

During all the years that Bradford conducted his paper, he was most loyal to those in authority. Yet Bradford, at heart, undoubtedly was in favor of the freedom of the press and supported in his columns many things simply because he needed the salary which he received as "Printer to the Province of New York," and which he would doubtless have lost had he adopted the motto of *The New-York Chronicle*, the tenth paper in New York, which read: "Open to all Parties and Influenced by None." Had *The New-York Gazette* been open to the Popular Party, it is a matter of doubt whether John Peter Zenger would have started *The New-York Weekly Journal* in 1733.

The newspaper war which arose between *The New-York Gazette* and *The New-York Weekly Journal*, the next paper of the colony, made Bradford's newspaper unpopular with the common people and assisted in a most material way to put Zenger's paper on a firm basis.

Bradford retired from the newspaper world on November 19, 1744, with the last issue of *The New-York Gazette*. For some time the paper had been published under the joint imprint of William Bradford and Henry De Foreest. After Bradford's retirement, De Foreest changed the name of the paper to *The New-York Evening Post*, with the next issue on November 26, 1744. Bradford died May 25, 1752.

ZENGER AND HIS PAPER

The second newspaper in the city was *The New-York Weekly Journal* first issued Monday, November 5, 1733, — incorrectly dated October 5, — by John Peter Zenger, a German who had come to New York in 1710 with a group of Palatines sent over by Queen Anne. Robert Hunter, at that time "Governor-in-Chief of New York, New Jersey, and Territories Depending Thereon in America," apprenticed Zenger on October 26, 1710, for eight years to William Bradford the printer whose newspaper has just been mentioned. Zenger, after he had become fairly proficient at his trade, ran away from his employer and drifted first into Pennsylvania and later into Maryland. Upon his return to New York he formed a partnership with Bradford. His association with his former partner was brief, for in 1726 he set up his own print-shop first on Smith and then later on Broad Street.

At this time New York had no newspaper to speak for the Popular Party, as Bradford's *Gazette* was practically a Government organ and its editor had to follow the directions of the Government "under the penalty of losing 50 pounds per annum salary and the title of the King's Printer for the Province of New York." As Zenger was poor and barely able to make both ends meet, there can be no doubt that when he brought out *The New-York Weekly Journal* on November 5, 1733, he was assisted financially by those opposed to the ruling powers. Among these was one James Alexander, who, in modern newspaper language, would be called the chief editorial writer. Most of the contents of *The Journal* was contributed matter, as may be learned by any one who cares to turn to the files of the early numbers. Zenger's contributions are easily discovered by their poor spelling and by their grammatical errors. Nevertheless, *The Journal*, which was folio in size, was much better printed than Bradford's *Gazette*, and so popular were some of the articles in the early issues that more than one edition had to be run off.

Zenger told of the success of his venture in the twelfth issue which appeared on January 21, 1734 (3), in which he said: —

To my Subscribers and Wellwishers;
Now when Forreign News is not to be had and all other News Writers in these countries are at a Loss how to continue their Papers, and what to fill them up with; I must acknowledge my Obligation to you to be such, that you do so plentifully supply me, that tho' for some Weeks past I have used my smallest Letter, and to put as much into a Paper as was in my Power, yet I have now Supplies sufficient to fill above seven weekly Papers more. This I mention that my Correspondents whose Works have not presently a Place in my Journal may know the cause of it and excuse it for a Time, assuring them that Justice shall be done to their Labours as soon as I possibly can, at least so much of them as I am advised I dare safely print and in order to do Justice to every one, I have thought of publishing a Thursdays Journal weekly for the Next Quarter, if my Subscribers for this Mondays Journal, will on their first Quarters Payment signify their desire of it either by Letter or Subscription for that purpose on the like Terms as this Paper, which I beg they'll consider of and signify their Inclinations, and if a sufficient Number to bear the charge approve of it, it shall (God willing) be done.

I am
Your obliged humble Servant
J. Peter Zenger.

An interesting comparison of *The Gazette* and *The Journal* was made by a correspondent who, writing under the *nom-de-plume* "Upon," gave the following reasons for his selection: "Zenger rides too fast and sticks in the spur when he ought to make use of the reins."

ZENGER'S TRIAL

An editor with such characteristics was bound to get into trouble with the authorities in colonial days. In his second num-

ber, Zenger published an article on "The Liberty of the Press."
This was followed by other articles radical in tone. In November, 1734, an issue of *The Weekly Journal* was omitted. The reason Zenger gave in his next issue, Number 55, for Monday, November 25: —

To All My Subscribers and Benefactors Who take My Weekly Journall.
Gentlemen, Ladies, and Others;
As you last week were Disappointed of My Journall I think it Incum-
bent upon me, to publish My Apoligy which is this. On the Lords Day,
the Seventeenth of this Instant, I was Arrested, taken and Imprisoned
in the common Goal of this Citty, by Virtue of a Warrant from the
Governour, and the Honorable *Francis Harrison*, Esq; and others in
Council of which (God Willing) yo'l have a coppy whereupon I was
put under such Restraint that I had not the Liberty of Pen, Ink, or
Paper, or to see, or speak with People till upon my Complaint to the
Honourable the Chief Justice, at my appearing before him upon My
Habias Corpus on *Wednesday* following. Who discountenanced that
Proceeding and therefore I have since that Time the Liberty of Speak-
ing through the Hole of the Door to My Wife and Servants by which
I doubt not yo'l think me sufficiently Excused for not sending my last
weeks *Journall*, and I hope for the future by the Liberty of Speaking
to my Servants thro' the Hole of the Door of the Prison to entertain
you with My Weakly *Journall* as formerly.

And am your obliged
Humble Servant
J. Peter Zenger.

Writing from his prison on December 20, 1734, Zenger not
only defended himself in replying to an attack made in Bradford's *Gazette*, but also criticized its writer for recalling the fact
that he was brought over at the expense of the Crown. To quote
Zenger's words: —

There is a great Noise made in that ridiculous Letter in Mr. Bradford's last *Gazette* about setting the Province in Flames, raising of Sedition and Tumults, etc. I know of none, either past or intended; if my
Adversaries know of any, they'l do well to discover them, and prevent
the Consequences . . . That I was brought over at the charitable
expense of the Crown is the only Truth that groaping Fumbler found
when he studied that clumsy Performance — I acknowledge it; Thanks
to QUEEN ANNE whose Name I Mention with Reverence, her Bounty
to me and my distress'd Country Folks to be gratefully remembered. If that Author has contributed any Thing towards it, I begg to
be inform'd, I assure him that my Acknowledgement shall not be want-

ing, not with standing his Ill Treatment: If he has not, I begg leave to tell him, that it is mean for him to twit me with Benefits that I am no ways beholden to him for.

Because of his attack on the arbitrary and corrupt administration of the British Colonial Governor Crosby, Zenger had been arrested on the charge of seditious libel. In the trial which followed, Zenger was fortunate in having to defend him Andrew Hamilton, probably the ablest lawyer of Philadelphia. During the most interesting trial several departures were made from the legal procedure of the past in libel suits. These have been outlined by Melville E. Stone, General Manager of the Associated Press, as follows: —

First, the jury took the bit in their teeth and asserted their right to be the sole judges of both the law and the facts. Second, they decided that the oldtime rule that "the greater the truth the greater the libel" was an unwise one. Zenger was acquitted. And so it came about that there was a famous revolution in the colonial law. The judge ceased to be the sole arbiter of an editor's fate, and the truth when published from good motives and justifiable ends became an adequate defence for the journalist brought to bar. This meant that for the first time in the world's history the freedom of the press, so far as such freedom was consistent with public rights, was established. The seed which John Milton had sown a century before, when he wrote his famous plea for "unlicensed printing," had come to fruition. Gouverneur Morris said this verdict was "the dawn of that liberty which afterward revolutionized America."

END OF ZENGER'S CAREER

Zenger was made Public Printer for the Province of New York in 1737, and a year later was given the same office for the Province of New Jersey. He continued, however, to bring out his *Weekly Journal* and lived to see the suspension of his rival, *The New-York Weekly Gazette*. *The New-York Evening Post*, the first paper of that name in the city, told of the end of Zenger's career when it published the following obituary notice on August 4, 1746: —

On Monday Evening last, departed this Life Mr. John Peter Zenger, Printer, in the 49 year of his Age; He Has left a Wife and six children behind, he was a loving Husband, and a tender Father, and his Death is much lamented by his Family and Relations.

The New-York Weekly Journal, however, continued to be published by Zenger's wife and son, John Zenger, Jr., until March 18, 1751, — or possibly a few weeks longer, — though no copies are known of a later date than the one just given.

Mother and son, however, experienced the greatest difficulties in making the paper pay expenses, and at various times printed in *The New-York Weekly Journal* notices requesting subscribers who did not have the ready money to send in hams, butter, cheese, poultry, flour, etc., in payment for their subscriptions in order that the "poor printer" might bring out his newspaper. The family was reduced to such straits financially that New York printers had to come to its aid: James Parker, for example, in his *Post-Boy*, advertised in the issue for November 11, 1751, that "a small Number of the Charters of the City of New York, printed by the late Mr. Zenger, for the Benefit of his Widow, are to be Sold by the Printer hereof, Price 3 Shillings."

Simply as a matter of record the author has compiled the following table of the twelve newspapers which appeared in New York before the outbreak of the Revolution:

(1) *The New-York Gazette* (1725); publisher, William Bradford.
(2) *The New-York Weekly Journal* (1733); publisher, Peter Zenger.
(3) *The Weekly New-York Post-Boy* (1743); publisher, James Parker.
(4) *The New-York Evening Post* (1744); publisher, Henry De Foreest.
(5) *The New-York Weekly Mercury* (1752); publisher, Hugh Gaine.
(6) *The New-York Gazette* (1759); publisher, William Weyman.
(7) *The American Chronicle* (1762); publisher, Samuel Farley.
(8) *The New-York Pacquet* (1763); publisher, Benjamin Mecom.
(9) *The New-York Journal; or General Advertiser* (1766); publisher, John Holt.
(10) *The New-York Chronicle* (1769); publisher, James Robertson.
(11) *Rivington's New-York Gazetter; or, The Connecticut, New-Jersey, Hudson's River and Quebec Weekly Advertiser* (1773); publisher, James Rivington.
(12) *The Constitutional Gazette* (1775); publisher, John Anderson.

CHAPTER V

BEGINNINGS IN COLONIES (*continued*)

IN the printing-plants of the newspapers mentioned in the preceding chapter were trained many of the pioneers who founded newspapers in the other colonies. Especially was this true of the plant owned by Benjamin Franklin who, on several occasions, helped his apprentices to establish their newspapers. Just what financial relations existed between Franklin and these printers must be a matter of conjecture. The partnership agreement of *The Pennsylvania Chronicle* showed that a third interest had been set aside for Franklin should he desire to avail himself of the offer. This policy of Franklin really made him the first owner of a "string of newspapers." The reason why New Jersey did not have a printed newspaper until after the Colonial Period closed is easily given: there was no demand, for the New York and Pennsylvania papers met all the needs. The Revolution, however, changed matters, and New Jersey came forward with financial assistance for the establishment of its own newspaper. Mention has been made in an earlier chapter of the written newspaper publicly posted in a tavern which supplemented in New Jersey the printed sheets from other colonies. The expressed hope of an early Governor of Virginia that his colony would not have a newspaper "these hundred years" was not fulfilled: the success of the newspapers in other colonies led to the establishment of *The Virginia Gazette.*

GENERALLY A GAZETTE

The mention of the term *Gazette* recalls the popularity of this word as a title for a newspaper. In nine of the thirteen colonies the first paper was a *Gazette:* these colonies were Connecticut, Georgia, Maryland, North Carolina, New Hampshire, New Jersey, New York, Rhode Island, Virginia. In the four remaining colonies where the first newspaper had another name, the second paper to be established had the word *Gazette* in its title.

The second favorite as a title for a newspaper during the colonial days was *The Journal*.

PARKS'S PAPER IN MARYLAND

William Parks, who had learned his trade in England, was the founder of journalism in two of the colonies. To him belongs the honor of bringing out the first paper not only in Maryland, but also in Virginia. In setting up his press in the former colony in 1726 he had been made "Public Printer to Maryland." One year later he began, on September 19, *The Maryland Gazette* at Annapolis. As the colony was but sparsely settled at the time he had great difficulty not only in getting subscribers, but also in securing advertisements: at times his paper contained no advertising save the notices inserted by himself about the things for sale in his print-shop. He was, however, more energetic in the matter of attempting to gather the news than many of the pioneer printers, and while visiting England in 1730, he made arrangements "by which upon all Occasions, I shall be furnished with the freshest Intelligence both from thence and other parts of Europe." Finding it financially impossible to continue his paper, Parks discontinued *The Gazette* in 1731, but on December 8, 1732, he brought out the paper again under the title *The Maryland Gazette Revived*. Associated with him in the revival of the paper was Edmund Hall, but evidently the partnership lasted only one year, for the imprint of December 28, 1733, showed that William Parks was again the sole proprietor. Some time between March and April of that year, the word *Revived* was dropped from the title and the paper came out simply as *The Maryland Gazette*. In December the paper was irregular in appearance and finally was totally discontinued.

GREEN'S GAZETTE

Another newspaper with the same title, *The Maryland Gazette*, was started at Annapolis, January 17, 1745, by Jonas Green, one of the greatest editors of the Colonial Period. Consequently, his account of what he hoped to make *The Maryland Gazette* may be quoted in full to show what the best publishers of that time wanted their papers to be: —

md - 1727

OUR Intend therefore, is to give the Public a Weekly Account of the most remarkable Occurrences, foreign and domestic, which shall from time to time come to our Knowledge; having always a principal Regard to such Articles as nearest concern the American Plantations in general, and the Province of Maryland in particular; ever observing the strictest Justice and Truth in Relation of Facts, and the utmost Disinterestedness and Impartiality in Points of Controversy.

AND in a Dearth of News, which, in this remote Part of the World, may sometimes reasonably be expected, we shall study to supply that Deficit, by presenting our Readers with the best Materials we can possibly collect; having always in this Respect, a due Regard to whatever may conduce to the Promotion of Virtue and Learning, the Suppression of Vice and Immorality, and the Instruction as well as Entertainment of our Readers.

WE take this Opportunity of making Application to our Learned Correspondents, whose ingenious Productions, if with such we shall at any Time be favoured, will ever find a Place in this Paper, and lay the Printer under greatest Obligations; provided whatsoever is transmitted of this Kind, be consistent with Sobriety and good Manners.

TO render Our GAZETTE useful, as well as entertaining, we shall present our Readers with the best Directions in the Culture of Flax and Hemp, especially the former, in the plainest Manner; which we hope will be of public Advantage to the Community in the present Situation of Affairs, when we can't always be certain of Supplies, and they are not to be had at all but at such Prices as the Generality of the People are not able to give for them.

AS the prosecuting and carrying on an Undertaking of this Kind has been much wished for, and long desired, and must necessarily be attended with considerable Trouble and Expence; we doubt not of meeting with a due Encouragement from the good People of this Province, in a sufficient Number of Subscriptions whereby the Printer may be enabled to carry on and continue it's Publication.

THOSE Gentlemen who are pleased to commence Subscribers, may depend on the most safe and speedy Conveyance of their respective Papers, by having them forwarded to the Court-Houses, and other the most public Places, of the several Counties in which they reside; especially where Want of Opportunity renders it impracticable to send them to the Houses of such Subscribers.

THE Price of this Paper to Subscribers, will be Twelve Shillings, Maryland Currency, per annum, unsealed; or Fourteen Shillings if sealed and directed. It will be Printed on good Paper, and a beautiful new Letter, the same with this Specimen.

ADVERTISEMENTS, of a moderate Length, will be taken in at the Printing-Office in Annapolis, and carefully inserted in this Paper, at Five Shillings each, the first Week; and One Shilling for every succeeding Week, so long as continued therein.

Green at the time he started *The Gazette* was Public Printer to Maryland, having been appointed to that office in 1740. He came from that New England family which was often distinguished as printers in colonial journalism, and in addition to his home training in the trade, he had worked on both Bradford's and Franklin's papers in Philadelphia before coming to Maryland. It is not strange, therefore, that he made his *Gazette*, in typographical appearance at least, the rival of any newspaper of his day.

Upon Green's death, April 11, 1767, *The Maryland Gazette* was published by his widow, Anne Catharine Green, until the first of 1768 when she took her son William into partnership. The latter died in August, 1770, and his mother again became the publisher until her death, March 23, 1775. Two sons, Frederick and Samuel, then continued *The Gazette*, which, during the War of the Revolution, did much to keep up the courage of the Maryland patriots. The paper was last published in 1839.

JOURNAL FIRST IN SOUTH CAROLINA

Eleazer Phillips, a New England printer, went to South Carolina in 1730 where he established a book and stationery shop in "Charles Town." Associated with him was his son, Eleazer Phillips, Jr. The latter established, on or near March 4, 1730, *The South Carolina Weekly Journal*. The paper, however, failed to get enough subscribers to warrant a continuous publication and suspended in about six months.

WHITMARSH AND TIMOTHY

The most important colonial paper in South Carolina was *The South Carolina Gazette* founded January 8, 1732, by Thomas Whitmarsh. Whitmarsh died of yellow fever in the summer of 1733, and *The Gazette* suspended publication on September 8 of that year. It was revived, however, a year later by Lewis Timothy (printed in the first few issues, "Lewis Timothee"), a printer from Philadelphia who had learned his trade in the plant of Benjamin Franklin. Timothy brought out the first number of the revival on February 2, 1734. Timothy was killed in an accident in December, 1738. For about six years his

S.C. 1730
S.C. Gazette 1732

paper was run by his widow, Mrs. Elizabeth Timothy. She then sold her interest to her son, Peter Timothy, who published *The South Carolina Gazette* uninterruptedly until May 7, 1772, when, on his appointment as Deputy Postmaster-General for the Southern Provinces of North America he leased the plant to Powell, Hughes & Company. With the issue for November 8, 1773, Timothy resumed control of *The Gazette* and was its publisher until 1775, when the paper temporarily suspended on account of the Revolutionary War. Timothy again revived *The Gazette* on April 9, 1777, with the following change in title, *The Gazette of the State of South Carolina.* When Charleston fell into the hands of the British in 1780, *The Gazette* was forced to suspend another time and its editor went into exile in St. Augustine, Florida. Shortly after his release from St. Augustine he was drowned, but his wife revived the paper on March 28, 1785, with another change in title, *The State Gazette of South Carolina.* Mrs. Timothy, following the example set by her mother-in-law, sold the paper in 1790 to her son, Benjamin Franklin Timothy, who changed the name to *The South Carolina State Gazette and Timothy and Mason's Daily Advertiser.* Timothy was associated with the paper until its final suspension in 1802.

Not to be confused with the paper just mentioned was *The South Carolina Weekly Gazette* at "Charles Town," started by Robert Wells, on November 1, 1758. Wells was on good terms with the British, for when the city fell into their hands he was allowed to continue publication of his paper under the title, *The Royal Gazette.* Volume I, Number 1, of The Royal Edition appeared on March 3, 1781. A year later, when Charleston was evacuated by the British, the paper ceased publication.

J. FRANKLIN IN RHODE ISLAND

After James Franklin, the founder of *The New-England Weekly Courant,* left Boston, he went to Newport, Rhode Island, where on September 27, 1732, he established *The Rhode Island Gazette.* It was the first newspaper in that State, and while it made a heroic struggle for existence, it only lasted eight months. After Franklin's death his wife, Anne Franklin, made several unsuccessful attempts to revive the paper.

The Franklin imprint, however, appeared on the second newspaper in Rhode Island, *The Newport Mercury*, founded in Newport on June 19, 1758, by James Franklin, Jr. When the son died in 1762, his mother, Anne Franklin, continued *The Mercury* for a brief time until she went into partnership with Samuel Hale. Upon her death in 1763 Hale ran the paper most successfully, as he was one of the first editors and publishers to realize that advertising depends upon circulation for its value.

GODDARD'S FIRST PAPER

William Goddard, a name frequently found in colonial journalism, started the third paper in Rhode Island on October 20, 1762. He called his paper *The Providence Gazette and Country Journal*. Goddard had difficulty as usual in collecting payments for subscriptions, and on May 11, 1765, was forced to suspend temporarily, but intended to revive the paper six months later, providing the stamp duties did not make such a resumption impossible. The permanent revival, however, did not begin until August 9, 1766, and an editorial note informed the reading public that the paper was now in the hands of Sarah Goddard & Company. Leaving his paper thus in the hands of his mother, William Goddard went to New York to seek employment, but sent Samuel Inslee, who later became a publisher of a New York colonial paper, to Providence to help Mrs. Goddard. On November 12, 1768, the paper passed into the hands of John Carter, who had worked in the office of Benjamin Franklin in Philadelphia, and later became a partner of Mrs. Goddard in the business. Carter made numerous improvements in the paper and ordered new type from England. Before it could reach Providence, however, the Revolutionary War was well on its way, so that when the type finally reached New York it was confiscated by the custom-house authorities of that city. *The Gazette* was one of the first papers to realize the importance of the battle of Lexington. In an account, which occupied nine inches of space in *The Gazette*, its editor made this significant statement: "Thus is commenced the American Civil War."

VIRGINIA — MOTHER OF GAZETTES

One reason why Virginia did not have a newspaper earlier than 1736 will be found in an assertion of Sir William Berkeley who was Governor of the Colony for thirty-eight years. In his report to the Lords of the Committee for the Colonies in 1671 he said: "I thank God we have not free schools nor printing; and I hope we shall not have these hundred years. For learning has brought disobedience and heresy, and sects into the world; and printing has divulged them and libels against the government. God keep us from both." On August 6, 1736, however, William Parks brought out at Williamsburg *The Virginia Gazette*. This first paper in Virginia has been described as "a small dingy sheet, containing a few items of foreign news, the ads of Williamsburg shopkeepers, notices of the arrival and departure of ships; a few chance particulars relating to persons or affairs in the colony; and poetical effusions celebrating the charms of Myrtilla, Florella or other belles of the period."

Parks was made "Printer to the Colony," at a salary of two hundred pounds — payable in tobacco, the currency of the time. If he was unsuccessful in establishing his paper on a permanent basis, it was through no fault of his, but due to the opposition to a free press in the colony. In his announcement Parks stated a subscription price of fifteen shillings per annum, and after commenting on the newspapers published in the other colonies, he said: "From these examples and the encouragement of several gentlemen on the prospect I have of success in this ancient and best settled colony of Virginia, I am induced to send forth weekly newspapers here, — not doubting to meet with as good encouragement as others, or at least as may enable me to carry them on."

The Gazette published by William Parks is not to be confused with *The Virginia Gazette* started on January 3, 1751, by William Hunter — though the latter may be in a certain sense considered as a revival of the first paper in Virginia. With issue Number 52, on December 27, 1751, Hunter said: —

This paper concludes the first year of *The Gazette* publication and as I have been at a great expense, as well in printing as sending them to different parts of the country, by special messengers, I hope my customers will favor me with their subscription money as soon as possible that I may be enabled to continue them — I am sensible there are many who complain of not getting their papers so regular as they desire, but hope they will be kind enough to excuse it, when they consider the many inconveniences the colony labours under both in this and other respects, for want of regular post through the country. However, as we daily expect the arrival of a postmaster-General, we have no reason to doubt, but that the Post-Office will be regulated in such a manner as will give content. In the mean time, as I shall do all in my power to dispatch the Gazettes, as well by different posts, as favourable opportunities, hope my customers will continue their favours, and oblige their very humble servant, The Printer.

The second *Virginia Gazette* was a great improvement on the first. Hunter was postmaster and had better opportunities to gather news. In addition, his *Gazette* was better edited. In its columns appeared some of the best-written essays of the Colonial Period. For instance, in 1757 a man, under the signature of "The Virginia Sentinel," published a contribution which showed that Virginia in spite of its early opposition to the press was not without literary talent.

A third *Virginia Gazette* was brought out in Williamsburg in May, 1766, by William Rind with a motto "Open to all Parties, Influenced by None." Rind began his *Gazette* with the coöperation of Thomas Jefferson, who considered the old *Gazettes* too much under the influence of the Government.

A fourth *Gazette* was started in Williamsburg on February 3, 1775, by Alexander Purdy and was conducted by him until 1779. Its motto was, "Always for Liberty and the Public Good." This particular *Virginia Gazette* has the honor of being the first American newspaper to print the full text of the Declaration of Independence which it did on July 26, 1776.

EARLY CONNECTICUT PAPERS

The Connecticut Gazette, the first paper in Connecticut, made its appearance on April 12, 1755, at New Haven. The first number bore the imprint, "Printed by James Parker at the Post-Office near the Sign of the White Horse." Benjamin Franklin had been induced by President Clap to purchase a printing-plant with a view to establishing the former's nephew, Benjamin Mecom, in business at New Haven. The material arrived in the fall of 1754, but Mecom changed his plans and Parker was secured to take up the work. Associated with Parker in *The Connecticut Gazette* was John Holt, who had the title of editor and was a junior partner of the firm of James Parker & Company. In 1764 *The Gazette* was suspended for a short time, but was afterwards revived by Benjamin Mecom on July 5, 1765. In an editorial announcement Mecom added the following statement about subscriptions: "All kinds of Provisions, Fire Wood and other suitable country Produce will be taken as pay of those who cannot spare money, if delivered at the Printer's Dwelling House, or at any other place which may accidentally suit him."

On August 8, 1758, Timothy Green the second brought out *The New London Summary, or the Weekly Advertiser*, at New London. Green died on the 3d of August, 1763, and the paper was suspended for three weeks. Afterward it was revived by Timothy Green, the third printer of that name in New London, under the title, *The New London Gazette*.

More important than either of these two Connecticut papers was *The Connecticut Courant*, first printed by Thomas Green at the Heart and Crown, near the North Meeting-House in Hartford, on Monday, October 29, 1764. This first issue was prospectus, having the number of 00. The first regular issue, however, was on December 3, 1764. During the War of the Revolution *The Connecticut Courant* occupied a rather important place in the journalism of the time. The British troops who took possession of New York had driven from that city all the patriotic printers, with the result that the circulation of *The Courant* was greatly increased, so much so that in all probability it was greater than that of any other colonial newspaper then printed. The paper has continued down to the present time and now bears the title of *The Hartford Courant*.

On October 23, 1767, Thomas and Samuel Green brought out in New Haven the first number of *The Connecticut Journal and New Haven Post-Boy*. After passing into the hands of many publishers the paper was discontinued on April 7, 1835. On July 3, 1776, *The Connecticut Journal* published the following note: "We are very sorry that we cannot procure a sufficiency of paper to publish a whole sheet; — but as there is now a paper-mill erecting in this town, we expect after a few weeks, to be supplied with such a quantity as to publish the Journal regularly on a uniform sized paper, and to be able to make ample amends for past deficiencies." In spite of its fairly long life the paper passed through the usual newspaper difficulties of the period. Some of the earliest issues were even smaller than that of the common letter paper.

Pretentious, at least in name, was *The Norwich Packet and the Connecticut, Massachusetts, New Hampshire, Rhode Island Weekly Advertiser*, first brought out on September 30, 1773, by Alexander Robertson, James Robertson, and John Trumbull. Three years later Trumbull became the sole proprietor and the Robertsons began publishing papers elsewhere.

ATTEMPTS OF DAVIS IN NORTH CAROLINA

In 1755 Benjamin Franklin, then Postmaster-General for the Colonies, appointed James Davis, who had emigrated from Virginia, to North Carolina, postmaster at Newbern. Following the example set by the colonial postmasters of Boston, the latter established the same year *The North Carolina Gazette*. It bore the following imprint: "Newbern: Printed by James Davis, at the Printing-office in Front Street; where all persons may be supplied with this paper at Sixteen Shillings per annum: And when Advertisements of a moderate length are inserted for Three Shillings the first Week and Two Shillings for every week after. And where also Book-Binding is done reasonably." Published on Thursdays, it usually appeared on a sheet pot size folio. Number 200 of this paper was dated October 18, 1759, and did not colonial editors frequently skip a week and often mix up their numbering it would be an easy matter to figure out by the help of old almanacs the Thursday in 1755 when this, the first paper in North Carolina, made its bow to Newbern. It was published about six years.

Davis made his second attempt to found a paper in 1764. He called the new venture *The North Carolina Magazine, or Universal Intelligencer*. (Its name was somewhat misleading, as the sheet appeared weekly on Fridays.) The first number was dated Friday, June 1, to Friday, June 8, 1764. The price per copy was four pence: at the end of 1764 there was a reduction in size of one half, but no reduction in price.

Evidently the second venture was not so successful as the first, for on May 27, 1768, Davis revived *The North Carolina Gazette*. This second *Gazette*, with intermittent publication, lasted a little over ten years. The word "intermittent" is used, since the issue for March 27, 1778, asserted that the third day of April next completed a year of publication since the paper was *last resumed*. The last known issue has the date of November 30, 1778.

Davis made still another attempt to found a *North Carolina Gazette*. The last was on August 28, 1783, two years before his death. His reason sheds considerable light on North Carolina journalism for the Colonial Period: "There has not been a newspaper published in North Carolina for several years." This third *Gazette* by Davis was an interesting example of newspaper-making, for it had neither headlines nor column rules. Possibly the reason why Davis was so unsuccessful in establishing a permanent paper may be found in the fact that he printed so little local news. Associated with Davis in this last enterprise was Robert Keith, who came from Pennsylvania. The full name of the paper was *The North Carolina Gazette, or Impartial Intelligencer and Weekly General Advertiser*.

STEWART — "PRINTER TO THE KING"

The second newspaper publisher in North Carolina was Andrew Stewart. Born in Belfast, Ireland, he, like many of the early printers, had come to America to seek his fortune, and in 1758 or 1759 had set up a press in Lætitia Court, Philadelphia, where he ran a bookstore along with his print-shop. Reaching Wilmington, North Carolina, June 24, 1764, with a part of his Philadelphia equipment, he announced himself as "Printer to the King." There is good reason to believe that his bluff worked and that he got part of the public printing. In September, 1764, he brought out the first number of *The North Carolina Gazette and Weekly Post-Boy*. Wilmington was a better news center than Newbern, and Stewart printed, for the time, many local items, but the paper did not take with the public and was discontinued for lack of support in 1767.

The second newspaper in Wilmington was *The Cape Fear Mercury* and was published by Adam Boyd. Number 7 had the date of November 24, 1769, and if there were no omissions in weekly publication, the first appearance must have been on October 13, 1769. An examination of the early issues shows that Boyd was not a practical printer, as his typography was very poor: yet the paper survived till the War of the Revolution broke out, being printed on the press and with the type that formerly belonged to Stewart.

ORIGIN OF JOURNALISM IN NEW HAMPSHIRE

New Hampshire got its first newspaper in a rather unique way. Daniel Fowle, after he left *The Independent Advertiser* of Boston, opened a small shop on Anne Street, where he sold books and pamphlets in addition to doing odd jobs on his press. Arrested in 1754 on the suspicion of having printed "The Monster of Monsters," said to be a reflection on the House of Representatives, and later sent to jail for having sold a few copies, he became disgusted with the Government of Massachusetts. At the psychological moment, to use a modern expression, a call came from New Hampshire to come over and start a paper in that colony. The call was answered by his removal to Portsmouth where he brought out Volume I, Number 1, of *The New Hampshire Gazette* on October 7, 1756.

On November 1, 1765, *The Gazette* came out with the usual black border, like so many other papers of the same time, and announced that it would cease publication because its printers were unwilling to pay the obnoxious stamp tax. During the War of the Revolution the paper was published rather irregularly and only slightly leaned toward the American cause. In 1776 it printed a communication urging the Provincial Congress not to establish an independent government because such a proceeding might be taken as a desire to throw off British rule. The editor was at once summoned before the Provincial Congress, severely censured, and admonished never in the future to publish articles reflecting upon the Continental Congress or the cause of American independence.

PAPER OF PATRIOTS

The Portsmouth Mercury and Weekly Advertiser, the second newspaper, came from the press of Thomas Ferber at his "New Printing Office Near the Parade," in Portsmouth, on January 21, 1765. The paper was started because of dissatisfaction of some of the ardent patriots who thought the first paper was not sufficiently strong for American rights. In spite of the fact that the new paper said it stood "Ever ready in exposing arbitrary powers, public injuries and all attempts to prevent the liberties of the people — dearer to them than their rights," it did not carry out its policy and consequently failed to obtain sufficient circulation to make the venture profitable. It was accordingly discontinued in about three years.

FIRST VENTURES IN DELAWARE

James Adams, a native of Ireland, was the publisher of *The Wilmington Chronicle*, the first newspaper in Delaware. After working for about seven years in the office of Franklin & Hall in Philadelphia, he set up a press in that city, but a year later (1761) he moved to Wilmington, where he first printed books and almanacs. In 1762 he started *The Chronicle*, but failed to get enough subscribers to make the venture profitable and after six months discontinued the sheet.

The second newspaper was also started in Wilmington in June, 1785, by Jacob A. Killen. He called his paper *The Delaware Gazette; or The Faithful Centinel*. The few copies of the early issues which have been preserved show that the paper had numerous variations in its title. From 1787 to 1791 the publishers were Frederick Craig & Company. On March 5 of the latter year, the partnership was dissolved and the paper continued by Peter Brynberg and Samuel Andrews — "late partners with Frederick Craig." The editorial policy of *The Gazette* was outlined in its issue for April 2, 1791, as follows: "Particular attention will be paid to agriculture and all communications (post paid) will be gratefully received and punctually attended to. Political pieces, with spirit and candor, in which *measures* rather than *men*, are attacked will always have a place in this paper. For the poet — a corner is ever open: and the mathematician will not be neglected." In September, 1795, the paper became a semi-weekly. With the issue of March 8, 1796, the imprint became "Printed for Robert Coram by Bonsal & Starr," and the same year it was again changed to "Printed by W. C. Smyth, rear of the New Fire-Engine, Shipley Street, opposite Capt. O'Flinn's Tavern." *The Gazette* was discontinued with the issue of September 7, 1799. The last issue, however, announced a successor in *The Mirror of the Times*, to be published a little later by James Wilson. After the failure of *The Chronicle*, James Adams took his son Samuel into partnership and started the third paper, *The Delaware Courant and Wilmington Advertiser*, in September, 1786. It appeared weekly and survived about three years.

The fourth paper, *The Delaware and Eastern Shore Advertiser*, was established in Wilmington on May 14, 1794, by S. and J. Adams and W. C. Smyth. With the issue of March 18, 1795, Smyth withdrew from the partnership in order to associate himself with *The Delaware Gazette*, as has already been mentioned. On Thursday, August 1, 1799, the paper appeared without the name of the publisher and in all probability that issue was the last.

PAPER POORLY SUPPORTED

The Mirror of The Times and General Advertiser, mention of which was made in the last issue of *The Delaware Gazette*, was the fifth paper in Delaware, and was started in Wilmington, Delaware, on November 20, 1799, by James Wilson as a Federal paper. It incidentally attracted a great deal of attention because it was the first newspaper in America to be printed on pure white paper especially prepared by a bleaching process discovered by Thomas D. Gilpin, of Wilmington. Its motto told the following tale: —

> Here sovereign truth for man's just rights contends,
> Alike unawed by foes, unswayed by friends.

Wilson, like other colonial printers, had the same "hard-luck tale" to record in his paper. In 1802, shortly after the New Castle County election, he announced to his friends and patrons that he would spend the day at Captain Caleb Bennett's Tavern, in New Castle, where he "would wait with his account-books open," hoping that all subscribers will call on him and inquire after the condition of his purse which was affected by a lingering consumptive complaint. The lingering complaint evidently proved fatal, for publication was suspended on August 22, 1806.

GAZETTES IN GEORGIA

For thirty years, after Georgia was founded, the colony depended for its news upon the papers of South Carolina, and its merchants were forced to advertise their goods in Charleston papers. On April 7, 1763, however, the first number of *The Georgia Gazette* was issued at Savannah by James Johnson at his printing-office on Broughton Street. On November 21, 1765, it suspended publication on account of the Stamp Act, but was revived again on May 21, 1766, and lasted as late as February 7, 1776, — possibly a little longer.

The second paper is not to be confused with the first, although it bore a somewhat similar title. It was called *The Royal Georgia Gazette* and was started in Savannah on January 21, 1781, by John D. Hammerer and survived until well along in 1782. From 1781 the paper was published by James Johnson — a fact which has caused some confusion because he was the founder of the first paper.

On January 31, 1783, Johnson started *The Gazette of the State of Georgia* — the third *Gazette* with which he was connected. He later shortened the name to *The Georgia Gazette*, the name of his first-born paper. Under this title the paper long continued to be published save for a temporary suspension on account of the great Savannah fire in 1796.

Such, in brief, was the history of the journalism enterprises in Georgia until the colonies secured their independence.

TARDY PAPERS IN NEW JERSEY

The first printed newspapers did not appear in New Jersey until the War of the Revolution had started. But it is not hard to explain this tardy appearance: Philadelphia and New York newspapers circulated then, as they do to-day, through New Jersey. The suspension of some of these papers, the removal of others to distant points, the increase in subscription price, the poor delivery by post-riders, many of whom were in active military service — all these things, coupled with the exciting events of the War, created an independent demand for news on the part of the patriots of New Jersey. Its Governor, William Livingston, knowing, in addition to the facts just mentioned, how useful a newspaper could be to arouse local public sentiment, made the following plea in a message to the Colonial Legislature October 11, 1777: —

Gentlemen: It would be an unnecessary Consumption of Time to enumerate all the Advantages that would redound to the State from having a Weekly News-Paper printed and circulated in it. — To facilitate such an Undertaking, it is proposed that the first Paper be circulated as soon as seven hundred subscribers, whose Punctuality in paying may be relied upon, shall be procured: Or if Government will insure seven hundred subscribers who shall pay, the Work will be immediately begun; and if at the End of six Months there shall be seven hundred or more subscribers who will pay punctually, the Claim upon the Government to cease. But if the subscribers fall short of that Number, Government to become a subscriber so as to make up that Number. The Price in these fluctuating Times can hardly be ascertained, but it is supposed it cannot at present be less than Twenty-six shillings per Year, which will be but six Pence a Paper.

STATE-SUBSIDIZED NEWSPAPER

A committee, to whom the matter was referred, brought in the following recommendations which were adopted: (1) A paper to be printed weekly, in four folio pages, and entitled *The New-Jersey Gazette;* (2) price to be twenty-six shillings per year; (3) the Legislature to guarantee seven hundred subscribers within six months; (4) a cross-post to be established from the printing-office, to the nearest Continental post-office at the expense of the State; (5) the printer and four workmen to be exempted from service in the militia. The printer selected for this State-subsidized newspaper — one of the very few in the history of American journalism — was Isaac Collins, who already had a plant at Burlington. He was a native of New Castle County, Delaware, where he was born "2d mo. 16, 1746" (Old Style). Learning his trade in the shop of James Adams, Wilmington, Delaware (see "Delaware Papers"), he had gone to Williams-burg, Virginia, to work for William Rind (see "Virginia Papers"). His most practical experience, however, he had obtained in Philadelphia while in the employ of William Goddard, the pub-lisher of *The Pennsylvania Chronicle.*

Collins, immediately after his selection for the position, began to make preparation to bring out the paper, but owing to the unsettled condition of the country he was not able to "pull" the first number off his press until December 5, 1777. With the issue of March 4, 1778, he took *The New-Jersey Gazette* to Tren-ton. Contrary to his expectations, the paper was not better supported at that place and at last suspended publication in July, 1783. Collins, however, was a plucky editor and made an attempt to revive *The Gazette* on December 9, 1783. He strug-gled along until November 27, 1786, when he brought out the last issue. He still continued his shop at Trenton, for the politi-cal plum of public printing had fallen into the lap of his apron.

Before he discontinued *The New-Jersey Gazette,* he was selling at his printing-office medicinal preparations, dry goods, groceri-ies, etc.: a complete list would read like an advertisement in a country four-corners store. He also received a commission on the negro boys and wenches whose sales he effected through the columns of his paper. He died at Burlington, New Jersey, March 21, 1817.

"JERSEY JOURNAL"

Two circumstances account for the appearance of the second newspaper in New Jersey. One was that when New York fell into the hands of the British the newspapers which continued publication there were loyal to the Crown: the second was that the army of General Washington at Morristown wanted a paper to tell the news of what the colonies outside of New Jersey were doing. Undoubtedly the latter was the more important, for Shepard Kollock, a printer at Chatham, who, like Collins, had learned the trade with James Adams at Wilmington, started, at the suggestion of General Knox, *The New-Jersey Journal* on February 16, 1779. The soldiers only five miles away subscribed liberally, considering how pitifully small were the wages received, and the officers often furnished, in exchange for army printing, the paper upon which *The Journal* was printed.

At the end of the Revolution, Kollock, finding himself in a place too small to support a newspaper, went to New Brunswick, where, on October 14, 1783, he started, with Shelly Arnett, *The Political Intelligencer and New-Jersey Advertiser* "at the Barracks," a building used to shelter British troops in colonial days. The partnership was dissolved in July, 1784, and he became the sole owner. On April 20, 1785, Kollock brought out his newspaper in "Elizabeth Town." With Number 134, or on May 10, 1786, he changed its title to *The New-Jersey Journal and Political Intelligencer*. It still survives as *The Elizabeth Daily Journal*. The change in name from *The New-Jersey Journal* was made when the paper became a daily on July 17, 1871.

Philip Freneau started *The Jersey Chronicle* at Mt. Pleasant, May 2, 1795, but discontinued publication on April 30th of the following year. For Freneau's *National Gazette* see page 122. The first paper in Newark was *The Centinel of Freedom*, brought out on October 5, 1796, by Daniel Dodge and Company. John Woods started a *Gazette* in Newark on May 19, 1791. On May 15, 1787, *The Weekly Mercury* was established at Trenton. *The New Jersey State Gazette*, begun in Trenton on March 5, 1799, was published by George Sherman and John Mershon. On March 26, 1799, Isaiah Thomas, a nephew of Isaiah Thomas of *The Massachusetts Spy*, became a member of the firm. On July 1, 1800, the paper united with *The Federalist*, which had been established on July 9, 1798, by Gershon Craft and William Black and which was one of the leading party papers of New Jersey at a later period.

CHAPTER VI

COLONIAL PERIOD

1704—1765

THE colonial editor, to whom journalism was a trade rather than a profession, found many difficulties in publishing his paper. In the first place, it was hard for him to get stock, for most of the paper on which he printed the news was imported from Europe, or was secured with difficulty from the few paper-mills established in this country. The year 1690, which saw the appearance in Boston of *Publick Occurrences*, also saw the establishment at Germantown, Pennsylvania, of the first paper-mill in the colonies. Other mills were erected so that the town became the early home of the paper industry in America. In one of them, William Bradford by 1697 had a fourth interest. When he came to New York and started his *Gazette*, he met the same difficulty in getting paper for his press that he had previously experienced in Philadelphia, but found relief by starting in 1728 a paper-mill at "Elizabeth Town," New Jersey. In 1730 a paper-mill was erected at Milton, Massachusetts, and soon had a monopoly of the trade around Boston. Sometimes the newspaper had to establish its own mill. Such was true of *The Connecticut Courant*, at Hartford. While this newspaper secured its own paper from Norwich, the droughts in summer or ice in the river in winter frequently curtailed the size of the sheet. Other newspapers, by inserting advertisements of "Rags Wanted," supplied the mills with material from which the paper was made.

TYPOGRAPHY OF PAPERS

The size of the newspaper has been so frequently given in connection with the mention of individual papers that little more needs to be said. From 1704 to 1765 newspapers were generally printed on half-sheets. Shapes and sizes varied greatly, not only because of the scarcity of news of the various towns, but more frequently because of the scarcity of paper. In spite of his meager equipment the colonial printer seldom found it necessary, even when he gave his reader two whole sheets, to use more than one variety of type. Newspapers, however, varied much in their style of typography. One distinctive mechanical characteristic of the colonial newspaper was the frequent use of a large initial letter for the leading news item or essay. From the beginning of the printed newspaper in this country down to the time when Franklin gave up writing for his newspaper, all nouns were capitalized, and it seemed generally permissible to capitalize any other word, at the printer's discretion. Extracts from colonial newspapers have been given frequently enough in the preceding pages to give the reader a fairly accurate idea of the orthography of the period. Some editors, usually of other birth than English, evidently compiled a dictionary of their own for office use. John Peter Zenger, for example, invariably spelled "Monday" in his date line, "Munday," but frequently allowed contributors to spell the word "Monday."

PRESSES AND INKS

In the tools of his trade the colonial printer was under a severe handicap. Both press and type had to be imported from England, and in many instances the printer because of his poverty had to purchase second-hand outfits. Such presses as were used were built practically of wood, and were often so constructed that only one page of even the small-sized colonial newspaper could be printed at one time. This handicap made four pulls necessary on the part of the printer before he could produce a printed newspaper of a whole sheet. Even in the case of the larger presses, two impressions were necessary for every copy of the paper. In other words, the output of a press was equal to one half the number of pulls a printer could give in an hour. It took so much muscular strength to pull the lever of the old-fashioned press that the services of a man were required. The only help a boy could be in the colonial print-shop was to ink the type: this he did, in many instances, with the help of a deerskin ball filled with wool and nailed to a stick of hickory. Not until 1750 were printing-presses manufactured in America: in that year, Christopher Sower, Jr., began to turn out hand-presses at Germantown, Pennsylvania. Handicapped by the lack of skilled labor, he was even then only able to manufacture presses inferior to those imported from Europe.

Reliable printing-ink also came from abroad. Substitutes were frequently attempted by the early printers and were manufactured from wild berries. The fading of the impression in some of the early colonial papers may be traced directly to the use of such substitutes. Not until the close of the first half of the eighteenth century was there a manufacture of a printers' ink that was worth the name.

MAKERS OF TYPE

Much of the poor printing in the Colonial Period was due to the fact that the type had become badly worn from frequent use. Often, the type had been used for years in printing colonial documents and pamphlets before it was employed to print the news. To get new type it was frequently necessary for the printer to make a special trip to England. The first attempt to cast type was made in Boston about 1768 by a Scotchman by the name of Michelson. With the scant materials available, he did the best that could be expected, but his type lacked the wearing qualities of the imported variety. Christopher Sower, Jr., of whom mention has already been made in connection with the manufacture of printing-presses, began to cast type in 1772 at his foundry in Germantown, but was compelled to secure his raw material in Germany. One of Sower's workmen, Jacob Bey, started the second type foundry in Germantown, and made several improvements in the composition of the metal employed in the manufacture of type. The most important type foundry was that established by Benjamin Franklin in 1775. For years Franklin had been whittling type out of wood and had been making cuts of metal, but not until the outbreak of the Revolution did he make a business of casting type. In charge of his foundry he put his son-in-law, B. F. Bache, who later figured in Philadelphia journalism.

WINTER WEATHER AND NEWS

Winter always brought its difficulties to the colonial printer. His shop often being poorly heated in severely cold weather the paper froze while it was being prepared for the press and caused endless delays. The colonial printer was forced to wet his paper before he could put it on the press. Winter also interfered seriously in the delivery of newspapers: post-riders who acted as mail-carriers frequently had to abandon their routes because the roads were closed by snowdrifts. Such irregularity in delivery frequently caused subscribers to discontinue their papers until the roads were open for travel again in the spring. This custom occasionally caused the colonial publisher so much annoyance that he threatened to move his paper to another town unless readers would subscribe for the paper for the entire year.

Possibly some of these discontinuances during the winter season were the fault of the colonial editor. Rural subscribers cared more for local news than they did for reprints from English papers. During the winter months when ships neither arrived nor departed from the ports, early American editors had a hard time to fill their columns. Few of them, however, were as frank as William Bradford, of *The New York Gazette*, who, on one occasion, explained the presence of an abstruse discussion in his columns as follows: "There being a scarcity of Foreign News, we hope the following Essay may not be unacceptable to our READERS." Severely cold weather was often accepted by the colonial printer as the excuse for omitting an issue entirely. Benjamin Franklin was always equal to any emergency. He frankly admitted that when news was dull during the winter season, he amused the customers of *The Pennsylvania Gazette* by filling the vacant columns with anecdotes, fables, and fancies of his own. To these "fillers" he gave such an air of truth that he not infrequently deceived his own readers. Many of his anecdotes, written only to amuse and entertain, were quoted as Gospel truth by European writers on American affairs.

FARLEY, PROGRESSIVE PUBLISHER

One attempt during this period to get the news while it was still news should not be overlooked. Samuel Farley, the son of a Quaker printer of Bristol, England, brought out the seventh paper in New York City on March 20, 1762. He called his paper *The American Chronicle*, and being energetic he tried to make it live up to its name. In his efforts to gather news more quickly he tried to secure from *The Pennsylvania Journal* and from *The Pennsylvania Gazette* advance sheets of these newspapers, but in each instance he was unsuccessful, as the two Philadelphia publishers positively refused to let him have copies of their papers before the usual time for city delivery. The refusal showed the spirit that then prevailed among American newspapers. Not until the early part of the nineteenth century did newspapers coöperate in sharing the burden of news-gathering.

Farley did, however, introduce into *The American Chronicle* a department called "The Lion's Mouth," which attracted much attention for its day. Some idea of this innovation may be obtained from the announcement of the feature in the fourth issue, April 12, 1762: —

In order to convey such Papers to the Publisher of *The Chronicle* as may be of general entertainment and Instruction, in the most secret Manner; and to prevent all such authors as chuse to remain incog. from being known even to the Printer, he has procured a young Lion, thro' whose Mouth (which stands immoveably expanded) the said Compositions may be conveyed with the utmost Secrecy; and such of them as shall be deem'd acceptable to the Public, and are free from all Defamation and personal Reflection, and come properly recommended, shall be inserted in *The Chronicle*. The Lion will be seated in the Day Time near the Window fronting the Dock, and to prevent his annoying any of his Majesty's Liege Subjects (tho' he is extremely tame and good natured) he will be chained securely to the Post of the Window. . . In the Night Time, to prevent his taking cold by the noxious Dew of this Northern climate, he will be placed on a Pedestal in the Entry just behind or so near the Door, that any Materials may be conveyed into his Mouth (which is always open) thro' a Hole in the Upper Door which leads direct to his Jaw.

N.B. He will Roar at no honest man whatsoever.

NEWS OF MODERN FLAVOR

Some of the news items published as early as 1747 had a modern flavor. But for the color of the paper and the spelling of the words a second glance for the date-line is almost necessary. When the American colonies were raising men to defend northern frontiers against invasions by the French and Indians and were voting appropriations with modern prodigality, there were newspapers which brought charges of graft against the men furnishing supplies to the troops. Parker's *New-York Gazette and Weekly Post-Boy* boldly printed an item which alleged that many of the guns purchased were out-of-date and practically useless, and that the beef for soldiers was more effective than powder because its odor would drive away the enemy. An editorial contributor, who had a keen sense of humor, offered the explanation that the guns were supplied by Quakers, who had scruples against the taking of human life, and that the loss on the meat could more easily be borne by the colonies than by the original owners. Veiled attacks were made that favoritism was shown in the selection of men to lead the troops and that incompetency was common, especially among the British officers sent over to defend the colonies.

NEWS "BOILED DOWN"

The colonial editor was often a master of his trade in "boiling down" the news: he did not use three columns when three lines would tell the story. *The Pennsylvania Gazette* on January 7, 1752, saw no "sensational copy" in its item, "We hear that within these few Days, near 400 Five-penny Loaves have been seized among the Bakers of this City, by the Clerk of the Market, for wanting greatly in their due Weight"; nor did it place any "scare" headline over this one on February 25 of the same year: "Last Week William Kerr (lately mention'd in this Paper) was indicted and convicted at the Mayor's Court, of uttering counterfeit Mill'd Pieces of Eight, knowing them to be such, for which he receiv'd Sentence as follows: To stand in the Pillory one Hour To-morrow, to have his Ear nail'd to the same, and the Part nail'd cut off; and on Saturday next to stand another Hour in the Pillory, and to be whipt Thirty-nine Lashes, at the Cart's Tail, round two Squares, and then to pay a Fine of Fifty Pounds."

COLONISTS SLOW PAY

Franklin, in his "Autobiography," has left a permanent record that the colonists were not especially interested either in newspapers or in books. To quote from the pen of this distinguished editor of the Colonial Period: "At the time I established myself in Philadelphia — 1723 — there was not a good bookseller's shop in any of the colonies to the southward of Boston. In New York and Philadelphia the printers were indeed stationers, but they sold only paper, almanacs, ballads, and a few common school-books. Those who loved reading were obliged to send for their books to England."

Even those most interested in reading preferred to buy their books and newspapers from England. This fact may explain why so many of the colonial editors reprinted pieces from English papers: in other words, they attempted to give readers what the latter wanted. Then, too, the colonists often followed the English custom of reading their newspapers at the public taverns. Other conditions prevented a paper from having a large circulation in rural sections. Subscribers living at a distance from the place of publication had to pay not only the subscription price of the paper, but also the cost for distribution by the mail-carrier. The pine knot, the tallow candle, or the bit of bear oil burning in a saucer afforded poor light for the perusal of a newspaper by a farmer, already tired by the day's toil of clearing forest land.

The fervent appeals of colonial editors to delinquent subscribers show how hard it was for the poor printer to raise the necessary funds in cash to meet the cost of his materials sent from abroad. To judge by the notices, the colonial editor experienced much the same difficulty in getting his subscribers to part with provisions in exchange for newspapers. Yet the colonial printer was willing to take almost anything in exchange for subscriptions. Firewood, homespun cloth, butter, eggs, poultry — almost anything was acceptable to "ye printer."

Some of the dunning appeals to subscribers were most unique. One printed by Thomas Fleet in *The Boston Evening Post* brought results even if some delinquents did not renew: "The Subscribers for this Paper, (especially those at a Distance) who are shamefully in Arrear for it, would do well (methinks) to remember those Apostolical Injunctions, Rom. xiii. 7, 8. *Render therefore to all their dues; — and Owe no man any thing.* — It is wonderful to observe, that while we hear so much about *a great Revival of Religion in the Land;* there is yet so little Regard had to *Justice and Common Honesty!* Surely they are *Abominable Good Works!*"

PRINTER CAPITALIZES MOTHER-IN-LAW

Thomas Fleet, who has been mentioned in the preceding paragraph, found many ways to supplement the income from *The Boston Evening Post*. One of these was from the sale of "Mother Goose Rhymes." Fleet, who had married Elizabeth Goose, was very much amused at the nursery jingles with which his mother-in-law amused his children at night. After he had put them into type he found it necessary to print several editions to meet the demand. So far as can be learned Fleet was the first man to capitalize his mother-in-law.

COST OF PRODUCTION

Fleet also left a memorandum which illustrated trade conditions of his day. In it he said: "In the days of Mr. Campbell (the founder of *The Boston News-Letter*), who published a newspaper here, which is forty years ago, Paper was bought for eight or nine shillings a Ream, and now tis Five Pounds; his Paper was never more than half a sheet, and that he had Two Dollars a year for, and had also the art of getting his Pay for it; and that size has continued until within a little more than one year, since which we are expected to publish a whole sheet, so that the Paper now stands us in near as much as all the other charges." For the sake of comparison of the cost of production of *The Boston Evening Post* with that of a similar paper published later in the century, the figures may be given for 1798. In that year the editor of *The Northern Budget,* a weekly paper published at

Troy, New York, asserted that he could, with the utmost economy, conduct his paper at thirty dollars a week. His estimate was somewhat lower than that of other editors of his time because he was able to get paper cheaper on account of the fact that a paper-mill had been built in Troy about five years previous.

ADVERTISEMENTS OF PERIOD

When John Campbell brought out *The Boston News-Letter* on April 24, 1704, he announced that "Persons who have any Houses, Lands, Tenements, Farms, Ships, Vessels, Goods, Wares or Merchandizes, &c. to be Sold, or Let; or Servants Runaway, or Goods Stole or Lost; may have the same inserted at a Reasonable Rate, from *Twelve Pence* to *Five Shillings*, and not to exceed: Who may agree with *John Campbel* Post-master of *Boston*." This list is fairly typical of the advertisements inserted in colonial newspapers. In many instances the Boston post-office was made the clearing-house: the first advertisement in the second number of *The News-Letter* offered a reward for the return of two iron anvils, weighing between one hundred and twenty and one hundred and forty pounds each, which had been lost "Off Mr. Shippen's Wharff," provided they were returned to John Campbell, Postmaster. Many of the advertisements contained the stereotyped expression, "For further information, inquire of John Campbell, Postmaster."

The third number of *The News-Letter* contained the following advertisement: —

A t Oysterbay on *Long-Island* in the Province of *N. York*, There is a very good Fulling-Mill, to be Let or Sold, as also a Plantation, having on it a large new Brick house, and another good house by it for a Kitchin, & work house, with a Barn, Stable, &c. a young Orchard and 20 Acres clear Land. The Mill is to be Let with or without the Plantation: Enquire of Mr. *William Bradford* Printer in *N. York* and know further.

This insertion in the third number showed quick action on the part of Bradford when it is considered how long it took to get a letter from New York to Boston at that time: it also showed that Bradford was familiar with, and was doubtless watching with much interest, the attempt to found a newspaper in Boston.

Advertisements similar to the following were found in colonial papers: —

Captain *Peter Lawrence* is going a Privateering from *Rhode-Island* in a good Sloop, about 60 Tuns, six Guns, and 90 Men for *Canada*, and any Gentlemen or Sailors that are disposed to go shall be kindly entertained.

The first advertisements of any size were those announcing the sale of books and pamphlets — especially those dealing with religious topics, or giving the sermons of noted divines. After the colonial publishers had reprinted extracts from *The London Gazette*, *The London Flying Post*, *The London Post-Boy*, etc., they advertised these English newspapers for sale at greatly reduced prices.

Franklin especially knew the value of *The Pennsylvania Gazette* as an advertising medium, and used it frequently, not only for himself, but also the members of his family. His wife, for example, sold in the print-shop a so-called very fine grade of toilet soap, said to have been imported from abroad, but doubtless manufactured by Franklin's father in Boston. He occasionally put into his "house" advertisements some of the humor found in "Poor Richard's Almanac." The following advertisement of this character was taken from *The Pennsylvania Gazette*: —

TAKEN out of Pew in the Church some months since, a Common Prayer Book, bound in red, gilt, and lettered D.F. (Deborah Franklin) on each cover. The Person who took it is desired to open it and read the eighth Commandment, and afterwards return it into the same Pew again, upon which no further Notice will be taken.

Another advertisement, inserted by Franklin in 1742, must have given his subscribers the impression that he was in the importing as well as in the printing business: —

JUst import'd from Lond and to be sold by B. Franklin, at the Post-Office, near the Market in Philadelphia.

All sorts of fine Paper, Parchment, Ink-powder, Sealing Wax, Wafers, fountain Pens, Ink and Sand Glasses with Brass Heads, Pounce, and

Pounce Boxes, Curious, large Ivory Books and Common ditto, large and small slates, Gunters Scales, Dividers, Protactors, Pocket Compasses, both large and small, fine Pewter Stands proper for Offices and Counting Houses, fine Mezzotinto and grav'd Pictures of Mr. Whitefield.

Where may be had great Variety of Bibles, Testaments, Psalters, Spelling Books, Primers, Hornbooks, and other sorts of stationery ware.

Even James Franklin, Benjamin's brother, was a good advertiser of the products of his press. Before he started *The New-England Courant*, and while he was still printing *The Boston Gazette* for Postmaster Brooker, he inserted this advertisement in the latter paper on April 25, 1720: —

The Printer hereof prints Linens, Calicoes, Silks, &c., in good Figures, very livily and durable colours, and without the offensive Smell which commonly attends the Linens printed here.

PILLS AND POWDERS SOLD AT PRINT-SHOPS

Even the most successful of the colonial printer-editors had to supplement the income from their presses by work in other fields. Attention has already been called to how frequently they were postmasters, or employed in the postal department. Almost invariably they were booksellers and stationers, especially of their own presses. To read the list of things which might be obtained at the print-shop gives one the impression that the colonial editor practically ran a store. Often he sold over the counter the goods accepted in payment for subscriptions. He seemed to make a specialty of selling quack medicines: he early discovered the value of his own newspaper as an advertising medium for such nostrums. The colonial editors of New York practically acted as wholesale distributors for such nostrums and encouraged their brother editors in other colonies to put pills and powders alongside of the Bibles and printed sermons on the shelves of the print-shop. Some of these nostrums "cured diseases not to be mentioned in the newspaper"; for full details sufferers might call at the office of the colonial papers and editors would answer any questions asked. In the North, most of these so-called remedies were imported from Europe and frequently bore the endorsement of royal persons;

in the South, most of the proprietary medicines offered for sale by local printers were manufactured from herbs after prescriptions furnished by Indian doctors. Typical of the latter *The South Carolina Gazette* advertised in January, 1744: —

The Seneka-Rattle-Snake-Root, so famous for its effectually curing of Pleurisy; and an excellent Eye-Water, to be sold by the Printer hereof.

TALES TOLD BY ADVERTISEMENTS

Save for their headlines, advertisements were frequently set up like regular reading matter. They were usually small in size, and not infrequently limited in size by the printer. Occasionally, one finds a colonial printer using the margins for an advertisement which came in late. Strange as it may seem, however, these advertisements when read to-day are almost as interesting as the text. They tell a story which needs but little by way of interpretation. They tell us of the fads and fancies in the matter of dress of the colonial period. If there were no mention of the prevalence of smallpox in the colonies, one would know that it was common because the word "pock-fretten" was used in describing a slave who had run away and for whom a reward was offered in the local press. The advertisements of servants and apprentices, who, like the slaves, had run away from their masters, recall a time when people were sold in bondage for a limited time until the money owed for their passage across the ocean, or for debts incurred after their arrival, was paid in full. The amount of the reward offered was often small — six cents. Such small rewards, however, are explained by the fact that masters were required by law to advertise runaway servants and slaves.

The advertisements of the colonial department stores — if that term may be used correctly — need to-day a glossary in order that articles described may be intelligible, even to women. How many readers of this book, for example, are familiar with the items listed by Isaac Jones, when in 1752 he advertised in *The Pennsylvania Gazette* to be sold cheap the following things?

Boiled and common camblets, single and double alopeens, broad and narrow shaloons, tammies, durants, plain and corded poplins, duroys, calimancoes, common and silk sagathies, florettas, bearskins, common and hair grazets, tabbies, ducapes, stay galloon and twist, men's and women's thread, dowlas, ozenbrigs, etc.

LIVE NEWS IN ADVERTISEMENTS

Charles Dudley Warner, who was connected for many years with *The Courant* of Hartford, Connecticut, once asserted that the colonial newspaper was a "broadside of stale news with a moral essay attached." Whatever may be true of the news, the advertisements in these old papers were rather interesting reading. There was nothing stale in this item inserted at regular rates in the columns of *The New-York Gazette* for 1734: —

Whereas James Moor of Woodbridge has advertised in this *Gazette*, as well as by Papers sent out and posted up, that his Wife, Deliverance, has eloped from his Bed and Board. These are to certifie, that the Same is altogether false, for She has lived with Him above Eight Years under His tyranny and increditble Abuses, for He has several times attempted to murder Her and also turned Her out of Doors, shamefully abusing Her, which is well known to the Neighbors and Neighbourhood in Woodbridge.

An advertisement in *The New York Weekly Post-Boy* in 1756 showed that Barnum was not the first to discover that the American people liked to be fooled once in a while: —

To be seen at the sign of the Golden Apple, at Peck's Slip, price sixpence, children four coppers, a large snake-skin, 21 feet long and four feet one inch wide. It was killed by some of Gen. Braddock's men by firing six balls into him, close by the Allegheny Mountains, supposed to be coming down to feed on dead men. When it was killed, there was found in its belly a child, supposed to be four years old, together with a *live* dog! It had a horn on its tail seven inches long, and it ran as fast as a horse. All gentlemen and ladies desirous to see it may apply to the subscriber at Peck's Slip.

ADVERTISING AGENCY IN POST-OFFICES

In many localities, advertisements for colonial papers might be left at the local post-office. In some instances the local post-office would accept advertising copy for publication in papers in other places: it did so with the permission of the postal authorities. Sometimes the post-office made public in print standing announcements similar to the following which appeared during the middle of the eighteenth century in *The Pennsylvania Gazette* at Philadelphia: "Advertisements for the German and English Gazettes printed at Lancaster by Miller and Holland are taken at the post-office." In fact, the colonial post-office always stood ready to help the newspaper when the postmaster was not financially interested in the printing-plant. William Bradford, the publisher of the first colonial weekly in New York, made an arrangement with Richard Nichols, postmaster in 1727, whereby the latter accepted advertisements for *The New-York Gazette* at regular rates and sold single copies of the paper at what to-day would be the stamp window.

FREE POSTAGE AT FIRST

When John Campbell first sent out his written news-letters to colonial Governors, they were mailed without cost. Later, when he printed his letters under the title, *The Boston News-Letter*, he undoubtedly was able to mail many of them free and only had to pay a nominal charge in other cases. One of the reasons why the colonial printer-editor desired to be postmaster was undoubtedly the opportunity that was afforded by such an office to make advantageous arrangements with local post-riders to deliver newspapers. Certainly, the postmaster-editor possessed better facilities for the distribution of his paper than rival editors; Benjamin Franklin and William Weyman have already borne testimony to this fact.

Franklin was a master at the art of securing free distribution of his *Pennsylvania Gazette*. In his issue for January 28, 1735, he published the following item: "By the indulgence of the Honorable Colonel Spotswood, Post-Master-General, the printer hereof is allowed to send the *Gazettes* by the post, *postage free*, to all parts of the postroad, from Virginia to New England."

REGULATIONS OF FRANKLIN

But as newspapers increased, a change from the plan just outlined was made. In 1758 Franklin and Hunter were in charge of the general post-office for the colonies, and on March 10 of that year they issued the following statement: —

Whereas the News-papers of the several Colonies on this Continent, heretofore permitted to be sent by the Post free of Charge, are of late years so much increased as to become extremely burthensome to the Riders, who demand additional Salaries or Allowances from the Post Office on that Account, and it is not reasonable that the Office which receives no Benefit from the Carriage of News-papers, should be at any Expence for such Carriage; and Whereas the Printers of News-papers complain that they frequently receive orders for News-papers from distant Post-Offices, which they comply with by sending the Papers tho they know not the Persons to whom the Papers are to be directed, and have no convenient Means of collecting the Money, so that much of it is lost; and that for Want of due Notice when distant Subscribers die, become Bankrupt, or remove out of the County, they continue to send Papers some years directed to such Persons, whereby the Posts are loaded with Many Papers to No Purpose, and the Loss so great to the Printers, as that they cannot afford to make any Allowance to the Riders for carrying the Papers; And whereas some of the Riders do, and others may demand exorbitant Rates of Persons living on the Roads, for carrying and delivering the Papers that do not go into Any Office, but are delivered by the Riders themselves.

To remedy these Inconveniences, and yet not to discourage the Spreading of News-papers, which are on many Occasions useful to Government, and advantageous to Commerce, and to the Publick; You are, after the first Day of June Next, to deliver No News-paper at your Office (except the single Papers exchang'd between Printer and Printer) but to such Persons only as do agree to pay you, for the Use of the Rider which brings such papers a small addition Consideration *per Annum*, for each Paper, over and above the Price of the Papers: *that is to say*, For any Distance not exceeding 50 miles, each Paper is carried, the Sum of 9d. Ster. *per Annum*, or an equivalent in Currency: For any Distance exceeding 50 miles, and not exceeding One Hundred Miles the Sum of One Shilling and Six Pence Ster. *per Annum;* and in the same proportion for every other Fifty Miles which such Paper shall be carried; which Money for the Rider or Riders, together with the Price of the Papers for the Printers, you are to receive and pay respectively once a Year at least, deducting for your Care and Trouble therein a Commission of *Twenty per cent.* And you are to send no Order to any Printer for Papers, except the Persons, to whom the Papers are to be sent, are in your Opinion responsible, and such as you will be accountable for. And you are to suffer no Rider employed or paid by you to receive more than the rates above for carrying any Papers by them delivered on their respective Roads: Nor to carry and deliver any Papers but such as they will be accountable for to the Printers, in consideration of an Allowance of the same Commission as aforesaid for Collecting and paying the Money.

And as some of the Papers pass thro' the Hands of several Riders between the Places where they are printed and the Place of Delivery; You are to pay the Carriage-money you collect for the Riders to the several Riders who have carried such Papers in Proportion, as near as conveniently may be made, to the Distance, they have been carried by each Rider respectively.

(Signed) FRANKLIN AND HUNTER.

This order remained in force until the relations between the colonies and England and the postal service became interrupted on account of the approaching conflict of the Revolution. Then many of the newspaper publishers arranged for a private distribution of their papers to country subscribers.

The reforms of Franklin and Hunter in the reorganization of the colonial post-office and in the increase of post-roads had two effects on the journalism of the period. First, there was an increase in letters among correspondents in the several colonies, and as these letters often contained news items of considerable importance, they not infrequently found their way into the newspapers under some such caption as "From a Gentleman Residing in Virginia"; second, the newspapers were placed on a better subscription basis, and the exchange papers, being more regular in their receipt, not only improved the news service, but also aroused a news interest in what was going on in all the colonies. Without this awakened interest, it might have been impossible to have persuaded the colonies to unite for common defense in the Revolutionary Period.

LOST — ELEVEN DAYS

Readers who turn the files of colonial newspapers for 1752 are often surprised at the irregularity in the matter of dating found in the papers for the first week of September of that year. The fifth issue of *The Mercury*, published by Hugh Gaine at New York, was dated August 31, 1752: seven days later, the sixth was dated September 18. Yet no mistake had been made; eleven days had simply been wiped out of existence by the change to the Gregorian style in figuring time, adopted the first week of September, 1752. Several writers have thought that Benjamin Franklin skipped a week in publishing his *Pennsylvania Gazette* at Philadelphia in the September of 1752. The irregularity here, as elsewhere, was due to the change to the Gregorian system of time.

B. FRANKLIN, CARTOONIST

Benjamin Franklin, who introduced many innovations into the American press, was the first to print the cartoon in his *Pennsylvania Gazette*. The occasion was a memorable one in American history. The government of the New York colony, on the recommendation of the Lords of Trade, issued on December 24, 1753, a call for a meeting in Albany of the British colonies in America and announced the date for that meeting for June 14, 1754. Rumors of a possible war with the French was the immediate cause of the action. The rumors were not without some foundation, for on May 9, 1754, Franklin, who was one of the three commissioners to attend the Albany convention on behalf of Pennsylvania, published in *The Pennsylvania Gazette* an "advice" for Major Washington that the fort in the Forks of the Monongahela had been surrendered to the French. To increase the force of his appeal for "our common defense and security," he inserted a cartoon which represented a snake cut into eight parts: the head represented New England, and the seven other parts stood for New York, New Jersey, Pennsylvania, Maryland, Virginia, North Carolina, and South Carolina. By way of a caption Franklin inserted under the cartoon the words "Join or Die."

INFLUENCE OF FIRST CARTOON

The power of the cartoon was at once recognized by the other editors of colonial papers. Before the end of the month, the snake cartoon had been copied in *The New-York Gazette*, *The New-York Mercury*, *The Boston Gazette*, and *The Boston News-Letter*. *The Boston Gazette* improved the original by putting the following words into the mouth of the snake, "Unite and Conquer." The influence of the cartoon was not entirely confined to the papers already mentioned. *The South Carolina Gazette*, for example, doing the best it could with the mechanical facilities at its disposal, printed a "near-snake" with straight lines to represent its parts. Even *The Virginia Gazette* spoke of a "late ingenious emblem" which was arousing the colonies. The snake of this cartoon was not allowed to die, but in its charmed life it appeared twice more in the newspapers at critical periods in American history. After a sleep of eleven years the snake appeared when the British Stamp Act was scheduled to go into effect, and after another rest it appeared at the outbreak of the Revolution.

TAXES ON NEWSPAPERS

During the Colonial Period two attempts were made to tax newspapers. The first was in Massachusetts, the second in New York. In both instances the tax was designed simply to raise revenue for the colony and not to restrict in any way the publishing of a newspaper. In each colony the tax was paid by the ultimate consumer and not by the producer of the newspaper.

FIRST IN MASSACHUSETTS

The Provincial Legislature of Massachusetts published on January 13, 1755, an act, passed on January 8 of that year, which imposed a tax of a halfpenny on every newspaper printed on and after April 30, 1755. The act was to cover a period of two years, from April 30, 1755, to April 30, 1757. There were three papers published in Boston: all of these appeared with "the little red stamp," save those preserved for office files. The stamp, usually put on the lower part of the right-hand margin of the paper, was a bird with outstretched wings. Of it *The Boston Evening Post* spoke as follows in its issue for May 5, 1755: —

> *The little pretty Picture here,*
> *O' the Side looks well enough;*
> *Though nothing to the purpose 't is,*
> *It will serve to set it off.*

As has already been intimated, the subscribers rather than the printers paid for the adornment of "the little red bird" which stood for the tax. *The Boston News-Letter* in its issue for April 24, 1755, published the following announcement: —

As the Stamp-Duty takes Place on Wednesday next, the 30th Current, the Publisher of this Paper desires such of his good Customers in Town or Country, who intend to take in on the Terms lately advertised, and have not yet given notice thereof, to do it on or before the said Day, that he may know what Number to print off.

The Boston Evening Post, shortly before the bird flew away when the tax ceased to be levied, May 1, 1757, printed this note for the benefit of its customers who were to benefit by the reduction in price: —

As the Stamp-Act will expire the second Day of May next, (after which there will be some Abatement of the present Price, notwithstanding the very high Price of Paper, &c. since the War) the Publisher thinks it proper to inform you that he will send out no Papers to any one who does not clear off all Accounts to that Time.

SECOND IN NEW YORK

The colony of New York passed on December 1, 1756, an act which went into effect on January 1, 1757, and which placed a halfpenny weekly tax on newspapers. The act originally was for one year, but it was renewed in December, 1757, and again in December, 1758, for one year. The purpose of this tax was practically the same as that of the one just mentioned in Massachusetts: it was to raise funds to help defray the cost of running the local government.

The subscribers in New York, as in Massachusetts, had to pay this tax. The situation was thus explained by *The New-York Weekly Mercury* for December 20, 1756: —

Consider that the Sum to be raised by the Stamp Office is to be laid out in the Defence of their Country; and that the Advanced Price of the Paper is not extorted from them by the Printer, but is owing to the Act, legally passed by the three different Branches of the Legislature of this Province.

When the New York provincial tax on newspapers ceased to be collected at the end of the year 1759 the papers, including *The Mercury*, went back to subscription rates asked before they were adorned with the red halfpenny stamps.

TYPOGRAPHICAL DEVICES

At the right of its title, *The Boston Gazette* inserted in 1719 a cut of a ship, and at the left, one of a postman. *The New Hampshire Gazette* used several such devices. Early issues of *The New York Gazette* had a device of the arms of New York supported by a human figure on either side with a crown for a crest. By April 24, 1727, it was using a similar cut at the left of its title and one of a post-boy at the right. *The American Mercury* of Philadelphia, naturally had its Mercury. T. and J. Fleet in their *Boston Evening Post* took the trade-mark placed by their father over the door of his shop, but replaced it later by the "Bible and Heart." Edes and Gill of Boston in their *Gazette* adopted a device which represented Minerva seated before a pedestal on which was a cage — her left hand held a spear topped with the cap of liberty and her right hand had liberated a bird flying to a city in the distance. Samuel Hall decorated his *Essex Gazette* with a cut of two Indians. Rogers and Fowle of Boston made the title of their *Independent Advertiser* show Britannia liberating a bird tied by a cord to the arms of France. Cuts of the King's arms were frequently used by newspapers sympathizing with the Tories. After the Revolution most of these allegorical figures disappeared.

LITERARY INFLUENCES

Moses Coit Tyler, in his "History of American Literature," has thus summed up the literary influence of the newspapers of the first era: —

Our colonial journalism soon became, in itself, a really important literary force. It could not remain forever a mere disseminator of public gossip or a placard for the display advertisements. The instinct of critical and brave debate was strong even among those puny editors, and it kept struggling for expression. Moreover, each editor was surrounded by a coterie of friends, with active brains and a propensity to utterance; and these constituted a sort of unpaid staff of editorial contributors, who, in various forms — letters, essays, anecdotes, epigrams, poems, lampoons — helped to give vivacity and even literary value to the paper.

CHAPTER VII

REVOLUTIONARY PERIOD

1765—1783

THE Revolutionary Period really began on March 22, 1765, when on that date the British Parliament passed its obnoxious Stamp Act to take effect on November 1 of that year. By this act, newspapers published in the colonies were scheduled to pay a halfpenny tax for one half-sheet or less and a one-penny tax for anything over one half-sheet, but not exceeding one whole sheet "for every printed copy thereof." Any advertisement inserted in their columns must, according to the terms of the act, pay a duty of two shillings. The newspaper taxes imposed by the Provincial Legislatures had been paid without a great deal of protest, but colonial printers fought this act, not only because they were opposed to taxation without representation, but also because they feared that subscribers and advertisers would not be willing to pay the increased cost of production. In self-defense the newspapers, even those still loyal to the Crown, united in a spirit of coöperation against the act: legislators were advised to "take good care of the freedom of the press," and the columns of the newspapers reproduced lively discussions on "the rights of the people" in the matter of taxation. Distinguished patriots, acting as occasional contributors to the press, changed editorial policies from static to dynamic influences.

NEWSPAPER VS. STAMP ACT OF 1765

While a few of the newspapers in America did actually suspend publication on account of the Stamp Act, most of them simply threatened to do so and then went ahead and brought out their issues with or without their regular official titles. For two or three weeks after the act went into effect several newspapers appeared with such heads as "No Stamped Paper To Be Had," "Recent Occurrences," etc. In Philadelphia *The Penn-*

Thursday, October 31, 1765.   THE   NUMB. 1195.

PENNSYLVANIA JOURNAL;
AND
WEEKLY ADVERTISER.

EXPIRING: In Hopes of a Resurrection to LIFE again.

I AM sorry to be obliged to acquaint my Readers, that as The STAMP-ACT, is fear'd to be obligatory upon us after the First of November ensuing, (the fatal To-morrow) the Publisher of this Paper unable to bear the Burthen, has thought it expedient to stop a while, in order to deliberate, whether any Methods can be found to elude the chains forged for us, and escape the insupportable Slavery, which it is hoped, from the just Representations now made against the said Act, may be effected. Mean while, I must earnestly Request every Individual of my Subscribers, many of whom have been long behind Hand, that they would immediately Discharge their respective Arrears, that I may be able, not only to support during the Interval, but be better prepared to proceed again with this Paper, whenever an opening for that Purpose appears, which I hope will be soon.   WILLIAM BRADFORD.

Remember, O my friends! the Laws, the Rights,
The generous plan of power deliver'd down,
From age to age, by your renown'd fore-fathers;
O let it never perish in your hands!
But piously transfmit it to your children.
Cut thus, great Liberty, inspire our souls,
And make our lives in thy possession happy,
Or our death glorious in thy defence.
ADDISON'S Cato.

LIBERTY is one of the greatest Blessings, which human beings can possibly enjoy: When we are deprived of this earthly happiness, we are fettered with the Chains of inimical servitude. Nations, who are born for the mutual support of each other, should preserve a steady attachment to the welfare and happiness of that nation with whom they are united, that their mutual alliance of friendship might be sincere and permanent. When this union is separated by the illegal encroachments on that Liberty, which is the Soul of Commerce, and the Support of Life, it degenerates into implacable Enmity, which in time grows inveterate, and finally recoils upon those who have been the means of its unhappy dissolution. The Liberty of the Press has very justly been esteemed one of the main Pillars of the Liberty of the People. While this is maintained, the first Steps to Oppression are detected, and the Attention of the People seasonably awakened. When this is suppressed, the Suspicion of the People, and their Ruin may admit of so sudden a transition, as renders the Success of the first impracticable...

And in all political Disorders the more contented we are under them, so much the worse are they, and so much the worse are we for them. It is a very happy Circumstance attending public Virtue and public Spirit, that the more it is vilified, the more illustrious it always appears...

Adieu, Adieu to the LIBERTY of the PRESS.

MORTUARY ISSUE OF BRADFORD'S *PENNSYLVANIA JOURNAL*
ON OCCASION OF THE STAMP ACT
(Reduced)

sylvania Journal and *The Pennsylvania Gazette* were typical examples of papers which adopted such a scheme. The former, in its issue for October 31, 1765, was the edition *par excellence* of the Stamp Act days. Reproduced on another page, it did much to arouse the colonists to drastic action, but it was the appearance of the paper typographically rather than what it said editorially that made this issue so influential. *The Maryland Gazette*, another paper which issued a "Doom's-Day Number," appeared in deep mourning, with the skull and crossbones, representing the stamp, on the lower right-hand corner of the front page, and printed in deep black type the words, "The Times are Dreadful, Dismal, Doleful, Dolorous, and Dollarless." Though this newspaper had announced in its issue of October 10, 1765, that it would suspend publication, it was kept before the people of Maryland by "apparitions" which closely resembled the real thing. For example, on January 30, 1766, there appeared *The Maryland Gazette Reviving:* on February 20, 1766, *The Maryland Gazette Revived*, and by March 6, 1766, *The Maryland Gazette*. These "apparitions" proved that *The Gazette* was "not dead but only sleepeth." After the date last mentioned, the paper resumed regular publication. Even *The South Carolina Gazette* had in place of its title the usual imprint, "No Stamped Paper To Be Had."

Other newspapers took just as decided a stand against the act. Hugh Gaine printed in his *New-York Weekly Mercury* on October 28, 1765, a notice that his paper "must now cease for a Time and the Period of its Resurrection is uncertain," but that "when it is revived the Printer hopes for a Continuation of the Favour of his Friends." He made — as did many other printers who issued a similar announcement — an appeal to patrons to pay what was due on subscriptions. A little later a New York mob compelled the surrender of all stamped paper in that city, and thus Gaine, when he printed a news-sheet on November 4, with "No Stamped Paper To Be Had" as its title, literally told the truth. All papers which adopted some subterfuge in the matter of headings resumed their old titles after the first few weeks of the Stamp Act.

A most diligent and careful search has not revealed among the thirteen original colonies a single newspaper which appeared on stamped paper. The stamp, however, was used by two or three papers elsewhere. A copy of *The Halifax Gazette* for February 13, 1766, for example, has on the upper left-hand corner of the fourth page the red halfpenny stamp with the word "America" also in red above it. *The Boston News-Letter*, in its issue for December 26, 1765, printed an item from Philadelphia in which a mention was made of the arrival in that city from Barbados of a "Stamped News-Paper of 2d. of November," and an announcement was given that the newspaper was "exposed to Public View at the Coffee-House." The paper was later suspended from an iron chain and burned.

REPEAL OF STAMP ACT

When the news reached Boston on Friday, May 16, 1766, that the British Parliament had repealed the Stamp Act on March 18, the papers of that city united and published an "extra" of the fact with the head, "Glorious News." To quote its conclusion: "Printed for the Benefit of the PUBLIC by Drapers, Edes & Gill, Green & Russell, and Fleets. The Customers to the Boston Papers may have the above gratis at the respective Offices." In the same spirit at least, the newspapers in other colonies published the "Glorious News."

SNAKE CARTOON AGAIN

At the time the British Stamp Act was attracting so much attention in the press, there appeared on September 21, 1765, *The Constitutional Courant*. The name of its editor was not given and the place of its publication was not mentioned. While there was only one issue, there were at least three different editions, which seems to indicate that there was simultaneous — or nearly so — publication in different cities. The paper was devoted principally to an attack on the Stamp Act, and two of the editions reprinted the snake cartoon which Franklin had inserted in *The Pennsylvania Gazette* in 1754. The sale of *The Constitutional Courant* was unusually large. It was hawked on the streets of New York by newsboys and was distributed along all the postroads by colonial riders. *The Boston Evening Post*, in publishing an account about *The Courant*, had the snake cartoon, already mentioned, reproduced in its columns on October 7, 1765.

The snake cartoon was reproduced a second time during this period. In 1774 John Holt, fighting editor, dragged it out of its newspaper hole and put it into the title of his paper, *The New-York Journal or General Advertiser*. The snake now had nine parts — Georgia had entered the combination. A slight change was made in the caption so that it read, "Unite or Die." Toward the close of the year, Holt's snake shed its skin and appeared coiled and united. On it were printed the following words: —

UNITED NOW FREE AND ALIVE FIRM ON THIS BASIS LIBERTY SHALL STAND AND THUS SUPPORTED EVER BLESS OUR LAND TILL TIME BECOMES ETERNITY.

Holt kept the united snake in the title of his paper until he was compelled to flee from New York on August 29, 1776, on account of the occupation of the city by the British.

The cartoon snake in its largest form stretched itself out on July 7, 1774, in *The Massachusetts Spy*, a paper published in Boston by Isaiah Thomas. It appeared directly under the title and occupied practically the entire width of the newspaper. However, a little space at the extreme right was saved in which appeared a dragon, representing Great Britain. Thomas asserted in his "History of Printing" that the snake cartoon appeared in each succeeding issue so long as *The Spy* was printed in Boston. The snake finally reached Philadelphia again, but for some unaccountable reason, instead of creeping back into its old hole, *The Pennsylvania Gazette*, it sunned itself in the title of *The Pennsylvania Journal*, a rival paper published by William Bradford. Its first appearance in *The Journal* was on July 27, 1774; its last was on October 18, 1775.

PET OF PATRIOTS

The Boston Gazette, the third paper of that name in Boston, and established April 7, 1755, by Edes and Gill, was the especial "pet of the patriots." In its pages were fought the New England editorial battles for American freedom: its contributors numbered such patriots as Samuel Adams, Joseph Warren, John Adams, Thomas Cushing, Samuel Cooper, etc. The paper was a good reporter of such important events as the Stamp Act, the Boston Massacre, the Boston Tea Party, etc.

The account of the Tea Party, from *The Boston Gazette*, is reproduced to show the improvement in the handling of news since the days of the Colonial Period: —

On Tuesday last the body of the people of this and all the adjacent towns, and others from the distance of twenty miles, assembled at the Old South Meeting-house, to inquire the reason of the delay in sending the ship Dartmouth, with the East-India Tea, back to London; and having found that the owner had not taken the necessary steps for that purpose, they enjoined him at his peril to demand of the collector of the customs a clearance of the ship, and appointed a committee of ten to see it performed: after which they adjourned to the Thursday following, ten o'clock. They then met, and being informed by Mr. Rotch, that a clearance was refused him, they enjoined him immediately to enter a protest and apply to the Governor for a passport by the castle, and adjourned again till three o'clock for the same day. At which time they again met, and after waiting till near sunset, Mr. Rotch came in and informed them that he had accordingly entered his protest and waited on the Governor for a pass, but his excellency told him he could not consistent with his duty grant it until his vessel was qualified. The people finding all their efforts to preserve the property of the East-India Company and return it safely to London frustrated by the tea consignees, the collector of the customs, and the Governor of the Province, DISSOLVED their meeting. — But, BEHOLD what followed! A number of brave and resolute men, determined to do all in their power to save their country from the ruin which their enemies had plotted, in less than four hours, emptied every chest of tea overboard, the three ships commanded by Captains Hull, Bruce, and Coffin, amounting to 342 chests, into the Sea!! without the least damage done to the ships or any other property. The masters and owners are well pleased that their ships are thus cleared; and the people are almost universally congratulating each other on this happy event.

REVERE, ENGRAVER OF CUTS

When the four victims of the Boston Massacre of 1770 were buried, *The Boston Gazette*, in its issue for March 12, 1770, illustrated its account of the event with cuts of four coffins. Evidently there must have been some one else who was expected to die, for Paul Revere, the leading Boston engraver, but better

Cornwallis TAKEN !

BOSTON, (Friday) October 26, 1781.

This Morning an Exprefs arrived from Providence to HIS EXCELLENCY the GOVERNOR, with the following IMPORTANT INTELLI-GENCE, viz.—

PROVIDENCE, Oct. 25, 1781. Three o'Clock, P. M.

This Moment an Exprefs arrived at his Honor the Deputy-Governor's, from Col. Chriftopher Olney, Commandant on Rhode-Ifland, announcing the important Intelligence of the Surrender of Lord CORNWALLIS and his Army ; an Ac-count of which was Printed this Morning at Newport, and is as follows, viz.—

NEWPORT, October 25, 1781.

YESTERDAY Afternoon arrived in this Harbour Capt. Lovett, of the Schooner Adventure, from York River, in Chefapeak Bay, (which he left the 20th inftant,) and brought us the glorious News of the Surrender of Lord Cornwallis and his Army Prifoners of War to the allied Army, under the Command of our illuftrious General ; and the French Fleet, under the Command of His Excellency the Count de Graffe.

A Ceffation of Arms took Place on Thurfday the 18th Inftant in Confequence of Propofals from Lord CORNWALLIS for a Capitulation.—His Lordfhip propofed a Ceffation of Twenty-four Hours, but Two only were granted by His Excellency General WASHINGTON. The Articles were compleated the fame Day, and the next Day the allied Army took Poffef-fion of York Town.

By this glorious Conqueft, NINE-THOUSAND of the Enemy, including Seamen, fell into our Hands, with an im-menfe Quantity of Warlike Stores, a Forty-Gun-Ship, a Frigate, an armed Veffel, and about One Hundred Sail of Tranfports.

Printed by B. Edes and Sons, in State Street.

A BROADSIDE OF EDES
A Revolutionary "Extra" of *The Boston Gazette*
(Reduced)

known for his midnight ride, rendered a bill to *The Boston Gazette* for engraving "5 coffings for a massacre." The coffins, with their skulls and crossbones, did much to arouse the Sons of Liberty to action.

GAINE AND HIS PAPERS

In all probability Hugh Gaine was the first newspaper publisher to employ newsboys to deliver papers. *The Mercury* for September 14, 1761, contained an advertisement for a nice boy to deliver papers to city patrons; "he will not be employed for more than two Hours every Monday Morning." *The Mercury* again asked on August 24, 1772, for "a clever honest Fellow to carry *The New York Gazette and Weekly Mercury* to Part of the Customers in the City, four Hours every Monday will do the business."

After New York had been abandoned by the Continental army, there were two editions for a short time of Hugh Gaine's *New-York Gazette*. One edition was brought out in New York City, another was brought out in Newark, in East New Jersey. The New York edition favored the Tory cause, and the Newark edition, that of the Whigs. In the past the assertion has been made that Gaine brought out both of these editions and was simply watching to see which side would probably be successful before he cast his lot. Such, however, was not the case. After the battle of Brooklyn, Gaine removed part of his presses and type to Newark. Here, on September 21, 1776, he brought out Number 1301 of his *Gazette*. This and the following issues spoke of "the Honourable Continental Congress," and the issue of Number 1306 showed that he enjoyed the confidence of Governor Livingston of New Jersey. What happened in New York was this: General Howe, upon his arrival found that there was no newspaper in the city and appointed Ambrose Serle, a Royalist, to bring out a paper. Serle promptly appropriated the type and presses which had been left at "The Bible and Crown" and brought out on September 30, Number 1301 of *The New York Gazette* with Gaine's imprint upon it. With the next issue, however, Number 1302, Searle changed the imprint. Gaine, however, did have a change of faith and returned to New York and

resumed charge of his old *New-York Gazette* with the issue of
November 11, Number 1307. How Gaine made his peace with
the British authorities was never told. He did, however, remain loyal to the Crown until the end of the war. For this
change to the Royalist cause, Philip Freneau the poet of the
Revolution, hurled a scorching poem at Gaine. But Gaine was
never trusted by the Royalists, for they appointed James Rivington "Printer to the King's Most Excellent Majesty," and
made *Rivington's New-York Loyal Gazette*, started after the office
of *The Gazetteer* had been wrecked, the official paper. They even
prevented Gaine from printing in his sheet the more important
items of news. After the evacuation of New York, by the
British, Gaine suspended his *Gazette* on November 10, 1783,
crossed out the word "Crown" in his imprint, "Bible and
Crown," and confined himself principally to the printing and
selling of books.

EXTRAMURAL PUBLICATIONS

During the War of the Revolution, whenever the British succeeded in occupying a strategic city there was nothing left for
the patriotic printer to do but to suspend publication or take his
newspaper elsewhere. John Holt, the publisher of *The New York
Journal*, for example, was forced to remove his paper to Kingston when New York fell into the hands of the British. His first
issue of *The Journal*, with the Kingston date-line was July 7,
1777. In making its bow to Kingston, *The Journal* said: —

After remaining, for ten months past, overwhelmed and sunk, in a
sea of tyrannic violence and rapine, *The New York Journal*, just emerg-
ing from the waves, faintly rears its languid head, *to hail its former friends
and supporters*, — to assure them that unchanged in its spirit and principles, the utmost exertions of its influence, as heretofore, will ever be
applied, with a sacred regard to the defence and support of American
rights and freedom, the advancement of true religion and virtue and
the happiness of mankind.

Holt found it necessary to make another change. After he had
brought out an issue on October 13, 1777, Kingston was burned
by the British three days later, and he removed to Poughkeepsie where he revived his *Journal* with the date-line on May 11,

1778. He discontinued publication in Poughkeepsie on January 6, 1782, and returned the latter part of 1783 to New York, where he again brought out his paper on November 22 of that year. Other publishers of the period were forced to make similar arrangements. Edes took his *Gazette* from Boston to Watertown; Thomas, his *Massachusetts Spy* from Boston to Worcester; Loudon, his *New-York Packet* to Fishkill; Southwick, his *Newport Mercury* to Attlebury; Dunlap, his *Pennsylvania Packet* from Philadelphia to Lancaster, etc.

NEWSPAPER OFFICE MOBBED

The Royalist papers, published under the protection and the encouragement of the British authorities, continued to issue their numbers, but they experienced difficulties and hardships almost equal to those of the patriotic papers, for local citizens, sympathizing as they did with the cause of national independence, positively refused to support journals with Tory editorial policies. But of these Tory sheets, possibly the most hated as well as the most feared was *Rivington's New-York Gazetteer; or the Connecticut, New Jersey, Hudson's River and Quebec Weekly Advertiser*, which James Rivington, once a member of a famous English publishing house of his name, established in New York April 22, 1773. So bitter became the feeling against this newspaper that its shop was twice mobbed during 1777. The second time a thorough job was done; a group of armed men on November 27 rode into New York, broke into the building, destroyed the press, and carried away the type, which was later melted into bullets for the use of the "Rebels," as Rivington called the Whigs. But Rivington, securing from England new press and type, brought out *The New-York Loyal Gazette*, which became, as has already been asserted, the official organ of the British in New York.

AID FROM ARMY

Because the New York newspapers were supervised by the British authorities, New Jersey as a "war measure" promoted the establishment of *The New-Jersey Journal* at Chatham. The Revolutionary forces under Washington at Morristown, five miles away, helped its publisher, Shepard Kollock, with "Nine Hundred Wt of old Tent Unfitt for service," and later with "Eight Hundred Three Quarters & Twelve pound old Tent Cloath," and still later, "Two Bundles Old Tent Rags wt Two Hundred One Quarter," also "One Other Bagg wt Two Hundred One Quarter old tent Rags"; these rags and old tents were for the manufacture of paper which Kollock so sadly needed. In addition, the army out of its scanty stores actually furnished a very large amount of white paper in order that the soldiers might have a newspaper which told of the progress of struggles in other colonies.

PHILADELPHIA PAPERS

During the last few years of the American Revolution, the most important newspaper in Philadelphia was *The Freeman's Journal; or The North-American Intelligencer*. It first appeared on April 25, 1781, and was edited and printed by Francis Bailey. Its policy was thus announced editorially: "To encourage genius, to deter vice, and disrobe tyranny and misrule of every plumage." Its most distinct service, however, was in reporting the progress of the war. In its issue for October 24, 1781, it announced the surrender of General Charles Earl Cornwallis in lines which reached clear across the page. In addition to its patriotic news was its satire. Philip Freneau, who later achieved prominence through his editorship of *The National Gazette*, contributed to *The Freeman's Journal* numerous bits of satirical verse. Another paper in Philadelphia started during the War was *The Pennsylvania Evening Post*, established January 24, 1775, by Benjamin Towne. During the early part of the War the paper was very friendly to the American cause, but later changed its editorial policy when the British occupied Philadelphia. After the evacuation of that city *The Evening Post* again announced its devotion to the Whig principles, but was forced to suspend for want of popular support, due to its policy while the British were in the city. *The Pennsylvania Journal*, established December 2, 1742, as *The Weekly Advertiser, or The Pennsylvania Journal*, by William Bradford, was in many respects, and these the most essential, more independent in tone than *The Pennsylvania Gazette* and was much the better newspaper during the Revolutionary Period.

When the British occupied Philadelphia a local printer took his printing-press and went to Egg-Harbour where he published *The Minute Intelligencer*. Evidently the Tory press was not the only one which published sensational news, as the following item quoted from *The Minute Intelligencer* will show: —

It is said the English Ministry, having no hopes of subduing America by force of arms, whilst the inhabitants retain their native virtue, have instructed the officers in their army to try a more certain method of success; by debauching the morals of the men, and seducing the virtue of the women. For this purpose play-houses are opened, gaming-tables established, and balls promoted, in a city languishing under a scarcity of the necessities of life.

In striking contrast to *The Minute Intelligencer* was *The Pennsylvania Ledger, or The Virginia, Maryland, Pennsylvania and New-Jersey Weekly Advertiser*, — Heaven save the name, — started in Philadelphia on January 28, 1775, by James Humphreys. He was extremely loyal to the Crown, and because of his somewhat rabid tendencies he was forced to suspend publication in November, 1776. When the British, however, took possession of the city, Humphreys seized the opportunity to resume publication of his sheet which he as promptly discontinued when they left.

SOUTHERN SHEETS

While the British were in control of Charleston, several printers in the army conducted a newspaper called *The Royal South Carolina Gazette*, printed by Roberts, MacDonald, and Cameron. Revolutionary forces in South Carolina also had an army printing-press and issued many "near-newspapers" telling of the activities of Green's army. *The Royal Gazette* always referred to them as *The Rebel Gazette*. But when the British evacuated Charleston, December 14, 1782, there was no newspaper left to tell the news of the place. This condition did not obtain long, for on February 15, 1783, Nathan Childs brought out *The South Carolina Weekly Gazette;* on January 18, 1786, the paper appeared as a daily under the name, *The Charleston Morning Post and Daily Advertiser* — later changed to *The City Gazette, or Daily Advertiser.* Associated in the publication of this paper was Peter Freneau, a brother of Philip Freneau who was the poet of the Revolution and later the editor of *The National Gazette.*

A SCOOP

On September 3, 1783, *The Gazette* of Providence, Rhode Island, printed one of the great scoops of the period when it announced: "By the brig Don Golvez, Capt. Silas Jones, arrived in the river from London, we have received a copy of the long looked-for Definitive Treaty, which we embrace the earliest occasion of handing to the public."

EDITORIAL CHANGES

If editorial expression before the Revolutionary Period was feeble and timid, as has been so often asserted, it was not because the colonial editors were weaklings or cowards, but because they knew that the publication of any criticism of the Government meant the suppression of their papers on account of the censorship. After the Stamp Act the newspapers became more critical and debates became more numerous. When the printer found, as he did in the case of the Stamp Act, that he could now violate the censorship with impunity, he became braver and more critical in his editorial expression, and enjoyed for the first time a freedom which rapidly changed the character of the American press.

HANDLING OF NEWS

In spite of the fact that daily newspapers did not make their appearance until after the Republic had been established, the newspapers showed unusual enterprise in printing the news of the more important battles. Instead of waiting to insert such accounts in regular issues, they printed handbills which were hawked on the streets and carried by the post-riders much the same as extra editions are to-day. These handbills, of which possibly *The Boston Gazette* issued the largest number, did not hesitate to employ large type whenever the Americans were victorious. When Lord Cornwallis surrendered at Yorktown, provision must have been made for the prompt dispatch of the news because many of the handbills contained the expression, "by special express." Benjamin Towne, even after he had suspended publication of *The Pennsylvania Evening Post*, occasionally printed handbills under the head, "All the News for Two Coppers." These he sold on the streets of Philadelphia. In spite of the stereotyped words, "Important Intelligence," many of these handbills gave the gist of the news in large headlines across the page.

ADVERTISING OF PERIOD

During the early part of the Revolutionary Period, editors not only increased the stock of patent medicines carried on their shelves, but did a more extensive business in the selling of slaves. The following advertisement from Hugh Gaine's *Weekly Mercury* for January 25, 1768, is typical: —

To be sold an excellent negro Wench about twenty years old, with a male Child about three months old; the Wench has had the Smallpox, can cook, wash and iron, can be well recommended, and is sold for no other fault than being too fruitful. Enquire of H. Gaine.

This advertisement was followed by another also offering a slave for sale, but in this case one should "enquire of the printer" — Hugh Gaine. Strange as it may seem, the editorial trade in slaves was possibly the largest in Boston. Many of the advertisements of runaway slaves differed slightly from those of the Colonial Period in that personal descriptions included such items as "an iron collar around his neck," "manacles on his wrists," "three scars on his back where he was burned for running away two years ago," etc. The interpretation of such items belongs to another history than that of journalism.

Many of the papers fairly bristled with advertisements like the following: "I intend to leave this Colony immediately. Payment of all debts to me should be made at once. (Signed ⸻ ⸻)" A collection of these advertisements would make a fairly good index of the leading Tories who fled to foreign countries to avoid the disorders of the Revolution.

Toward the close of the period, advertisements of lotteries occupied much space in the newspapers. In most cases these lotteries were conducted not for personal gain, but for village and city improvement. Especially interesting to-day are those advertisements which announced lotteries for the benefit of churches and colleges. If these advertisements were truthful, — and there is no reason to suppose they were otherwise, — lotteries equipped the libraries of our higher institutions of learning, remodeled houses of worship, put bells in the steeples of churches, repaired roads, erected bridges over rivers, and did many other things for which communities to-day are commonly taxed.

An advertisement in *The Virginia Gazette* showed that a local church had gone into the wholesale tobacco business and was evidently trying to market through the columns of the press the nicotia leaves turned in by parishioners in payment for subscriptions to the rector's salary.

Benjamin Franklin has already been mentioned as an able writer of advertisements. An excellent example of his work will be found in an advertisement which he wrote for George Washington, inserted in the first number of *The Maryland Journal and The Baltimore Advertiser*, which William Goddard brought out on Friday, August 20, 1773. Most vividly did Franklin tell how Washington, "having obtained patents for upwards of twenty thousand acres of land on the Ohio and Great Kanhawa Rivers," was going to lease sections upon moderate terms — a number of years rent free provided settlers cleared, fenced, tilled, laid down good grass for meadow, and set out at least fifty good fruit trees. Franklin did not hesitate to add for Washington this concluding bit of comment: —

And it may not be amiss further to observe, that if the scheme of establishing a new government on the Ohio, in the manner talked of, should ever be affected, these must be among the most valuable lands in it, not only on account of the goodness of soil, and the other advantages above enumerated, but from their contiguity to the seat of government, which more than probable will be fixed at the mouth of the Great Kanhawa.

This advertisement, it may be remarked incidentally, was exceedingly profitable to Washington.

PRINTING-PRESSES OF PERIOD

Newspapers continued to be printed on the ordinary flat-bed hand-press. The size of the editions of some papers had become so large that the man who pulled the levers complained of back-aches. To overcome this difficulty, inventors had already started to find some way out of the difficulty. Before the close of the period, Benjamin Dearborn, publisher of *The New Hampshire Gazette*, had invented a wheel press which would print the whole side of a sheet at one pull of the lever. No great mechanical improvement in the printing-press was made, however, until the beginning of the next century when a revolving cylinder was substituted for the lever.

SMALL CIRCULATION

The circulation of individual papers during the Revolutionary Period still remained small. James Rivington, with Number 78 of *The New-York Gazetteer; or the Connecticut, New Jersey, Hudson's River and Quebec Weekly Advertiser*, boasted in October, 1774, that he sent his paper to every colony of North America, and announced with pride that it had a circulation of thirty-six hundred. As Rivington's paper later came to be known as *The Lying Gazette*, it is barely possible that he was also a "circulation liar." His paper did have, however, one of the widest distributions of any of the period.

POST VS. PRESS

John Holt, in his *New York Journal* for October 30, 1766, complained most bitterly that his rival, James Parker, prevented the post-riders of New Jersey from distributing his paper to customers and had substituted in its place the newspaper published by Parker, "as his Paper is printed in the same Form, and under the same Title that mine used to be, it is probable many of my Customers may not have attended to the Difference of the Printer's Name. The Meanness and Dishonesty of this Proceeding, I shall leave to the Resentment of my Customers, who will determine, whether to encourage such a Man, by accepting his Papers, or whether to adhere to the Printer, they voluntarily thought fit to employ." Holt then complained that Parker, his rival printer who had control of the post-office, ought not have such authority, "an arbitrary power, greater than that ever exercised in England."

At the time William Goddard started his *Maryland Journal*, August 20, 1773, newspapers were under an espionage: if they contained any reflection on the Royal Government they were promptly destroyed. Postmasters loyal to the British Government carefully examined all copies offered for transmission through the mails. In order to get around this annoyance, Goddard ran his own post to Philadelphia. Leaving his sister, Mary K. Goddard, in charge of his newspaper, Goddard in October, 1773, made a tour through the Northern colonies. While on this trip he arranged for "an American post office system on constitutional principles" to put into effect his plan for the distribution of newspapers from Massachusetts to Georgia.

FIRST STRIKE OF PRINTERS

During the time that the British were in control of New York times were unusually hard, especially for printers. The price of provisions had been repeatedly advanced. On account of the blockade the supply of firewood, the only fuel of the time, was greatly reduced, and what there was, sold for a price beyond the purse of the printer. Rents had been raised, and local taxes had been increased. Consequently, there was some justification for a meeting of printers for the expressed purpose of insisting upon an advance in their wages. Meeting at the home of one of their number, they fixed upon what they considered a fair remuneration for their work and presented their demands to the newspapers by which they were employed. The newspapers consented to the increase, except the one owned by James Rivington. Upon his refusal to grant the increase the printers for his paper refused to work any longer at the old wage. Finding himself unable to print his newspaper, Rivington at last yielded, and the printers came back. In all probability this was the first strike of printers in America. Justification for this strike will be found in the fact that the printers were receiving a wage of less than one dollar per day.

PAPER FOR PRESSES

The war automatically ended the importation of white paper from abroad. Paper-mills had increased until there were over forty in the country. Several of these were laid waste by British soldiers, and others lay idle because employees had enlisted in the army. The remaining mills were unequal to supply the demand, so that during the latter part of the Revolutionary Period and for some time later the newspapers experienced great difficulty in securing the paper on which to print the news.

Several sheets were forced to refuse subscriptions until conditions should improve. *The New Jersey Gazette* on April 23, 1778, announced, "No more Subscriptions can be received at the present by this GAZETTE for Want of Paper." The Supreme Executive Council of Pennsylvania was very anxious to subscribe for *The New York Packet*, which had been established in New York, January 4, 1776, but was then published at Fishkill, New York. In answering the request Samuel Loudon reported that on account of the scarcity of paper he had printed but few sheets for the past three months, but that a parcel was now on its way to him and that in two weeks he would begin to forward the papers to the Council.

ADVERTISEMENTS FOR RAGS

Advertisements for rags for the paper-mills continued to appear frequently in papers of all sections of the country where presses had been established. Especially urgent were these appeals in such papers as *The Boston Gazette*, *The Providence Gazette*, *The Albany Gazette*, *The Maryland Gazette*, *The Hudson Gazette*, *The New-Jersey Gazette*, *The North Carolina Gazette*, *The Fayetteville Gazette* — to use simply the *Gazettes*. The *Fayetteville Gazette* asserted "that the economical Housewife who supplies the paper mill with rags, serves her country in her sphere as well as the soldier who fights for it does in his." *The Chelsea Courier*, at Norwich, Connecticut, suggested that every husband should say to his wife, "Molly, make a rag bag — and put it under the shelf where the family Bible lies." *The Massachusetts Spy* at Worcester expressed much the same thought when it requested "the fair Daughters of Liberty not to neglect to serve their country by saving for the Paper Mill all Linen and Cotton Rags," and remarked, "If the Ladies should not make a fortune by this piece of Economy, they will at least have the Satisfaction of knowing they are doing an essential Service to the Community, which, with the ten Shillings per pound, the price now given for clean white rags, they must be sensible will be a sufficient reward." *The North Carolina Gazette* urged young ladies to send to the paper-mill "Any old handkerchief no longer fit to cover their snowy breasts." *The Boston Gazette* printed a "Rag Lesson" for children and servants, especially girls, and respectfully submitted to the consideration of all "Parents, Masters, and Mistresses, but particularly to the Women of every House: you all know that Paper is made of Rags. You will therefore do much good, if you will promote the Manufacture of that useful article by saving all Rags, fine or coarse, of whatever colour, made of Linen or Cotton — Don't sweep them into the Fire, or out of the House: but be prudent, and attend to the Direction and Advice of the wisest and best Person that ever lived — 'Gather up the fragments, that nothing be lost.' Although the Quantity you may save should be but small and you should think it of little Consequence in itself, consider that when it is put together with other Savings, it will increase the heap; and that, as the Scotch Proverb says, 'Many Mickles Make a Muckle.' " *The New-Jersey Gazette* expected "Storekeepers who wish well to their Country to lend their Assistance in taking Rags in and to whom a Compensation will be made." An advertisement in *The Providence Gazette* announced: "Four Coppers per Pound will be given for fine linen and cotton Rags, and two Coppers for coarse, by John O. Waterman, at the Paper Mills in Providence, and by the Printer of *The Gazette:* A cart from the Paper Mills will go through the Town of Providence once a Month for the Purpose of Collecting Rags." Hugh Gaine early in the Revolutionary Period experienced such difficulty in getting paper for his press that he offered prizes to persons who delivered the most rags to the office of his paper in New York. The prizes were ten dollars, eight dollars, and five dollars, and were in addition to the regular price paid for rags. On account of the scarcity of paper, numerous newspapers were forced to raise their subscription price.

The paper from American mills was of inferior quality, because in the rush to supply the demand it had to be taken wet from the machines and was often unfinished by the workmen. The poor printing of the latter part of the period was due, in many cases, to the poor quality of the paper put on the press.

SEIZURE OF PLANT

John Holt established a plant at Norfolk, Virginia, about 1775. In charge of this paper, *The Virginia Gazette, or The Norfolk Intelligencer,* he placed his son, John Hunter Holt. Governor John Murray, Fourth Earl of Dunmore, had been transferred in 1772 from New York to Virginia. Provoked by *The Gazette,* Dunmore ordered the seizure of the press. Protests over his action promptly appeared in newspapers outside of Virginia. One correspondent asked: —

How could you dare deprive the public of a press by which their wrongs are made known and through which all knowledge is conveyed? Must *Genius* bow the neck and court the smiles of *Nero* while *Fair Science* sits melancholy, deploring her unhappy state?

The following item — dated Norfolk, October 1, and published in *The Pennsylvania Gazette* for October 18, 1775 — told of the seizure: —

Yesterday came on shore about 15 of the King's soldiers, and marched up to the printing-office, out of which they took all the types and part of the press, and carried them on board the new ship *Eilbeck,* in presence, I suppose, of between two and three hundred spectators, without meeting with the least molestation; and upon the drums beating up and down the town, there were only about 35 men to arms. They say they want to print a few papers themselves; and they looked upon the press not to be free, and had a mind to publish something in vindication of their own characters. But as they have only part of the press, and no ink as yet, it is out of their power to do anything in the printing business.

To complete the mention of Holt made on page 89 it may be said that he died in New York, January 30, 1784. Isaiah Thomas said of him: —

Holt was a man of ardent feelings, and a high churchman, but a firm whig, a good writer, and a warm advocate of the cause of his country.

CHAPTER VIII
PERIOD OF EARLY REPUBLIC
1783—1812

WHEN the American colonies secured their independence and faced the problem of self-government, the conditions were extremely favorable for a revival of papers which had suspended publication during the war and also for the establishment of many new journals to mirror the radical changes of the times. The few Tory sheets which had survived through the coöperation of British arms now changed their policies and became loyal supporters of the new Republic. The people, ever mindful of the past, refused to subscribe or to support such papers. After brief struggles for existence they discontinued publication and their publishers made a living as booksellers, stationers, job printers, etc.

Controversies which soon arose between States became so bitter as almost to lead to civil war. They changed even the colorless and purposeless newspaper into a fighting organ. Editorial policies were largely determined by geographical location. To this stimulus may be attributed the influence secured by the local press — an influence even greater than that of the Revolutionary Period.

The debates over the adoption of the Constitution broke down the geographical lines and divided the press as well as the people into two groups, one which favored and the other which opposed. Some of the newspapers which had been most urgent in demanding nothing but absolute independence from England were among those which sought to delay or even to defeat the adoption of the Federal Constitution. The subsequent death of some of these journals was due to the fact that however sincere they might have been they took what later proved to be the unpopular side of this great issue. Others, often new publications, met with immediate favor because of the fervor with which they advocated the needs of such a document.

NEWSPAPERS CHIEFLY POLITICAL TRACTS

After the Constitution was adopted political leaders found that they needed mouthpieces for a wider expression of their views. They divided themselves into parties of which the common people knew little or nothing. To get the people to take sides on political questions they founded newspapers which, while giving a little news, did more to advance and spread the doctrines of party leaders, for politics tended to make the journals of the period not newspapers in the modern sense of the term, but chiefly political tracts: the moral essay of the Colonial Period was omitted and in its place was substituted a coarse and frequently vulgar attack upon a rival. Papers conceived amid intense political feeling and born simply to be bulletin boards for party leaders, continued to increase in number in spite of a high death-rate. At a political meeting it was considered quite proper to pass a resolution calling upon "our party newspapers to attack at once the reputations of all the leading Federalists in the State," or *vice versa*, for most papers were either Federal or Republican.

PERSONAL ATTACKS OF PRESS

In view of such conditions the newspapers of the last decade of the eighteenth century — with here and there an exception only to prove the rule — abounded in little else than libelous and scandalous personal attacks. The new freedom of the press promoted not truth but calumnies and falsehoods. Chief Justice McKean, in a libel case (1798) against William Cobbett, of *Peter Porcupine Gazette* in the City of Brotherly Love, remarked:

Every one who has in him the sentiments either of a Christian or a gentleman cannot but be highly offended at the envenomed scurrility that has raged in pamphlets and newspapers printed in Philadelphia for several years past, insomuch that libelling has become a national crime, and distinguishes us not only from all the states around us, but from the whole civilized world. Our satire has been nothing but ribaldry and billingsgate; the contest has been who could call names in the greatest variety of phrases; who could mangle the greatest number of characters, or who could excel in the magnitude of their lies; hence the honor of families has been stained, the highest posts rendered cheap and vile in the sight of the people, and the greatest services and virtue blasted.

This opinion had already been held by Benjamin Franklin who said in a comment on the political change in the press: —

Now many of our printers make no scruple of gratifying the malice of individuals by false accusations of the fairest characters among themselves, augmenting animosity even to the producing of duels, and are, moreover, so indiscreet as to print scurrilous reflections on the government of neighboring states, and even on the conduct of our best national allies, which may be attended with the most pernicious consequences.

PASSAGE OF SEDITION LAWS

That the American press from 1790 to 1800 was probably as powerful in its influence as at any time in its history, is not to be denied. But the violence and vituperation of the party press led to the first attempt on the part of the American Government to regulate the newspaper press. The year of 1798 saw the passage of the Alien and Sedition Laws. A section of the latter enacted:—

That if any person shall write, print, utter, or publish, or shall cause or procure to be written, printed, uttered or published, or shall knowingly and willingly assist or aid in writing, printing, uttering, or publishing any false, scandalous and malicious writing or writings against the government of the United States, or either house of the Congress of the United States, or the President of the United States, with intent to defame the said government, or either house of the said Congress, or the said President, or to bring them, or either of them, into contempt or disrepute; or to excite against them, or either or any of them, the hatred of the good people of the United States, or to stir up sedition within the United States, or to excite any unlawful combinations therein, for opposing or resisting any law of the United States, or any act of the President of the United States done in pursuance of any such law or of the powers in him vested by the Constitution of the United States, or to resist, oppose, or defeat any such law or act, or to aid, encourage, or abet any hostile designs of any foreign nation against the United States, their people or government, then such person, being thereof convicted before any court of the United States having jurisdiction thereof, shall be punished by a fine not exceeding $2,000, and by imprisonment not exceeding two years.

EDITORS JAILED

There were several prosecutions under this act. Abijah Adams, publisher of *The Boston Chronicle,* officially called bookkeeper at that time, was indicted for libeling the Massachusetts Legislature, found guilty, sentenced to jail for thirty days, and forced to give bond for one year of good conduct. The editor of *The Chronicle* was Thomas Adams, who was confined to his bed at the time, but he wrote for his paper the following note: — "The patrons of *The Chronicle* may still depend on the regular supply of their papers. The Editor is on the bed of languishment and the bookkeeper is in prison, yet the Cause of Liberty will be supported amid these distressing circumstances."

Charles Holt, publisher of *The Bee* at New London, Connecticut, spent three months in jail and paid a fine of two hundred dollars because he censured the President and urged men not to enlist in the army. *The Bee* was a party opponent of John Adams, and after Holt had served his time and paid his fine, he took his paper to Hudson, New York. Fifty years later Congress refunded the fine with interest. James Thompson Callender, editor of *The Richmond Examiner*, paid the same fine as Holt, but was sentenced for three times as long in jail for defaming the press. When Jefferson became President, he pardoned Callender and had the fine remitted.

David Frothingham, editor of *The Argus*, of New York, was indicted for libel and found guilty by a jury which recommended, however, the mercy of the court. He was fined only one hundred dollars, but received a sentence of four months. Henry Croswell, editor of *The Wasp*, was indicted for printing a "scandalous, malicious and seditious libel concerning Thomas Jefferson." Alexander Hamilton was one of the lawyers who appeared for Croswell. In spite of these and other convictions, the attempt of the Government to reform the press only made bad matters worse.

Anthony Haswell, editor of *The Vermont Gazette*, at Bennington, Vermont, paid, a year after his indictment, a fine of two hundred dollars and spent sixty days in jail. Benjamin Franklin Bache, of *The General Advertiser*, probably escaped a still more severe sentence because his death ended a suit. Incidentally it may be remarked that because of the abuse his newspaper had heaped upon Washington, he had been thrashed by Clement Humphrey.

WASHINGTON ATTACKED

Even Washington once was led to remark that "the publications in Freneau's [*The National Gazette*] and Bache's [*The General Advertiser*] papers were outrages on common decency." They were, especially the latter. When Washington retired from the presidency *The General Advertiser*, in its issue for Monday, March 6, 1797, incorrectly dated March 5, thus expressed itself in an editorial comment disguised as correspondence: —

"Lord, now lettest thou thy servant depart in peace, for mine eyes have seen thy salvation," was the pious ejaculation of a man who beheld a flood of happiness rushing in upon mankind — If ever there was a time that would license the reiteration of the exclamation that time is now arrived; for the man who is the source of all the misfortunes of our country, is this day reduced to a level with his fellow-citizens, and is no longer possessed of power to multiply evils upon the United States — If ever there was a period for rejoicing this is the moment — every heart in unison with the freedom and happiness of the people ought to beat high with exultation, that the name of Washington from this day ceases to give a currency to political iniquity, and to legalize corruption — a new era is now opening up upon us, an era which promises much to the people; for public measures must now stand upon their own merits, and nefarious projects can no longer be supported by a name: when a retrospect is taken of the Washingtonian administration for eight years, it is a subject of the greatest astonishment that a single individual should have cankered the principles of republicanism in an enlightened people, just emerged from the gulf of despotism, and should have carried his designs against the public liberty so far as to have put in jeopardy its very existence — Such, however, are the facts, and with these staring us in the face, this day ought to be a Jubilee in the United States.

Yet this comment was mild compared with the coarser utterances of previous issues which ought not to be reprinted because of their vulgarity. Federalists were accustomed to speak of *The General Advertiser* as being "misconducted" first by "Bennie Bache" and later by "Willie Duane."

PRESS DIVIDED OVER BRITISH TREATY

Much of this newspaper hostility toward Washington, it may be remarked incidentally, grew out of the British Treaty of

1794 which divided the American press very distinctly in the matter of editorial opinion. Practically every Federal newspaper gave a column or two in support of the treaty. On the other hand, the Republican-Democratic press fairly teemed with criticism which was both coarse and spiteful in its attacks on the Administration. These editorial reproaches, expressed — to quote Washington's own words — "in such exaggerated and indecent terms as could scarcely be applied to a Nero, to a notorious defaulter, or even to a common pickpocket," did much to strengthen his determination to retire to Mount Vernon, for Washington had become extremely sensitive to newspaper rebuke. Perceiving this, Jefferson, toward the last, did what he could to stem the torrent of newspaper abuse, but the flood was at high tide and could not be dammed. Federal newspapers, however, were more successful in their attempts to dam the Republican press.

PRESIDENTS VS. PRESS

When John Adams became President in 1797 he was even more severely attacked in the press than Washington had been. But his Administration fought the attacks. Armed by the Sedition Law, which was passed the following year and which has already been outlined, it sought to annihilate the Republican papers which it could not force to surrender. In the fight, which lasted four years, the Federal Party lost, for the people rallied to the support of the papers and defeated Adams in the election of 1800 by putting Thomas Jefferson in the presidential chair. Jefferson remitted many of the fines imposed upon Republican editors, but was later forced to commence suits for libels upon himself by Federal editors.

Federal papers bitterly attacked Jefferson for the Louisiana Purchase on the ground that he had trampled on the Constitution which granted him no such power to acquire additional territory: some of the most radical sheets suggested that the States where the Federals were in the majority should secede from the Union. Jefferson's Embargo Policy alienated some of his own party organs — especially in Virginia where the tobacco-growers had been hard hit by the Embargo. Jefferson suffered the same personal abuse from newspaper editors as did Washington. Federal editors spoke of him as "a cold thinking villain whose black blood always runs temperately bad."

EDITORIAL CHANGES

One important change occurred during the Period of the Early Republic, in the matter of editing newspapers. In the Colonial Period the editor was almost invariably a practical printer who depended upon his trade for a living, and where this was not possible, he supplemented the income from his press by ways which have already been outlined in a preceding chapter. He spoke of himself in his columns not as an "editor," but as a printer, undertaker, author, and other terms. Such editorial matter as appeared in his columns was from the pen of other contributors. During the Period of the Early Republic, when papers were founded chiefly for political purposes, the editor came into his own. He was either a printer seeking an office or he was a politician who hired a printer to run his paper. In the Colonial Period the pamphlet was the medium for editorial expression, but with the change just mentioned, to use the newspaper for political purposes, the pamphlet disappeared and its contents were printed in the newspaper. Toward the close of the period men of real ability were hired to edit newspapers in which they had no financial interest. Communications from other pens were welcomed, but they were no longer given first place in the paper.

PESTILENCE AND PRESS

The prevalence of yellow fever in Philadelphia during several seasons toward the close of the eighteenth century, and an epidemic of a malignant fever in New York City in the early part of the nineteenth century, caused several papers in both cities to suspend publication. The fever devastation in Philadelphia may have been one of the reasons why Freneau failed to resume publication of *The National Gazette*. For fear that it might return, Joseph Gales, at the suggestion of his wife, who had been a sufferer from the fever in a previous year, sold his *Independent Gazetteer*, in 1799, to Samuel Harrison Smith, who, in 1800, moved the journal to Washington, as has been mentioned elsewhere in this book, and gave it the name of *The National Intelligencer*. Gales then went to Raleigh, North Carolina, where he started another paper, *The Raleigh Register*, a name which suggested itself from his first-born newspaper venture, *The Sheffield Register*, of England. After the malignant fever had attacked New York City in 1803, *The Evening Post* of that city pledged itself "to pursue the discussion of the origin of the late pestilence to a regular and satisfactory close." William Coleman, the editor of that paper, had evidently seen a vision that a newspaper might do something more than merely print the news of political squabbles.

NEWSPAPERS DISINFECTED

At times when epidemics similar to those just named in the preceding paragraph were appearing in the larger cities, the publishers of newspapers disinfected their sheets before delivering them to newsboys and post-riders. Frequently, in order that the sheets might not be carriers of disease, they were put into stoves and thoroughly smoked before being wrapped for delivery. In the South, where yellow fever often spread very rapidly, special stoves, built of sheet iron, were designed for this purpose and used tobacco as fuel, but the process was slow, as only one sheet "smoked" at a time. The plan of "smoking" by wholesale from resinous woods was probably more commonly employed in the North than in other sections of the country because of the great infection feared from smallpox. The academic and pedantic newspaper critics, who, like the poor, have been ever present, used to assert at such times that a publisher would perform a much more useful service for the public if he would pay more attention to disinfecting the contents of his papers and less to disinfecting the sheets themselves. The latter, so the critics asserted, could be done when necessary by the reader in his own home.

FREEDOM OF PRESS

For some unaccountable reason the American colonies, after they established their independence and had drawn up their

Constitution, did not make provision for the freedom of the press. Each colony, however, as it drew its State Constitution, passed some resolution to the effect that the press being essential to State freedom ought to be inviolably preserved. As new States and Territories drew their own constitutions, they incorporated some similar resolution to protect the press from the censorship to which it had. been subjected during the colonial period. Even the first Congress saw the mistake of its omission and passed an Amendment that Congress shall make no law abolishing the freedom of speech or of the press. In spite of this constitutional guarantee, the Alien-Sedition Laws were passed.

HILDRETH ON PRESS OF PERIOD

Hildreth, in speaking of the influence of the press upon American politics in 1812, thus explains the rise of this period of black journalism: "The demand for printers and editors, especially in the middle states could not be supplied from domestic sources and as many of these political exiles had been connected with the press at home, many of them having been driven into exile in consequence of publications prosecuted by the Government as libelous and seditious, they had adopted the same calling in America."

LOCATION OF LEADING PAPERS

According to the census of 1800 there were in the United States only eleven cities or towns which had a population of over five thousand. Of these, only two, Philadelphia (70,287) and New York (60,489), had more than fifty thousand: three, Baltimore, Boston, and Charleston, had between twenty and thirty thousand: three, Providence, Savannah, and Norfolk, had between five and ten thousand: just over the five thousand limit were Portsmouth, New Hampshire, Albany, New York, and Richmond, Virginia. As the total population, as given in the census, was about five million, three hundred thousand, the city population, therefore, constituted only about five per cent. Newspapers had greatly increased in number since 1783, but they were still largely agricultural, except in the eleven cities just mentioned. The temporary location of the seat of the Government at Philadelphia had given that city a most influential place in journalism. Its papers were not only the largest in circulation, but they had the widest distribution and were the most frequently quoted. When the Government removed to Washington this newspaper preëminence went from Philadelphia to New York. Already the latter had made itself felt in a political way, and its newspapers, especially its dailies, took first place not only in local, but also in national, influence. The political battle between Alexander Hamilton and Aaron Burr assisted materially in giving an impetus to New York journalism.

MASSACHUSETTS STAMP ACT OF 1785

During the Period of the Early Republic an attempt to put a stamp tax on newspapers was made in Massachusetts. That State, on March 18, 1785, passed an act imposing duties on licensed vellum, parchment and paper including "for every newspaper two-thirds of a penny." Nothing could have aroused greater opposition on the part of the press, to which the very name of "stamp act" was most offensive. Whereas, there was no evidence that the State Legislature desired in any way to abridge the liberties of the press, the newspapers promptly took that point of view and filled their columns with tirades against this obnoxious act.

The *Massachusetts Centinel* was especially bitter in its denunciation. To quote from the issue of May 4, 1785: —

The Stamp Act, passed the last session of the General Court, meets opposition throughout every part of the Commonwealth; that part laying a duty on newspapers particularly so. The cloven foot in it appears too visible to escape notice. To clog the currents of information, — and to shackle the means of political knowledge and necessary learning, — are discordant notes to the general ear. But its danger is not the whole of its evil consequences. It is deemed *impolitic* and *unequal*, — *impolitic*, as it will encourage our sister States to send their papers into this commonwealth cheaper than they can possibly be afforded here, to the ruin of a set of artizans, whose exertions in the late revolution deserve a more liberal fate: — *unequal*, as the revenue arising from newspapers must (while but a mite in the general treasury) operate, in a great degree, to the destruction of the present printers of these publications.

The Boston Gazette in its issue for April 18, 1785, printed the following item: —

The General Court in their last Session was pleased to pass an Act, generally called the STAMP ACT, a Name heretofore held in an approbious light, and highly disgustful to us.

A clause in said Act says, "For every NEWS-PAPER, *two thirds of a Penny.*"

Should the *Stamp* on NEWS-PAPERS take place, the price will be enhanc'd and the poor, by being unable to take the same, will be deprived of the pleasure of affording themselves and their children the advantages attendant on the perusal of this vehicle of entertainment and political knowledge; — and who will say, it will not be a disadvantage to the State in general, for the majority of the inhabitants thereof to be politically ignorant?

And will not this *Stamp* on NEWS-PAPERS, if held in force, tend thereto?

It is therefore hoped and expected by many, that the Honorable Members of the General Court, in their next Session will take the above mentioned Clause in the said Act into mature consideration repeal the same, and free the public from that bar to political wisdom.

On August 12, 1785, under a Philadelphia date-line, was published an article entitled "A Libel Some Will Say." From it, the following paragraph was taken: —

Every man in the thirteen states from New Hampshire to Georgia, should pour out incessant execrations on the devoted heads of those miscreants in Massachusetts who machinated, advised, aided, abetted, or assisted in laying sacriligious hands upon that most invaluable of all blessings — THE FREEDOM OF THE PRESS — that palladium of all the rights, privileges, and immunities, dear or sacred to any body of men worthy to rank above the brute creation! — that dispeller of the — till then — impenetrable clouds which overspread the world for ages anterior to the auspicious aera of its discovery! That scourge of tyrants whether *monarch, aristocrats*, or *demagogues.*

TAX ON ADVERTISING

Because of the unpopularity of this act, the Massachusetts Legislature repealed it on July 2, 1785. But another was passed, putting a duty on advertisements of six pence on each insertion. Some of the Massachusetts newspapers, notably *The Massachusetts Centinel*, were willing to accept this substitute on the ground that it was no infringement of the liberty of the press and that it "contributed thousands to the exigencies of the State." But most of the papers continued their opposition to the measure. *The Massachusetts Spy* said that it had to suspend publication on account of the act. Of this circumstance, *The American Herald* of Boston in its issue for April 3, 1786, said: —

The Massachusetts Spy (which it is acknowledged has been very essential to this Commonwealth in particular, before, at, and since the late Revolution) is now languishing with a *dangerous Wound*, given it by the *Legislature* of *Massachusetts* on the second day of July last. Humble and united application has been made for a particular kind of *Court Plaister*, which could speedily have wrought a *Cure;* but as that *Power*, only, which gave the *Wound*, could apply the *Remedy*, with *effect*, it could not be obtained! — The wound grows worse daily — *mortification* has taken place, and in all probability will soon prove fatal to the existence of that *Old Public* Servant — "Alas *Poor SPY*."

MODERN METHOD TO EVADE LAW

While the Massachusetts papers of this period could scarcely have afforded the services of modern corporation lawyers, some of them knew how to get around the law that was so offensive to them. The way in which it was done is outlined in this announcement from *The Boston Gazette:* —

The sixteenth article of our Bill of Rights says "The Liberty of the Press is essential to the security of Freedom in a State: It ought not therefore to be restrained in this commonwealth."

While the papers of the other states are crowded with advertisements, (free of duty) those of this state are almost destitute thereof; which justly occasions the oppressed printers of those shackled presses to make their separate complaints, as many do, owing to their being prohibited advertising in their own papers their own Books and Stationery without incurring a penalty therefor. We, for the same reason that our brother Typographers use, forbear publishing that *Bibles, Testaments, Psalters, Spelling-Books, Primers, Almanacks, &c.* besides *Stationery and all kinds of Blanks*, may be had at No. 42, Cornhill.

The duty on advertisements also prevents our publishing that we have lately reprinted an excellent moral Discourse, entitled, "The Shortness and Afflictions of Human Life illustrated," for the price of said book being but *eight pence*, it will take away the profits of too many; and perhaps encourage government to continue this burthen.

ADVERTISING TAX WITHDRAWN

Such methods to make the law ineffectual doubtless had much to do with its repeal in 1788. The House Committee in reporting on the act, announced that the imposition on the newspapers was not worth the small return from the tax (£250) so long as the papers from New York, New Hampshire, Rhode Island, and Connecticut might circulate freely in Massachusetts. Several of the papers which had suspended publication on account of the act reappeared. *The Massachusetts Spy* in resuming publication on April 3, 1788, offered this salutation of thankfulness: —

The Printer has the happiness of once more presenting to the Publick, the MASSACHUSETTS SPY, or the WORCESTER GAZETTE, which at length is restored to its *Constitutional Liberty*, (thanks to our present Legislature), after a *suspension* of *two years*. Heaven grant that the FREEDOM of the PRESS, on which depends the FREEDOM of the PEOPLE, may, in the United States, ever be guarded with a watchful eye, and defended from Shackles of every *form* and *shape*, until the trump of the celestial messenger shall announce the final dissolution of all things.

After Massachusetts had repealed the act which taxed newspaper advertising, no State, because of the odium attached to a Stamp Act, attempted to impose a duty upon newspapers until the fifth decade of the next century. On September 30, 1842, an act of the Virginia Legislature imposed a tax on newspapers which amounted to the subscription price for each paper.

POSTAL REGULATIONS OF PERIOD

Newspapers multiplied so rapidly that they became a burden to post-riders. In order to make sure that copies reached subscribers, newspapers were forced to pay the carriers on the post-roads an extra allowance. This charge meant an increase in the subscription price. Madison "viewed with alarm this newspaper tax" as he called it. On June 12, 1792, he wrote Jefferson: "I am afraid the subscriptions will soon be withdrawn from the Philadelphia papers unless some step be speedily taken to prevent it. The best that occurs seems to be to advertise that the papers will not be put into the mails, but sent, as heretofore, to all who shall not direct them to be put into the mail. Will you hint this to Freneau?" Federal postal acts of 1793 permitted every printer of a newspaper to send one copy without charge to every printer of a newspaper in the United States. Other provisions permitted newspapers to be carried in separate bags from letters at a fixed rate of one cent for a distance not over one hundred miles. Papers going farther were charged a cent and one half, but a restriction was made that postage on a single newspaper in a state where it was published should not exceed one cent. An additional act, the same year, insisted that newspapers should be dried by the publisher before being turned over to the postmaster for transmission: the Postal Department objected to carrying too much water in its mail-bags. No distinction was made in the matter of weight of the different newspapers; whether they were large or small they paid the same price per copy.

READERS BUT NOT BUYERS OF PAPERS

During this period, newspapers when sent regularly through the mail seemed to be more or less common property like umbrellas left in the hallways. The complaints about non-delivery of papers were frequent. Even George Washington had to complain on this matter, and in a letter to a Philadelphia printer who was about to establish a paper he made the following request: "It has so happened, that my *Gazettes* from Philadelphia, whether from inattention at the Printing or Post offices, or other *causes*, come very irregularly to my hands. Let me pray you therefore to address those you send me, in the appearance of a letter — The common paper, *usually* applied, will do equally well for the cover. — It has sometimes occurred to me, that there are persons who, wishing to read News Papers without being at the expense of paying for them, make free with those which are sent to others; under the garb of a letter it is not presumeable this liberty would be taken."

AN ADDITIONAL DUTY OF POST-RIDER

The post-rider was not only a carrier of the *Gazettes* in the early days of the Republic, but he was also a collector of subscriptions. The following advertisement of the post-rider from Providence to Connecticut is taken from *The Gazette* of the former place for April 2, 1803: —

PAY THE POST, THAT HE MAY PAY THE PRINTER

I who have been TWO YEARS at most
(Strange as 't may seem) a RIDING POST
And worn my poor old DOBBIN'S shoes out
With riding hard, to bring the news out,
And made wry faces at the storm,
While yet the news was moist and warm,
That you might read, before the fire,
Of battles fought, and sieges dire,
What politician now is vest,
Who's dead, and who is married next,
And such like entertaining story,
Which I have always laid before ye, —
Solicit, my friends, the amount
Of what is due ON OLD ACCOUNT.

ALBE STONE.

COMBINATION OF PUBLISHERS TO RAISE PRICES

In 1803 several papers in New York City made an attempt to get together to fix prices. *The New York Evening Post*, in its issue for December 1 of that year, told of this attempt as follows: —

At a meeting of the Publishers of the following Daily Newspapers printed in the City of New-York, viz. *Daily Advertiser, Mercantile Advertiser, Daily Gazette, American Citizen, Commercial Advertiser,* and *Evening Post* held at Lovett's Hotel on Saturday 5th November, 1803 it was unanimously Resolved:

That the sum of eight dollars per annum, at present paid as the price on Subscription for a Daily Paper, is inadequate to the expences of Paper, Printing, and Publication: and that the same be increased to Ten Dollars from and after the first day of January next.

That the price of those papers which are issued twice a week for the country, shall, from and after the first day of January, be Four Dollars per annum.

In a note to the public *The Evening Post* gave some of the reasons, which were found in the "rise which labor and every article employed in the printing shop had experienced since the terms of the subscriptions were last fixed." Printers' wages had increased from six dollars to eight and nine; salaries of clerks and collectors had risen from three hundred and three hundred and fifty to four hundred and five hundred dollars a year. The item of paper, in quality and size, amounted in its blank state to more than one half of the proceeds of all subscriptions. Type had risen twenty-five per cent and all other materials in about the same proportion. Attention was called that these items including that of labor required prompt payment, while newspapers gave more extensive credit than was allowed in any other business — "an evil sorely felt by the proprietors." While *The Evening Post* admitted that subscriptions in amount had quadrupled, it asserted that they were not sufficient to support a newspaper establishment, and frequently confessed that it was the advertisers who provided the paper for the subscribers, and went so far as to say that without a very extensive advertising support, a publisher of a newspaper received less reward for his labor than the humblest mechanic. While the subscription rates were scheduled for a raise, those of advertising remained the same as before.

The scheme did not work out as planned. *The Evening Post*, in a column and a half editorial in its issue for December 9, expressed surprise that both *The Mercantile Advertiser* and *The New-York Gazette* had receded from the project which they had stood pledged to support and that *The Morning Chronicle* had declined to come into the measure, not because the price of subscriptions was high enough, but because, being the youngest establishment in the city, it was not prepared to encounter shock of the loss of subscribers. The same editorial in *The Post* denied that there had been any improper combination among the printers. The previous price of *The Evening Post* had been eight dollars per year to city subscribers and nine dollars to country subscribers.

PARTY SUPPORT OF PRESS

During the era of the party organ, not only the politicians but also the voters were expected to subscribe to the paper which supported partisan principles, regardless of the representative merit of such publications. Occasionally, a paper of the rival party became so energetic in the matter of gathering news or in its ability to express more forcibly its editorial opinions that it secured circulation among all parties. Such a paper was *The Phœnix*, started in Providence, Rhode Island, on May 11, 1802, to help the organization of the Republican Party, then under the leadership of Thomas Jefferson, and to assist the political activities of the Honorable Theodore Foster, then United States Senator from Rhode Island. This paper became so popular with the voters of Providence that *The Gazette* published a complaint in its columns that *The Phœnix* had not only the largest circulation, but also the largest advertising patronage in spite of the fact that it was a Republican paper in a Federal town.

NEWSPAPER DIVISION ALONG PARTY LINES

In 1810 Isaiah Thomas published, in his "History of Printing," a list of the American newspapers. His list of three hundred and sixty-six papers — while not complete — showed fairly well the relative distribution of papers along party lines. Of the twelve in New Hampshire, eight were Federal and two, Republican; of the thirty-two in Massachusetts, twenty were Federal and eleven, Republican; of the seven in Rhode Island, four were Federal and three, Republican; of the twelve in Connecticut, ten were Federal and one, Republican; of the fifteen in Vermont, nine were Federal and six, Republican; of the sixty-seven in New York, twenty-nine were Federal and twenty-seven, Republican; of the eight in New Jersey, three were Federal and five, Republican; of the seventy-three in Pennsylvania, thirty-four were Federal and twenty-nine, Republican; of the three in Delaware, two were Republican; of the twenty-one in Maryland, nine were Federal and eleven, Republican; of the six papers in the District of Columbia, two were Federal and three, Republican; of the twenty-three in Virginia, seven were Federal and fifteen, Republican; of the ten in North Carolina, five were Federal and three, Republican; of the ten in South Carolina, four were Federal and four, Republican; of the thirteen in Georgia, three were Federal and seven, Republican; of the seventeen in Kentucky, two were Federal and fourteen, Republican; of the six in Tennessee, one was Federal and five were Republican; of the fourteen in Ohio, three were Federal and eight, Republican; of the four in Mississippi, one was Federal and one, Republican; of the ten in Territory of Orleans, five were Federal and one was Republican. Of the single papers in Michigan, Indiana, and Louisiana, Thomas did not give the party affiliation. Of the scattering neutral papers, most of them were agricultural in character. The figures already given show how closely the newspapers were divided on party lines, for politics and press were in close partnership. Often the party in control sought support through the advertising at its disposal; at other times it held before the editor the promise of political office. This partnership reached its closest affiliation in the next period.

CONCLUSION

The contribution of the period was the constitutional guarantee of the freedom of the press. The value of such freedom was emphasized by the First Continental Congress in an address to the inhabitants of Quebec (October 28, 1774):

The last right we shall mention regards the freedom of the press. The importance of this consists, besides the advancement of truth, science, morality, and arts in general, in its diffusion of liberal sentiments in the administration of government, its ready communication of thoughts between subjects and its consequential promotion of union among them, whereby oppressive officers are shamed or intimidated into more honorable and just modes of conducting affairs.

Virginia in its Declaration of Rights (June 12, 1776) boldly asserted:

That freedom of the press is one of the great bulwarks of liberty, and can never be restrained but by despotic governments.

How other States made similar declarations is mentioned on page 108. In Federal Convention (August 20, 1787) a motion proposing a guarantee was lost. One delegate remarked that the power of Congress did not extend to the press. But popular demand brought about the first amendment:

Congress shall make no law ... abridging the freedom of speech, or of the press.

CHAPTER IX

FIRST DAILIES AND EARLY PARTY ORGANS

As the cities increased in size and became more commercial centers, the newspapers became more valuable as advertising mediums. The publishers soon became rivals in the matter of publishing the news of the stores and began to issue their papers more frequently, — first, semi-weekly, and later, tri-weekly. From this it was only a step to bring out a paper every day in the week save Sunday.

BEGINNINGS OF DAILY JOURNALISM

The first daily newspaper appeared in Philadelphia on Tuesday, September 21, 1784; it was entitled *The Pennsylvania Packet and Daily Advertiser* and was published by John Dunlap and David C. Claypoole. From 1791 to 1793 Dunlap was the sole publisher, but in the latter year Claypoole again became a partner until December, 1795, when Dunlap withdrew. From that time it was published by David C. and Septimus Claypoole, under the title of *Claypoole's American Daily Advertiser*, until the death of Septimus in 1798. When, on September 30, 1800, it was sold to Zachariah Poulson, Jr., it became *Poulson's American General Advertiser*. On December 30, 1839, the paper was merged into the present *North American* of Philadelphia. Such, in brief, was the history of the first daily paper in this country.

CONTENTS OF FIRST DAILY PAPER

Because *The Pennsylvania Packet and Daily Advertiser* was the beginning of daily journalism in America, a word or two may not be out of place in this connection about the contents of the first issue. It was a four-page sheet of four columns to the page and sold for four pence per copy. The first page and the last were filled entirely with advertisements. The third page consisted half of advertisements and half of text. Of the two columns devoted to news, fully one half of the column related to information about vessels dismasted. Of the three fourths of the column in which the news of Philadelphia was given, fully one half came from the naval office and told about the entries at the Port of Philadelphia — inward and outward. There was a little over a stick of type about the arrival of vessels at Newburyport, Massachusetts; three sticks or thereabouts told the news of New York. The only page which did not contain an advertisement was the second; of this "The Errors of the Press," an essay reprinted from *The London Public Advertiser*, occupied a column and a half; the rest of the page contained some intelligence based upon European papers just received at the printing-office. The paper was simply a development of a tri-weekly sheet of the same name, save in the place of *General* was the word *Daily* in the title. The tri-weekly, "Published on Tuesdays, Thursdays and Saturdays by David C. Claypoole," had sold for six pence a copy.

SECOND DAILY IN AMERICA

The second daily in the United States was the outgrowth of the second paper to be established in Charleston after the evacuation of that city by the British at the close of the Revolution. At the start the precursor was called *The South Carolina Gazette and General Advertiser* and appeared from two to four times each week, but not regularly on the same days of the week. Its editor and publisher was John Miller, an English publisher who had been forced to come to this country because of his "defying and exposing the wickedness and the folly of the cursed American war." Upon reaching Philadelphia and explaining the circumstances under which he had been forced to leave England, he was invited by the South Carolina delegation, then in attendance at the Continental Congress, to come to Charleston and establish a newspaper in that city — an invitation which he accepted. From irregular publication on several days of the week it was only a step to bringing the paper out daily. This was done on Wednesday, December 1, 1784. Papers in London frequently referred to Miller as "Printer to the States of

America." This error is doubtless due to the fact that Miller had been made, immediately upon his arrival in Charleston, "Printer to the State." He continued to publish his daily until it was purchased a year or two later by *The State Gazette of South Carolina*, when it was merged with that paper. Miller then removed to Pendleton, South Carolina, where he published a weekly, *The Merger*, until his death in 1809.

NEW YORK HAS NEXT DAILY

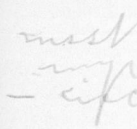

The third daily paper in the United States was *The New York Daily Advertiser*, first published on Thursday, March 1, 1785, by Francis Childs. Not being the outgrowth of another paper, it was, at least in its early days, rather poorly supported by advertisers: yet its publisher made an earnest attempt to secure such business and offered to insert advertisements at three shillings each. It had no sooner been established than it became engaged in a quarrel with Holt's *New York Journal*. Colonel E. Oswald, of the latter paper, asserted that the daily had been started simply to injure Widow Holt. Philip Freneau contributed to the columns of *The Daily Advertiser*, but was never its editor, simply a writer of political articles. *The Advertiser* was the special organ of the Hartford Convention; in fact, its editor, Theodore Dwight, was secretary of the Convention. In its columns he told rather fully the story of New England's opposition to the War of 1812. Although the first daily paper in New York, it did not lead in circulation other dailies which were later established — due, doubtless, to its political beliefs. By 1820 it was credited with a circulation of thirteen hundred, but probably it had less than that amount. It finally united with *The Express*, then a morning, but later changed to an evening, newspaper.

FIRST DAILY OF BOSTON

Boston did not have a daily paper until October 6, 1796, when *The Polar Star and Boston Daily Advertiser* arose on the horizon. Its editor was John Burk, who had fled from Ireland where he had become involved in trouble on account of his connection with a rebellious band called the "United Irishmen."

In some of his early numbers Burk published an account of his trial before the University of Dublin on the charge of Deism and Rebellionism. Shortly after, he addressed an advice "to the editors of the several newspapers in Boston" about the "vices that existed in newspaper establishments." In it he said, "The period of election is ushered in by bickerings, by personalities, by squabbles and scurrilities, by feuds, by heart-burnings and heart-scaldings, by animosity, by contentions and quarrels, which reflect a disgrace on the amiable character of Liberty, and are unworthy the literary advocates of a free people." Because of these and other criticisms, Burk became unpopular and was forced to suspend his paper early in 1797. Leaving Boston, Burk came to New York, where he helped *The Time Piece*, established by Philip Freneau, March 13, 1797, to keep going in a political way. Because of his political editorials in this paper, he was one of those editors arrested for publishing a libel contrary to the provisions of the Sedition Law.

FIRST APPEARANCE OF "THE FEDERALIST"

In promoting the adoption of the Constitution of the United States *The Independent Journal*, established November 17, 1783, in New York City, rendered a distinct service by printing a collection of essays advocating that measure under the general caption "The Federalist." Of these essays, eighty-five in number, the first seventy-six appeared in *The Journal*, starting on October 27, 1787, and stopping on April 2, 1788. Signed by "Publius," they were addressed to the voters of New York, and urged the necessity of supporting the proposed Constitution. Alexander Hamilton, John Jay, and James Madison were the real authors of these semi-editorial essays, though all wrote over the common name of "Publius." The series was copied in many of the other newspapers and had much to do with the adoption of the Constitution, not only by New York, but also by other States. No other one thing during the early days of the Republic showed more the power of the controversial press than the appearance of "The Federalist." The essays have since been reprinted in book form and are still studied by the students of political history. In 1788 *The Independent Journal* became *The*

New York Daily Gazette: it was absorbed by *The New York Journal of Commerce* in 1840.

HAMILTON AND JEFFERSON AS JOURNALISTS

Alexander Hamilton and Thomas Jefferson, though usually classified in histories as statesmen, were also journalists by proxies. Their names are associated with possibly the two best illustrations of the party press and the personal organs — *The Gazette of the United States* and *The National Gazette.* The first of these, edited by John Fenno, was the leader of the Federal press and was the political organ of Hamilton; the second, edited by Philip Freneau, was the leader of the Republican press and was the personal organ of Jefferson. Both editors were employed by the Government: Fenno was "the printer" to the Treasury Department at a salary of twenty-five hundred dollars a year; Freneau held a "clerkship for languages" in the State Department at a salary of two hundred and fifty dollars a year.

ORGAN OF HAMILTON

The Gazette of the United States was the older publication, being established in New York City on April 11, 1789, when that city was still the seat of the Government. As soon as the Government removed to Philadelphia, in 1790, *The Gazette of the United States* followed it and appeared with a Philadelphia imprint on April 14, 1790. Hamilton was thus the first in the field with a personal organ.

ORGAN OF JEFFERSON

Jefferson, perceiving that *The Gazette of the United States* was, to quote his own words, "a paper of pure Toryism, disseminating the doctrine of monarchy, aristocracy, and exclusion of the people," desired a paper that would be a "Whig vehicle of intelligence," and if he did not bring Freneau to Philadelphia, he at least sympathized with the latter's ambition to start a paper which should be distinctly Republican in policy. *The Gazette of the United States* soon had a rival in *The National Gazette* which Freneau established in Philadelphia on October 31, 1791. From the start it had a national rather than a local circulation: in this respect, as in several others, it followed Jefferson's plan. Naturally *The National Gazette,* being a party and personal organ, opposed Hamilton and most of the things for which he stood. At first, Hamilton let Fenno defend the attacks, but when the latter, in *The Gazette of the United States,* began to call the editor of *The National Gazette* a "blackguard," "bedlamite," "fauning parasite," etc., Freneau, who was a master of satirical verse, replied as follows: —

Since the day we attempted *The Nation's Gazette*
Pomposo's dull printer does nothing but fret;
Now preaching,
And screeching,
Then nibbling
And scribbling,
Remarking
And barking,
Repining
And whining
And still in a pet
From morning till night with *The Nation's Gazette.*

Instead of whole columns, our page to abuse,
Your readers would rather be treated with news;
While wars are a-brewing
And kingdom's undoing,
While monarchs are falling
And princesses squalling,
While France is reforming
And Irishmen storming —
In a glare of such splendor, what nonsense to fret
At so humble a thing as *The Nation's Gazette!*

No favours we ask'd from your friends in the east;
On your wretched soup — meagre I left them to feast;
So many base lies you have sent them in print,
That scarcely a man at our paper will squint:
And now you begin
With a grunt and a grin
With the bray of an ass,
And a visage of brass.
With a quill in your hand, and a lie in your mouth
To play the same trick on the men of the south.

One National Paper, you think is enough
To flatter and lie, to pallaver and puff;
To preach up in favor of monarchs and titles,
And garters and ribbons, to prey on our vitals:

Who knows but our Congress will give it in fee,
And make Mr. Fenno the grand patentee!
Then take to your scrapers
Other national papers —
No rogue shall go snacks
And the newspaper Tax
Shall be puff'd to the skies
As a measure most wise —
So a spaniel, when master is angry and kicks it,
Sneaks up to his shoe and submissively licks it.

From this time on, political discussions in both papers became more heated. Fenno's *Gazette of the United States* stood for the Hamiltonian doctrine of Federal control, modeled after that of England: Freneau's *National Gazette* came out just as strongly for the Jeffersonian principles of popular control dictated by the will of the people. Space does not permit a discussion of these widely divergent principles of Jefferson and Hamilton — principles upon which two great political parties were built.

PRESS BATTLE OF STATESMEN

While it was undoubtedly true that both Hamilton and Jefferson were sincere in their desire to avoid an open quarrel, it soon became evident that the newspaper articles must bring about a fight to a finish. The break came when Hamilton, incensed by the ironical and satirical thrusts of Freneau, published in July, 1792, the following letter in *The Gazette of the United States:* —

Mr. Fenno:
    The editor of *The National Gazette* receives a salary from the government. *Quære:* Whether this salary is paid for translations or for publications the design of which is to vilify those to whom the voice of the people has committed the administration of our public affairs, — to oppose the measures of government and by false insinuation to disturb the public peace?
    In common life it is thought ungrateful for a man to bite the hand that puts bread in his mouth, but if the man is hired to do it, the case is altered.

Freneau's reply may be found in the following item: —

Whether a man who receives a small stipend for services rendered as French Translator to the Department of State and as editor of a free newspaper admits into his publication impartial strictures on the proceedings of the government, is not more likely to act an honest and disinterested part toward the public than a vile sycophant who, obtaining emoluments from the government far more lucrative than the salary alluded to, [Fenno was printer to the Treasury Department at a salary of twenty-five hundred dollars a year finds his interest in attempting to poison the mind of the people by propagating and disseminating principles and sentiments utterly subversive of the true interest of the country and by flattering and recommending every and any measure of government, however pernicious and destructive its tendency might be to the great body of the people?

JEFFERSON DEFENDS FRENEAU

The fact must not be lost sight of that the struggle was no longer between the editors of the two *Gazettes*, but between Hamilton and Jefferson. The fight became so open that Washington found it necessary to call his two secretaries together and ask them to cease their attacks one upon the other, making his appeal that the interests of the country demanded that such attacks as were appearing in the two papers could not work for the good of the Commonwealth. Washington even asked Jefferson to dispense with the services of Freneau. This, the Secretary of State refused to do. His defense may be quoted at length as it disproved the charge so often made that Jefferson was an actual contributor to *The National Gazette:* —

While the government was at New York I was applied to on be-half of Freneau to know if there was any place within my department to which he could be appointed. I answered there were but four clerkships, all of which I found full and continued without any change. When we removed to Philadelphia, Mr. Pintard, the translating clerk, did not choose to remove with us. His office then became vacant. I was again applied to there for Freneau and had no hesitation to promise the clerkship to him. I cannot recollect whether it was at the same time or afterwards, that I was told he had a thought of setting up a paper there. But whether then or afterwards, I considered it a circumstance of some value, as it might enable me to do what I had long wished to have done, that is to have the material parts of *The Leyden Gazette* brought under your eye, and that of the public, in order to possess yourself and them of a juster view of the affairs of Europe, than could be obtained from any other public source. This I had ineffectually attempted through the press of Mr. Fenno, while in New York, selecting and translating passages myself at first, then having it done by Mr. Pintard, the translating clerk, but they found their way too slowly into Fenno's paper. Mr. Bache essayed it for me in Philadelphia, but his being a daily paper did not circulate sufficiently in other states. He even tried, at my request, the plan of a weekly paper of recapitulation from his daily paper, on hopes it might go into the other states, but in this, too, we failed. Freneau, as translating clerk and the printer of a periodical paper likely to circulate through the states (uniting in one person the parts of Pintard and Fenno) revived my hopes that they could at length be effected. On the establishment of his paper, therefore, I furnished him with *The Leyden Gazettes* with an expression of my wish that he could always translate and publish the material intelligence they contained, and have continued to furnish them from time to time as regularly as I have received them. But as to any other direction or any indication of my wish how his press should be conducted, what sort of intelligence he should give, what essays encourage, I can protest in the presence of Heaven that I never did by myself or any other, or indirectly say a syllable nor attempt any kind of influence. I can further protest in the same awful presence, that I never did by myself or any other, directly or indirectly write, dictate, or procure any one sentence or sentiment to be inserted in his or any other gazette, to which my name was not affixed or that of my office. I surely need not except here a thing so foreign to the present subject as a little paragraph about our Algerian captives, which I once put into Freneau's paper.

Freneau's proposition to publish a paper having been about the time that the writings of Publicola and the discourses of Davilla had a good deal excited the public attention, I took for granted from Freneau's character, which had been marked as that of a good Whig, that he would give free place to pieces written against the aristocratical and monarchical principles these papers had inculcated. This having been in my mind, it is likely enough I may have expressed it in conversation with others, though I do not recollect that I did. To Freneau I think I could not, because I still had seen him but once and that was at a public table, at breakfast at Mrs. Elsworth's, as I passed through New York the last year. And I can safely declare that my expectations looked only to the chastisement of the aristocratical and monarchical writings, and not to any criticism on the proceedings of government. Colonel Hamilton can see no motive for any appointment but that of making a convenient partizan. But you, sir, who have received from me recommendations of a Rittenhouse, Barlow, Paine, will believe that talents and science are sufficient motives with me in appointments to which they are fitted, and that Freneau as a man of genius, might find a preference in my eye to be a translating clerk and make a good title to the little aids I could give him as the editor of a *Gazette* by procuring subscriptions to his paper as I did some before it appeared, and as I have done with pleasure for other men of genius. Col. Hamilton, alias

"Plain Facts," says that Freneau's salary began before he resided in Philadelphia. I do not know what quibble he may have in reserve on the word "residence." He may mean to include under that idea the removal of his family; for I believe he removed himself before his family did to Philadelphia. But no act of mine gave commencement to his salary before he so far took up his abode in Philadelphia as to be sufficiently in readiness for his duties of his place. As to the merits or demerits of his paper they certainly concern me not. He and Fenno are rivals for the public favor. The one courts them by flattery, the other by censure, and I believe it will be admitted that the one has been as servile as the other severe. No government ought to be without censors; and where the press is free, no one ever will.

FIGHT OF FRENEAU FOR EDITORIAL FREEDOM

Freneau was extremely bitter against any secrecy on the part of national legislation. Taking as its target the act of the Senate in holding its sessions behind closed doors, *The National Gazette* fired the following shot in an editorial in February, 1792: —

A motion for opening the doors of the senate chamber has again been lost by a considerable majority — in defiance of instruction, in defiance of your opinion, in defiance of every principle which gives security to free men. What means this conduct? Which expression does it carry strongest with it, contempt for you or tyranny? Are you freemen who ought to know the individual conduct of your legislators, or are you an inferior order of beings incapable of comprehending the sublimity of senatorial functions, and unworthy to be entrusted with their opinions? How are you to know the just from the unjust steward when they are covered with the mantle of concealment? Can there be any question of legislative import which freemen should not be acquainted with? What are you to expect when stewards of your household refuse to give account of their stewardship? Secrecy is necessary to design and a masque to treachery; honesty shrinks not from the public eye.

The Peers of America disdain to be seen by vulgar eyes, the music of their voices is harmony only for themselves and must not vibrate in the ravished ear of an ungrateful and unworthy multitude. Is there any congeniality excepting in the administration, between the government of Great Britain and the government of the United States? The Senate supposes there is, and usurps the secret privileges of the House of Lords. Remember, my fellow citizens, that you are still freemen; let it be impressed upon your minds that you depend not upon your representatives but that they depend upon you, and let this truth be ever present to you, that secrecy in your representatives is a worm which will prey and fatten upon the vitals of your liberty.

But for the attacks of Freneau the Senate might possibly be still holding its sessions behind locked doors.

END OF BOTH GAZETTES

In spite of the fact that Freneau published at the end of the first six months a most flattering notice about the success of *The National Gazette*, the paper on October 26, 1793, brought out its last issue and published the following notice: —

With the present number (208) conclude the second volume and second year's publication of *The National Gazette*. Having just imported a considerable quantity of new and elegant type from Europe, it is the editor's intention to resume the publication in a short time — at the opening of the next Congress.

Please send in subscriptions.

Printers of newspapers may no longer send in exchange until further notice.

This notice left a loophole so that Freneau might resume publication of his *Gazette* in case he could raise sufficient funds — something he was evidently unable to do. The fact that the yellow fever plague broke out in Philadelphia this same year may have had something to do with the death of *The Gazette*. One other thing may have been a factor in the decision: Jefferson at this time resigned his office of Secretary of State and automatically Freneau ceased to be the official translator of the Government.

Freneau's paper led all the organs of the same political faith. Seldom during these years did a Republican paper get out an issue in which there was not at least one quotation from *The National Gazette*.

The Gazette of the United States continued to be the Federal organ and was bitterly opposed to the attempt of France to involve the United States in war. Fenno remained editor of the paper until his death in 1798 when he was succeeded by his son, John Ward Fenno. The paper later became *The United States Gazette* and was finally consolidated with *The Philadelphia North American* in 1847.

POLITICAL LEADER OF PRESS IN NEW ENGLAND

Of the early political papers of the period, the most interesting and also the most conservative was unquestionably *The Massachusetts Centinel and The Republican Journal* founded on March 24, 1784, by Benjamin Russell. In the first number he printed the following conditions under which he hoped to bring out his paper: —

(1). This paper shall be printed with a legible type, on good paper, to contain four quarto pages, demi. (2). The price of this paper (will) be *Twelve Shillings*, the year, one quarter to be paid on subscribing. If agreeable to the custom in the cities of London, New-York and Philadelphia, the subscribers should choose to pay *per* number, the price will be *Two Pence*. (3). The papers in the town of Boston, shall be delivered to the subscribers as early as possible on publication days. (4). Advertisements shall be inserted at as low a price as is demanded by any of their brethren in the art, and continued, if desired in Six Numbers. (5). Gentlemen in the country may be supplied with this paper at the above price, (postage excepted) which is cheaper than any other papers, if the advantage of receiving them twice in the week is considered. The publishers engage to use every effort to obtain, and the most scrutinous circumspection in collecting whatever may be thought of public utility, or private amusement: Variety shall be courted in all its shapes, in the importance of political information — in the sprightliness of mirth — in the playful levity of imagination — in the just severity of satire — in the vivacity of ridicule — in the luxuriance of poetry — and in the simplicity of truth. We shall examine the regulations of office with candor — approve with pleasure — or condemn with boldness. *Uninfluenced by party, we aim only to be just.* The assistance of the learned, the judicious and the curious is solicited: Productions of public utility, however severe, if consistent with truth, shall be admitted; and the modest correspondent may depend on the strictest secrecy. Reservoirs will be established in public houses for the reception of information, whether foreign, local or poetical.

RUSSELL'S DEVICES TO ATTRACT ATTENTION

In spite of this rather pretentious announcement for a paper, *The Centinel* increased in circulation, not because of the amount or the quality of its news, but because its publisher was the first to realize the value of dramatized and illustrated features for his subscribers. He was extremely fertile in devices and never hesitated to use pictures or mechanical arrangement in types to attract the attention of readers. He fought for the adoption of the Constitution, but was bitterly opposed to the return of confiscated property to those who had left America during the War to live in England or any of the colonies. No paper in Massachusetts was more bitter toward the tax on newspapers passed by the State Legislature in 1785 than was *The Centinel.*

Russell took special delight in printing allegories in his paper. Of these, one of the best was entitled "The Federal Ship," published shortly after the inauguration of Washington in 1789: —

Just *launched* on the *Ocean of Empire*, the Ship COLUMBIA, GEORGE WASHINGTON, Commander, which, after being thirteen years in *dock*, is at length well *manned*, and in very good condition. The Ship is a *first rate* — has a good *bottom*, which all the Builders have pronounced *sound* and *good*. Some objection has been made to parts of the *tackling*, or *running rigging*, which, it is supposed, will be *altered*, when they shall be found to be incommodious, as the Ship is able to make very good *headway* with them as they are. A *jury* of *Carpenters* have this matter now under consideration. The *Captain* and *First Mate* are universally esteemed by all the Owners, — Eleven [1] in number — and she has been *insured*, under their direction, to make a good *mooring* in the *harbor* of Public Prosperity and Felicity — whitherto she is bound. The Owners can furnish, besides the Ship's Company, the following materials: — *New-Hampshire*, the Masts and Spars; *Massachusetts*, Timber for the Hull, Fish, &c.; *Connecticut*, Beef and Pork; *New-York*, Porter and other Cabin stores; *New-Jersey*, the Cordage; *Pennsylvania*, Flour and Bread; — *Delaware*, the Colors, and Clothing for the Crew; *Maryland*, the Iron work and small Anchors; *Virginia*, Tobacco and the Sheet Anchor; *South-Carolina*, Rice; and *Georgia*, Powder and small Provisions. Thus found, may this *good Ship* put to sea, and the prayer of all is, that GOD *may preserve her, and bring her in safety to her desired haven.*

On June 16, 1790, *The Centinel* was enlarged and the word *Columbian* was substituted for that of *Massachusetts.*

RUSSELL'S OFFER TO CONGRESS

One incident in the career of Russell should not be omitted. When Congress held its first session, the country was almost bankrupt. In view of this fact, Russell offered to publish in his

---

[1] Only eleven States had then adopted the Constitution. North Carolina and Rhode Island are not recognized as owners of the Ship.

paper all the laws and other legal advertisements without pay. Toward the close of Washington's inauguration, he was asked for a bill and promptly sent a receipted account of the indebtedness of the Government to him. When Washington learned of the fact, he remarked: "This must not be. When Mr. Russell offered to publish the laws without pay, we were poor. It was a generous offer. We are now able to pay our debts. This is a debt of honor, and must be discharged." Russell was later sent a check for seven thousand dollars, the amount of his receipted bill.

WORDLESS JOURNALISM

Russell, more than any other editor of the period, recognized the value of wordless journalism. He made the pictures in *The Centinel* serve the same purpose that the cartoon does to-day. His device of "The Federal Pillars" attracted much attention. Whenever a new State adopted the Constitution he added another pillar to the "Federal Edifice." In the early part of August, 1788, when eleven States had approved the Constitution, he ran in his paper a device showing conditions then obtaining. The eleven States were represented by the corresponding number of perpendicular pillars. North Carolina's pillar was raised to an angle of forty-five degrees, while the one for Rhode Island appeared broken above its base. Hope for the latter was held out in the inscription at the right of the capital: "☞ The foundation good — it may yet be saved." Evidently Russell had no doubt about the final action of North Carolina, for over the pillar which represented that State was the encouraging news: "Rise it will." Written testimony shows how eagerly readers of *The Massachusetts Centinel* watched the rise of columns in the "National Dome."

THE GERRYMANDER CARTOON

It was this same Russell who printed the Gerrymander cartoon, though it was drawn by Gilbert Stuart. The struggle between the Republicans and the Federalists for the control of the State of Massachusetts was extremely bitter. In 1811 the former had not only elected Elbridge Gerry Governor, but also carried both houses of the Legislature. To retain this supremacy in the future, that there might be no doubt about the election of a United States Senator, the Republicans remapped the senatorial districts and divided the power of their political opponents by paying no attention to county boundaries. In Essex County the arrangement of the district in relation to the town was most singular and absurd. Russell had opposed such a political move, and after it had become a law he had taken a map of Essex County and colored the towns according to senatorial districts. The strange map hung on the walls of his editorial sanctum. One day as Stuart gazed at the map he remarked to Russell that the towns as they had been colored resembled some monstrous animal. A few touches of his pencil added a head, wings, and claws. "There," said Stuart, according to the report, "that will do for a salamander." Editor Russell looked at the revised map only a minute and then exclaimed, "Salamander? Better call it Gerrymander." In describing this incident in his "Reminiscences," Joseph T. Buckingham said: "The word became a proverb, and, for many years, was in popular use among the Federalists as a term of reproach to the Democratic Legislature, which had distinguished itself by this act of political turpitude. An engraving of the Gerrymander was made, and hawked about the State, which had some effect in annoying the Democratic Party." Republicans had by this time come to be known as Democrats — a term first used by the Federalists in ridicule.

NECESSITY OF CHANGE IN NAME

When Washington retired to Mount Vernon, *The Centinel* became a faithful supporter of John Adams and his policies. The term *Republican Journal* in the second part of the title of the paper was in a certain sense a misnomer. It was later changed to *The Massachusetts Federalist*. While a great Federal organ, *The Centinel* reported European news much better than its contemporaries. Russell subscribed to the leading foreign journals and reprinted in condensed form the more important items. This practice made the paper a wholesale distributor of news for the country printers of New England. Russell did not hesitate to rebuke the sensational press because it had "ejected mud, filth, and venom," in the political campaigns and had "attacked and blackened the best characters the world ever boasted." Nevertheless, being the editor of a Federalist organ, Russell was forced, much against his will, to support De Witt Clinton of New York and to oppose James Madison. In proportion as the Federalists lost in influence, *The Centinel* — now called *The Columbian Centinel* — lost in subscription. Toward the close of 1828 Russell retired from newspaper work and in 1840 *The Centinel* became a part of *The Boston Daily Advertiser*.

FIRST FEATURE PAPER

Before the close of the eighteenth century, American journalism had a "feature" paper, the departments of which attracted more attention than its "latest intelligence both foreign and domestick." This paper was started, not in one of the larger cities, but in the little country village of Walpole, New Hampshire. Its promoters were Isaiah Thomas, publisher of *The Worcester Spy*, and David Carlisle, a native of Walpole, and at one time an apprentice in the office of Thomas at Worcester, Massachusetts. Taking a printing-press and type which had seen good service on *The Spy*, Carlisle brought out in April, 1793, *The New Hampshire Journal*. In this sheet may be found the precursor of the modern newspaper "colyum" in a department furnished by Royal Tyler, whose humorous squibs were headed "From the Shop of Messrs. Colon and Spondee." No paragraphers of the nineteenth century ever surpassed Tyler in skillful alliteration, of which he was unusually fond. Tyler had a rival in Isaac Storey, a graduate of Harvard College of the Class of 1792, who signed his political effusions, "Peter Quince." Thomas Green Fessenden, upon his graduation from Dartmouth College, began, under the signature of Simon Spunkey," a series of political lampoons which in Hudibrastic style satirized the French and the Republican politics. David Everett, also a graduate of Dartmouth College, wrote a prose department of clever essays, "Common Sense in Dishabille." These humorous essays were so popular that they were not only republished in many of the newspapers, but were afterwards collected and printed in a small volume. Other clever features were supplied by writers, doubtless college-bred, and were signed, "The Rural Wanderer," "The Medler," "Peter Pencil," "The Hermit," etc. The most popular department in the paper was the one which had for its caption "The Lay Preacher." For it Joseph Dennie wrote lay sermons which went the rounds of the rural press and even found their way into the columns of the city newspapers. Such was the demand of readers for these lay sermons that editors were sometimes forced to insert them even when pressure was so great on the newspaper columns that advertisements had to be omitted. For some reason, possibly because his associates were so fond of showing their scholastic attainments, Dennie went out of his way to lampoon both Harvard and Dartmouth Colleges. More and more these special features crowded out the news until the paper finally became almost a satirical weekly. Because of the popularity of *The New Hampshire Journal* two extra post-riders had to leave Walpole in order to distribute the paper.

TWO OLDEST DAILIES IN NEW YORK

Two dailies founded in New York with political backing deserve special mention. Both papers were founded as Federal organs and were inspired by Alexander Hamilton, who was endeavoring to strengthen the grip of his party on the City of New York.

NOAH WEBSTER AN EDITOR

The earlier, *The Minerva*, now *The Globe and Commercial Advertiser*, was established on December 9, 1793, and induced Noah Webster, the lexicographer at Hartford, to become its editor. It was published "every day, Sundays excepted, at four o'clock or earlier if the arrival of the mail will permit." Webster, in outlining the editorial policy of his paper, said that it would be "The Friend of Government, of Freedom, of Virtue, and every Species of Improvement." His editorials were undoubtedly on the highest plane of any of the period and the paper was the ablest edited of any Federal daily. He was the first editor to advocate no entangling alliances. "I have defended the administration of the national government because I believe it to have been incorrupt and according to the Spirit of the Constitution. I have advocated the Constitution because, if not perfect, it is probably the best we can obtain, and because experience teaches us, it has secured to us important rights and great public prosperity. . . . I have cautioned my fellow-citizens against all foreign intrigues, because I am aware of the fatal dissensions they would introduce into our councils, and because I hold it proper for us to attach ourselves to no foreign nation whatever, and be in spirit and truth *Americans*." In another editorial, he tried to prove that slave labor was less productive than that of freemen.

Connected with *The Minerva* was *The Herald, Gazette for the Country*, a semi-weekly paper made up of extracts from the daily and printed solely for national circulation. Webster wielded more power through the columns of *The Herald* than he did through those of *The Minerva*, just as Horace Greeley later moulded public opinion chiefly through his weekly rather than his daily edition of *The Tribune*. *The Herald*, however, also changed its name before the close of the period to *The New York Spectator*, but its relation to the daily continued the same. When Webster retired on July 1, 1799, Zachariah Lewis became the editor and held that position until April 11, 1820, when Colonel W. L. Stone, of *The Albany Daily Advertiser*, assumed editorial control.

COLEMAN STARTS "EVENING POST"

The second was *The Evening Post*, which was first set up on November 16, 1801. Its editor was William Coleman. This paper must not be confused with several others of the same name. The first *Post* was that of the Colonial Period and was the fourth paper in the city; the second was *The New York Gazetteer; or Daily Evening Post*, published by Kollock, Carroll, and Patterson from August 24, 1786, until December 18 of that year, when its title was changed to *The New York Gazetteer and Public Advertiser;* the third was *The New York Evening Post*, a tri-weekly started on November 17, 1794, by L. Wayland, and discontinued May 25, 1795; the fourth was the Federal daily of

1801. Coleman was a lawyer who had attracted the attention of the Federal leaders and had had some experience on *The Gazette* at Greenfield, Massachusetts. Coming to New York in 1798, he had been given an appointment in the Circuit Court, but in the political upheaval about the middle of 1801 he, along with many other members of his party, had been removed from his office.

BRYANT TELLS STORY OF "POST"

The story of *The Evening Post* from 1801 to 1812 was well told by William Cullen Bryant in an editorial prepared for the semi-centennial of that paper in 1851. The original prospectus, though somewhat measured in style, was well written. The editor, William Coleman, while avowing his allegiance to the Federal Party, announced that "In each party are honest and virtuous men" and expressly persuaded that the people needed only to be well informed to decide public questions rightly. He contemplated a wider sphere than most secular papers of that day and spoke of his designs "to inculcate just principles in religion" as well as in "morals and politics." He even made some attempt to carry out this intention, for in an early number he printed a communication in reply to a heresy avowed by *The American Citizen*, a Republican daily paper, which had been maintaining that the soul was immaterial and that death was a sleep of the mind as well as of the body. At the outset, Coleman made a sincere effort to avoid those personal controversies so common among the conductors of party papers, and with which their columns were so much occupied. In a "leader" in the first number, he expressed his abhorrence of "personal virulence, low sarcasms, and verbal contentions with printers and editors" and his determination not to be deviated from the line of temperate discussion — a resolution he found difficult to keep.

The Evening Post occasionally indulged in a comment in a lighter vein. On May 18, 1802, it answered a female correspondent, who had asked why the paper, like other papers, had not censored the style of ladies' dress then in vogue: "Female dress of the modern Parisian cut, however deficient in point of the ornament vulgarly called clothing, must at least be allowed to be not entirely without its advantages. If there is danger of its making the gentlemen too prompt to advance, let it not be unobserved that it fits the lady to escape. Unlike the dull drapery of petticoats worn some years since, but now banished to the nursery or kitchen, the present light substitute gives an air of celerity which seems to say — Catch me if you can." During the first decade of *The Evening Post* there was much discussion of public questions; its editorial articles, even when brief, seldom if ever seemed to think that it was their sphere to pronounce prompt judgment on every question of a public nature the moment it arose. The annual message of Jefferson to Congress in 1801 was published in *The Evening Post* on December 12 of that year without comment. Not until December 17 was there any discussion, but when it started it lasted until April 8 of the following year. Though Coleman was styled Field-Marshal of the Federal Party he was opposed to the famous Hartford Convention. Mention has been made that Coleman found it impossible because of the times to keep personalities out of *The Post*. By way of illustration, its editorial comment of December 2, 1803, may be quoted: "Cheetham's *New York Watch-Tower* [connected with *The American Citizen*] has recently come to hand in an entire new dress — in such a strange habit, in fact, that it was almost as much unknown as the notorious swindler who disguised himself by putting on a clean shirt. But Cheetham has been cautious, while altering his manner, not to improve his *matter*. Falsehoods appear in the columns of *The Watch-Tower* as numerous as usual, with no other difference, than that they shew *a face more bold*." For the benefit of the lay reader, it may be said that "bold face" is a term used to designate a certain kind of type, as well as to describe the actions of individuals.

Coleman, of *The Evening Post*, had to defend himself not only against the attacks of Cheetham in *The American Citizen*, a continuation of Holt's *New York Journal*, but also against those of Duane in *The Aurora*, a continuation of Bache's *Philadelphia Advertiser*. This newspaper war was typical of the period. Coleman edited a Federal paper and Cheetham and Duane, Republican sheets. Sometimes Coleman attacked his rivals separately, but not infrequently he attempted to kill, editorially, both editors with one stone. For instance, here is a quatrain which he once hurled at his rival editors: —

> Lie on, Duane, lie on for pay,
> And, Cheetham too, lie thou too;
> More against truth you cannot say
> Than truth can say 'gainst you.

LITERARY DAILY OF THE TIME

At the beginning of the nineteenth century the foremost literary newspaper in New York was unquestionably *The Morning Chronicle*, which first appeared on Friday, October 1, 1802, with Peter Irving as managing editor. In his opening prospectus he announced that "while he intended to give the earliest commercial intelligences and to advocate with manly freedom genuine Republican principles, he also intended to blend the interests of literature with those of commerce and politics and to enrich its columns with scientific information." He asserted that "malignity, detraction and scurrilous abuse should never be permitted to stain its pages." Its literary contents comprised criticisms, letters, selections, and extracts from the *literati* of the day. *The Chronicle* was not without its lighter vein department. Irving promised in his introduction "sportive effusions of wit and humor" which materialized with a series of papers on plays and players, fashionable foolishness, and the passing humors of the hour. These were signed with the *nom-de-plume* of "Jonathan Oldstyle" and were thought for a long time to come from the pen of Peter Irving, but in reality they came from that of his younger brother, Washington. Another brother, John Treat Irving, contributed to the columns of *The Chronicle* bits of verse in which he satirized the party conflicts of the day. Still another brother, William Irving, the eldest of the family, told in the columns of *The Chronicle* his experiences as an Indian trader on the Mohawk and later published pungent satire about the doings of the day. James K. Paulding, whose sister had married William Irving, became a contributor of verse. *The Morning Chronicle* was a warm supporter of Aaron Burr and devoted much space to defending the charges brought against him in the columns of *The Evening Post*. The death of Hamilton not only killed Burr socially and politically, but also killed *The Chronicle*. Its remains were purchased in 1805 by *The Poughkeepsie Journal*.

FIRST PAPER WITH TWO EDITIONS

The year 1796 saw an innovation in the shape of two editions, morning and evening, of the same paper. In that year Samuel H. Smith, who afterwards achieved more distinction in the field of journalism as the editor of *The National Intelligencer* at Washington, published *The New World* at Philadelphia "every morning and evening, Sundays excepted." In reality the paper had only one edition, for the sheet was printed all at the same time and was then divided; one half went to the customer in the morning and the second to him in the afternoon. *The New World*, being a novelty, attracted considerable attention for a short time, but subscribers, not satisfied with the paper, discontinued their subscriptions and the venture was abandoned after a few months. Nevertheless, here was the beginning of a system which, in the twentieth century, yields in some of the metropolitan cities an edition of the same paper almost every hour.

"COURIER" OF CHARLESTON

One of the most influential papers in the South during the early part of the nineteenth century was *The Courier* established at Charleston, South Carolina, on January 10, 1803, as a Federal organ. Its publisher was Loring Andrews, who had previously been connected with *The Herald of Freedom* in Boston, *The Western Star* in Stockbridge, Massachusetts, and *The Sentinel* in Albany. On the death of Andrews on October 19, 1805, *The Courier* passed into other hands and became one of the most enterprising newspapers of the State. In its calm discussion of political matters it set an example worthy of imitation by other papers. *The Courier*, though being one of the most influential papers of the State, refused to yield to the public demand for editorial support of the Ordinance of Nullification passed at the Nullification Convention, but being a real newspaper it did give its readers somewhat fully an account of the acts of the Convention.

CHAPTER X

PARTY PRESS PERIOD

1812—1832

THE American press commonly spoke of the War of 1812–15 as "Madison's War." The newspapers of New England, where the war was unpopular, were especially bitter in personal attacks. The burning of the public buildings at Washington and the reward offered by British agents for scalps of Americans — including women and children — fanned the press to an editorial fury in which many of the papers, heretofore opposed to Madison, joined. As a matter of simple justice, it should be noted that both of these acts of barbarism were severely denounced and to a certain extent repudiated by the press of England.

The newspapers published west of the Alleghanies were more active in their support of Madison. By 1812 the professional press in the new settlements was already exerting considerable political influence. Some of the papers were making a sincere attempt to get the news while it had a timely interest. Among the most enterprising of these sheets was *The Reporter* started at Lexington, Kentucky, in 1808 by Worseley and Overton, but later conducted exclusively by Worseley. William Worseley was not satisfied with simply the news service of the weekly post-rider. On Friday, for example, he sent his negro servant — commonly called "Worseley's Man Friday" — to meet the mail-carrier on the Overland Trail, then to hurry back to the newspaper office with the Washington letter and the Eastern exchanges. *The Reporter* was unusually active, not only in the gathering of its news, but during the War of 1812 it went outside of merely printing the news to collect clothing, etc., which it forwarded to the Kentucky volunteers in the army. To *The Reporter*, therefore, belongs the credit, possibly, of being the first to be something more than a mere newspaper.

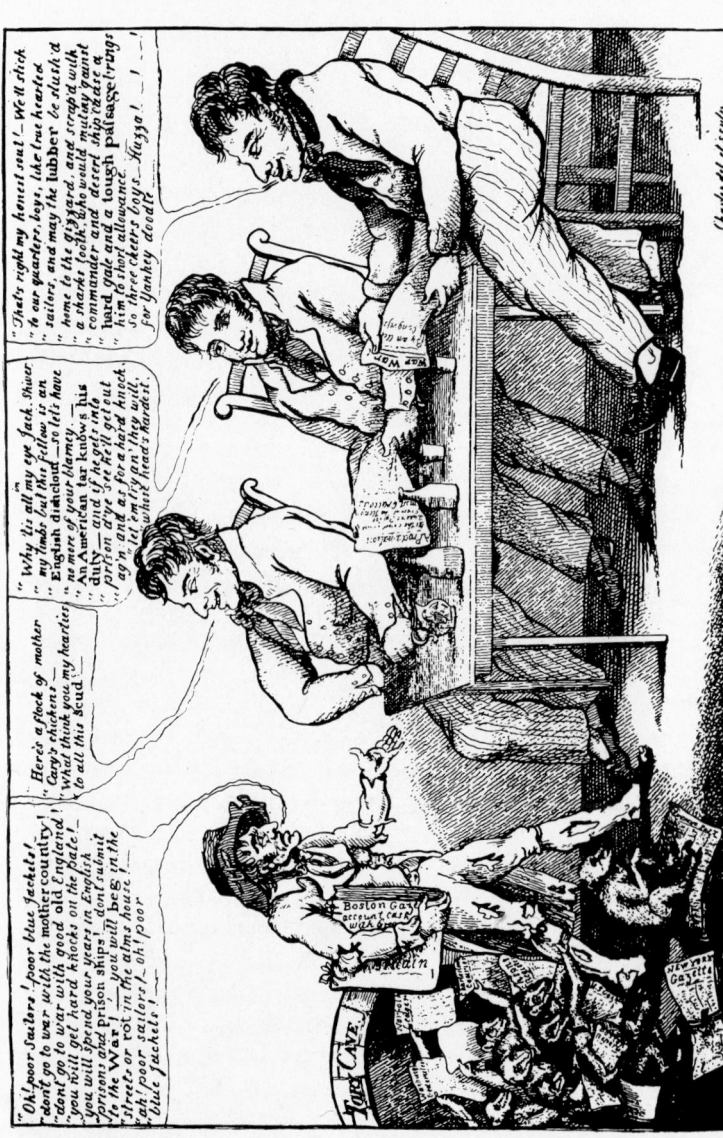

THE TORY EDITOR and his APES *Giving their pitiful advice to the* AMERICAN SAILORS

CARTOON BY WILLIAM CHARLES

THE TORY PRESS

Papers which opposed taking up arms against England came to be known as the Tory press and held much the same position as that of the Copperhead press during the War of the States. The Tory press was severely rebuked, not only by rival newspapers, but also by William Charles, the real cartoonist of the War of 1812. One of his cartoons had for its title "The Tory Editor and His Apes Giving Their Pitiful Advice to the American Sailors." From the Tory cave, shown in the illustration, came the editor of *The Boston Gazette*, who was the chief spokesman of the Tory press. His advice to the sailors was — according to the cartoon — as follows: — "Oh! Poor Sailors: Oh! Poor Blue Jackets! Don't go to war with the mother country! Don't go to war with good old England! You will get hard knocks on the pate! — You will spend your years in English prisons and prison ships! — Don't submit to the War! — You will beg in the streets or rot in the alms house! — Oh! poor sailors! — Oh! poor blue jackets!" A reply from one of the sailors in the cartoon was: "We'll stick to our quarters, boys, like true hearted sailors, and may the lubber be slushed home to the gizzard, and scrap'd with a shark's tooth, who would mutiny 'gainst commander and desert ship 'cause a hard gale and a tough passage brings him to short allowance. Three cheers for Yankee doodle."

Some of the papers which Charles put in the Tory class and made to ape *The Boston Gazette* were *The New-York Gazette*, *The Charleston Courier*, *The Washington Federalist*, *The Norfolk Ledger*, *The New York Evening Post*, *The Boston Reporter*, etc. His cartoon, though crudely drawn, presented in its dialogue the editorial attitude of the two sections into which the American press was divided on account of the war.

PRESS ON HARTFORD CONVENTION

Republican papers made no end of fun of the Commissioners appointed at the Hartford Convention to go to Washington for the purpose of protesting against the distribution of the Federal taxes and of arranging for better protection of the seaports on the Atlantic Coast. The Commissioners, reaching Washington at about the same time that the Treaty of Peace was made public, and finding that their mission had been in vain, almost immediately left the city. One newspaper, *The National Advertiser*, printed the following amusing advertisement under the headline "MISSING": —

Three well-looking, respectable men, who appeared to be travelling towards Washington, disappeared from Gadsby's Hotel on Monday evening last, and have not since been heard of. They were observed to be very melancholic on hearing the news of the peace, and one of them was heard to say with a sigh, "Poor Caleb Strong!" They took with them their saddlebags, so that no apprehension is entertained of their having any intention to make away with themselves. Whoever will give any information to the Hartford convention of the date of the unfortunate and trustful gentlemen by letter (post-paid) will confer a favor upon humanity. The newspapers, particularly the Federalist newspapers, are requested to publish this advertisement in a conspicuous place and send in their bills to the Hartford convention.

P.S. One of the gentlemen was called Titus Oates or some such name.

The Federal press, after the Hartford Convention, steadily declined in influence. Some of its most radical organs which had opposed the war with England were forced to suspend publication. Other papers, to escape a similar fate, changed parties — an act which often meant a change in name, for *Federalist* as a title for a newspaper was almost as common at the time as was *Gazette* in the Colonial Period. By 1820 the Federal Party was without a single electoral vote.

NEW YORK PAPERS AT CLOSE OF WAR

At the close of the War of 1812, New York had seven daily newspapers. A statement of the circulation of these various papers will not only give an idea of how many papers the leading dailies of the period were printing, but also show to what extent newspapers were being read in the city. *The Mercantile Advertiser* had a circulation of 2000; *The Gazette*, 1750; *The Evening Post*, 1600; *The Commercial Advertiser*, 1200; *The Courier*, 920; *The Columbian*, 870; *The National Advocate*, 800. In other words, one person out of every fifteen was a newspaper subscriber. The small circulation of the last few papers in the list may be explained by the fact that they had been but recently established in the city. *The Columbian* was started in 1808 by Charles Holt, after he had set *The Bee* buzzing first at New London, Connecticut, and later at Hudson, New York. It was an organ of Jefferson and later of Madison. *The National Advocate* had only just appeared. It was started by Tammany Hall in order that that organization might have an official organ. The Republican newspapers, not only in New York, but in the other cities, lost no opportunity to criticize the British practice of impressing American seamen into service. It is rather remarkable that a little later they should have so completely ignored the French decree about the confiscation of American goods, as this decree was only a little short of being a declaration of war.

ERA OF "BLACK JOURNALISM"

The darkest period in the history of American journalism was that which began at the close of the second war with England, a time truthfully characterized as the "period of black journalism," when a greater depth of degradation was reached than was ever touched in the so-called "yellow" period of recent times. Those who look over the papers of this era will find that all of the customary courtesies of life were put aside; that the papers of both parties employed the vilest, grossest epithets found in the English language; that the newspapers advanced the most atrocious charges against those holding public offices and even so forgot themselves as to attack wives and sisters in their disgraceful accounts of the personal activities of office-holders.

But the pendulum began to swing the other way. Its first push toward the legitimate function of the newspaper was given by Charles Hammond of *The Gazette* of Cincinnati. He refused to make his paper simply an organ for a great party leader and turned it into a medium for the discussion of the great principles of the Republican Government. In him there was an inborn love of truth for its own sake. Hammond once expressed his opinion of the violent personal journalism of the period as follows: "I am afraid my quondam crony, Mr. Shadrach Penn, of *The Louisville Public Advertiser*, has kept a great deal of bad company since the days of our political intimacy. He seems to mistake vulgarity for wit and misrepresentation for argument;

errors from which, in days of yore, he was as free as most men. I am sometimes constrained, upon better acquaintance, to think and speak well of men whom I once reprobated. I have never yet felt disposed to vituperate a man that I once esteemed and commended. If such sink into vicious courses, I leave their exposure to others. I should as soon think of assassination as attacking a friend because he differed from me in politics." Incidentally, it may be remarked that *The Public Advertiser* just mentioned had started as a weekly in 1818, but became on April 4, 1826, the first daily paper in Kentucky. It was then edited by Shadrach Penn, Jr.

The coarseness, the shallowness, the distortion of news, the use of the press to avenge private wrongs, — all this and much more could be excused, but no reason can be found to justify the papers which so often during this period were little short of being blackmailers and blackguards. But such newspapers, as during the periods which followed, were but a mirror of the times, and their editors were no better, or no worse, than the other men of the day. Even the books of the period were at times so full of scandal and untruth that they had to be suppressed or their publishers, being afraid that they would be prosecuted for libel, either removed the title-pages or cut their names from the imprint. It is important to bear in mind that no better criterion exists by which to judge any particular period than the newspapers published during the same era. Before hasty judgment is passed upon newspapers, a study should be made of the times in which they were published.

PRESS A MIRROR OF TIMES

Personal fights between editors cannot be understood to-day without a knowledge of the condition of the times. It was a period of personal encounters in the home and of fights in the streets. New York newspapers told of the fights between the Battery boys and the Lispenard Hill's: Boston papers recorded in detail the encounters between the North-Enders and the Charlestown Pigs; Philadelphia papers published the fights between the Chestnut Street boys and the crowd which called themselves the Northern Liberties. Roughly speaking, there was a "hot time in the old town," regardless of where the "old town" was located. Such times were naturally mirrored in the press. In the matter of excellence, possibly the newspapers of Boston came first, those of Philadelphia second, and those of New York well down the list. For instance, James G. Brooks, who had edited *The Minerva*, one of the foremost literary papers of the early nineteenth century, but then editor of *The Courier*, publicly posted on the walls and fences of New York a bulletin which said, "I publish M. M. Noah of *The Enquirer* as a coward. — James G. Brooks." It is an interesting comment to record that these two New York papers later became more friendly and united under the title, *The Courier and Enquirer*, on May 25, 1829.

CONTENTS OF NEWSPAPERS

To the party press a most important piece of news was always the report of the official proceedings of Washington. Somehow it never occurred to the typical partisan editor of this period that he might make these reports more interesting if they were pruned of less important items, but instead he gave the routine detail of Congressional debates, no matter how exciting might be the news of his local community, and evidently thought that which came from Washington had additional news value because of its source. Even advertising space was sacrificed to make room for the speech of some representative at Washington who liked to hear himself talk and who was spurred on to talk the longer because his words would probably appear in print. The columns of the party newspaper were always open for communications from politicians of the same political faith — a courtesy which was usually greatly abused both to the annoyance of some readers and many advertisers. In addition, there were usually long-winded editorials which often included a repetition of the matter already stated in other columns. But if it had not been for such full reporting in party organs it would have been extremely doubtful whether the deliberations of Congress would have been preserved for posterity.

Next to giving his readers all the political gossip of the time, the editor of the period thought he ought to provide a choice miscellany of all sorts. There was more excuse for the insertion of such matter, for the magazines had not yet come into their own and books were still too expensive for purchase by any save the rich. In almost every newspaper, regardless of party affiliation, there was a column or more for original verse through which local poets rode wild-shod, for poets and politicians were great seekers, then, as now, for publicity. Incidentally, it may be remarked that much of the poetry of the day dealt with political topics, so that subscribers might get good measure in political matters. The most interesting reading, even in some of the most important papers, was found in the letters of old inhabitants who had left to seek their fortunes beyond the Alleghanies and then had written about the new settlements of the West. Letters were expensive because of the high rate of postage; consequently their writers boiled down the news. Not yet had editors realized the real news value of local happenings.

FIRST HIGH TARIFF PAPERS

In spite of the fact that the press of the period was bitterly partisan in character, independent papers began to spring up in various sections of the country, chiefly in New England. Here, professing absolute neutrality in politics, they became the advocates of a strong protective policy for American industries. Especially important was *The Manufacturers' and Farmers' Journal and Providence and Pawtucket Advertiser*, which first issued from the printing-office of Miller and Hutchins in the Old Coffee-House in Providence on January 3, 1820. Instead of being a party organ, it was the official spokesman for the Rhode Island Society for the Encouragement of Domestic Industries. It was at the start published semi-weekly and because of its non-partisan character had a circulation among those of all political faiths. So carefully did it avoid having any connection with political parties that even when so important a matter as the Missouri Compromise was before the people it made no mention of the bill save in its reports of the proceeding of Congress. Its name was later shortened to *The Providence Journal*, and because of its constantly increasing patronage it was able to appear daily on and after July 21, 1829, — one day later than the first appearance of *The Daily Advertiser* in Providence.

The Journal from that time on continued to be one of the most influential papers of Rhode Island and during the great European War which broke out in the second decade of the twentieth century it often "scooped" in its news items the majority of the larger papers of the metropolitan cities.

At the time *The Manufacturers' and Farmers' Journal and Providence and Pawtucket Advertiser* appeared, the tariff question was attracting considerable attention in the press. The papers along the Atlantic Coast, from *The Argus* in Portland to *The Enquirer* of Richmond, were taking up in their columns the discussion of protection of industries. *The Boston Courier* was started with the help of Daniel Webster as a daily newspaper in Boston on March 2, 1824, to protect "infant manufacturers and cotton and woolen clothes and all agricultural and mechanical products against foreign competition." The leading exponent in New York of protection to American industries was *The Statesman*. These early papers devoted to protection were most severely criticized, on the ground that they were advocating a Japanese system of economy and would eventually shut out America from commercial intercourse with other nations. A few years, however, showed a very radical change in the attitude of many Northern papers toward the subject of protection. At the beginning of the period the great majority of the Republican newspapers, strange to say, was in favor of a high tariff because of political hostility felt toward Great Britain, while the Federal press was in favor of unrestrictive commerce. The "Tariff of Abominations," passed by Congress during the Session of 1827–28, brought about a very radical change in the tone of the press. Editorial policies were completely reversed: protection became popular in New England and free trade in the South. Some of the oldest papers in the country were included in this change: *The Pittsburgh Gazette* which had been started in a log house on the Monongahela River on July 29, 1786, and was the first paper published west of the Alleghanies, had long been a Federal organ in favor of free trade, but became an earnest advocate of a protective tariff and the purchase of home-made goods. This change in journalism was practically simultaneous with the change of heart on the part of many prominent statesmen of the period.

PARTY ORGAN IN MAINE

Party organs had sprung up in new territory. In Maine, for example, *The Eastern Argus* was established at Portland on September 8, 1803, by Calvin Day and Nathaniel Willis to promote the interest of the Republican Party — called by *The Argus* and many other papers the Jacobin Party after the liberalists of France. When Willis about a year later, November 8 to be exact, became the sole publisher, he was so radical in his political comment that he landed in jail — a circumstance that greatly added to the popularity of *The Argus*. Week by week he printed in his paper: "[Such and such] week of the imprisonment of the editor for daring to avow sentiments of political freedom." With every week of imprisonment the circulation of *The Argus* increased. On January 7, 1808, Willis took in Francis Douglas as partner, but later, wanting to make *The Argus* a religious newspaper and not receiving enough encouragement from the clergy in Portland, he sold out his interest and went to Boston to carry out this idea in *The Recorder*, started on January 3, 1816, possibly the first religious weekly in the country. Douglas ran *The Argus* from October 6, 1808, until his death September 3, 1820, when his widow took into partnership Thomas Todd. *The Argus* became a semi-weekly in 1824, a tri-weekly in 1832, and daily in 1835. *The Argus* during the Civil War Period was a severe critic of Greeley because of his dictatorial attitude toward the Administration. Greeley retaliated with this editorial comment on September 20, 1862 about *The Argus*: "Boy: take the tongs and throw the foul sheet out of the window and never let another come into the Office." It is now the oldest newspaper in Maine.

PRESS AND POLITICS

After the Tariff of Abominations had been passed in Congress, some of the most bitter papers in the South urged a separation from the Union and a few even recommended an alliance with Great Britain. The suggestion was even made that a few seats in the House of Commons should be set aside for the American delegates. If newspaper accounts may be believed, and there is no reason to doubt them, the suggestion was not unkindly received in England: it was asserted that seats in Parliament might be secured upon the condition that no formal endorsement of slavery would be demanded. This condition completely changed the editorial tone of the papers which advocated the alliance.

The party organs of Jackson bitterly assailed the Administration of John Quincy Adams, on account of its so-called extravagance and waste of public funds. An "awful howl" appeared in the press when the charge was found for "payment of blacking the boots of the Indian delegates at Washington." These delegates wore only moccasins.

The papers which sprang up to support the nomination and then the election of Andrew Jackson were literally too numerous to mention. Some notice must be made, however, of a most loyal party organ, *The Patriot*, of Portsmouth, New Hampshire. Its editor, Isaac Hill, was rewarded for service rendered to Jackson by the nomination of Second Comptroller of the Treasury. The Senate, however, refused to confirm the nomination, but New Hampshire later retaliated by electing Hill United States Senator. *The Patriot* was thus placed in a strategic position, to start the war upon the United States Bank. Of this war, more will be said later in the chapter.

PART PLAYED BY PRESS IN POLITICS

The way party organs controlled politics in New York was fairly typical of that in other States. The political leaders would have a conclave at Albany at which they would decide upon a man to run for Governor. Some little party organ in a rural section would then be selected to be the first to suggest the fitness of such a man for the position. The suggestion would then be taken up by other rural organs in various parts of the State. Such a nomination would be warmly seconded, even though coming from the rural sections, by the party organs in the "upstate cities." The chief party organ at Albany would then sum up the situation somewhat as follows: "From all over the state comes a unanimous demand for the nomination of ―― ――. While he is not the first choice of this newspaper, there seems to be such an overwhelming demand that the paper is forced to yield to the will of the majority. He should get the nomination and should receive the loyal support of every member of the party at the coming election." A cut-and-dried editorial in praise of the man would then be inserted in the Albany organ. This editorial would then be reprinted with other kind words of commendation by all the party organs of the State. The party voter, thus convinced of the universal demand of the man as Governor, would promptly fall in line. The party press had done its work — and done it well.

PARTY PRESS IN ALBANY

Since the newspapers prior to 1830 were political mouth-pieces and were filled chiefly with political squibs and reports of stump speeches, Albany, the Capital of New York State, was an important news center. *The Albany Register*, established in 1788 by John and Robert Barber, was the spokesman for De-Witt Clinton. When he left office the paper soon after "went into his big ditch," the Erie Canal. It was revived, however, in 1818 by Israel W. Clark who had previously published *The Watch Tower*, a Democratic paper started at Cherry Valley, New York, in 1813, but removed to Cooperstown, New York, in 1814. Under his editorship it fed once again at the State printing crib.

Martin Van Buren needed some one to preach partisan gospel in Albany, and so with Jesse Buel in the pulpit he started *The Albany Argus* on January 1, 1813. Van Buren knew whereof he spoke when he asserted, in 1823: "Without a paper, thus edited at Albany, we may hang our harps on the willows. With it, a party can survive a thousand convulsions." In that year Edwin Croswell became the editor of *The Argus*, and while always mindful of his master's voice he succeeded in injecting a literary taste and some journalistic skill into the vulgarity of the acrimonious political journalism of the time. *The Argus* was a member of the famous Van Buren triumvirate; its other two members were *The Globe*, edited by Blair at Washington, and *The Enquirer*, edited by Ritchie at Richmond, Virginia.

THE GREAT NEWS DISTRIBUTOR

The most important newspaper of the era was not a daily, or even a semi-weekly; it was *The Weekly Register* established at Baltimore, September 7, 1811, by Ezekiah Niles, an editor of *The Evening Post* of that city. In its pages the political and economic news of the country was reported with a fairness and fidelity which characterized no other paper of the time. It achieved a national circulation and was extensively quoted by other papers. In fact, it was a sort of general distributor of news for its contemporaries. So accurate was it that it has been quoted by historians and other writers upon American history more than any other single newspaper in the history of this country. Niles conducted it until 1836 when it was continued by his son, William Ogden Niles, who had attempted to establish *The Journal* at Albany, New York, — not the present *Evening Journal* of that city, — in 1825, but who, upon the failure of that sheet, became associated with his father on *The Register* in 1827. The younger Niles conducted the paper until June 27, 1849. Its motto was, "The Past — the Present — for the Future." The entire series of *The Weekly Register* has been reprinted in seventy-five volumes and its advertisements told the truth when they asserted that no library was complete without it. *The Register* was discontinued because the newspapers of the country more and more performed the same service for their readers. The nearest approach to *The Register* which may be found to-day is *The Literary Digest*.

NATIONAL REPUBLICAN ORGAN

A political organ which attracted much attention in New York was *The American*, an evening paper established by Charles King March 3, 1819. (Its daily edition began March 8, 1820.) At the start *The American* was distinctly a Tammany sheet, or, what amounted to the same thing, a buck-tail paper. It was a loyal supporter of Van Buren, but later was forced to withdraw from its affiliation with the Democratic Party. A new Tammany sheet, *The New York Patriot*, was started largely through the instrumentality of John C. Calhoun. *The American* then became a National Republican paper until February 16, 1845, when it united with *The Courier and Enquirer*. During all this time King was editor of *The American* and after the merger took place became associated with James Watson Webb and Henry J. Raymond in the editorial direction of *The Courier and Enquirer* until he was called to the presidency of Columbia College. King was an exceptionally able editorial writer, but he failed to recognize the value of news — something to which the penny press was then devoting a great deal of attention. *The American* felt quickly this competition with the one-cent papers and on May 1, 1843, reduced its price from six to two cents per copy. The change in price, however, failed to increase the circulation and the paper united with *The Courier and Enquirer*, as has already been mentioned. At one time, however, it exerted great political influence among the more aristocratic circles of New York on account of its able editorials.

EMBREE AND GARRISON

The first abolition paper did not appear in the North, but was started in Tennessee in 1820 — ten years before William Lloyd Garrison brought out *The Liberator* in Boston. On April 30, 1820, Elihu Embree, a member of the religious Society of Friends, started in Jonesboro, Tennessee, *The Emancipator*, a radical exponent of the abolition cause. One of the cardinal principles of the Society of Friends was that no member in good standing could ever hold a person in bondage. Embree was the son of a Quaker preacher and lived in Pennsylvania, before he came to Tennessee to make his home in Washington County. Of him a leading Tennessee paper said at the close of the war: "He was the stuff of which martyrs are made." After teaching and preaching the doctrine of emancipation he started *The Emancipator*, which he continued for eight months when sickness and death finally overcame him. In every possible way he sought to increase the circulation of this paper. To the Governor of each of the States he sent a copy gratis. The Governors of Georgia, Alabama, North Carolina returned their copies sealed, so that Embree must pay letter postage, which, in the case of the package from the Governor of North Carolina, amounted to one dollar, the subscription price of the paper. When other men to whom he had sent sample copies turned the same trick, he gave them a free advertisement, in which, after mentioning what had been done, he concluded with "Without entering into any nice dispositions to discover whether such conduct is any better than pocket-picking, I leave my readers to judge." The South as a matter of strict accuracy has of late been more prompt to accept the honesty of purpose of this pioneer of the abolition of slavery than has been the North.

In striking contrast with the paper just mentioned was a daily started on August 1, 1831, at Charleston, South Carolina. In view of its editorial policy, it was correctly named *The State's Rights and Free Trade Evening Post*. It had at the head of its editorial column the following quotation from Thomas Jefferson, "Nullification is the rightful remedy," and was a prophecy of what the press of South Carolina was to be at a later time when it became the source of inspiration for the secession press.

In the North the most violent advocate of the abolition of slavery was *The Liberator*, started in Boston on January 1, 1831. Its editor, William Lloyd Garrison, was one of the most fearless men who ever sat in an editorial chair. Threatened repeatedly with applications of tar and feathers, mobbed in the streets of Boston, hung in effigy all over the country, he kept up an incessant fight for the freedom of slaves until victory was his. Important as was *The Liberator* in American history, it was not distinctly a newspaper, and its influence has been told over and over again in general histories. Such works, however, have overlooked the fact that this influence was exerted very often through the editorials in the secular press which commented either pro or con about the contents of *The Liberator*. The coarseness of the editors' invectives was characteristic of the period. *The Liberator* was discontinued on December 29, 1865.

WANDERING JEW JOURNALIST

One of the most interesting characters in the history of American journalism was Mordecai Noah, a journalist of fertile imagination. He conceived the idea of bringing the scattered tribes of Israel to an American settlement; he also believed that the Indians were descendants of the lost tribes and proposed that a certain part of the land should be set aside for them. He had other idiosyncracies of which it is no editorial fib to say that they were too numerous to mention. One of them, however, deserves special notice: he seemed to want to edit as many papers as possible. He began his newspaper career in 1810 by editing *The City Gazette* in Charleston, South Carolina. When Tammany Hall, quite a different organization from the present one of that name, repudiated its organ and established another, *The National Advocate* secured Noah as the second editor of that paper. In 1826, after a quarrel with the publishers, Noah started another paper with the same name. Prevented by legal steps in this attempt to have two papers of the same name, he called his paper *Noah's New York National Advocate*. Again getting into legal difficulties, he made another change and called the sheet *The New York Enquirer*. When this paper was merged in 1829 with *The Morning Courier*, Noah still kept up an editorial connection with the union as its associate editor. In 1834 he established *The New York Evening Star*, a Whig organ to support William Henry Harrison. When *The Star* united with *The Commercial Advertiser*, Noah became editor of *The Morning Star*. In 1842 Noah edited a Tyler organ in New York called *The Union*. It lasted about a year, and then he commenced in 1843 *Noah's Weekly Messenger* which after a short time united with *The Sunday Times*. He remained editor of this paper until his death in 1851.

FIRST STAR REPORTER

Henry Ingraham Blake, the Father of American Reporting, belonged to this period. Connected with *The New England Palladium*, a Boston paper started on January 1, 1793, as *The Massachusetts Mercury*, but later, in January, 1801, changed to *The Mercury and New England Palladium*, he was the first to go after news without waiting for items to come to the newspaper office. Though he occasionally reported local matters in and around the city, he made his reputation as a gatherer of ship news. Newspaper tradition in Boston still asserts that he knew the names of the owner, the captain, and most of the crew of every boat that docked in Boston Harbor in his day. Instead of going to the coffee-houses to get the news retold there by sea captains, he would go down to the wharves, get into a boat, and often go out alone to meet the incoming vessels without regard to what the weather was or to what time of day the vessel would dock. After getting the news from the captain or some member of the crew, he would rush back to the office of *The Palladium* and there, with the help of his wonderful memory and by a few notes on his cuffs or on his finger nails, he would put the matter into type as he sang to himself in a monotone. If the item was unusually important he never hesitated to stop the press of the paper in order to secure its insertion. In this way he secured for the Marine Department of *The Palladium* a reputation which put the shipping news of the other Boston papers in the "also-ran" column. Scant justice has been done to "Harry" Blake, who was the father of reporting in the modern sense of this term. After he left *The Palladium*, the paper lost its most valuable asset and soon began to lose its subscribers, who no longer found its ship news worth reading. *The Palladium* passed through various hands until it became in 1840 a part of *The Boston Daily Advertiser*, which had been started on March 3, 1813, and was the first daily paper of any importance in New England.

POULSON OF PHILADELPHIA

The grand old man of the period was Zachariah Poulson, Jr., the editor and publisher of *Poulson's American Daily Advertiser* in Philadelphia. His life links the journalism of the Early Republic with the Era of the Penny Press. In September, 1800, Poulson purchased for ten thousand dollars *The American Daily Advertiser*, the first daily paper in America, and gave it his own name and continued to publish it until December, 1839, when he sold it to the owners of the youngest Philadelphia daily, *The North American*. When his paper was merged with *The North American*, *The Saturday Evening Post* published this tribute to Poulson: "No man probably in this country has ever enjoyed so undisturbed a connection with a newspaper as Mr. Poulson. Commencing at a time when competition for public favor was unknown, he has strictly pursued the even tenor of his way, without departing from the rules which he adopted in the outset of his course. While his younger brethren were struggling and striving with each other — adopting all means to secure patronage — enlarging their sheets, and employing new and extraordinary means to win success — he looked calmly on, and continued as he commenced, nothing doubting that his old and tried friends would adhere to him. Nor was he disappointed in this expectation, since up to the moment of his dissolution *The Daily Advertiser* has neither abated in usefulness, interest, or profit." Mr. Poulson's greatest contribution to American journalism was the training which he gave to a large number of journalists who later went east and west to establish papers upon the sound principles learned while working on *Poulson's Daily Advertiser*. Though a strong Whig, Poulson had a natural propensity to look at political questions from all angles, and in his political criticism he was unquestionably honest and remarkably free both by conviction and by sentiment from using the press to advance personal aspirations.

UNITED STATES BANK AND PRESS

Notwithstanding what academic historians may say on the subject, one of the worst corruptors of the press toward the close of the period was the Bank of the United States at Philadelphia. Its directors knew that its charter was soon to expire and began to count its friends in the press. In spite of its best efforts it encountered so much newspaper opposition and so little favorable comment that it finally passed, on March 11, 1831, a resolution authorizing its president, Nicholas Biddle, to print what he chose to defend the Bank and to pay for the same without accountability. Between that date and the end of 1834 Biddle spent "without vouchers" $29,600 — a sum that would go much farther in those days than now in corrupting the press. When Biddle was accused of using the whole press of the country to aid him in his fight with President Jackson and was charged with being criminally profuse in his accommodations to newspapers which favored a new charter for the Bank, he pointed to a number of papers to which loans had been made and which, when the notes were given, were opposed to rechartering the Bank. Among these were *The Washington Telegraph*, edited by General Duff Green, and *The New York Courier and Enquirer*, edited by Mordecai Manuel Noah and James Watson Webb.

At the time Green applied for the loan to *The Telegraph* he intimated that the accommodation should carry with it no change in the editorial policy of his paper. To this Biddle replied: "The Bank is glad to have friends from conviction; but seeks none from interest. For myself, I love the freedom of the press too much to complain of its occasional injustice to me." He even went so far as to indicate that he would be willing to write on the notes, "Editorial indorsement of the Bank not necessary."

Nevertheless, after the loan *The Telegraph* did change its policy and came out for the Bank. When word of the change was taken to President Jackson he wrote — in an unpublished letter: "I have barely time to remark that the conduct of General D. Green is such as I suspected. . . . The truth is he has professed to me to be heart and soul against the Bank but his idol" — John C. Calhoun to whom Green owed his position on *The Telegraph* — "controls him as much as the shewman does his puppets, and we must get another organ to announce the policy and defend the administration, in his hands it is more injured than by all the opposition." The new "organ" was *The Washington Globe* started December 7, 1830, and edited by Francis P. Blair. Political office-holders, in a none too delicate way were given to understand that they should subscribe to *The Globe* and to do everything in their power to promote its circulation.

No sooner was *The Globe* revolving nicely than one of the officers of the Bank offered to pay Mr. Blair whatever might be the charge for the insertion of a report prepared by Biddle. Blair refused to accept any compensation, but did print, as a public document, the statement prepared by the Bank. Later a friend of the Bank left with a member of President Jackson's

Cabinet a large check to be given to Mr. Blair "as an expression of the respect the donor entertained for the labors of the editor of *The Globe*." The check was returned and Blair continued his attacks on the Bank.

In New York *The Courier and Enquirer* in a savage and almost brutal attack, had charged the Bank with "furnishing capital and thought at the same moment," with "buying men and votes as cattle in the market," and with "withering, as by a subtle poison the liberty of the press." After these charges had been made, the Bank of the United States continued to loan money to *The Courier and Enquirer* until the notes of that newspaper totaled $52,975. When the press published the figures the Bank attempted to justify its position by claiming that the loans were considered a "safe and legitimate business transaction." In 1833 notes for part of the paper's indebtedness ($18,600) were protested by the Bank: two years later *The Courier and Enquirer* offered to settle for "ten cents on the dollar." James Gordon Bennett, who was at the time connected with *The Courier and Enquirer*, once made this résumé of the situation for that newspaper in particular and for others in general: "*The Courier and Enquirer* was in some financial difficulty at the period the war was made by the Bank, and Mr. Noah when he saw the breeches pocket of Mr. Biddle open, entered it immediately and presented the chief exemplar of inconsistency and tergiversation."

In defense of the Bank it may be said that the institution was fighting a life or death battle and was often unjustly attacked by a bitter and vindictive opposition press. The Bank was forced, so its defenders asserted, to fight enemies who held out to editors the appointments to office: it could only use in the conflict such means as it possessed — loans and subsidies to newspapers.

Thomas H. Benton, the spokesman for Jackson in the war against the Bank, charged that the institution was criminally profuse in its accommodations to editors who favored the granting of a new charter. In the newspaper war which grew out of the conflict *The New York Courier and Enquirer* found itself attacked for criticizing the Bank while at the same time being a debtor. At various times, as already mentioned, it borrowed sums until its total indebtedness amounted to $52,975. To justify this position *The Courtier and Enquirer* published a statement as to its financial condition. Whether the condition of the paper was sufficient to warrant such a loan is open to discussion. The statement, however, did show a number of interesting facts about publishing a blanket sheet. According to the memorandum compiled by Colonel Webb, there were 3300 daily subscribers who paid an annual subscription price of $10; 2300 hundred weekly or semi-weekly subscribers whose average subscriptions amounted to $4.50; 275 yearly advertisers at the flat rate of $30. The annual gross income amounted to $60,750, from which the annual expenses of $35,000, when subtracted, showed a profit — at least on the books — of $25,750. According to Colonel Webb, *The Courier and Enquirer* was worth fully $150,000. If it were, it steadily lost in value, for at a later period it found itself unable to meet expenses and was finally absorbed by *The World.*

BULLETIN BOARDS — THEN AND NOW

Bulletin boards on which a résumé of the news was posted first appeared during the second decade of the eighteenth century. By 1815 *The New York Mercantile Advertiser* and *The New York Gazette* were posting on boards nailed to their front doors brief statements of the more important items which came to their offices. Other papers in distant cities soon followed the example set by the New York papers and the bulletin board became an established adjunct of American journalism. The Mexican War and the War of the States increased their usefulness. At one time most of the provincial press got its news of outside happenings from correspondents who visited these bulletin boards and then forwarded the contents to their respective papers first by letter and then later by wire. Not until the close of the nineteenth century did these pony reports for the smaller dailies completely disappear. The bulletin board has possibly reached its highest development in reporting athletic events. Because of the great interest taken by the American public in baseball, the bulletin board has frequently blocked city streets with its crowd of interested spectators who wanted the news even before it could appear in "Sporting Extras." The speed with which news has been told by metropolitan bulletin boards is one of the most remarkable mechanical achievements of American journalism. In a baseball game when the ball has been batted out into the field and has been caught by the center-fielder, this fact has been recorded on a bulletin board fifteen hundred miles away from the game before the ball could reach the home plate in an attempt to put out a man running bases after the fly had been caught.

PRINTING-PRESSES OF PERIOD

During 1822 steam was first used in America as the motive power to run a printing-press: this was seven years before steam turned the wheel of the first locomotive in England. Daniel Treadwell of Boston built the pioneer power press: its frame was constructed of wood and its mechanism was clumsy — but it worked. Another Yankee, Isaac Adams, perfected the press and made it more practical. Called to New York in 1827 to repair a Treadwell press, he soon saw the possibilities of im-provement and in 1830 he successfully put his own press on the market. Later, the demand was so great that he took his brother, Seth Adams, into partnership. The Adams press differed from the hand-press in that, after the type had been put on a flat bed, "the bed was raised and lowered by straightening and bending a toggle joint by means of a cam, thus giving the impression upon the iron platen fixed above it" — to quote a technical description. Isaac Adams "automatized the printing-press." Automatically his press inked the type; automatically it drew the sheet between the type-bed and the platen for the impression; automatically it took the sheet now printed from the type-bed; automatically it "flirted," after registering, the sheet to a pile by a "fly" invented by Adams and still used on cylinder presses. The various patents of Adams passed in 1858 to Robert Hoe, who by that time had made many improvements — but those make a story for another chapter. About one thou-sand sheets per hour was the maximum speed of the improved Adams press.

Up to the close of the period the use of steam, however, was still in the experimental state. Hand-power from "crank men," who turned a large wheel, was sufficient to print the papers even of the daily journals. Frederick Koenig, a Saxon, assisted by Thomas Bensley, a London printer, succeeded in printing from a revolving cylinder in 1812. To have a cylinder roll over a type-bed was bound to be faster than to press an iron platen against it. Robert Hoe, who had started to make printing-presses in New York in 1805, saw the advantage of the changes and began the construction of cylinder presses. In the earlier models that part of the cylinder not used in making the impression was "trimmed down" to allow the type to pass back and forth without touching it. The daily papers used the hand-turned, large-cylinder presses to print their editions. The old-fashioned hand variety still sufficed for provincial newspapers of small circulation.

POSTAL REGULATIONS OF PERIOD

Until the war increased the operating expenses of the Postal Department, newspapers circulated under the provisions of the first Federal Postal Act of 1793. Complaints about poor service were frequent in appearance, but nothing was done except to increase the postal routes. To increase the postage was the last thing the newspapers wanted, yet the first change made just such provisions.

From February 1, 1815, to March 31, 1816, postage on newspapers was increased fifty per cent to raise revenue on account of war expenses. In April of this year (1816), in spite of the reduction on letter postage, it was continued with the exception that postage would be reduced to one cent on papers delivered in the same State in which they were printed even though carried more than one hundred miles. By an act of 1825 newspapers were required to pay one quarter of the annual postage in advance.

A bill for the abolition of postage on newspapers was introduced in 1832. The committee on Public Offices to which it was referred reported adversely on May 19, 1832. In its report it said: —

The postage on newspapers is not a tax. It is no more in the nature of a tax than is the freight paid on merchandise. It is money paid for a fair and full equivalent in service rendered, and paid by the person for whose benefit and by whose venture the service is performed. The law does not require newspapers to be distributed by the mails. It only extends to their proprietors that privilege when it becomes their interest to avail themselves of it in preference to other and more uncertain and expensive modes of conveyance. There does not appear any sufficient reason why the public should pay for transporting printers' articles or merchandise to a distant market any more than the productions of other kinds of industry. In all cases the expense must be defrayed either by a tax or by the person for whom the service is performed; and the committee cannot perceive a more equitable way than for each one to pay for the services actually rendered to himself for his own benefit and by his own order.

Considerable complaint had been made by the papers published outside of the larger cities that the postal laws discriminated in favor of the metropolitan newspapers.

As newspapers increased in the amount of news printed, they did not add more pages, but simply increased the size of the sheet. The result was the publication of those mammoth newspapers which were commonly called "blanket sheets"; some of them in fact were about the size of a bed quilt. By the postal laws a small folio paper in the country paid the same rate as these larger papers printed in New York.

CONDITIONS AFFECTING PRESS

The "reign of Andrew Jackson" was an important one in the history of American journalism. The population had increased to over twelve millions — more than double what it was at the opening of the century. The area was more than twice what it was in Jefferson's day. The chapter on "The Beginnings of Journalism in States and Territories" not numbered among the thirteen original colonies shows how the printing-press had followed the trail blazed by the settler to his pioneer home. The frontier newspaper was but a repetition of the early journalism on the Atlantic Coast. In spite of migration westward the population in the cities had increased, due to the development of new industries and to the extension of the merchant marine.

Schools and colleges sprang up to supplement the work of older institutions. Courses both in the grammar and in the high schools were lengthened. Postal routes were extended. Stage lines were numerous and even the railroads started to carry passengers. Journalism, which is ever linked with the social and economic growth of a country, was bound to be affected materially by these changes. Education made more people readers of newspapers, and improved transportation facilities permitted not only a quicker, but also a larger distribution of the papers. Popularizing the newspaper, however, came from the reduction in cost. Journalism never fully came into its own until a newspaper could be purchased for a penny. Until Jackson's Administration only the wealthy could afford a daily paper. Till then it was a mark of distinction to subscribe to a newspaper, but after the day of the cheap press no such condition ever obtained.

TRANSITIONAL PARAGRAPH

The opening sentence in an editorial of *The New York Evening Post* for March 6, 1835, showed succinctly the journalism of the Party Press period: —

We devote the entire reading portion of our paper to-day, together with some additional columns borrowed from advertisements, to the proceedings of Congress on the two last days of the session.

The following resolution quoted in an editorial in the same newspaper for October 10, 1835, indicated the topic which later received more newspaper space than possibly any other in the history of American journalism:

Whereas, The course of *The Evening Post*, in continuing to discuss the Abolition question, in our opinion, meets the decided disapprobation of the Democracy of the City and County of New York, and of an overwhelming majority of the people of the North, and is decidedly contrary to the expressed opinion and views of this Committee; and whereas, the manner as well as the matter of its publications upon that question, are in our opinion dangerous to the peace and safety of the good people of the South, our brethren in the family of this great Republic: —

Resolved, That the proceedings of the Democratic Republican General Committee be no longer published in *The Evening Post*, and that this Resolution be signed by the Chairman and Secretary, and published in *The Times, Truth Teller, Jeffersonian,* and the German paper, *The New-York Gazette.*

CHAPTER XI

BEGINNINGS IN STATES

1783 — 1832

BEFORE taking up the origin of the penny press, some notice must be paid to the pioneer printers who had established newspapers in the States and Territories not included in the thirteen original colonies. Sons and apprentices of Massachusetts printers, especially from Boston, had left their cases and, taking old hand-presses and fonts of type, had founded papers in Vermont and Maine, settlements hardly yet populated enough to support such enterprises. Others, traveling along the old Mohawk Trail, had gone westward. Adventurous printers from New York and Pennsylvania had taken the Overland Trail through Pittsburgh into the Ohio Valley. Here, putting their outfits on flatboats and into dug-outs, they had floated to Mississippi frontiers. The political plum of Printer to the Territory was shaken into the leather apron of several and the rude log cabin at various outposts served, as in the Colonial Period, equally as well for a post-office as for a print-shop. Occasionally the frontier journalists were politicians who sought to repeat old tricks in new fields. Not infrequently lawyers who found their professional services not yet needed in a country, where every man was practically a law unto himself, were drafted from the bar — take either meaning of the word — into editorial chairs. In a volume of this size mention can be made only of those printers who founded the first papers. Unembarrassed by stamp taxes and unhindered by censorship of the press, they faced other problems in transporting their plants and in getting their supply of white paper equal in every respect to the difficulties of the pioneers on the Atlantic Coast. Individual hardships are given in the accounts of some papers, not because they were unusual, but because they were typical. Without these pioneer sheets to link the Territories and later the States together, it is extremely doubtful if a central form of government would have survived. In Florida and in Louisiana newspapers had been started when these Territories were not yet part of the United States. The beginnings of journalism in these two, therefore, may first be considered before taking the others.

EARLY JOURNALISM IN FLORIDA

Before the Revolutionary Period closed the first newspaper had already appeared in Florida. It was called *The East Florida Gazette* and was published at St. Augustine by William Charles Wells. No issues of *The East Florida Gazette*, so far as can be learned, have been preserved, but such a paper was mentioned several times by a few Southern papers of the Early Republic Period. Its severe criticism of "the good people of the States" was especially annoying to its contemporaries in those former colonies which had become integral parts of the United States. Associated later with William Wells in publishing *The Gazette* was, in all probability, his brother John, who had printed *The Royal Gazette* at Charleston, South Carolina. For this offense, he was ordered by State authorities to leave and went to St. Augustine, where he helped his brother to print books and possibly *The Gazette*. Florida being sparsely settled did not have another paper till late in the Party Press Period when *The Weekly Floridian* was established in 1828 at Tallahassee.

FRENCH AND ENGLISH PAPERS IN LOUISIANA

Among the refugees at San Domingo who settled at New Orleans was L. Puclot. After much difficulty he succeeded in getting the consent of Governor Carondelet to print in French the *Moniteur de la Louisiane*, which first appeared on March 3, 1794. A year later J. B. L. Fontaine became its editor and he continued to hold that position until 1814, during much of which time he was also the publisher. In 1797 the *Moniteur* became the official State paper and in its pages are to be found most of the facts we know about the early history of Louisiana, containing as it does "All the official documents, Spanish, French and American which relate to the changes of government and all officially issued territorial laws, decisions of the city council, municipal notices, consumption of flour by bakers, bills of mortality and the list of baptisms and marriages, etc." The last issue of the paper, Number 1641, was on July 2, 1814. Two days later Fontaine died. *The Louisiana Gazette* on July 7 of that year said of him: "He was an enemy to the revolutionary principles that so long deluged his native country in blood, and often (to his intimate friends) expressed the hope that he should live to hear of a Bourbon being on the throne of France. His hope was realized and he departed in peace, we trust to play his part in another and a better world."

Le Courrier du Vendredi was started at New Orleans on May 26, 1785, without the name of its editor in the imprint. It was the precursor of *The Louisiana Courier*, a tri-weekly published in French and English. *Le Télégraphe*, established December 10, 1803, was another weekly newspaper originally published all in French, but later a tri-weekly printed part in French and part in English. In its second issue it printed the terms of treaty by which Louisiana became a part of the United States. Formal possession of the Territory was taken December 20, 1803.

The Louisiana Gazette, the first paper in New Orleans to be printed in English, was established on July 27, 1804. Published twice a week, its editor was John Mowry. He started with only nineteen subscribers who paid an annual subscription of ten dollars. Several attempts were made to turn *The Gazette* into a daily newspaper: the first was on April 3, 1810. Possibly the reason that these attempts were not very successful was due partly to the fact that editors did not pay enough attention to local news and also to the large number of residents who could not read English.

THE CALL FROM VERMONT

In the rooms of the Vermont Historical Society at Montpelier is still preserved the press on which was printed the first newspaper in that State. The claim has been made that this press was the first to be used in the English-speaking colonies of North America and that it did the best work in a mechanical way, when set up in the house of Henry Dunster, the first president of Harvard College. But at any rate, it printed at Westminster, Vermont, on February 12, 1781, Volume I, Number 1, of *The Vermont Gazette, or Green Mountain Post-Boy*. From that day dates the beginning of journalism in what is now the State of Vermont. The paper, 17 x 12½, had for its motto:—

> *Pliant as Reeds where Streams of Freedom glide;*
> *Firm as the Hills to stem Oppression's Tide.*

Printed by Judah Paddock Spooner and Timothy Green, it lasted until the beginning of the year 1783.

The second paper was at Bennington: it bore the name of *The Vermont Gazette, or Freeman's Depository*, and first appeared June 5, 1783, from the shop of Anthony Haswell and David Russell. On January 5, 1797, it was continued as *The Tablet of the Times*. In spite of numerous changes both in name and ownership it survived until 1880. Possibly its period of greatest influence was during the days when it advocated Andrew Jackson for President of the United States.

George Hough bought the press and type used to print the first paper at Westminster, took in as partner Alden Spooner, who was a brother of Judah, and brought out at Windsor on August 7, 1783, the third paper, *The Vermont Journal and the Universal Advertiser*. It bore the motto —

> *From Realms far distant and from Climes unknown,*
> *We make the Knowledge of Mankind your own;*

and survived until about 1834.

Anthony Haswell printed on June 25, 1792, at Rutland the first issue of the fourth newspaper, *The Rutland Herald, or Rutland Courier*. Its immediate successor was *The Rutland Herald, or Vermont Mercury*, first published December 8, 1794, by Samuel Williams and a clergyman of the same name. It had the longest life of any paper in the State and is still published.

ORIGIN OF JOURNALISM IN MAINE

January 1, 1785, saw the first newspaper established in Maine: called *The Falmouth Gazette*, it was published by Benjamin Titcomb, who had learned his trade in a shop at Newburyport, Massachusetts, and Thomas B. Wait, who had been connected with *The Boston Chronicle*. Titcomb retired from the paper with the issue of February 16, 1786, and Wait changed the title to *The Cumberland Gazette* on April 7, 1786. When part of Falmouth was incorporated as Portland on July 4, 1786, the latter town soon appeared in the imprint, but on January 2, 1792, the title was changed, to avoid confusion with another Portland paper of a similar name, to *The Eastern Herald*. In 1796 John K. Baker bought the paper and consolidated it with *The Gazette of Maine*, on September 3, 1796. An attempt was made to make the paper a semi-weekly, but failed: subscribers would not pay the increased cost. On March 5, 1798, Baker admitted Daniel George as a partner, but left the paper himself with the issue of November 3, 1800. From December 29, 1800, till February 2, 1801 George had Elijah Russell as a partner in the enterprise, but after the latter date he ran the paper until discontinued on December 31, 1804. Such, in brief, was the history of Maine's first newspaper.

The Gazette of Maine was brought out on October 8, 1790, at Portland by Benjamin Titcomb, Jr., but was consolidated with *The Eastern Herald* which has already been mentioned. Howard S. Robinson started *The Eastern Star* at Hallowell on August 4, 1794. It had a short life, being followed the next year by *The Tocsin*, but not until *The Kennebeck Intelligencer* had been established November 21, 1795, by Peter Edes in what is now called Augusta, but what was then Hallowell. Though discontinued with the issue of June 6, 1800, it was revived as *The Kennebec Gazette* on November 14, 1800. A fire in the printing-office caused a suspension of the paper from February 11, to March 28, 1804. A second suspension from November 21, 1804, to January 16, 1805, was due to a lack of financial support. On August 8, 1805, Edes took in his son Benjamin as a partner, but as the paper could not support both, the son was forced to leave. Changing the character of his paper and making it more a party organ, Edes, on February 13, 1810, adopted the title of *The Herald of Liberty* for his paper. In 1815, probably with an issue in September, Edes suspended *The Herald of Liberty* and left Augusta, where he had "sunk property by tarrying so long with so little encouragement," and went to Bangor, where he brought out *The Bangor Weekly Register* November 25, 1815, and "could make out to live if nothing more." Like his father, B. Edes, of *The Boston Gazette*, P. Edes failed to secure popular support, possibly because he was too ardent a Federalist. With the issue of August 23, 1817, Edes ceased to bring out a paper and sold his plant to James Burton, who on March 7, 1817, had started *The Augusta Patriot*, but who had evidently failed to make the paper a successful venture. Burton, however, did not resume the publication of *The Bangor Weekly Register* until December 25, 1817. The space that Edes had used to advocate a separation of Maine from Massachusetts, Burton employed to advertise lottery tickets. *The Bangor Register* lasted until August 2, 1881.

Possibly *The Tocsin*, established at Hallowell in 1795 by Thomas B. Wait, Howard S. Robinson, and John K. Baker, may have antedated *The Kennebeck Intelligencer*, but little is known of this newspaper save that it had a short life. Incidentally, it may be remarked that it was too much to expect a Maine newspaper at this period to support three men.

The first daily newspaper in that State, however, was *The Courier* established in Portland in 1829 by Selba Smith, the original Jack Downing of "Jack Downing Letters" fame. The second was *The Portland Daily Advertiser*, first issued regularly as a daily in 1831, having as its first editor, James Brooks, who later founded *The Express* in New York City. Its most distinguished editor was James G. Blaine, who used journalism as a stepping-stone to politics. The first morning daily in Portland was *The Times* brought out in 1836 by Charles P. Ilsley.

LOCAL AID GIVEN BY KENTUCKY

Although Kentucky was first organized as a part of Virginia, it had its eyes upon admission as a State by the time the Federal Constitution was being adopted. To promote its admission, Lexington, at that time the most important town, voted in July, 1786, a free lot to John Bradford, a Virginia planter who had come to Kentucky after the War of the Revolution. On the site given him by the town of Lexington,

Bradford put up a log print-shop and on April 11, 1787, brought out the first number of *The Kentucke Gazette*. The delay in bringing out this paper was due to the difficulty in getting the press, type, and paper from Philadelphia. This equipment had to come by wagon over the post-road to Pittsburgh, and then by flatboat down the Ohio to Maysville, and then "by nag" over the trail recently blazed to Lexington.

In the first number, Bradford issued this apology for the appearance of his paper: —

My customers will excuse this, my first publication, as I am much hurried to get an impression by the time appointed. A great part of the types fell into pi in the carriage of them from Limestone to this office, and my partner, which is the only assistant I have, through an indisposition of the body, has been incapable of rendering the smallest assistance for ten days past.

The partner mentioned in the quotation just given was Bradford's brother, Fielding.

The initial number of *The Kentucke Gazette* was a single sheet, two pages (10 x 19½), three columns to the page. Fielding Bradford retired with the issue of June 7, 1788, and from that time its publisher until 1802 was John Bradford. The peculiar spelling of "Kentucke" was changed to the modern form, "Kentucky," on March 14, 1789. An attempt was made on January 4, 1797, to make the paper a semi-weekly, but a year later, or on January 3, 1798, it changed back to a weekly again. Daniel Bradford succeeded his father as editor and publisher of the paper on April 2, 1802. *General Advertiser* was added to the title at the beginning of 1803. Another attempt to make the paper a semi-weekly was made on February 19, 1806, but was not successful and a change to a weekly publication was resumed on January 3, 1807. *The Kentucky Gazette and General Advertiser* passed out of the control of the Bradford family on October 3, 1809, when Thomas Smith became the publisher. Smith, enlisting for service in Canada in August, 1812, turned the paper over to his brother-in-law, William W. Worseley, but still kept his own name in the imprint as publisher. A month later, however, he took in John Bickley as partner, but a little over a year later sold the paper to Fielding Bradford, Jr. It was published for about three years by him and then sold to John Norvel & Co. The "Co." was dropped with the issue of February 7, 1818, but on March 5, 1819, the paper was transferred to Joshua Norvel & Co., which later became, on October 6 of that year, Norvel & Cavins. The latter partner, however, became the sole proprietor on July 27, 1820. *The Kentucky Gazette* ceased publication some time in 1848.

The second paper in Kentucky was also started in Lexington by Thomas H. Stewart, who, on or near February 17, 1795, brought out *Stewart's Kentucky Herald*. After ten years *The Herald* became a part of *The Kentucky Gazette*.

The family of Bradford was connected with the first three papers in Kentucky. In 1802 John Bradford was the publisher of *The Kentucky Herald*, just mentioned; on November 7, 1795, Benjamin J. Bradford brought out the third paper, *The Kentucky Journal*, at Frankfort.

OTHER PAPERS IN KENTUCKY

Other early Kentucky papers were *The Rights of Man, or The Kentucky Mercury*, first published in May, 1797, at Paris, by Darius Moffett; *The Mirror*, August, 1797, at Washington, by Hunter & Beaumont; *The Guardian of Freedom*, by John Bradford & Son (this paper was really a branch of *The Kentucky Gazette* published at Frankfort in order to advocate Bradford as State Printer); *The Palladium*, August, 1798, at Frankfort, by Hunter (after *The Mirror* at Washington was discontinued, the earlier part of that year); *The Western American*, in 1803, at Bardstown, by Francis Peniston; *The Western World*, in 1806, at Frankfort, by Joseph M. Street; *The Candid Review*, in 1807, at Bardstown, by Peter Isler & Co.; *The Louisville Gazette*, in 1807, by Joseph Charles; *The Impartial Observer*, in 1807, at Lexington, by Guerin & Prentiss; *The Argus of Western America*, in 1808, at Frankfort, by William Gerard.

EARLY JOURNALISM IN WEST VIRGINIA

Dr. Robert Henry, physician, who had come to Berkeley County in 1792, started the first newspaper in West Virginia at Martinsburg in 1789. It was called The *Potomac Guardian and the Berkeley Advertiser* and had for its motto, "Where Liberty Dwells, There's My Stand." The earliest known issue is that of April 3, 1792, Volume 2, Number 73. It was a 9 x 15 sheet and the copy is preserved at the Capitol at Richmond, Virginia. Nathaniel Willis, father of Nathaniel Willis, who published *The Boston Recorder*, and grandfather of Nathaniel Parker Willis, who was the most distinguished literary man of his day, founded the second newspaper of West Virginia, also in Martinsburg in 1799. Willis called his paper *The Martinsburg Gazette.* The third newspaper in the State, again printed at Martinsburg, was started in 1800 and called *The Berkeley and Jefferson County Intelligencer and Northern Neck Advertiser*. Its publisher was John Alburtis. Wheeling had its first newspaper, *The Repository*, in 1807. Other early papers in Wheeling were *The Times, The Gazette, The Telegraph,* and *The Virginian.* In 1819 Herbert P. Gaines brought out the first newspaper at the Capital of the State, Charlestown, *The Kanawha Patriot*, and in 1820, Mason Campbell brought out the second, *The Western Courier.* Other papers followed until by 1850 there were three dailies and twenty-one weeklies in West Virginia.

INAUGURAL JOURNALISM IN DISTRICT OF COLUMBIA

Before the seat of government was permanently located in the District of Columbia, a number of newspapers had been published in Georgetown. The first of these was *The Times and Potowmack Packet*, established by Charles Fierer in February, 1789. Others were *The Weekly Ledger*, started by Alexander Doyle in March, 1790; *The Columbian Chronicle*, by Samuel Hanson in December, 1793; and *The Centinel of Liberty*, by Green, English & Company in May, 1796. The first paper actually printed in Washington City was *The Impartial Observer and Washington Advertiser*, the initial number of which Thomas Wilson issued on May 22, 1795. The paper was suspended about a year later on account of its owner's death. Its immediate successor was *The Washington Gazette* — a semi-weekly established on June 15, 1796. The relation between *The Impartial Observer* and *The Washington Gazette* is made clear by the following notice in the early issues of the latter: —

The printers of news papers in the United States are desirous to take notice that this is the only paper printed in the city of Washington, and issues from the office late the property of Mr. Thomas Wilson deceased, and since then a few weeks in the possession of Mr. John Crocker. They are requested to forward their papers to Benjamin More, or the printer of *The Washington Gazette* and may depend on having *The Washington Gazette* regularly forwarded to them.

The most important early paper was the tri-weekly, *The National Intelligencer and Washington Advertiser*, started on October 31, 1800, by Samuel Harrison Smith, who moved with the Government from Philadelphia to Washington and who has already been mentioned several times in these pages. He took into partnership in 1810 Joseph Gales, Jr., who dropped *The Washington Advertiser* from the title. After Smith became president of the Washington branch of the United States Bank, he retired from journalism and William W. Seaton became associated with Gales in the publishing of the paper now issued daily. Under the editorship of these two men the paper became the recognized Government organ — called by John Randolph "The Court Paper." It was the official reporter of Congress, and had it not been for the excellent work of Gales, who had been taught stenography by his father, it is extremely doubtful whether the great speeches of Webster, Clay, and Calhoun would have been preserved. These statesmen, incidentally, often wrote for the paper. *The Intelligencer* was the spokesman for the Presidents until the inauguration of Jackson, when *The United States Telegraph*, edited by General Duff Green, became the Administration organ. Because of Green's endorsement of the policies of John C. Calhoun, Jackson established *The Globe*. When William Henry Harrison was inaugurated in March, 1841, *The Intelligencer* came back into its own official position until the Whig Party was split by the death of the President, but it again became "The Court Paper" when Fillmore took the presidential chair on the death of Taylor. It continued to be published in Washington until January 10, 1870, when it was moved to New York, where it lasted only a short time. The reason for the removal was the fact that with the secession of the South the paper lost over two thirds of its entire circulation.

INITIAL PAPERS OF TENNESSEE

Very often the publisher of the first newspaper in any State was also the authorized printer to the Territorial or State Legislature. Such was the case in Tennessee, where George Roulstone first brought out, at Rogersville on November 5, 1791, *The Knoxville Gazette*. After issuing a few numbers he moved his plant to Knoxville, where he continued to bring out the paper until his death in 1804. He remained public printer all this time and his wife was later elected for two successive terms to fill the place.

The second paper in Knoxville was *The Register* founded in 1798 by John R. Parrington. Another early Knoxville paper was *Wilson's Gazette* begun in 1804 by George Wilson, and published until 1818, when Wilson went to Nashville to begin *The Nashville Gazette* in the interest of "Old Hickory." Working with Wilson as a journeyman printer was F. S. Heiskell, who, shortly before the former left for Nashville, started a second *Register* in August, 1816, which survived, though under many editors, until the outbreak of the War of the States.

The first paper in Memphis was *The Memphis Advocate and Eastern District Intelligencer*, which first appeared on January 18, 1827. *The Times* was established soon after and later the two papers were united with the title of *The Times and Advocate*.

Journalism began in Nashville in 1797, when *The Tennessee Gazette* appeared under the editorship of a Kentucky printer named Henkle. A year later the paper was sold and the name changed to *The Clarion*. *The Hamilton County Gazette*, which later became *The Chattanooga Gazette*, was brought from Knoxville to Chattanooga by flatboat in 1838. It suspended in 1859, but in 1864 was revived by James R. Hood and E. A. James.

OHIO AND ITS EARLY PAPERS

The distinction of being the first paper in Ohio belongs to *The Centinel of the Northwestern Territory*, brought out in the village of Cincinnati on November 9, 1793, by William Maxwell. Born about 1755 in New Jersey, he had come to Ohio by way of Pittsburgh. He brought with him a Ramage press and a few fonts of type which he set up in a log cabin print-shop at the corner of Front and Sycamore Streets. By way of a motto for his paper he borrowed that of *The New York Chronicle*, "Open to All Parties — But Influenced by None."

Speaking as the printer of *The Centinel of the Northwestern Territory*, he said in his opening issue: —

Having arrived at Cincinnati, he has applied himself to that which has been the principal object of his removal to this country, the Publication of a News Paper. This country is in its infancy, and the inhabitants are daily exposed to an enemy who, not content with taking away the lives of men in the field, have swept away whole families, and burnt their habitations. We are well aware that the want of regular and certain trade down the Mississippi, deprives this country in great measure, of money at the present time. These are discouragements, nevertheless I am led to believe that the people of this country are disposed to promote science, and have the fullest assurance that the Press, from its known utility, will receive proper encouragement. And on my part am content with small gains, at the present, flattering myself that from attention to business, I shall preserve the good wishes of those who have already countenanced me in this undertaking, and secure the friendship of subsequent population.

The paper, published on Saturday, was a four-page sheet and had three columns to the page. Having mislaid the subscription list Maxwell published a notice in the first issue that subscribers should call at the office for their paper and that subscriptions would be received "in Columbia by John Armstrong, Esquire; North-Bend by Aaron Cadwell, Esquire; Coleram by Capt. John Dunlap, and in New-Port by Capt. John Vartelle." At the very start Maxwell advocated the opening of the Mississippi to navigation and never ceased to be the pleader of this cause so long as he remained the editor. Having been appointed postmaster to Cincinnati, he sold *The Centinel of the Northwestern Territory* in 1796 to Edmund Freeman, who changed its name to *Freeman's Journal*. The latter continued its publication under that title until 1800 when he followed the seat of the Territorial Government to Chillicothe and brought out *Freeman's Journal* in that place. Upon his death, in 1801, Nathaniel Willis purchased the paper and combined it with *The Sciota Gazette*, a paper still published at Sciota.

The next paper, in order of establishment, in Ohio was *The Western Spy and Hamilton Gazette*, first published May 28, 1799, at Cincinnati by James Carpenter. Its name was changed to *The Western Spy* in 1806; three years later, April 13, 1809, to *The Whig*, and still later, June 13, 1810, to *The Advertiser*. Evidently, the changes in names did not add to the circulation of the sheet, for it was eventually forced to suspend publication. Incidentally it may be remarked that in September, 1810, Carpenter started *The Western Spy*, but early in 1819 he changed it to *The Western Spy and Cincinnati General Advertiser*. It united with *The Literary Cadet* on April 29, 1820, only to become *The National Republican and Ohio Political Register* on January 1, 1823. A change in name was made January 3, 1830, to *The National Republican and Cincinnati Daily Mercantile Advertiser*, and on July 11, 1833, to *The Cincinnati Republican and Commercial Register*.

The third paper in Ohio has already been mentioned, *The Sciota Gazette*. This influential sheet, so often quoted in New York, Philadelphia, and other papers, was established in Chillicothe April 25, 1800, by Nathaniel Willis, a family name often met with in the history of American journalism. *The Gazette* absorbed *The Fredonian* in August, 1815, and *The Supporter* in March, 1821.

Of the other early papers in Ohio mention may be made of *The Ohio Gazette and The Territorial and Virginia Herald*, the fourth paper in the Northwestern Territory established December 7, 1801, by Wyllys Silliman and Elijah Backus at Marietta; *The Liberty Hall and Cincinnati Mercury*, by John W. Browne, December 4, 1804, at Cincinnati; *The Ohio Herald*, by Thomas G. Bradford & Company, July 27, 1805, at Chillicothe; *The Fredonian*, by R. D. Richardson, February 19, 1807, at Chillicothe; *The Star*, by John McLean, February 13, 1807, at Lebanon; *The Commentator*, by Dunham and Gardiner, September 16, 1807, at Marietta; *The Supporter*, by George Nashee, September 29, 1808, at Chillicothe; *The Independent Republican*, by Peter Parcels, September 8, 1809, at Chillicothe; *The Impartial Observer*, by John C. Gilkinson & Company March 25, 1809, at St. Clairsville; *The Ohio Sentinel*, by Isaac G. Burnett May 3, 1810, at Dayton.

Ohio had in 1810 fourteen newspapers and by 1819, thirty-three.

INTRODUCTORY PAPERS OF MISSISSIPPI

As in other States, the first paper in Mississippi was *The Gazette*. It appeared on, or near August 1, 1800, at Natchez and was called *The Mississippi Gazette*. Its editor and printer was Benjamin Stokes. For a year, during 1801, the paper was published by Sackett & Wallace, but later, Mr. Stokes again assumed control and continued publication until about January 1, 1802.

On or near August 11, 1801, the second newspaper in Mississippi appeared at Natchez and was called *The Intelligencer*. Its printers were D. Moffett and James Farrell. Its life was short, and was followed by *The Mississippi Herald* on July 26, 1802. This by all means was the most important paper in this State during its early period. It was printed by Andrew Marschelk. Later, it became *The Mississippi Herald and Natchez Gazette*. The old files, which once belonged to Colonel Marschelk, show that he conducted the paper under the following titles: *Natchez Gazette*, *Washington Republican*, *Washington Republican and Natchez Intelligencer*, *State Gazette*, *Mississippi Republican*, *State Gazette*, *Natchez Newspaper and Public Advertiser*, *Mississippi Statesman*, *Mississippi Statesman and Natchez Gazette*, and finally *The Natchez Gazette*.

The next paper in Mississippi was *The Constitution Conservator*, which was founded on or near October 16, 1802, by John Wade at Natchez. On September 1, 1804, John Shaw and Timothy Terrill brought out *The Mississippi Messenger* at Natchez. The chief distinction of this paper was that many of its editorials were written in doggerel.

BEGINNINGS IN INDIANA

Journalism in Indiana began in Vincennes when Elihu Stout, a printer from Lexington, Kentucky, brought out the first number of *The Indiana Gazette* on July 31, 1804. The newspaper was produced under great difficulties. The paper was brought to Vincennes on pack-horses which traveled over the old Buffalo Trail. The plant itself had been brought from Frankfort, Kentucky, down the Ohio River and up to Wabash in what was then called "piroques." The printing-office burned out in about two years, and the paper was revived on July 11, 1807, by Stout under the title, *The Western Sun*. Stout was the Territorial Printer and conducted the paper until 1845 when he sold out after he received the office of postmaster.

Other early Indiana papers included *The Gazette*, established at Corydon in 1814; *The Plaindealer*, established at Brookville in 1816; *The Indiana Republic*, established at Madison in 1815; *The Indiana Register*, established at Vevay in 1816; *The Centinel*, established at Vincennes in 1817; *The Indiana Oracle*, established at Lawrenceburg in 1817; *The Intelligencer*, established at Charleston in 1818. The first directory of Indiana papers was a gazetteer, published in 1831 by the proprietors of *The Indiana Journal*, and listed for 1832 twenty-nine different newspapers.

Notices similar to the following — taken from *The Bloomington Post* — appeared frequently in Indiana papers: —

Persons expecting to pay for their papers in produce must do so soon, or the cash will be expected. Pork, flour, corn and meal will be taken at the market prices. Also, those who expect to pay us in firewood must do so immediately — we must have our wood laid for the winter before the roads get bad.

MAIDEN ATTEMPTS IN MISSOURI

Joseph Charless, a printer who had worked on *The Kentucky Gazette* at Lexington, was the founder of journalism in Missouri. Securing an old Ramage press and a few fonts of type he put his plant aboard a keel-boat on the Ohio and floated down that river to find a permanent location at what is now St. Louis, but was then only a little settlement of about one thousand inhabitants. Here, on July 12, 1808, he, with the help of Joseph Hinkle, a former printer on a Kentucky *Gazette*, pulled the first number of *The Missouri Gazette*. In this period in American history Congress had divided its recently acquired province into the Territories of Orleans and Louisiana. St. Louis was in Louisiana Territory, so on December 7, 1809, Charless changed the title from a local to a more general one and called his paper *The*

Louisiana Gazette. When Congress, however, again set off Missouri and Louisiana each as a separate territory, Charless on July 11, 1812, returned to the original name of *The Missouri Gazette.* Charless retired from the paper on September 13, 1820, when he sold it to James C. Cummins. On March 13, 1822, he, in turn, sold it to Edward Charless, the oldest son of the founder, who changed the name to *The Missouri Republican,* as a personal tribute to his Jeffersonian doctrines. It is now published as *The St. Louis Republic.*

In order to counteract the influence of *The Gazette* the political opponents of Charless raised a fund of one thousand dollars to start a Republican newspaper in St. Louis. An advertisement in *The Lexington Kentucky Reporter* brought them Joshua Norbell, of Nashville, Tennessee. Early in May, 1815, he started a rival sheet called *The Western Journal.* Two years later he was succeeded by Sergeant Hall, of Cincinnati, who issued the first number of his paper under the new name of *The Western Emigrant.* Two years later the paper became *The St. Louis Enquirer,* which once had for its editor Thomas H. Benton, who later forsook journalism for politics and became the United States Senator.

SPOKEN PAPER IN MICHIGAN

Journalism in Michigan began with that most interesting precursor, the spoken newspaper, conducted under the auspices of the Reverend Father Gabriel Richard, a priest of the Order of Sulpice, who came to Detroit in 1798 as resident pastor of the Roman Catholic Church of St. Anne. Mention has been made in an earlier chapter of how he appointed a town-crier whose duty it was on Sunday to stand on the church steps and to tell the public in general and the congregation in particular such news as was fit to speak. Advertising had its place in this spoken newspaper which told of the things for sale, etc. For the benefit of those absent at the spoken edition a written one was publicly posted near the church. For some time Father Richard was assisted in this way of publishing the news by Theopolis Meetz, who was at the time sacristan of St. Anne's Church, but who later became a printer and newspaper publisher.

FIRST PRINTED PAPER

Out of this spoken, and later written, newspaper, grew the first printed sheet in Michigan entitled *The Michigan Essay, or Impartial Observer*. It first appeared in Detroit on August 31, 1809. As editor and publisher Father Richard selected one of his parishioners, James M. Miller. The French section — not a half, as has so often been asserted, but about a column and a half — was undoubtedly written by the Father himself. An editorial announcement informed the public that the paper would be published every Thursday and handed to city subscribers at five dollars per annum, payable half-yearly in advance. It stated its policy in the following words: "The public are respectfully informed that the Essay will be conducted with the utmost impartiality; that it will not espouse any political party, but fairly and candidly communicate whatever may be deemed worthy of information, whether foreign, domestic, or local."

The second paper in Michigan was *The Detroit Gazette*, started on July 25, 1817, by Sheldon & Reed. This was the first permanent newspaper in Michigan, and like its predecessor, *The Michigan Essay*, it had to serve not only the English but also the French population of the city. One page was in French and the other three in English. It had an unusually hard time to make both ends meet, for in its issue of July 14, 1820, it asserted that only ninety of its one hundred and fifty-two subscribers had paid their subscriptions and not a single advertiser had yet met his bill. In spite of this fact, however, the paper survived until April 22, 1830.

The next paper was *The Michigan Herald*, also of Detroit, brought out on May 10, 1825, by H. Chipman and Joseph Seymour.

RUSH FOR ALABAMA

The first paper in what is now Alabama was unquestionably *The Mobile Sentinel*, published by Samuel Miller and John B. Hood at Fort Stoddert, May 23, 1811. These men were so determined to be the first in Mobile journalism that they started south before the city was annexed, but were compelled to stop for the printing outside in the neighborhood of St. Stephens, where they began to print *The Mobile Sentinel* while under the protection of Fort Stoddert. Sixteen issues of this paper at least were brought out, but whether a single one of them was actually printed in Mobile is not known.

Mobile under Spanish rule surrendered to General James Wilkinson, April 13, 1813. On April 28, 1813, a *Mobile Gazette* with an account of the affair was published. Its editor and publisher was George B. Cotton. Cotton, in selling out his interest, said in his farewell in the issue of June 23, 1819, that *The Mobile Gazette* was started under his management in the infancy of the town, and some have taken this assertion to mean that the paper was in existence while Mobile was under Spanish rule. This seems extremely doubtful.

The Commercial Register, the predecessor of the present *Mobile Register*, appeared on December 10, 1821. In 1823 *The Register* printed a brief note that it had purchased the title, interest, and property of *The Mobile Gazette*.

ORIGIN IN ILLINOIS

The year of 1814 saw the first newspaper in Illinois. It was called *The Illinois Herald* and was published at Kaskaskia by Matthew Duncan, Printer to the Territory and publisher of the Laws of the Union, 1815. Duncan was a native of Virginia and came to Illinois by way of Kentucky. The paper appeared on or near June 24, 1814, as Number 30 of Volume I is dated December 13, 1814. On April 24, 1816, the paper became *The Western Intelligencer* and was published by Robert Blackwell and Daniel P. Cook. On May 27, 1818, the paper became *The Illinois Intelligencer* and continued publication under that title until October 14, 1820, when it suspended, only to be revived on December 14 of that year at Vandalia which had become the Capital of the State.

The second paper, *The Illinois Immigrant*, appeared in Shawneetown on June 13, 1818, with Henry Eddy and Singleton H. Kimmel as editors. On September 25, 1819, it became *The Illinois Gazette*.

Difficulties of printing the early papers in Illinois are illus-

trated in the following editorial by James Hall, the editor of
The Illinois Gazette, in 1821: —

After a lapse of several weeks (three months to be exact) we are now
enabled to resume the publication of our sheet. Paper (the want of
which has been the cause of the late interruption) was shipped for us
early last fall, on board a boat bound for St. Louis — to which place,
owing probably to the forgetfulness of the Master, it was carried and
has but just now come to hand. . . . High and low water it seems are
equally our enemies — the one is sure to delay the arrival of some article
necessary to the prosecution of our labors, while the other hurries something of which we stand in the most pressing need, down the current
beyond our reach.

PARTY ORGANS IN ARKANSAS

Journalism began in Arkansas when William E. Woodruff
printed at the Post of Arkansas the first number of *The Arkansas Gazette* on November 20, 1819. A native of Long Island, he
had arrived at the Post on October 30, 1819, from Franklin,
Tennessee, bringing with him by canoes and dug-outs a press
and some type. Being the Printer to the Territory he ceased to
bring out *The Gazette* at the Post on November 24, 1821, and
went to Little Rock, which had been made the Capital. Here he
revived his paper on December 29, 1821, and continued it as
the official organ of the State until 1833. That year he refused
to let *The Arkansas Gazette* be simply a mouthpiece for Governor
Pope. Woodruff, like most of the early editors in the West, had
political aspirations and used his newspaper to help in their
achievement, but when elected State Treasurer in October, 1836,
he sold his paper to Cole & Spooner. The latter soon retired,
and going to Hartford, joined the staff of *The Courant;* the
former continued *The Gazette* until about 1840, when, for political
and other reasons, he had to withdraw from the paper, which
came again to Woodruff, its former owner. Three years later
he sold it to Benjamin J. Bordon, who changed it from a Democratic to a Whig paper. Chagrined at this change in policy of
The Arkansas Gazette, Woodruff started, with the help of John
E. Knight, in 1846, *The Arkansas Democrat*. Four years later
the two papers were combined under the title, *The Gazette and
Democrat*. The paper was eventually sold to Captain Columbus

Danley, who dropped the *Democrat* from the title when *The True Democrat* appeared. Save for its suspension in 1863–65, *The Arkansas Gazette* has continued publication until to-day.

The second paper in the State was *The Advocate* brought out at Little Rock in March, 1830, by Charles P. Bertrand, a native of New York City and a frontier lawyer of unusual ability. It was owned and edited by him until 1835 when it passed into the control of Albert Pike and Charles E. Rice. The same year that *The Advocate* was established, *The Democrat* was founded at Helena by Henry L. Biscoe: its editor, however, was William T. Yeomans. After the rupture between Governor Pope and *The Arkansas Gazette* Andrew J. Hunt, in December, 1833, started at Little Rock *The Political Intelligencer;* edited by Colonel John W. Steele, it became the official spokesman for Governor Pope until the end of his term. Later, becoming a Whig organ, it changed its name to *The Times.* On Hunt's death *The Times* and *The Advocate* joined forces under the leadership of Albert Pike. Charles T. Towne in 1839 called for a short time *The Witness* to the stand in behalf of the Democratic Party. C. F. M. Noland let loose *The Eagle* at Batesville in 1840 to cry for the Whigs. David Lambert let *The Star* first shine in Little Rock the same year.

TEXAS SIFTINGS

When Commodore Aury, Colonel Mina, and Captain Perry were stationed at Galveston Island in 1816 the military orders and others news were printed on a small sheet by Samuel Bangs, a peripatetic printer coming from Baltimore. While this sheet could hardly be called the first newspaper, it was a sort of precursor to journalism in Texas. Another precursor appeared in 1819 when the Long Expedition reached Nacogdoches and made that point its headquarters. During its stay Horatio Bigelow published a small sheet more or less regularly; it gave the history of the Expedition, however, rather than general news.

The first real paper of the Lone Star State was *The Texas Gazette,* which made its appearance September 29, 1829, and was published by Godwin Brown Cotten in San Felipe, Austin County. *The Texas Gazette* survived until 1832 when it was purchased by

D. W. Anthony and united with *The Texas Gazette and Brazoria Commercial Advertiser*, a paper started in 1830 by Mr. Anthony at Brazoria. The union was called *The Constitutional Advocate and The Texas Public Advertiser* and its first issue appeared on August 30, 1832. One year later Anthony died of the cholera in Brazoria. In July, 1834, F. C. Gray and A. J. Harris began in Brazoria the publication of *The Texas Republican,* a paper which continued until the invasion of Santa Anna in 1836. Of *The Advocate of the Peoples' Rights,* another paper started in Brazoria in 1834 by Oliver H. Allen, little is known, and not much more about *The Texian Advocate and Immigrants' Guide,* which appeared spasmodically during 1835–36 in Nacogdoches.

Mention is made on page 216 of the journalism in Texas after the revolt from Mexico. Any sketch of Texas journalism certainly should notice the establishment of *The Daily News* in Galveston by George H. French on April 11, 1842. His price for single copies was 6¼c. It later appeared under the imprint of various publishers, but after the War of the States was purchased by Willard Richardson. How Col. A. H. Belo joined him may be found on page 339. In May, 1846, John D. Logan and Thomas Sterne established *The Texian Advocate* in Victoria. They brought their equipment from Van Buren, Arkansas, on flatboats to New Orleans and thence by Mexican carts to Victoria. Being strangers in the country, they were assisted in an editorial way by John Henry Brown. Mr. Logan later published *The Herald* in San Antonio, where he died about 1875. The first paper in San Antonio, however, was *The Western Texian,* established in 1848 — soon followed by *The Ledger.* In 1849, James W. Latimer founded *The Dallas Herald,* which in 1885 was merged with another newspaper. *The Dallas News* was established in 1885. Soon after the Mexican War, *Bandera Americano* or *American Flag* was established at Brownsville by Edwin B. Scarborough and was conducted by him until his death in 1860. On February 19, 1880, Gail Johnson, a grandson of Gail Borden who had started *The Telegraph* at Houston in 1836, founded *The Houston Post. The Statesman* at Austin, established in 1871, now boasts that it is the second oldest paper in Texas.

CHAPTER XII

BEGINNINGS OF THE PENNY PRESS

THE precursor of the penny press was undoubtedly *The Daily Evening Transcript*, which was established in Boston on Saturday, July 24, 1830, by Lynde M. Walter, a graduate of Harvard. It was published the first two days of the next week, but was then suspended until August 27, 1830, since when it has appeared without a single break in its publication. While not sold on the streets at a penny a copy, it quoted the extremely low rate of four dollars per annum payable semi-annually in advance. In the preface it said that it was started to supply the " deficiency created by the surcease of *The Bulletin*," and asserted that it would not "mingle in the everyday warfare of politics nor attempt to control public bias, in abstract questions of Religion or Morality." Its political creed it outlined as follows: —

We believe that Duties imposed upon Imports, for the protection of domestic industry, are necessary and constitutional; that Congress has power to appropriate the public funds to works of internal improvement; — that the Bank of the United States is expedient to the preservation of a wholesome currency, and is warranted by the Constitution; — that the union of these States was decreed by the whole people, — will be maintained by the whole people, — and cannot be dissolved but by the will of a majority of the whole people voting each for himself, either personally or by special delegation.

It had two departments which attracted attention: one was headed, "Police Court"; the other, "Marine Journal." In connection with the latter the paper published a notice of indebtedness for "Facilities afforded by Mr. Topliff of Merchant's Hall for the memoranda inserted in our Marine Journal."

Walter, the first editor, occupied the chair until his death in 1842, when his sister, Cornelia Walter, assumed the editorship. During the first few years of Mr. Walter's régime, the most important matter of moment was the anti-slavery movement

While *The Transcript* could not be called an anti-slavery paper, it did give free access to its editorial columns to William Lloyd Garrison, then a young man, who wrote a great deal over the signature of W. L. G. In 1847 Epes Sargent, a well-known poet and author, became the editor and continued until 1853, when Daniel M. Haskell sat in the editorial chair until 1874. During the twenty-odd years that Mr. Haskell was editor, he was assisted by such men of literary excellence as E. P. Whipple, Charles Sumner, Wendell Phillips, etc. Since Mr. Haskell's death in 1874, various men have been editors of *The Transcript*, and each of these has kept the paper up to the high aims of independent journalism which was the keynote of its beginning.

FIRST DAILIES SOLD FOR CENT

Possibly the first daily paper which sold for a penny was *The Cent*, which started in Philadelphia the same year that *The Daily Evening Transcript* was established in Boston. *The Cent* has long been a lost newspaper coin of which little is known save that its circulation was small and its life was short. Its publisher, however, was Dr. Christopher Columbus Conwell, who died in 1832.

By mere coincidence the man who first conceived the idea of publishing a penny paper in New York was also a physician, Dr. Horatio David Shepard. As he walked through the Bowery and noticed how readily candy, peanuts, and other trinkets, which sold for a cent, were passed over the counter, the thought occurred to him that a newspaper sold at the same price would be successful. Enthused with the idea he went to several printers and tried to get them interested in his proposition to start a penny newspaper. At first he was unsuccessful, but finally persuaded Horace Greeley to join him in bringing out such a paper. Greeley, however, insisted that the price was too sudden a reduction from the six pennies ordinarily charged for a newspaper and insisted on doubling the proposed price. With a capital of only two hundred dollars and with a credit which was scarcely good for forty dollars' worth of type, *The Morning Post* started on January 1, 1833, as a two-cent paper with Dr. Shepard, Horace Greeley, and Francis W. Story as its printers and publishers. The date selected for bringing out the sheet was most inopportune; a snowstorm prevented the distribution of the papers. After one week's trial, in a vain effort to dispose of a daily edition of two or three hundred copies, the price was reduced to one cent. The change was made too late, however, for financial resources had been exhausted and no printer was willing to assume the burden of continuing publication. After three weeks *The Morning Post* was a tombstone in the journalism graveyard, already overcrowded in New York.

FOUNDER OF PENNY PRESS IN NEW YORK

But in September of that year, Benjamin Henry Day, a practical printer, who had learned his trade on *The Springfield Republican* and had taken a post-graduate course in the composing-room of *The New York Evening Post*, did establish in New York a penny sheet to which he gave the very appropriate name of *The Sun* — said to have been suggested by a compositor, David Ramsey. According to Day's statement he had first planned a penny paper in 1832, when, on account of the presence of cholera in New York, he had scarcely enough business for his print-shop to pay his running expenses. In the spare time thus afforded he roughly mapped out the plans for a daily paper to keep his presses busy. In an address in 1851 Mr. Day thus told of his early venture: —

In August, 1833, I finally made up my mind to venture the experiment, and I issued the first number of *The Sun* September 3. It is not necessary to speak of the wonderful success of the paper. At the end of three years the difficulty of striking off the large edition on a double-cylinder press in the time usually allowed to daily newspapers was very great. In 1835 I introduced steam-power, now so necessary an appendage to almost every newspaper office. At that time, all the Napier presses in the city were turned by crank-men, and as *The Sun* was the only daily newspaper of large circulation, so it seemed to be the only establishment where steam was really indispensable. But even this great aid to the speed of the Napier machines did not keep up with the increasing circulation of *The Sun*. Constant and vexatious complaints of the late delivery could not be avoided up to the time that I left the establishment and until the invention of the press which permitted the locking of the type upon the cylinder.

It was Day's plan to make a paper not for the classes which were already well served by the six-penny sheets, but for the masses who had no newspaper. Starting with a circulation of three hundred, *The Sun* rapidly prospered until very shortly it was pressing hard the old conservative sheets. True to his original plans Day turned out a paper which gave in a condensed form the mechanics and the servant-girls the tittle-tattle and the gossip of the town. To make both ends meet he had to keep down the size of his paper, which was four pages with three columns of ten inches to the page, but it is wonderful how much news he was able to boil down and print in his limited sheet. At the start *The Sun* was not edited with any great ability until Day secured George W. Wisner, who was one of the first American journalists to realize the value of the police court as a source of news. Already Wisner had been a police court reporter for the paper, for which service he received the magnificent wage of four dollars per week. To him the "assault and battery" cases of the police court were more interesting than the attacks of Jackson on the United States Bank.

In 1837 Day sold the paper to his sister's husband, Moses Y. Beach, for forty thousand dollars. *The Sun* remained in the Beach family, save for a temporary eclipse when it was published as a daily religious newspaper, until it was sold to Charles Anderson Dana and his associates, who assumed control on January 25, 1868. After Day retired from *The Sun* he became the publisher of *The True Sun*, which shed its light, such as it was, first on November 25, 1842. It shone for only a brief period of two years and then set. This second paper by Day should not be confused with *The True Sun* started on January 22, 1835, by W. F. Short and S. B. Butler, which suffered a total eclipse after four days.

EARLY LOCAL RIVALS

The success of *The Sun* led to the establishment of penny papers not only in New York, but also in all the other more important cities of the country such as Philadelphia, Boston, Baltimore, Albany, etc. The immediate rival of *The Sun* in New York was *The Transcript* started on March 14, 1834, by three composi-

THE  SUN.

NUMBER 1.]   NEW YORK, TUESDAY, SEPTEMBER 3, 1833.   [PRICE ONE PENNY.

PUBLISHED DAILY,

AT 222 WILLIAM ST............BENJ. H. DAY, PRINTER.

The object of this paper is to lay before the public, at a price within the means of every one, ALL THE NEWS OF THE DAY, and at the same time afford an advantageous medium for advertising. The sheet will be enlarged as soon as the increase of advertisements requires it—the price remaining the same.

Yearly advertisers, (without the paper,) Thirty Dollars per annum—Casual advertising, at the usual prices charged by the city papers.

☞ Subscriptions will be received, if paid in advance, at the rate of three dollars per annum.

FOR ALBANY—PASSAGE ONLY $1.

The large and commodious steamboat COMMERCE, Capt. R. H. Fitch, will leave the foot of Courtlandt street on Friday, at five o'clock, P. M. for Albany, stopping at the usual landing places to land and receive passengers. Passage $1. For particulars apply to the Captain on board.
REGULAR DAYS.
From New York, Mondays, Wednesdays, Fridays.
From Albany, Tuesdays, Thursdays, Saturdays.   a29

FOR NEWPORT AND PROVIDENCE.

The splendid steamboat BENJAMIN FRANKLIN, Capt. E. S. Bunker, and the PRESIDENT, Capt. R. S. Bunker, will leave New York at 5 o'clock, P. M. and Providence at 11 o'clock. M. every Monday, Wednesday and Friday. For further information apply to the Captain on board, foot of Courtlandt-st. or at the office, 14 Broad st.   a2

FOR HARTFORD—PASSAGE 1 DOLLAR.

THROUGH BY DAYLIGHT.
The splendid low-pressure steamboat WATER WITCH, Capt. Vanderbilt, leaves the foot of Catherine street every Tuesday, Thursday, and Saturday mornings, at 6 o'clock, and arrives in Hartford at 7 o'clock the same evening. Passage One Dollar—meals extra.
The above boat leaves Hartford on Mondays, Wednesdays, and Fridays, at the same hours.   s2 tf

FOR LONDON—To sail 10th of Sept.—The new packet ship Montreal, Champlin, Master, will sail on the 10th inst. For freight or passage, having elegant accommodations, apply to the Captain, on board, Pine-st. wharf, or to
JOHN GRISWOLD, Agent. 68 South st.   a2

FOR LIVERPOOL.—The fast-sailing ship Tallahasse, S. Glover, Master, will be ready to receive cargo in a few days, and have despatch. She has excellent accommodations for both cabin and steerage passengers. For freight or passage, apply to
WOOD & TRIMBLE, 157 Maiden-lane.   a2

FOR HAVRE.—The Packet ship Formosa, Orne, master, will sail on the 8th Sept. For freight or passage apply to the captain on board, or to
WM. WHITLOCK, Jr. 46 South st.   a2

FOR LIVERPOOL—Packet of the 8 Sept.—The packet ship Roscoe, J. C. Delano, master, is now in readiness to receive cargo. For freight or passage apply to the captain on board, foot of Maiden lane, or to
FISH, GRINNELL & CO. 134 Front st.   s2 t10

FOR KINGSTON, JAM.—Packet 10th Sept. The elegant coppered ship Orbit will sail as above. For freight or passage, having splendid accommodations, with state rooms, apply to
B. AYMAR & Co. 34 South st.   a2

FOR NEW ORLEANS.—Packet of the 8th September, the very fast-sailing coppered ship, Nashville, Capt. Rathbone, will sail as above. For freight or passage, having handsome accommodations, apply to   F. K. COLLINS, 68 South st.
N. B. A lighter is in readiness to receive cargo at Pine street wharf.   a2

FOR NEW ORLEANS.—Packet of Sept. 15, the ship Tennessee, Capt. Sears, will sail as above. For freight or passage, having handsome accommodations, apply to
SILAS HOLMES & CO. 62 South st.   a2
N B A lighter is in readiness to receive cargo.

AN IRISH CAPTAIN.

"These are as sweet a pair of pistols as any in the three kingdoms;" said an officer, showing a pair to a young student of his acquaintance, "and have done execution before now; at the slightest touch, off they go, as sweet as honey, without either recoiling or dipping. I never travel without them."

"I never heard of highwaymen in this part of the country."

"Nor I." replied the officer, "and if I had I should not trouble myself to carry the pistols on their account—Highwaymen are a species of sharks who are not fond of attacking us lobsters; they know we are a little too hard to crack. No, my dear sir, highwaymen know that soldiers have not much money, and what they have they fight for."

"Since that is the case, how come you to travel always with pistols?"

"Because," answered the officer, "I find them very useful in accommodating any little difference I may accidentally have with a friend, or which one friend may chance to have with another."

"Why, I was twice set before I arrived at your age.—The first time was with a relation of my own, who said he would see my courage tried before he would contribute with the others towards the purchase of my first commission; so I sent him word that I would be happy to give him one proof the very next morning, and when we met, I touched him so smartly in the leg, that he has halted ever since. But all his doubts being now removed, he cheerfully contributed his quota with the rest of my relations, and we have been very good friends ever since."

"Pray what gave you occasion for the second?" said the young student.

"How it began originally is more than I can tell," answered the captain; all I know is, that a large company of us dined together; we sat long, and drank deep, and I went to bed rather in a state of forgetfulness, and was awaked in the morning from a profound sleep, by a gentleman who began a long story, how I had said something that required explanation; and also, that I had accidentally given him a blow, but he supposed I had no intention to affront him, and so he continued talking in a roundabout kind of way, without coming to any point. So I was under the necessity of interrupting him, "upon my conscience, Sir, (said I,) I am unable to declare, with certainty, whether I had any intention of affronting you or not, because my head is still a little confused, and I have no clear recollection of what passed, nor do I fully comprehend your drift at present, but I conjecture that you wish to have satisfaction; if so, I must beg you will be kind enough to say so at once, and I shall be at your service." Finding himself thus cut short, he named the place and the hour. I met him precisely at the time. His first pistol missed fire, but I hit him in the shoulder. At his second shot, the bullet passed pretty near me, but mine lodged in his hip, and then he declared he was quite satisfied. So as I had given a blow the preceding night, and two wounds that morning, upon declaring himself satisfied, I said I was contented."

"You would have been thought very hard to please, if you had made any difficulty."

"I thought so myself," rejoined the captain, "and so the affair ended; he being carried home in a coach, and I marching from the field of battle on foot."

"Pray, may I ask if you ever was in a battle?"

"No," replied the captain with a sigh, "I never was; I never had that good fortune, though I would give all the money I have in the world, and all the money I am owing, which is at least treble the sum, to be in one to-morrow."

"Provided you had a good cause;" replied the student.

"I should not be squeamish respecting the cause, provided I had a good battle: that, my dear, is what is the more essential to a conscientious officer, who wishes to improve himself in his profession. I have much reason, therefore, to hope for a war; and at the present juncture, it would be much to the advantage of the nation in general, as it is dwindling into a country of ploughmen, manufacturers, and merchants. And you must know, too, that I am pretty fortunate, having already stood thirteen shots, and I never was hit but once."

"Thirteen: what, have you fought thirteen duels?"

"No, no!" replied the captain, "the last shot fired at me completed only my sixth duel."

Wonders of Littleness.—Pliny and Ælian relate that Myrmecides wrought out of ivory a chariot, with four wheels and four horses, and a ship with all her tackling, both in as small a compass, that a bee could hide either with its wings. Nor should we doubt this, when we find it recorded in English history, on less questionable authority, that in the twentieth year of Queen Elizabeth, a blacksmith of London, of the name of Mark Scaliot, made a lock of iron, steel, and brass, of eleven pieces, and a pipe key, all of which only weighed one grain. Scaliot also made a chain of gold, of forty-three links, which he fastened to the lock and key, and put it round the neck of a flea, which drew the whole with perfect ease. The chain, key, lock, and flea, altogether weighed but one grain and a half!

Hadrianus Junis saw at Mechlin in Brabant, a cherrystone cut into the form of a basket; in it were fourteen pair of dice distinct, the spots and numbers of which were easily to be discerned with a good eye.

But still more extraordinary than this basket of dice, or any thing we have yet mentioned, must have been a set of turnery shown at Rome, in the time of Pope Paul the Fifth, by one Shad of Mittelbrach, who had purchased it from the artist Oswaldus Norbitogerus. It consisted of sixteen hundred dishes, which were all perfect and complete in every part, yet so small and slender that the whole could be easily enclosed in a case fabricated in a peppercorn of the ordinary size. The Pope is said to have himself counted them, but with the help of a pair of spectacles, for they were so very small as to be almost invisible to the naked eye. Although his holiness thus satisfied his own eyes of the fact, he did not, we are assured, require of those about him to subscribe to it on the credit of his infallibility; for he gave every one an opportunity of examining and judging for himself, and among the persons thus highly favored, particular reference is made to Gaspar Schioppius Johannes Faber, a physician of Rome.

Turrianus, of whose skill so many wonderful things are related, is said to have fabricated iron mills, which moved of themselves, so minute in size, that a monk could carry one in his sleeve; and yet it was powerful enough to grind in a single day, grain enough for the consumption of eight men.

A Whistler.—A boy in Vermont, accustomed to working alone, was so prone to whistling, that, as soon as he was by himself, he unconsciously commenced. When asleep, the muscles of his mouth, chest, and lungs were as completely concentrated in the association, he whistled with astonishing shrillness. A pale countenance, loss of appetite, and almost total prostration of strength, convinced his mother it would end in death. If not speedily overcome, which was accomplished by placing him in the society of another boy, who had orders to give him a blow as soon as he began to whistle.

THE FIRST ISSUE OF *THE NEW YORK SUN*
(Reduced)

tors Hayward, Lynde, and Stanley. For a while in 1834 it looked
as though the new paper was going to eclipse *The Sun*, as it
achieved the larger circulation. Day and Wisner of *The Sun*
were once indicted for criminal libel for an attack on Attree,
the editor of *The Transcript*, so bitter did the fight become between these two papers. *The Transcript* then began to pay more
attention to political matters than *The Sun:* on December 4,
1834, it devoted its entire paper to the presidential message of
Andrew Jackson and did not print a single advertisement. Getting into the field of its six-penny contemporaries, *The Transcript*
soon lost its lead over *The Sun*, and when internal trouble arose
among its printers and owners it became on July 24, 1839, only
an epitaph in the newspaper graveyard.

Before *The Transcript*, however, another penny paper, *The
Man*, had been born in New York on February 18, 1834. It was
published in the interest of trade unions and endeavored to raise
the compensation for federated labor. Nothing it printed attracted half so much attention as the way in which the letters in
its name were drawn. This unique head when it first appeared
was thus described by *The Transcript*, on May 27, 1834: —

The Man, a penny paper published in this city, which advocates the
cause of the working man, has provided itself with a new head, quite
characteristic of its particular objects. This head is composed entirely
of farming utensils and mechanic instruments. There is a ploughshare,
a scythe, a rake, an axe, a hatchet, a saw, a hammer, an augur, a square,
a drawing-knife, a plane, a goose, a pair of shears, etc., etc. all arranged
and joined together so as to make THE MAN.

The Man died an early death.

One or two early penny papers in New York may be briefly
mentioned. Shortly after *The Sun* had risen in New York, *The
Daily Bee* came from the hive (located in Masonic Hall) of
John L. Kingsley on March 5, 1834. Devoted to "literature,
drama, police and court proceedings, news, etc.," it had a short
life, in its first appearance in 1834, and a not much longer in its
second in 1836. Kingsley later, however, rendered a more efficient service to American journalism by improving the method
for stereotyping page forms of newspapers. Women were not
neglected by the penny press. An attempt to reach them was

made on April 29, 1836, when *The Ladies' Morning Star*, price one cent, appeared above the newspaper horizon. A brief mention of all the newspapers which started in New York from 1830 to 1870 would fill a page of this volume and would make about as interesting reading as the catalogue of ships in Homer's "Iliad."

POPULARITY OF TRANSCRIPTS

For some reason *The Transcript* was an unusually popular name for these early penny papers, just as *The Gazette* had been for the early weeklies of the Colonial Period and *The Advertiser* had been for the first dailies of the Early Republic. Mention has already been made of *The Transcript* of Boston and New York; reference to *The Transcript* of Philadelphia will be made a little later. The first penny paper in Albany was *The Transcript*, started on October 12, 1835. Baltimore saw *The Daily Transcript*, a penny paper established on May 10, 1836. On May 17, 1837, *The Sun* was started at Baltimore under the editorship of Arunah S. Abell. Abell was present when *The Sun* first rose in New York and had helped make the first entry of *The Public Ledger* in Philadelphia. Within a year Abell's penny paper had a circulation of "more than twice as many copies as the oldest established journal" in that city. In 1842 *The Daily Whig* and *The National Forum* were established in Baltimore as penny papers to support Henry Clay in his presidential aspirations.

PENNY PRESS IN BOSTON

The success of *The Sun* in New York and that of its satellite, *The Orb*, in Philadelphia led to the establishment of *The 12 o'clock News* in Boston on March 13, 1834. Strictly speaking, the first newspaper to be sold in Boston for one cent was *The Daily Penny Post* which was first set up at 28 Franklin Street on Monday, August 26, 1833, with a motto of *Multum in Parvo*. *The News*, published by B. Hammatt Norton, was issued daily at twelve o'clock and after the second number appeared on March 17 the paper was printed regularly. At the start *The News* was similar to *The Sun* of New York, not only in its subject-matter, but also in its mode of treatment. As time went on, however, it paid less attention to the news and more to literary articles which it quoted from exchanges. Because of this fact it fell behind *The Sun* as a gatherer of news and became more of a literary publication for the elect of Boston.

A number of German printers who had been connected with *The Boston Daily Times* started in December, 1844, a morning newspaper of their own called *The American Eagle*. It was a penny sheet devoted, as its name implies, to the interest of the Native American Party. Successful at first, it was quietly expiring a slow death when its promoters decided to start a new evening daily which would be neutral in politics and to let the morning paper die unless it showed more signs of life. The new afternoon venture in Boston journalism was called *The Evening Herald* and first appeared with an edition of two thousand on August 13, 1846. For four months the editorial and reportorial staff consisted of only two men. Its first page was filled with literary matter and much of the other three consisted of material "lifted" from the columns of *The Morning Eagle*. *The Herald*, feeble as it was, managed to survive financial diseases concomitant with newspaper infancy, and at the beginning of 1847 it appeared with a new dress as *The Morning Herald* and *The Evening Herald*. An editorial spoke as follows about the penny press in Boston: "The competition of the penny press has caused a mental activity among all classes; rash and impulsive it may be, but, nevertheless, far preferable to the dignified stagnation which, in times of yore, was seldom broken by the larger and more expensive journals." A little later *The Boston Herald*, in an editorial on the "dignity of the penny press," said, among other things: "The time has come when the respectable portion of the community no longer looks to the big sixpenny, lying oracles of politics for just notions on government, exalted piety, or pure and chaste morality. The low price of the penny papers endows their publishers with a philanthropical spirit of disinterestedness, and a regard to the purity of public morals not dependent on pecuniary considerations. A cent is but a nominal price for a newspaper, and, therefore, the publishers and editor of a penny print are moved only by an earnest and

prayerful wish for the spiritual and temporal good of their readers. Much diurnal good may now be had at the very low price
of one cent. It would be folly to deny that a pure and refined
taste has been engendered by the cheap literature of the day."
This paper should not be confused with another member of the
penny family of Boston which had practically the same name,
The Boston Morning Herald, but which had been started earlier
and was edited by William B. English.

PENNY PRESS IN PHILADELPHIA

When Day started *The Sun* in New York in 1833, he had in his
employ three printers, A. S. Abell, A. H. Simons, and William
Swain. The last printer later became the foreman of its composing-room at twelve dollars a week. Worn out by having to
work overtime Swain was compelled to take a vacation; upon
his return he was not able to make satisfactory settlement for
the time he was absent, and withdrew from *The Sun*, taking Abell
and Simons with him. The trio, convinced of the wonderful possibilities of the penny press, but satisfied that New York was
already well served, went to Philadelphia where they brought
out, on March 25, 1836, the first number of *The Public Ledger*.
Being practical printers, they were unable to look after the editorial end of the paper and secured for this work Russell Jarvis,
whose work on *The United States Telegraph* had already attracted attention. The new paper adopted as its editorial policy:
"While *The Public Ledger* shall worship no man, it shall vituperate none. *The Public Ledger* will be fearless and independent,
applauding virtue and reproving vice wherever found, un-
awed by station, uninfluenced by wealth." *The Ledger* was not
quite so successful as *The Sun* in New York and at the start
was published under great handicaps, financially and otherwise.
But when it started to attack the United States Bank in the
days of the "Banking War," it became very popular and grew
in "stature and wisdom." *The Ledger* continued to be a penny
paper until 1864 when it was sold to George W. Childs who advanced the price to two cents on account of the greatly increased
cost of white paper.

A few days before *The Ledger* was started, *The Daily Tran-*

script, edited by Frederick West and published by William L. Drane, had made its appearance in Philadelphia. *The Transcript* soon united with *The Ledger*, in September, 1836, and the union was called *The Public Ledger and Daily Transcript*. *The Veto*, a distinctly campaign publication, had been started on April 17, 1834, at one cent a copy: it had for its motto, "Old Hickory, Home Spun, and Hard Money." *The Orb*, another penny paper founded about the same time, soon disappeared. *The Daily Focus*, a rival of *The Public Ledger* in the penny field, attacked Jarvis, the editor of the latter paper, so relentlessly and so bitterly that he finally brought suit against the owners of *The Focus*, Turner, Davis, and Balicau. The case was never reached on the docket and *The Focus* was hidden among the many other penny papers which attempted to dispute the supremacy of *The Public Ledger* for a time and then disappeared.

BENNETT AND HIS "HERALD"

In New York *The Sun* and *The Transcript* were being printed in 1835 on Ann Street in the plant of Anderson & Smith. Into their shop came James Gordon Bennett from Philadelphia where he had been connected with *The Pennsylvanian*. The final result of this conference was that the firm agreed to add another paper to their presses. Called *The New York Herald*, it was published by James Gordon Bennett & Company in the cellar of Number 20 Wall Street. On May 6, 1835, the first number appeared with Bennett as editor, publisher, advertising director, circulation manager.

The assertion has often been made that Bennett started *The Herald* with five hundred dollars, two wooden chairs, and an old dry-goods box. But he had something more: his chief asset was his newspaper experience — often bought dearly. He had been editor of a Sunday paper, *The New York Courier*, writer on political topics in *The National Advocate*, Washington correspondent for *The New York Enquirer*, associate editor of *The Courier and Enquirer*, and owner of *The New York Globe*, a two-cent campaign organ which he started on October 29, 1832, to support Jackson and Van Buren.

From the start *The Herald* had its own troubles. It sold for one cent a copy and consequently its circulation brought in only a very limited revenue. *The Sun* and *The Transcript* objected to being printed at the same plant as *The Herald* and soon withdrew from Anderson & Smith. A big fire on Ann Street August 12, destroyed the printing-plant and caused *The Herald* to suspend until August 31. But *The Herald* continued to grow and had to seek larger quarters. On April 6, 1836, it moved again, this time from Broadway to Clinton Hall Building. Four months later the price per copy was increased to two cents.

At the end of the year 1836 the following résumé was published: —

The surprising success of *The Herald* has astonished myself. I began on five hundred dollars, was twice burnt out, once had my office robbed, have been opposed and calumniated by the whole newspaper Press, ridiculed, contemned, threatened, yet here I am, at the end of fifteen months, with an establishment, the materials of which are nearly worth five thousand dollars, nearly all paid for, and a prospect of making *The Herald* yield in two years a revenue of at least thirty thousand dollars a year; yet I care not, I disregard, I value not money. I rise early, and work late, for character, reputation, the good of mankind, the civilization of my species. It is my passion, my delight, my thought by day, and my dream by night to conduct *The Herald*, and to show the world and posterity, that a newspaper can be made the greatest, most fascinating, most powerful organ of civilization that genius ever yet dreamed of. The dull, ignorant, miserable barbarian papers around me, are incapable of arousing the moral sensibilities, or pointing out fresh paths for the intellectual career of an energetic generation.

For the sake of comparison and for the purpose of showing the aim of the paper the following quotation is made from Volume I, Number 1: —

James Gordon Bennett & Co. commence this morning the publication of *The Morning Herald*, a new daily paper, price $3 a year, or six cents per week, advertising at the ordinary rates. It is issued from the publishing office, No. 20 Wall Street, and also from the printing-office, No. 34 Ann Street, 3d story, at both of which places orders will be thankfully received.

The next number will be issued on Monday morning — this brief suspension necessarily taking place in order to give the publishers time and opportunity to arrange the routes of carriers, organize a general system of distribution for the city, and allow subscribers and patrons to furnish correctly their names and residences. It will then be resumed and regularly continued.

In the commencement of an enterprise of the present kind it is not necessary to say much. "We know," says the fair Ophelia, "what we are, but know not what we may be." Pledges and promises, in these enlightened times, are not exactly so current in the world as Safety-Fund Notes, or even the U.S. Bank bills. We have had an experience of nearly fifteen years in conducting newspapers. On that score we can not surely fail in knowing at least how to build up a reputation and establishment of our own. In debuts of this kind many talk of principle — political principle — party principle, as a sort of steel-trap to catch the public. We mean to be perfectly understood on this point, and therefore openly disclaim all steel-traps, all principle, as it is called — all party — all politics. Our only guide shall be good, sound, practical common sense, applicable to the business and bosoms of men engaged in every-day life. We shall support no party — be the organ of no faction or coterie, and care nothing for any election or any candidate from president down to a constable. We shall endeavor to record facts on every public and proper subject, stripped of verbiage and coloring, with comments when suitable, just, independent, fearless, and good-tempered. If *The Herald* wants the mere expansion which many journals possess, we shall try to make it up in industry, good taste, brevity, variety, point, piquancy, and cheapness. It is equally intended for the great masses of the community — the merchant, mechanic, working people — the private family as well as the public hotel — the journeyman and his employer — the clerk and his principal. There are in this city at least 150,000 persons who glance over one or more newspapers every day. Only 42,000 daily sheets are issued to supply them. We have plenty of room, therefore, without jostling neighbors, rivals, or friends, to pick up at least twenty or thirty thousand for *The Herald*, and leave something for others who come after us. By furnishing a daily morning paper at the low price of $3 a year, which may be taken for any shorter period (for a week) at the same rate, and making it at the same time equal to any of the high-priced papers for intelligence, good taste, sagacity, and industry, there is not a person in the city, male or female, that may not be able to say, "Well, I have got a paper of my own which will tell me all about what's doing in the world. I'm busy now, but I'll put it in my pocket, and read it at my leisure."

With these few words as "grace before meat," we commit ourselves and our cause to the public, with perfect confidence in our own capacity to publish a paper that will seldom pall on the appetite, provided we receive moderate encouragement to unfold our resources and purposes in the columns of *The Morning Herald*.

The contents of the first issue of *The Herald* were in striking contrast not only to the previous work Bennett had done for newspapers, but also to the contributions he was soon to make to American journalism. Before he started *The Herald* he had contributed to the leading literary papers of the day; he had written heavy political editorials on men and matters of moment; he had lectured on political economy in the old chapel of the Dutch Reformed Church on the corner of Ann and Nassau Streets. Yet he made *The Herald* — to quote the language used at that time — "light and spicy."

NEW YORK PAPERS OF BENNETT'S TIME

His reasons for making *The Herald* what he did may possibly be found in the competition he had to meet at that time in New York. To sell his papers he had to bring out a publication that was different from those of his rivals already in the field. In 1835 New York had the following daily papers: *The New York American, The Mercantile Advertiser and New York Advocate, The New York Daily Advertiser, The Morning Courier and Enquirer, The New York Journal of Commerce, The New York Commercial Advertiser, The Business Reporter and Merchants' and Mechanics' Advertiser, The New York Times, The Evening Post, The Evening Star, The New York Sun, The Man, The Jeffersonian, The New York Gazette and General Advertiser*, and *The New York Transcript*. In addition to these fifteen daily papers there were eleven semi-weeklies and thirty-one weeklies in the city. New York, like Athens of old, has always been ready to hear the new thing — especially in newspapers.

FREE FIELD FOR BENNETT

No "sacred cows" browsed in Bennett's fields. He even attacked the church regardless of denomination. He wrote the first newspaper accounts of the annual meetings of the various religious organizations — much to the annoyance of both pulpit and pew. He reported the proceedings of the police court with a freedom which even enlarged the time-honored freedom of the press. In relating scandal with full particulars that filled columns of his paper, he seemed to think the more he shocked people the more they would read his paper. If he was assaulted either on the street or in his office, he gave a full report the next morning under the standing head, "Bennett Thrashed Again." The announcement of his engagement which he published in *The Herald* is one of the most interesting specimens of newspaper literature. In a certain sense, he often put his own private journals in his paper as may be found in the following editorial printed in 1836: —

We published yesterday the principal items of the foreign news, received by the Sheffield, being eight days later than our previous arrivals. Neither *The Sun* nor *The Transcript* had a single item on the subject. *The Sun* did not even know of its existence. The large papers in Wall street had also the news, but as the editors are lazy, ignorant, indolent, blustering blockheads, one and all, they did not pick out the cream and serve it out as we did. *The Herald* alone knows how to dish up the foreign news, or indeed domestic events, in a readable style. Every reader, numbering *between thirty and forty thousand daily*, acknowledges this merit in the management of our paper. We do not, as the Wall street lazy editors do, come down to our office about ten or twelve o'clock, pull out a Spanish cigar, take up a pair of scissors, puff and cut, cut and puff for a couple of hours, and then adjourn to Delmonico's to eat, drink, gormandize, and blow up our contemporaries. We rise in the morning at five o'clock, write our leading editorials, squibs, sketches, etc., before breakfast. From nine till one we read all our papers and original communications, the latter being more numerous than those of any other office in New York. From these we pick out facts, thoughts, hints and incidents, sufficient to make up a column of original spicy articles. We also give audiences to visitors, gentlemen on business, and some of the loveliest ladies in New York, who call to subscribe — Heaven bless them! At one we sally out among the gentlemen and *loafers* of Wall street — find out the state of the money market, return, finish the next day's paper — close every piece of business requiring thought, sentiment, feeling, or philosophy, before four o'clock. We then dine moderately and temperately — read our proofs — take in cash and advertisements, which are increasing like smoke — and close the day by going to bed always at ten o'clock, seldom later. That's the way to conduct a paper with spirit and success.

VITUPERATION OF TIME

But in order to understand Bennett and his newspaper, it is necessary to be familiar with the journalism of the time. Editors were just beginning to find out that the pen was mightier than the sword, the pistol, or the walking-stick. They filled their columns with malicious squibs and furious diatribes against each other. The vituperation of the press knew no bounds. By way of illustration the following epithets used by Park Benjamin in *The Signal*, by James Watson Webb in *The Courier and Enquirer*, and by M. M. Noah in *The Evening Star* may be given: "Obscene vagabond," "Loathsome and leprous slanderer and libeler," "Unprincipled conductor," "Rascal," "Rogue," "Cheat," "Veteran blackguard," "Habitual Liar," "Polluted wretch," "Foreign vagabond," "Foreign imposter," "Monster," "Daring infidel," "Pestilential scoundrel," "Venomous reptile," *ad infinitum*.

In answer to the charge that he was once a pedler in the streets of Glasgow, Bennett once replied in his paper as follows: —

I am, and have been, a pedler — and part of my name is Gordon. This I admit. From my youth up I have been a pedler, not of tapes and laces, but of thoughts, feelings, lofty principles, and intellectual truths. I am now a wholesale dealer in the same line of business, and people generally believe I have quite a run, and what is better, no dread of suspension. I was educated and intended for a religious sect, but the Almighty, in his wisdom, meant me for truth and mankind, and I will fulfil my destiny in spite of all the opposition made to me either in the old or new hemisphere. Yes, I have been a pedler, and am still a pedler of the thoughts, and feelings, and high imaginings of the past and present ages. I peddle my wares as Homer did his — as Shakespeare did his — as every great intellectual and mighty pedler of the past did — and when I shall have finished my peddling in this world, I trust I shall be permitted to peddle in a better and happier region for ever and ever.

Much has been made of two articles which appeared in *The British Foreign Quarterly Review* and which attacked most bitterly the newspapers of the United States in general and *The New York Herald* in particular. *The Westminster Review* answered these charges sufficiently when it remarked that American journalism was no worse than English. There is every reason to believe that the articles in *The Foreign Quarterly Review* were not written in good faith.

INNOVATIONS OF "THE HERALD"

What really made *The New York Herald*, however, yet remains to be outlined. In the second number a Wall Street feature was

added to the paper. Irregularly at first, these articles on finance
proved so popular that they became a regular department. In
addition to the comment about the money market, stock quotations were given. According to *The Herald*, it was "the only
paper in the city which gives authentic and daily reports of
Wall Street operations, stocks, and the money market." Until
1838 the department was conducted entirely by Bennett. In
reviewing the history of this department, he said in *The Herald*
of February 20, 1869: —

> The daily financial report was begun by us when we started *The
> Herald*. We made it personally. Getting through that part of our va-
> ried labors that could be done at an early hour, we went to Wall Street,
> saw for ourselves what was in progress there, and returned with our
> report sketched out in fragmentary fly leaves of letters or other handy
> scraps of paper. We told the truth, for we were in the interest of the
> public; and the truth of that locality was not complimentary in those
> days any more than it would be now. War was made upon us right and
> left by the men whose little games were spoiled whenever the public
> came to know what they were at; and, strangest of all things for a war
> originating in that quarter, it was a "moral war." We lived through it,
> however.
> Compelled to delegate our labor in the preparation of a financial
> report, we have always meant and still mean to keep that report as
> honest as it was in its origin; to constitute it a legitimate and exact
> record of what is honestly done in Wall Street, and an exposure — a lay-
> ing bare to the eyes of the public of what is dishonestly done there. We
> will compound none of the villainies with the fellows who trade on
> public credulity to abuse public confidence. One journal shall tell what
> Wall Street really is and what is done there.

Wall Street had some excellent newspaper stories, as Bennett
soon found out.

After the fire which destroyed the Ann Street printing-plant,
Bennett announced the policy which, carried out in every detail,
contributed much to the success of *The Herald*. That policy was:
"*In every species of news The Herald will be one of the earliest of
the early*." At the same time Bennett announced this policy he
also said: "We mean to procure intelligent correspondents in
London, Paris, and Washington, and measures are already
adopted for that purpose." When the Sirius and Great Western
crossed the Atlantic, with steam as the motive power, Bennett

enlarged the foreign correspondence of the paper. For years *The Herald* was first in foreign news. Bennett did not neglect local and national news. After he had found the value of such items to the paper he went over New York with a net and gathered in — with apologies to *The New York Times* — "all the news that's fit to print," along with some that was n't. He developed his own news bureau for the interior. He printed "news-slips" which were sent free by express mail to the newspapers in the interior. These "news-slips," which reached publishers one mail in advance of the regular issues of *The Herald*, took the place of the telegraph news service of the Associated Press of to-day. This free news service placed papers receiving the same under obligation to see that *The Herald* got all the worth-while news from their territory — and got it before the other New York papers.

In building up *The Herald*, Bennett had the active coöperation of Frederic Hudson, who had the honor of being managing director. Of the latter, Samuel Bowles, the elder, once said, while editor of *The Springfield Republican*, that Hudson was the greatest organizer of a mere newspaper that this country has ever seen.

PENNY PAPERS SOLD BY BOYS

The conservative *Journal of Commerce*, a six-penny paper, on June 29, 1835, published an account of the penny press in New York which described not only the conditions in New York, but those in other cities which had penny newspapers: —

It is but three or four years since the first penny paper was established. Now there are half a dozen or more of them in this city, with an aggregate circulation of twenty or thirty thousand, and perhaps more. These issues exceed those of the large papers, and, for aught we see, they are conducted with as much talent, and in point of moral character we think candidly they are superior to their six-penny contemporaries. . . . They are less partisan in politics than the large papers, and more decidedly American, with one or two exceptions. The manner in which their pecuniary affairs are conducted shows how much may come of small details. They are circulated on the London plan, the editors and publishers doing no more than to complete the manufacture of the papers, when they are sold to the newsmen or carriers at

67 cents per 100. The carriers distribute the papers, and on Saturday collect from each subscriber six cents, so that for each call their net income to the carriers is but one third of a cent. We wish our penny associates all success, hoping that they will grow wise, good, and great, until they make every sixpenny paper ashamed that tells a lie, or betrays its country for the sake of party, or does any other base thing.

For some reason the owners of the six-penny political sheets did not consider it strictly ethical to sell their wares on city streets. Subscribers received their papers by carriers, and transient purchasers had to go to the counters of newspaper offices. The penny press, however, did not wait to enroll annual subscribers, but tried to market its merchandise daily through boys. The pages of the early penny papers fairly bristled with advertisements of "Boys Wanted." The first issue of *The Public Ledger* in Philadelphia contained a small advertisement to this effect: —

50 MEN AND BOYS can make it an advantageous business to circulate this paper. Apply at the office of *The Ledger* Nos. 38–39 Arcade.

Early issues of *The Boston 12 o'clock News* contained this advertisement: —

WANTED 20 boys neatly dressed and excellent deportment to sell *The Daily News* — None need apply except those who intend to engage permanently. 30¢ for every 100 sold.

Possibly *The Sun* of New York was the first to use news boys in this way. Almost at the start that paper contained a notice: —

TO THE UNEMPLOYED. A number of steady men can find employment by vending this paper. A liberal discount is allowed to those who buy to sell again.

For the first time journalism was brought directly to the people. By making the daily papers easy to buy, the penny press brought something of a revolution into American journalism. Its system of marketing its products undoubtedly had much to do with its success.

The penny paper on account of its size was forced to give its news in small space. For example, the first issue of *The Sun* in New York gave an account of a revolution in Mexico in four lines which included a statement of the source of the item. For the most part, the penny sheet printed its news on inside pages: the first page was given over either to advertising or to articles usually quoted from exchanges. *The Sun*, to quote its first issue again, had on its front page a supposedly humorous story about an Irish captain and the duels he fought; early issues of *The New York Transcript* devoted their front pages to a continued story, "Edward and Julia; a Reminiscence of Forty Years Since"; page one of the first issue of *The Daily Evening Transcript* in Boston was composed entirely of advertisements. At the start the editor of the penny paper usually culled his material from the pages of his more verbose six-penny contemporary: later, he either went himself or sent a reporter to gather such items.

The chief distinction between the six-penny sheets and the penny papers was that the former featured the news of legislative chambers and the latter that of the courts. It must be frankly admitted that in some instances the penny press went to the extreme limit in reporting criminal cases, but in so doing it showed sound newspaper psychology. What makes a short piece of fiction so interesting is its account of some struggle or "scrap," whether it be the conflict in a character study where two natures battle against each other, or whether it be the fight of two rivals for the hand of Fair Ophelia. How well James Gordon Bennett knew this has been outlined elsewhere. In reporting the happenings of the police court the "scrap" element, which gave value to the accounts, was present in double strength: first, there was the story of the physical combat which brought the contestants to court; second, there was the legal battle between their lawyers. The penny papers went on the principle of what the Lord let happen ought to be printed in their sheets. Such contentions of the penny press brought upon it the severe criticism of the more cultured in the community. It was not uncommon for the subscribers of the more conservative papers to write letters similar to the following: —

Your paper should take a more dignified stand; and not condescend to notice the assaults of the degraded penny press. The price of your journal is such that it is taken only by readers of the more intelligent classes; readers who despise the vulgarity of the penny newspapers, and who have cause to feel themselves affronted when you give so large a space, or any space, indeed, to a refutation of their absurdities. It seems to me, that a proper respect for your own dignity, as well as a proper respect for those into whose hands your lucubrations chiefly fall, ought to restrain you from giving additional circulation to the trash of the minor prints, which are suited only to the taste and capacities of the lower classes of people.

It was in answer to just this letter that William Leggett replied: —

If it were true that the readers of the penny papers are chiefly confined to what our correspondent chooses to term the "lower classes," it would be no argument against them, but in their favour. Those who come within the embrace of that exotic phrase are in immense majority of the American people. It includes all the honest and labouring poor. It includes those whose suffrages decide the principles of our government; on whose conduct rests the reputation of our country; and whose mere breath is the tenure by which we hold all our dearest political, religious, and social rights. How ineffably important it is, then, that the intelligence of these "lower classes" should be cultivated; that their moral sense should be quickened; and that they should have the means within their reach of learning the current history of the times, of observing the measures of *their* public servants, and of becoming prepared to exercise with wisdom the most momentous privilege of free-men. This great desideratum the penny press supplies, not as well and thoroughly, perhaps, as the philanthropist could wish, but to such a degree as to be necessarily productive of immense benefit to society. It communicates knowledge to those who had no means of acquiring it. It calls into exercise minds that before rusted unused. It elevates vast numbers of men from the abjectness of mere animal condition, to the nobler station of intelligent beings. If usefulness constitutes the true measure of dignity, the penny press deserves pre-eminence, as well on account of the character of its readers, as the extent of its circulation. He who addresses himself to intelligent and cultivated minds, has a critic in each reader, and the influence of his opinions must necessarily be circumscribed. But he who addresses himself to the mass of the people, has readers whose opinions are yet to be formed; whose minds are ductile and open to new impressions, and whose intellectual characters he, in some measure, moulds. He becomes the *thinker*, in fact, for a vast number of his fellow-beings. His mind transfuses itself through many bodies. His station renders him, not an individual, but a host; not one, but legion. Is this not a vocation of inherent dignity? — to address, daily, myriads of men, not in words that fall on cold and inattentive ears, and are scarce heard, to be immediately forgotten; but in language clothed with all that undefinable influence which typography possesses over oral communication, and claiming attention not in the hurry of business, or amidst the distractions of a crowded assemblage, but when the thoughts have leisure to concentrate themselves upon it, and follow the writer in all the windings of his argument.

If the censures were well founded which are lavished on "The vile penny press," as some of the larger papers are prone to term their cheaper rivals, they should but provoke minds governed by right principles to a more earnest endeavour to reform the character of an instrument, which must be powerful, either for evil or for good. That they are so vile we do not admit. We have found, ourselves, honourable and courteous antagonists among them; and if those who apply to them the harshest epithets, would treat them instead, with respectful consideration, copying from their columns as readily as from those of other journals, when intrinsic circumstances presented no particular motive of preference, and contesting their errors of opinion on terms of equal controversy, they would do far more towards raising the character and increasing the usefulness of that important branch of popular literature, than general and sweeping condemnation can possibly do to degrade it. For ourselves, professing that our main object is to promote the cause of truth in politics and morals, we should consider ourselves acting with palpable inconsistency, if we were governed, in any degree, by so narrow a principle of exclusion as that which our correspondent recommends. That newspaper best consults its real dignity which never loses sight of the dignity of truth, nor avoids any opportunity of extending its influence.

SUCCESS OF NEW PRESS

Not all of the six-penny newspapers, however, were so charitable toward their younger brethren found in the penny press. They resented the strenuous competition which they must meet in the gathering and selling of news. The aristocrats of the day thought that the newspaper was their especial property and should be published for them exclusively. It was something of an honor before the establishment of the penny press to be a newspaper subscriber; it was somewhat similar to having a piano in the house; but when newspapers sold for a penny a copy, they crept into the pockets of the working-man to be glanced at hastily at his noonday lunch and to be read religiously after his evening meal. Naturally, politicians bitterly opposed this new press, and did what they could to prevent it from feeding at the political crib of State and National advertising. Nevertheless, the new journalism, opposed to politics and independent in spirit, continued to thrive. It was said that in ten years it did more good by exposure of municipal scandals than the older press had done in twenty. In the birth of the penny newspaper may be found the beginning of the independent press in America. The new press when it discussed politics did so without taking orders from Washington: it ceased to be a minor or a servant controlled by party class or personal clique.

CONTEMPORARY CRITICISM

A writer of the period has left the following comment about the control of the press: —

Before the year 1833, journalism, literary, commercial, or political, had been weak and unsystematized. The falsest estimates were placed upon the efforts of men in every department of letters. A few cliques ruled the whole country, and everything that emanated out of the limits of these was liable to be consigned to oblivion. One cannot but smile at the extravagant praises lavished upon writers and orators who are now almost forgotten, or whose works are oftener alluded to than read — men who had the public journals in their hands, and by means of them played their unjust games with the aspiring minds of the nation. In the political ranks, there were a large class of men whose deeds have been recorded in their official acts, and whose characters are the ablest comments upon the history of those times.

CHAPTER XIII

TRANSITION PERIOD

1832 — 1841

THE penny press brought several changes in the manufacture and marketing of newspapers. Among these were the use of steam to turn the press and the employment of boys to sell single copies in addition to distributing papers among regular subscribers. The greater demand for larger editions, the competition to be first in news, the better facilities for gathering items, the deeper interest taken in civic improvement, the changes in the body politic, the expansion of the country, the increase of literacy among all classes with the introduction of compulsory education — all these things brought readjustment in the printing and making of newspapers.

These changes came gradually, however, and will be taken up more in detail as they appear. They were concomitant with other transformations of American civilization. Many reforms grew out of the agitations of the penny press. In New York, for example, *The Sun* advocated the installation of a paid fire department. Under the volunteer system the chief aim of fire companies was to be first at the burning building rather than to extinguish the flames. One company never hesitated to destroy the apparatus of a rival if thereby it could be first at the fire. Rival gangs which formerly fought on city streets put on the red shirts of volunteer firemen and fought their battles for supremacy as before. In securing the introduction of horse-drawn engines and the adoption of a paid department, *The Sun* rendered a most distinct service to the city. *The Herald* performed just as distinct a service when it fought for the adoption of uniforms for the city police. Previously, members of the police department had been distinguished from civilians only by the presence of a badge worn on the coat. In case of trouble, it was not uncommon for a policeman to remove his badge and with the insignia in his pocket, watch the fracas as a spectator. The reforms in the police department brought about by *The Herald* added much to the respect for law and order in New York. Possibly the penny press of Philadelphia secured even greater reforms for that city. The press was again simply a mirror of the transformations of overgrown villages into metropolitan cities and of isolated States and Territories into a Nation.

GREELEY, SEWARD, AND WEED

During the time when the penny press was being established in the larger cities, Horace Greeley was interested in various newspaper enterprises. His entrance into New York City in 1831, because of his peculiarities of dress and mannerisms, might be paralleled to that of Benjamin Franklin into Philadelphia. From his savings as a journeyman printer, Greeley, as has already been mentioned, aided in the publication of what became the first one-cent newspaper in New York, *The Morning Post*. At the time *The Sun* was established he was running a job office which made a specialty of the advertising literature of lotteries, etc. In conjunction with Jonas Winchester he started on March 22, 1834, *The New Yorker*, in which he published the larger part of his editorial work, both original and selected writings, though he continued to write for *The Daily Whig*. He was a member of the political company, spoken of in the press as Seward, Weed, and Greeley. This company proceeded, after the political revolution of 1837 to start, under the auspices and by the direction of the Whig Central Committee of the State of New York on March 3, 1838, a campaign paper in Albany called *The Jeffersonian*. Funds for its establishment were contributed by the leading Whig politicians in amounts of ten dollars each. The paper, sold at fifty cents a year, was according to Greeley established "on the impulse of the Whig tornado to secure a like result in 1838 so as to give the Whig party a Governor, Lieutenant-Governor, Senate, Assembly, United States Senator, Congressman, and all the vast executive patronage of the State," then amounting to millions of dollars. For his services, Greeley received a remuneration of one thousand dollars, but he naturally expected to get some of those offices worth from three to twenty thousand dollars per year which Seward upon being elected Governor was handing out to his friends. In this he was disappointed: to quote his words, "I return to my garret and my crust."

In the Tippecanoe and Tyler campaign of 1840—known as the "Tip and Ty" campaign in the press — the same political firm brought out another campaign paper on May 2, 1840, entitled *The Log Cabin* published simultaneously at New York and Albany. Of this sheet Henry Jarvis Raymond, when editor of *The New York Times*, once said, "It was the best campaign paper ever published." It was designed only for a campaign sheet and was expected to expire with the twenty-seventh number: forty-eight thousand of the first issue were sold and subscriptions came in at the rate of seven hundred a day. *The Log Cabin*, both by its caricatures and by its editorials, promoted the raising of log cabins, formally dedicated with plenty of hard cider, as political centers and headquarters for Harrison and Tyler men.

The Whig tornado, mentioned by Greeley, started with Jackson's decision to remove the deposits of the Government from the Bank of the United States. Financial interests subsidized existing Whig organs and started new ones at strategic points. Democratic papers, alienated by Jackson, continued their opposition to his successor, Martin Van Buren. A group of papers, headed by *The Enquirer* of Richmond, was especially bitter toward Van Buren for not favoring the annexation of Texas and became even more violent in its denunciation when he accepted a nomination of a rival political organization. The sound money doctrines of Van Buren made the Whig campaign organs popular with the masses which wanted "higher wages and lower prices" so readily promised by these sheets in case of victory at the polls. Log cabins were frequently erected to be used as print-shops and the office mascot was invariably a live raccoon chained to the front doorpost or to the rude chimney of the structure. The popularity of the log cabin was due to the fact that Harrison was not only born in one, but also had one attached his house. Rival campaign weeklies existed for the Democratic Party with names as peculiarly appropriate as *The Log Cabin*. Two favorites were *The Coon Skinner* and *The*

Dry Cider Barrell. Of the Whig sheets, next to Greeley's *Log Cabin,* came *The Corn-Stalk Fiddle* and *The Whig Rifle.* Never again did the campaign weeklies, or dailies for that matter, play so important a part in presidential elections as in the "Tip and Ty" campaign of 1840.

GREELEY AND HIS DAILY

After Harrison had been elected, largely through the Whig Campaign organs of which *The Log Cabin* was the leader, Greeley naturally thought that Governor Seward would ask that the position of postmaster of New York be given to the editor of *The Log Cabin,* but he was unable not only to get this position, but also to get anything "in the scramble of the swell mob of coon-minstrels and cider-suckers which swarmed to Washington for offices." Of the residents from New York, City "no one in the crowd," to quote Greeley's own words in a letter to Seward, had done so much "toward General Harrison's nomination and election," as the editor of *The Log Cabin.* Unable to get political office Greeley started *The Tribune* in New York on April 10, 1841, on the very day of Harrison's funeral. The aim of this newspaper, published at one cent, was that it should be "removed alike from servile partisanship on the one hand and from gagged, mincing neutrality on the other." Though there were already numerous daily papers in New York there was still room for another local Whig paper. *The Courier and Enquirer, The New York American, The Express,* and *The Commercial Advertiser* were Whig papers, but circulated at the annual subscription price of ten dollars a year: *The Evening Post* of the same price leaned to the Democratic side of politics; *The Journal of Commerce,* while primarily a commercial daily favored entries approved by the Democrats. *The Signal, The Tattler,* and *The Star* were among the cheap papers which sat astride the political fence; *The Sun* had now achieved an enormous circulation, and while professing neutrality in politics always shone a little brighter for the Democrats; *The Herald* was still independent and had raised its price to two cents.

In his preliminary notice of publication, Greeley thus outlined the policy to be pursued by *The Tribune:* —

On Saturday, the tenth day of April instant, the subscriber will publish the first number of a new morning journal of politics, literature and general intelligence. *The Tribune*, as its name imports, will labor to advance the interests of the people, and to promote their moral, social and political wellbeing. The immoral and degrading police reports, advertisements and other matter which have been allowed to disgrace the columns of our leading penny papers will be carefully excluded from this, and no exertion spared to render it worthy of the hearty approval of the virtuous and refined, and a welcome visitant at the family fireside. Earnestly believing that the political revolution which has called William Henry Harrison to the Chief Magistracy of the nation was a triumph of right reason and public good over error and sinister ambition, *The Tribune* will give to the new administration a frank and candid, but manly and independent, support, judging it always by its acts, and commending these only so far as they shall seem calculated to subserve the great end of all government — the welfare of the people.

The success of *The Tribune* was immediate. The editor's personal and political friends had secured subscribers by the hundreds before the first issue of five thousand copies was printed. Though started as a penny paper, *The Tribune* began its second volume on April 11, 1842, at the increased price of nine cents a week, or two cents a copy. *The New Yorker* and *The Log Cabin* Greeley merged into *The Weekly Tribune*. *The Tribune* under Greeley's editorship has been commonly classed as a party organ, but he was fairly successful in his determination to "remove it from servile partisanship on the one hand and from gagged, mincing neutrality on the other"; no better illustration of this fact is found than his own words, "*The Tribune* will accept the party nominee but will spit upon the platform." Though *The Tribune* continued to be a pulpit from which Greeley preached daily the partisan gospel, according to St. Horace, it was also a platform for the early appearance of such distinguished journalists and publicists as Charles Anderson Dana, Henry Jarvis Raymond, George William Curtis, Carl Schurz, John Hay, Whitelaw Reid, Henry James, William Dean Howells, Bayard Taylor, George Ripley, Margaret Fuller, Edmund Clarence Stedman, Richard Grant White, Richard Hildreth, John Russell Young, Sidney Howard Gay, etc.

NEWSPAPER BATTLES

In the competition to be first on the streets with important news, papers spared neither labor nor expense — to use a hackneyed expression. In an age when politics attracted so much attention in the press it was natural that there should be the keenest rivalry in reporting political speeches. As these were often delivered at some distance from the place of publication, papers adopted various methods to rush the reports. If news had to come by boat, compositors and type cases were put on board, and as fast as copy was written on the trip it was put into type and made ready for the press. On the other hand, if news had to come by rail, a reporter, acting under instructions from his paper, hired a locomotive for his exclusive use and made a fast run with only the engineer as a companion. Such methods for the transmission of news were common until the telegraph proved quicker.

Such enterprises did much to develop the instinct for news, for speed soon became the distinguishing characteristic of American journalism. Boats on the Hudson river often carried a corps of compositors who could put into type a speech delivered at Albany and have it ready to lock up in a form by the time the boat docked in New York. One of the most remarkable beats in this connection was the report of a speech delivered by Daniel Webster in Boston. Several New York newspapers sent shorthand reporters who took down the remarks of Webster, as the address was an important one. Representing *The Tribune* was Henry J. Raymond, who, inexperienced in stenography, was somewhat handicapped, but he had provided for the emergency by taking with him a number of *Tribune* compositors. The latter, with the help of a miniature printing-plant which had been put on board the night boat out of Boston, were prepared to set the speech in type as fast as Raymond could write it. Employees of *The Tribune* met the boat when it landed at five the next morning and in one hour carriers were distributing copies of *The Tribune* which contained a full report of Webster's speech delivered in Boston the preceding afternoon. Greeley's paper that morning was the talk of the town, and his rivals on that occasion were simply "also rans."

STEAM EXPRESSES OF "THE SUN"

In running steam expresses to obtain early news possibly *The New York Sun* stood first. Its publisher once asserted that the secret of its success was mainly due to its enterprise in this direction. From 1842 to 1847 it spent over twenty thousand dollars in running such expresses — a large sum for the time when financial returns from advertising were not large. In justice to other Gotham papers it must be said that *The Sun* was not infrequently eclipsed in this field by *The Herald* or by *The Tribune*. A whole chapter could be devoted to interesting accounts of races between newspaper expresses. On one occasion to get the European news which was coming by way of Boston both *The Sun* and *The Herald* had a locomotive, but on rival tracks. The reporter of *The Sun* was the first to leave Boston, but he was no sooner out of sight than the reporter of *The Herald* sent his locomotive to the round-house and got out a special edition of *The Herald* in Boston on the press of *The Mail*. This special edition of *The Herald*, sent by train to New York, was the first to give the news, for *The Sun*, thinking that the express of *The Herald* had been wrecked when it did not arrive, had not rushed the news into type as rapidly as usual. On another occasion a representative of *The Tribune*, in order to have the exclusive use of an important item of news, deliberately stole an engine especially chartered by *The Herald* and then ran away with it to New York. In those days newspapers did not bother their heads with the nice questions of newspaper ethics: it was simply a fight to get the news and to get it first in print.

EDITORIAL COMBATS

During the days of personal journalism a large amount of editorial space was frequently given to abuse of rival editors. Some of these tilts between editors, though often unmannerly, were very interesting.

James Watson Webb, of *The Courier and Enquirer*, once took revenge upon Horace Greeley, of *The Tribune*, by attacking what he thought were some of the eccentricities of the latter. Greeley came back with the rejoinder in *The Tribune* which completely squelched Webb — at least for the time being. Webb on January 27, 1844, published the following editorial in *The Courier and Enquirer:* —

The editor of *The Tribune* would have all the world live upon bran-bread and sawdust. He seeks for notoriety by pretending to great eccentricity of character and habits, and by the strangeness of his theories and practices; we, on the contrary, are content with following the beaten path, and accomplishing the good we can, in the old-fashioned way. He lays claim to greatness by wandering through the streets with a hat double the size of his head, a coat after the fashion of Jacob's of old, with one leg of his pantaloons inside and the other outside of his boot, and with boots all bespattered with mud, or possibly, a shoe on one foot and boot on the other, and glorying in an unwashed and unshaven person. We, on the contrary, eschew all such affectation as weak and silly; we think there is a difference between notoriety and distinction; we recognize the social obligation to act and dress according to our station in life; and we look upon cleanliness of person as inseparable from purity of thought and benevolence of heart. In short, there is not the slightest resemblance between the editor of *The Tribune* and ourself, politically, morally, or socially; and it is only when his affectation and impudence are unbearable, that we condescend to notice him or his press.

Greeley, equal to the occasion, on the next day printed the following reply in *The Tribune:* —

It is true that the Editor of *The Tribune* chooses mainly (not entirely) vegetable food; but he never troubles his readers on the subject; it does not worry them; why should it concern the Colonel? It is hard for philosophy that so humble a man shall be made to stand as its exemplar, while Christianity is personified by the hero of the Sunday duel with Hon. Tom Marshall; but such luck will happen. As to our personal appearance, it does seem time that we should say something. Some donkey, a while ago, apparently anxious to assail or annoy the Editor of this paper, and not well knowing with what, originated the story of his carelessness of personal appearance; and since then, every blockhead of the same disposition, and distressed by a similar lack of ideas, has repeated and exaggerated the foolery, until, from its origin in *The Albany Microscope*, it has sunk down at last to the columns of *The Courier and Enquirer*, growing more absurd at every landing. Yet, all this time, the object of this silly raillery has doubtless worn better clothes than two-thirds of those who thus assailed him, — better than any of them could honestly wear if they paid their debts otherwise than by bankruptcy; while, if they are indeed more cleanly than he, they must bathe very thoroughly not less than twice every day. The Editor of *The Tribune* is the son of a poor and humble farmer; came to New York a minor, without a friend within two hundred miles, less than ten dollars in his pocket, and precious little besides; he has never had a dollar from a relative, and has, for years, labored under a load of debt. Henceforth he may be able to make a better show, if deemed essential by his friends; for himself he has not much time or thought to bestow on the matter. That he ever affected eccentricity is most untrue; and certainly no costume he ever appeared in, would create such a sensation in Broadway, as that James Watson Webb would have worn, but for the clemency of Gov. Seward. Heaven grant our assailant may never hang with such weight on another Whig executive! — We drop him.

In order to understand the latter part of Greeley's comment about Webb, some mention should be made of the latter's willingness to defend his opinions, not only in the columns of his paper, but also on the "field of honor." One such duel had involved Webb in legal difficulties and he had only escaped a jail sentence through the courtesy of Governor Seward.

For the sake of the contrast of juxtaposition, an editorial tilt of a later period, when journalism had become impersonal, may be inserted. As *The Tribune* had the better of it in the editorial controversy just recorded, an illustration may be used which reverses the honor. Long after *The Courier and Enquirer* had become a part of *The World*, a Democratic President made a very poor appointment to an office at his disposal. *The Tribune*, thinking that it might embarrass its neighbor, asserted that it would leave the explanation of this appointment to the official Democratic spokesman, *The World*. The antiphonal rejoinder of *The World*, after reprinting the comment, was, "It would be a great deal better for the readers of *The Tribune* if that newspaper left all matters to *The World* to explain." Nothing shows more the tremendous advance which American journalism has made than the two editorial controversies just given.

FIRST NEWSPAPER CORPORATION

William Leggett, in summing up the newspaper press of 1835, made a special plea for the corporational newspaper — a prophecy of what the coming newspaper in America was to be. Mr. Leggett thought that newspapers thus established would then be able to stand "the assaults of prejudice, now fatal in the unassisted hands of single and comparatively indigent individuals." He pointed out that in England the principal newspapers were joint-stock property, many having hundreds and some thousands of owners whose interests are attended to by a committee of directors of their own selection. By way of contrast, Mr. Leggett added: —

Among us, the newspapers are the property of single individuals; and it is found that administering to the depraved tastes and appetites of the community, consulting the passions and caprice of the hour, and guiding their course by the variable breath of the multitude, is a more profitable, as well as an easier task, than steering undeviatingly by fixed principles, referring all subjects to the touchstone of truth, and addressing themselves with inflexible constancy to the judgments of men. It is not to be wondered at, however much it is to be deplored, that they adopt the readiest and most lucrative mode of discharging their functions, and forego the glorious opportunity their vocation affords, of effectually advancing the great interests of mankind.

The first paper to be thus published by a stock company was *The New York Tribune*. On January 1, 1849, a meeting was called for the purpose of distributing the stock among its employees. Every one was placed on a salary from editor-in-chief down to printer's devil. This system of association ownership was especially pleasing to Greeley because of its socialistic aspect.

PRESS MODESTY OF POLITICIANS

During the first half of the nineteenth century, even the ablest statesmen delivered their speeches primarily for home consumption. They did not care to have their utterances given widespread publication. They were to be reported in the friendly organs of the political parties. Henry Clay, for example, when he was about to make a speech at Lexington, Kentucky, was told that a reporter of the Associated Press was present. The great Kentucky statesman then promptly refused to go on with his address until the reporter had folded up his paper and left the grounds. Clay was deeply insulted — and did not hesitate to say so in picturesque language — that a writer for newspapers unknown to him should have the audacity to report his speech without first securing special permission to do so. The reporter, fortunately, was Richard Smith, who later became associated with *The Commercial Gazette* of Cincinnati. Being a good newspaper man, he hung around until the speech was over, and then obtained an excellent résumé of the address from a friend who knew the politics of the State and who remembered the salient points of the speech. Until the politician learned that he must speak to a larger audience than that around the stump, the reporter was regarded as an impertinent intruder.

JOURNALISM IN THE REPUBLIC OF TEXAS

When Texas, being dissatisfied with Mexican rule, revolted in 1835, its most important newspaper became *The Telegraph and Texas Register* which first appeared at San Felice, October 10, 1835, published by Gail Borden, Joseph Baker, and Thomas H. Borden. It was not only one of the foremost papers devoted to the revolutionary cause, but also practically the official organ of the Provincial Government: it continued to be published at Austin until March 24, 1836, when General Santa Anna sent forward an advance guard which forced the staff to take the press apart, break up the forms, pack the type, etc., and to flee to Harrisburgh, where another attempt was made to print another edition of *The Telegraph*. As a matter of fact, one issue was put into type and six sheets had been actually taken off the press when another advance guard from Santa Anna entered the place, seized the press, pied the type, and held the printers as prisoners. Later, the troops from Santa Anna threw the press and type into the Buffalo Bayou, from which they were later taken, cleaned, and used in Houston to print *The Morning Star*, which first appeared on April 8, 1839, and boasted of being the first daily paper in the Republic of Texas.

After the battle of San Jacinto, Gail Borden went to Cincinnati, where he bought another printing outfit which he used in resuming publication of *The Telegraph* on October 2, 1836, at Columbia on the Brazos, then the temporary seat of the Government. On April 11, 1837, *The Telegraph* was moved to Houston, at that time the seat of the Government, where Dr. Francis Moore became its editor. On June 20, 1837, Gail Borden sold his interest to Jacob W. Cruger and the publishers now became Cruger and Moore: they were also Public Printers and continued to hold that office even after the Capital had been removed to Austin. At the latter place they established, on January 15, 1840, *The Texas Sentinel*, but continued *The Telegraph* at Houston. Gail Borden, after selling his interest in the paper, eventually returned to his native State and founded in New York City the great milk company which bears his name.

Of the journalism conditions in Texas while a Republic the following résumé has been left by "an emigrant, late from the United States": "That the Texians are a reading people is manifested by the fact that there are now twelve newspapers published in the Republic. One of these is a daily paper published at Houston, and one or two others are, during the sessions of Congress, semi-weekly ones. In a population so small, and with such imperfect post routes, to sustain so many papers must be admitted to be an astonishing circumstance."

TOPLIFF'S "NEWS-ROOM"

Possibly Samuel Topliff made the first attempt to gather news to be retailed among several newspapers. Establishing his headquarters in a "news-room" in the Coffee Exchange in Boston he made a specialty of the reports of the market and the commercial news of Boston Harbor. He kept a logbook in which captains of boats which had just arrived wrote the news they had picked up at foreign ports. This logbook was available to the Boston newspapers — for a consideration. Mention has already been made of how *The Boston Transcript* availed itself of such an opportunity when it brought out its first issue in 1830.

PRESS PIGEONS OF CRAIG

While Topliff was busy in Boston, Arunah S. Abell, of *The Baltimore Sun,* and D. H. Craig were busy experimenting the possibility of using pigeons to carry news. Headquarters were established in Baltimore and here the pigeons were trained: at one time over four hundred were kept in a house on Hamstead Hill near the Maryland Hospital for the Insane. The pigeon express first ran — or rather flew — from Washington to Baltimore: later, Washington dispatches were carried by pigeon relays to Baltimore, Philadelphia, and New York. The headquarters at the last place was a coop on top of *The Herald* building. Incidentally, it may be remarked that it was not until the beginning of the twentieth century that *The Herald* did away entirely with its carrier pigeons: until fifteen years ago that newspaper had one of the best cages of these remarkable birds for exigencies.

D. H. Craig also experimented in Boston with pigeons as carriers of news. Securing a number of African carrier pigeons, he kept them in a special building near his house in Roxbury until they had become thoroughly domesticated. Upon the expected arrival of an English mail steamer in Halifax he, with his winged carriers, would go there, get the latest British papers, and then take passage to Boston. While at sea he would write on thin manifold paper a summary of the most important European news. Then when the steamer was about fifty miles from Boston he would liberate his pigeons with the news fastened to wing or foot. They would reach home several hours before the steamer docked and the news they carried would, after being promptly put into type, be published as an extra of *The Boston Daily Mail*. When the edition had been run off, the title of *The Daily Mail* was removed and that of *The New York Herald Extra* was substituted and the press again started. The second edition, after being promptly forwarded to New York by Sound steamers, was put into the hands of newsboys by James Gordon Bennett, proprietor of *The New York Herald*. Because of the intense rivalry between *The Herald* and *The Sun*, Bennett at one time offered five hundred dollars an hour for every hour that Craig could furnish *The Herald* with news ahead of rivals. So bitter became this fight for the honor of being first in the news that questionable methods of interference were often adopted: even the pigeons which carried the news were shot by men hired by newspapers outside the service of the winged carriers. Craig later became connected with the Associated Press of New York.

HALE AND HALLOCK

In New York the first pretentious step to gather news while it was news was made by Arthur Tappan who had founded *The Journal of Commerce* as a semi-religious newspaper to combat the growing evil influences of the theater. To get the European news he used to meet the incoming vessels with a rowboat and thus save time in getting the news into print. Later, he sold his paper to the Boston newspaper men, David Hale and Gerard Hallock. These men, familiar with the news enterprise of Samuel Topliff, built a fast news-yacht which they called "The Journal of Commerce" after their newspaper. *The Courier and Enquirer*, not to be outdone, promptly put into commission another news-boat, "The Thomas H. Smith." *The Journal of Commerce*, true to the principles of its founder, refused to collect the news on the Sabbath and appealed to the more provincial subscriber to excuse lack of news on Monday. *The Journal of Commerce* also built a semaphore telegraph at Sandy Hook by means of which it relayed news from its news-boat to Staten Island where items were promptly taken to its New York office. In this way the paper was able to be first in maritime news for some little time. Whenever important items arrived it got out extra editions in order that it might be first on the streets. Aroused by the enterprise of the penny press, the conservative blanket sheets — called "our bed-quilt contemporaries" by the penny papers — were not always beaten in the publishing of notable news.

PRIMITIVE PONY EXPRESS

While other papers shared in the honor of its development, the pony express was really started by *The Sun*, of Baltimore, Maryland. Local newspapers had supplied their customers with the President's messages as follows: they purchased supplements previously printed in Washington, but bearing the title of their papers, and then distributed them upon their arrival to their readers. In December, 1838, however, *The Sun* hired a representative to bring, with the help of "a Canadian pony as nimble as a goat and as swift as the wind," a copy of the message to *The Sun* office on Light Street. Within five minutes after its arrival forty-nine compositors were hastily putting it into type and in two hours this newspaper had the message on the streets of the city. This was the beginning of the famous pony express of *The Sun*.

From that time forward, until the invention of the telegraph, the pony express was used to bring the messages of the Presidents to Baltimore; from this point they were relayed by fresh expresses to New York and other cities. Through the help of its horses *The Sun* was enabled to give its readers President Harrison's Inaugural Address on the same day that it was delivered. But it was in the war with Mexico that the pony express reached its highest development.

FIRST FLIGHT OF "BROOKLYN EAGLE"

When Harrison was elected President, politicians of the rival party at once began to make preparations for the defeat of the Whig Party at the next presidential election. Many papers were established for the sake of influencing votes. Among those thus founded for political causes was *The Eagle*, of Brooklyn, New York. For some years previous to 1841 the county in which Brooklyn is located had been Whig: the Democrats sought an excuse for being in the minority by asserting that they had no party organ to represent them. A few of the leaders, therefore, in the hopes of wresting control of the county from the Whigs, formed a company to start a new daily newspaper: the result of their efforts was the establishment of *The Brooklyn Eagle and The Kings County Democrat* on October 26, 1841, with Isaac Van Anden as its first editor and publisher. After the county had been swung into the Democratic ranks, most of the men who had started *The Eagle* thought that, as the object for which the journal had been founded had been obtained, the paper might be well discontinued. Mr. Van Anden, however, thought otherwise, and as a protest against discontinuing the sheet he offered to purchase the interest of the others in the paper. In this way he became its sole owner and conductor. Though founded as a party organ, *The Eagle* both in national and local campaigns has supported in its editorial columns both

Republican and Democratic candidates when these candidates stood for a policy that best represented the interests of the people. As Brooklyn grew, *The Eagle* shared in its prosperity: it has carried an amount of advertising which has been exceeded by only two other newspapers in the City of New York. Among its distinguished editors has been the poet, Walt Whitman, and the late St. Clair McKelway. In spite of the competition of the penny papers of New York, *The Eagle* succeeded in keeping the home field to itself, even though it charged three cents per copy.

COOPER'S WHOLESALE LIBELS

The only man who has ever sued the newspapers for libel on a wholesale scale was the distinguished American novelist — James Fenimore Cooper. Returning from a long residence abroad, he retired to the old homestead at Cooperstown, New York. During his absence, the villagers had used a piece of property belonging to the novelist as a sort of recreation spot. It was one of those numerous points which run out into Otsego Lake and was near enough to the village to be ideal for picnic purposes. Acting strictly within his legal rights Cooper forbade trespassing upon this piece of property. The resentment of the village was so bitter that it attracted the attention of the many newspapers of the State, including that of a Whig organ at Norwich, New York, which told how the Cooper books had been removed from the village library and burned. The local Whig organ at Cooperstown reprinted the item from its Norwich contemporary and was promptly sued for libel by Cooper, who "recovered the verdict and collected it by taking the money — through a Sheriff's officer — from the editor's trunk." Various Whig papers, not only in the vicinity of Cooperstown, but also New York City, promptly took up the fight. Not content with merely criticizing Cooper's action in his home town, it proceeded to criticize very severely Cooper's criticism of American ways and manners found in his two books, "Homeward Bound" and "Home as Found."

Among the New York newspapers which thus criticized Cooper were *The Courier and Enquirer*, edited by James Watson

Webb, and *The Commercial Advertiser*, edited by William L. Stone. Cooper promptly brought suit against them both. In his action against Colonel Webb, his suit was for criminal libel and the jury returned the verdict of not guilty. Cooper found that it was much harder to send a man to jail for libel than it was to collect monetary damage for a reputation. Cooper therefore had better success when he brought suit against Thurlow Weed, the editor of *The Albany Evening Journal*, who published several unfavorable notices about Cooper and his books. Weed at the time of the suit was unable to be present on account of sickness in his family and a verdict of four hundred dollars against him was given to Cooper. Weed sought in vain to have the case reopened. Finding himself unsuccessful, he proceeded to set forth his case in a letter to *The New York Tribune* published on November 17, 1841. For the publication of this letter Cooper brought suit against Greeley for libel. The jury, after several ballots, finally returned the verdict of two hundred dollars. Greeley having attended the trial in person proceeded to report the event for his own paper. The report came within three quarters of a column of filling the entire inside of *The Tribune*, which he headed "The Cooperage of *The Tribune*." Extracts were printed in more than two hundred papers and the novelist proceeded to bring suit for a new libel — several of them, in fact. Greeley, now thoroughly aroused, prepared to take the suits more seriously and hired the Honorable William H. Seward as his attorney. The latter, by various hearings on demurrer and by numerous expensive interlocutory proceedings, prevented the case coming to trial.

PRESS RESTRICTIONS OF THE SENATE

The Senate in 1841 attempted to exclude reporters from its Chamber on the ground that the regulations provided only for the admission of representatives from Washington newspapers. This attempt of exclusion was the last stand to favor the party organs of the Capital. For years these organs had been making enormous sums for printing the reports of Congress. Henry Clay asserted that $420,000 was thus paid to the three Washington organs, *The Globe*, run by Blair and Rieves, *The National In-*

telligencer, run by Gales and Seaton, and *The Madisonian*, run by Thomas Allen. James Gordon Bennett, of *The New York Herald*, promptly attacked this favoritism and announced that he was willing to give daily reports at the Senate without any remuneration. Out of his efforts grew the "freedom of the press" for all newspaper correspondents at Washington.

SENSATIONAL NEWS OF THE PERIOD

In 1843 *The United States Gazette* published the statistics of the murders and other crimes recorded in its pages from January to July of that year. The account showed over nine hundred accidental deaths, of which fully one half came from drowning. There were two hundred and fifteen murders by guns, pistols, bowie-knives, etc.; there were fifty-six deaths by firearms which were imprudently handled; forty-five died from clothing taking fire; forty-six were struck by lightning; forty-three were killed by falling from horses or by the upsetting of carriages, etc.; eighty-three committed suicide. From this account, which was copied by many newspapers to show that they had not been beaten in recording such catastrophes, it is evident that the newspapers even at this time were not neglecting the so-called sensational news.

PARTY PATRONAGE VS. "THE POST"

As late as 1835 the National Government still exerted a tremendous influence through its patronage in moulding American newspapers. Party organs were kept strictly in line by the threat which continually hung over them of "Stop the Government advertising." Bribes for party support were fairly numerous. Criticism of any department of the Government was dangerous. For example, because *The New York Evening Post* criticized the seditious doctrines of the Postmaster-General in the matter of the destruction of Northern papers circulated in the South, the official list of letters uncalled for in the New York Post-Office was transferred to *The New York Times* (not the paper which bears that name to-day). Because *The New York Evening Post* believed the tone of a letter of the Secretary of the Treasury to the President of the United States Bank was undignified, the Treasury Department withheld its advertising in *The Post*. Because *The New York Evening Post* thought the Secretary of the Navy had acted with gross partiality in a naval court-martial, advertising from that department in *The Post* was promptly cancelled. Because *The Evening Post* exposed the duplicity of the Collector of the Port of New York, it lost the advertising supplied by the Custom House. In view of the "Government patronage" of the day, independence of the press was very expensive in 1835, but William Leggett hewed to an upright line in his *Evening Post* and let the Government patronage chips fall where they would.

ADVERTISING OF THE PERIOD

Before the advent of the penny press the advertiser usually took a "square" in the newspaper for which he paid thirty dollars a year: this amount also included a subscription to the newspaper. After the first year the advertiser sometimes paid and not infrequently he neglected to do so. As the number of advertisers increased, the size of the sheets was enlarged until they became too bulky to hold conveniently in the hands. For this reason they were called by the penny papers "our bed-quilt contemporaries."

The first penny papers asked the same rate of thirty dollars per year for advertising, but the squares were smaller, and the sum did not include a subscription to the paper. Later, the penny papers adjusted their prices for advertising according to a more modern rate card and insisted that advertisers change their copy more frequently. They developed a new field with the small advertiser: what is now called "classified advertising" began to make its appearance.

In their first issues penny papers reprinted somewhat more desirable advertising, such as railroads, steamboats, stagecoaches, etc., and inserted a notice similar to the following — taken from *The New York Daily Bee* : —

The advertisements inserted in this number we insert gratuitously, hoping to obtain the patronage of the advertising public, as this will be our greatest support. We would respectfully request those persons whose advertisements are inserted, if they wish to have them continued to call and make it known.

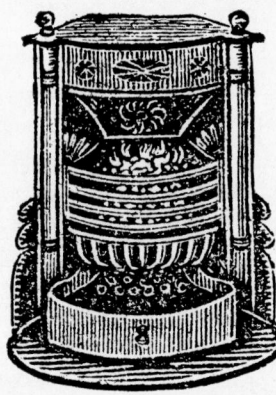

PHILADELPHIA
STOVE
MANUFACTORY,

No. 189 N Second street, two doors below the sign of the Barley Sheaf, between Race and Vine streets.— HENRY J. FOUGERAY respectfully informs the citizens of the U. States that he continues to manufacture an extensive assortment of his Patent Stoves, for burning Lehigh and Schuylkill Coal, for Churches, Halls, Parlours, Kitchens, Offices, &c. together with Nine Plate, Open and Cabin Stoves, Cambouses, Backs, Jams, &c. All of which he will dispose of at low prices.

N.B. Cash given for Old Stoves and Scrap Iron, or taken in exchange.   aug 18-6m

---

Approved Cook Stoves Perpetual Oven, &c.

No. 111 North Second street, Philadelphia.

GEO J. FOUGERAY informs the citizens of the United States that he continues to manufacture his approved Cook Stoves, to burn coal and wood, with stoves for churches, halls, offices, stores, &c.

Also, Perpetual Ovens.

N. B. All kinds of old Stoves and Iron taken in exchange.

ADVERTISEMENTS IN *THE PHILADELPHIA AURORA*
Showing free use of Cuts before the Invention of Cylinder Presses
(*Enlarged*)

The Cartoon

P.T.Avery

English 22

March 20,1928.

Sunday morning in the fraternity. Newspapers strewn all
over. Members perched here,there and everywhere smoking pipes and cigar-
ettes and"looking over"the news. But,strange to say,the real"newsy" parts
of the papers seem to be everywhere.but in the hands of the members. A
glance around shows that everyone is reading the comic cartoons or the
pictorial sections. Silence reigns except for an occasional "next on

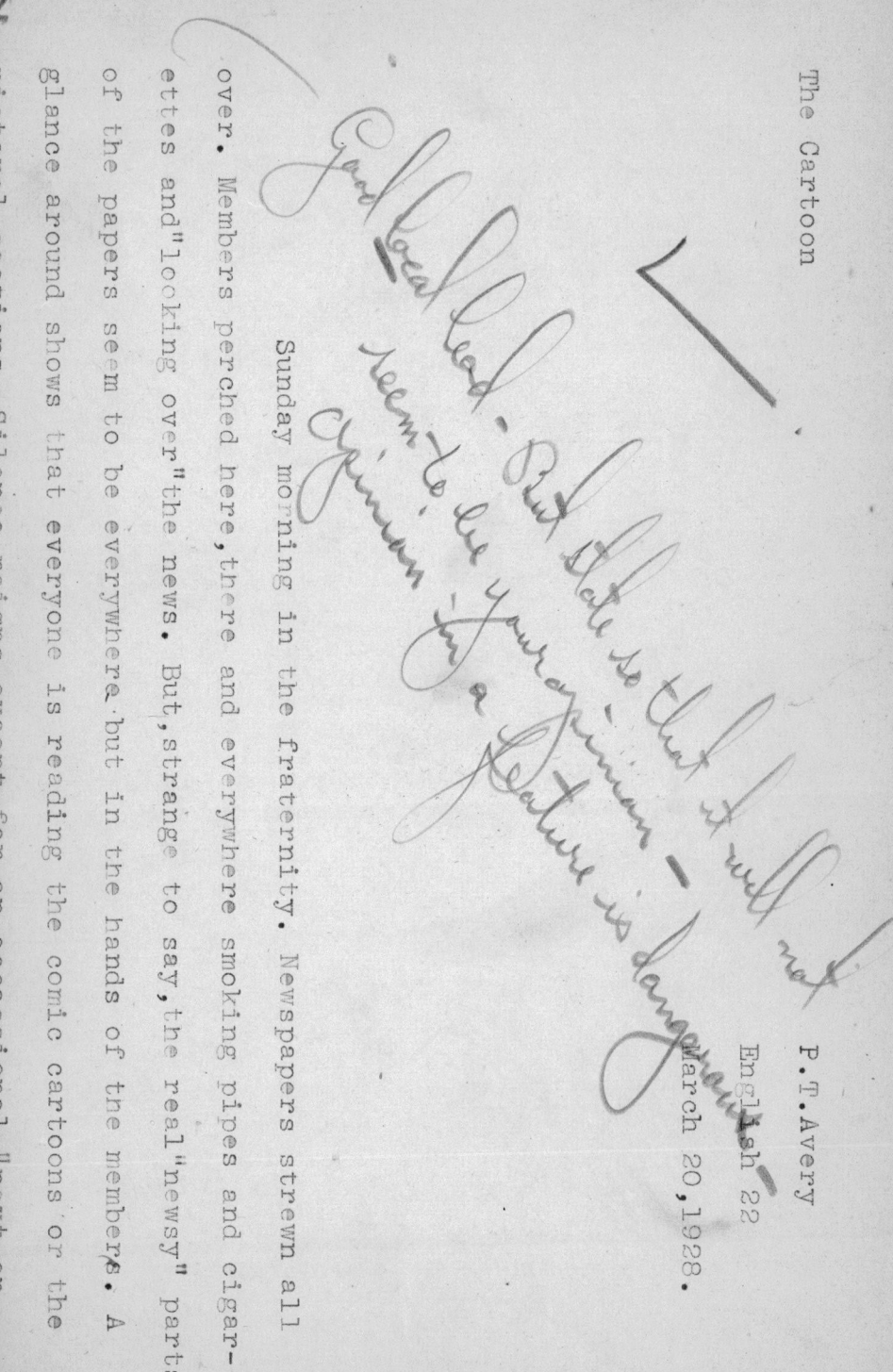

appeal for the union of the colonies for their common defense and security he inserted a cartoon which represented a snake in eight parts. The
parts represented the eight colonies. As a caption he inserted under the
cartoon the words "Unite or die." *[handwritten: period always until quotes]*

This was the first cartoon printed in American papers.
It appeared several times at critical periods in that century. No other
cartoon appeared until after the Revolutionary war. During the period of
the ratification of the Constitution Benjamin Russel of the Massachusetts
Centinel printed a cartoon showing a number of pillars, some standing erect
and some leaning and some prone. Those upright represented the states that
had ratified the Constitution; those leaning were the states who showed
favorable signs of ratifying and those prone were the states which had
made no move of that sort. The roof which the pillars were supporting

represented the union.

During the War of 1812 a good many of the newspapers were active in opposing the war and heaping insults on Madison and his government. They even went so far as to advise the people not to fight even in defense of their country. William Charles, the cartoonist of that period made fun of these opposing papers in his cartoons. These cartoons werer crudely drawn and nowhere near as mechanically perfect as the cartoons we read today but they evidently served their purpose.

Cartoons became more numerous as the American press grew older. Today every issue of every paper contains some cartoons. They are undoubtedly one of the best means of conveying news but how slow they were to develope is evident in their past history.

various sections. There is always this first rush for the "picture papers?"
and then the news gets its share of attention.

This story seems to be true of every house into which a
Sunday paper finds its way. Pictures come first and then the news of the
day. But if we were to go back two hundred years in newspaper history what
a difference we would find. There was no rush for picture sections then
because there were no picture sections. The newspapers contained merely
the actions of the government, some shipping news and some advertisements.
It was not until 1754 that a cartoon or picture of any sort was printed
in the American papers. This was printed by Benjamin Franklin in the
Pennsylvania Gazette.

In 1753 the government of New York issued a call for a
meeting in Albany of the British colonies in America. Rumours of a possible war with France was the cause of this action. Franklin was one of
the three commissioners chosen to represent Pennsylvania. As a forceful

Legal notices found in six-penny contemporaries were reprinted by the cheaper papers and bills mailed to county officials. Although unauthorized, these bills were paid because politicians did not dare to offend the penny sheets who were in a position to expose the petty grafts of the period. Before the type-revolving cylinder press made its appearance, many of the newspapers were so profusely illustrated that they resembled catalogues rather than newspapers. Some of the more fastidious sheets seriously objected to the use of these cuts which gave such a black appearance to the newspaper, and charged extra for their insertion even though no extra mechanical labor was involved.

EPIDEMIC OF MEDICINAL ADVERTISING

During the Colonial Period the newspaper publisher was often a seller of medicines. There were several reasons for this; one was that the colonial printer was forced by necessity to supplement the income from his press by that from other sources; medicinal preparations, then, as now, allowed large profits. In the second place, the early settler was forced by isolation to be his own doctor. What was more natural, therefore, than that the post-rider who brought *The Gazette* should also bring household remedies for cases of emergency. It made matters easier when both these items could be purchased at the same shop. The American, forced by necessity to be his own doctor, soon came to be his own doctor from choice. All that was needed to increase the sale of pills and powders was an epidemic of bodily ills. This "curse" came at about the time that the masses were getting the penny press. An epidemic of dancing swept across the country. Previously, balls had been confined to the more aristocratic gatherings, but dances became popular with the mechanics, the gatherers of ashes, the clerks in shops, etc. Economists who have studied this period of American history say that the amount spent on balls by all manner of society was simply enormous. Dancing was prolonged into the morning hours. Ventilation of ballrooms was then so poor that the result was a flood of almost all ills to which the human body is heir. Manufacturers of proprietary medicines found they could reap a fortune by advertising their nostrums in the public

press. They did so and on the profits of the sales of such medicines were founded some of the large fortunes of later years.
Some of the concoctions of this period were simply colored water
and were absolutely harmless; but others contained absolute
poisons. The injurious effect of such widespread doping was
checked by threatened legislation by various States. In this way
the worst of the positively injurious "remedies" were eliminated
from the advertising columns, but the press, not only in the
rural sections, but also in the cities, continued its partnership
in dosing the American people. Many newspaper men actually
wrote the advertisements; for instance, Henry Jarvis Raymond,
who later became the distinguished founder of *The New York
Times*, increased his income by writing daily advertisements of
medicinal pills for a quack doctor for which he received a remuneration of fifty cents for each piece of copy.

As late as 1881 Charles Dudley Warner complained that the
newspaper columns "outshine the shelves of the druggist in the
display of proprietary medicines." Many excellent newspapers,
for thirty years after this remark, continued to be, so far as the
advertising columns were concerned, directories of patent medicines until Samuel Hopkins Adams, in a series of articles in
Collier's Weekly, entitled "The Great American Fraud," exposed
the chicanery of patent medicine manufacturers and the worth-
lessness of many of their concoctions.

FEDERAL SUPERVISION ADVOCATED

By a ruling of the Postmaster-General, Amos Kendall, in 1835,
the coaches having mail contracts were not permitted to carry
passengers on their Western trips until provision was made for
all the mail matter addressed to the West. Similar restrictions
were placed upon the mail routes along the Atlantic seaboard.
When the newspapers in the North began to advocate the abolition of slavery it raised a howl of protest in the South. Charleston, in South Carolina, particularly objected to the circulation of
such newspapers. The postmaster in that city held such newspapers in his office pending instructions from the Postmaster-
General. The latter side-stepped the question by saying that he
had no legal authority to issue instructions on this technical

point. Before the Department handed out a ruling, a public meeting was held and a resolution unanimously adopted that all incendiary newspapers held at Charleston should be burned and that the mails in the State should be searched and every attempt be made to suppress inflammatory newspapers, and suggested the propriety of passing a law that would prohibit under severe penalties the circulation in Southern States of newspapers which tended to instigate the slaves to insurrection.

President Jackson, in his Inaugural Message, advocated the right of Federal supervision of newspapers. This recommendation by President Jackson was referred by the Senate to a committee of which the chairman was John C. Calhoun, of South Carolina. Speaking for the committee, Calhoun reported on February 14, 1826, that it was not up to Congress to decide when newspapers were incendiary, for they might also decide they were not, and thus laden the mails of the South with papers advocating abolition. He insisted that it belonged to the Southern States and not to Congress to determine what newspapers should circulate in that section. He also proposed that it should not be lawful for any postmaster in any State or Territory of the United States knowingly to deliver to any person any newspaper touching the subject of slavery. Calhoun's recommendations were put in a bill which was ordered to a third reading in the Senate by a vote of 18 to 16, but it failed to pass.

STATISTICAL RÉSUMÉ

The Postal Department requested *The Globe* to publish the following information — doubtless to be paid for at regular rates — about the newspapers and periodicals published in the United States, July 1, 1839: —

Maine	41
New Hampshire	26
Vermont	31
Massachusetts (at Boston, 65)	124
Rhode Island	14
Connecticut	31
New York (at New York City, 71)	274
New Jersey	39

Maryland (at Baltimore, 20)	48
Pennyslvania (at Philadelphia, 71)	253
Delaware	3
District of Columbia (at Washington, 11)	16
Virginia (at Richmond, 10)	52
North Carolina	30
South Carolina	20
Georgia	33
Florida Territory	9
Alabama	34
Mississippi	36
Louisiana (at New Orleans, 10)	26
Arkansas	4
Tennessee	50
Kentucky	31
Ohio (at Cincinnati, 27)	164
Michigan	31
Wisconsin Territory	5
Iowa Territory	3
Indiana	69
Illinois	33
Missouri	25
	1555

The account then went on to say that of the above publications, 116 were daily newspapers, 14 tri-weeklies, 30 semi-weeklies, and 991 weeklies. The rest were semi-monthlies, monthlies, and quarterlies — principally magazines and reviews. Mention was also made of the fact that many of the daily papers were also publishers of the tri-weeklies, semi-weeklies, and weeklies. Of the newspapers, 38 were in the German language, 4 in French, and 1 in Spanish. Attention was also called to the fact that several of the New Orleans papers were printed in French and English.

The statistics of the newspaper press made an interesting feature in the returns of the Seventh Census. From that it appeared that the whole number of newspapers and periodicals in the United States, on the first day of June, 1850, amounted to 2800. From calculations made on the statistics returned, it appeared that the aggregate circulation of these 2800 papers and periodicals was about 5,000,000.

The following table, taken from an abstract of the Census Report, shows the numbers of daily, weekly, monthly, and other issues with the aggregate circulation of each class in 1850: —

```
350....Dailies.............................750,000....Circulation
150....Tri-weeklies........................75,000....     "
125....Semi-weeklies.......................80,000....     "
2000...Weeklies...........................2,875,000....   "
50.....Semi-monthlies.....................300,000....     "
100....Monthlies..........................900,000....     "
25.....Quarterlies.........................20,000....     "
```

W. T. Coggeshall, State Librarian of Ohio in 1856, compiled the following table, which shows approximately newspaper statistics from 1776 to the close of the period: —

	1776	1810	1828	1840
Maine			29	36
Massachusetts	7	32	78	91
New Hampshire	1	12	17	27
Vermont		14	21	30
Rhode Island	2	7	24	16
Connecticut	4	11	33	33
New York	4	66	161	245
New Jersey		8	22	33
Pennsylvania	9	72	185	187
Delaware		2	4	6
Maryland	2	21	37	45
District of Columbia		6	9	14
Virginia	2	23	34	51
North Carolina	2	10	20	27
South Carolina	3	10	16	17
Georgia	1	13	18	34
Florida		1	2	10
Alabama			10	28
Mississippi		4	6	30
Louisiana		10	9	34
Tennessee		6	8	46
Kentucky		17	23	38
Ohio		14	66	123
Indiana			17	73
Michigan			2	32
Illinois			4	43
Missouri			5	35
Arkansas			1	9
Wisconsin				6
Iowa				4
Total	37	359	861	1403

CHAPTER XIV

BEGINNINGS IN STATES AND TERRITORIES

1833—1873

ALL the editors who had joined the Westward advance in journalism had one characteristic in common: they had the most sublime faith that the section where they settled was to become an influential part of the country at large. In the code of these pioneer editors, optimism was ever present. Such a quality was necessary, for often preparations were made to bring out a newspaper before a sufficient number of subscribers to support the enterprise had arrived on the scene. The homes of these pioneer newspapers were at the start to be found in the rude tent of the camper, the dug-out of the prairie, and the log cabin of the mountain.

Often the story of these beginnings is more interesting than the contents of the newspapers. But few copies of the earliest papers in the territory covered in this chapter have been preserved. The greatest loss, however, was not that of the printed sheets, but that of the written precursors which were sold on the mountain trails and paid for with gold taken in tin pans from the bed of a neighboring stream. In the South printing materials came by way of Mexico: in the Far West they went with the immigrant train over the desert: on the Pacific Coast they came by ship around Cape Horn.

Before making any criticism of the contents of these early papers, one must remember that the men who blazed the trail through Western wilds were not discriminating readers. They cared more for interesting subject-matter than for literary mode of treatment. Their respect was commanded only by the editor who could fight with his gun as well as with his pen. Illustrations in proof of the assertion just made will be found in the pages which follow.

EARLY WISCONSIN WEEKLIES

The frontier printer occasionally started his paper before the arrival of other settlers. With intuitive foresight he seemed to know probable locations of settlements along rivers and at the junction of smaller streams. Typical of papers thus established was *The Mirror* of Newport, one of the pioneer papers of Wisconsin, but by no means the first. Its editor, Alanson Holly, very graphically mirrored the Westward movement of journalism in his salutatory greeting: —

' We are doing what, perhaps, has never been done in the United States before — We are printing *The Wisconsin Mirror* in the woods. Not a dwelling, except our own, within half a mile of us, and only one within a mile. The forest oaks hang over our office and dwelling, the deer and rabbits shy around us, and the partridges and quails seek our acquaintance, by venturing nearer and nearer our doors. The noble Wisconsin is bearing onward its immense burdens of ice, majestically and silently, within sight of our windows; and the snow-capped hills, covered with scattering oaks and pines, peer up in the distance. There is romance and reality in all this, and we feel almost willing to publish a paper in such a location, just for the excitement of the thing. But most of the romance is soon to be spoiled. Already, several dwellings are in progress near us and before many weeks they are to be occupied by enterprising neighbors, and when spring and summer shall come, we expect such a chatter of axes and spades, and trowels, and saws, and hammers, that we shall hardly be able to write our editorials without introducing more or less confusion. The fact is, we expect a large village, yea, a city, to grow up rapidly around us; and that is why we are here — printing in the woods.

Mr. Holly was in error when he thought his paper was the first to be printed "in the woods." Other papers had been started under conditions even more primitive with the type set under the oaks themselves.

Not infrequently the paper was published to advertise the attractions of the settlement and to promote immigration. For these reasons D. H. Richards founded in July, 1836, *The Milwaukee Advertiser*, the first paper in the city and the third in the State. Incidentally, *The Advertiser* was also issued to advance the interest of the Milwaukee and Rock River Canal. In March,

1841, Richards sold the paper to Josiah A. Noolan, who changed its name to *The Courier*. The latter was succeeded by *The Wisconsin*.

Pioneer papers were invariably begun as weeklies, but even then they were often irregular in appearance. Such was the case of *The Green Bay Intelligencer*, the first paper in Wisconsin Territory, begun on December 11, 1833, by John V. Suydam and Albert Ellis. The following year the latter, becoming the sole proprietor, continued as publisher until June 1, 1835, when he accepted C. P. Arndt as a partner. In August, 1836, *The Intelligencer* united with *The Wisconsin Free Press*, which had been in existence just a year and was the second paper in Wisconsin, to form *The Democrat*. In the spring of 1840 the paper last mentioned went to Kenosha, where it was published as *The Telegraph*.

GENESIS OF KANSAS JOURNALISM

Kansas ever has been, and is, a great newspaper State. Its journalism, in the strict sense of that term, dates from March 1, 1835, when there appeared at the Baptist Mission *The Shawanoe Sun*. Published exclusively in the Indian language, it was a small quarter-sheet edited by the Reverend Johnston Lykins and printed on the Mission press by Jotham Meeker. In the spring of 1837, when Meeker went to the Ottawa Mission in Franklin County, the paper was printed by J. G. Pratt until 1839, when it was discontinued on account of the illness of its publisher. The old-fashioned press of the Mission was later taken to Prairie City and used to print *The Freeman's Champion* first issued on June 25, 1857, in a home-made tent, the gift of the women of that place.

The earliest English newspaper in Kansas was *The Kansas Weekly Herald*, first brought out in Leavenworth on September 15, 1854, by Osborn Adams. It was started before there was a single permanent building in Leavenworth: only four temporary tents had been raised before a type-setter was at work, under an old elm tree, on the first number. An editorial remark in the first issue said: "Our editorials have been written and our proof corrected while sitting on the ground with a big shingle for a table." In 1859 it became a daily, but suspended in 1861 on the death of its owner.

The same year that *The Kansas Weekly Herald* was started, a second paper, *The Pioneer*, was begun at Kickapoo. The next year saw three established at Lawrence. The first of these, started on January 5, 1855, by John Spear, was *The Kansas Tribune.* In November it suspended for a few weeks and later removed to Topeka. On January 6, 1855, just one day after *The Tribune* was founded, *The Herald of Freedom* appeared at Lawrence under the direction of George W. Brown. One number of the paper, dated October 21, 1854, had been printed at Wakarusa, Pennsylvania. After publishing this issue, Brown moved to Lawrence, where, with the help of a few settlers, he set up a log printing-office. The third paper to be established at Lawrence in 1855 was *The Kansas Free State.* Both *The Free State* and *The Herald of Freedom* figured conspicuously in the exciting times of '55 and '56.

In striking contrast to these papers published at Lawrence was *The Squatter Sovereign*, started on February 3, 1855, at Atchison by John H. Stringfellow and Robert S. Kelly. In a way the paper was the successor of *The Democratic Platform,* which Kelly had published at Liberty, Missouri, in the interest of slavery. *The Squatter Sovereign* was practically the organ of the Border Ruffians and fought most bitterly the Free State papers then in existence in "bleeding Kansas." After the exciting years of '55 and '56, *The Squatter Sovereign* passed into the hands of other owners who gave it another name and reversed its editorial policies. One of the earliest, if not the first, daily paper published west of the Missouri River was *The Daily Kansas Freeman* begun at Shawnee on October 24, 1855. The times were evidently too exciting and the threats of the Border Ruffians to destroy the paper were too frequent to warrant a continuance of the sheet, for it suspended on November 7.

DAWN OF NEW MEXICO JOURNALISM

In strict accuracy the first newspaper printed in New Mexico was *El Crepusculo (The Dawn)* and was first published by Antonio José Martínez in Taos, November 29, 1835. But four numbers of *El Crepusculo* were issued and these were on paper the size of foolscap. The paper failed to pay expenses and was suspended after the four issues.

The first newspaper, however, to be printed in English, either in whole or in part, was *The Santa Fé Republican*. This paper was a four-page weekly in two parts — two in Spanish and two in English — and made its appearance in Santa Fé on September 4, 1847. Its publishers were Hovey and Davies and its editor, G. R. Gibson.

The New Mexican was started at Santa Fé on December 1, 1849, by Davies and Hones. This paper, however, is not to be confused with the present *New Mexican*, started by Charles Leiv on January 22, 1863.

INITIAL PAPERS OF IOWA

The first paper in Iowa was *The Dubuque Visitor*, brought out at the Dubuque Lead Mines, at that time in Wisconsin Territory, by John King on May 11, 1836. He had founded the Dubuque Lead Mine in 1834 and was satisfied that the little village would grow and become a prosperous city. Having purchased in Cincinnati a hand-press, some type, and material sufficient to issue a small weekly paper, he returned to Dubuque. William Carey Jones, a young printer from Chillicothe, accompanied King to take charge of the mechanical side of the paper. On June 3, 1837, a new owner changed the title to *The Iowa News*, and the name of the paper was again changed on August 1, 1841, to *The Miner's Express*. When on April 19, 1851, a new publication, *The Dubuque Herald*, appeared, *The Miner's Express* made preparation to bring out a daily paper. On August 19 of that year it published the first daily paper north of St. Louis or west of the Mississippi. *The Herald* met this move by also changing to a daily paper and the competition became so keen between the two that a merger became necessary and on October 26, 1854, the two papers united under the title, *The Daily Express and Herald* — later changed to *The Daily Herald*. On August 27, 1901, the paper absorbed *The Dubuque Daily Telegraph*. The paper is now continued as *The Telegraph and Herald*.

The second paper in Iowa was started at Mount Rose in 1836 by Dr. Isaac Glalland. He called his paper *The Western Adventurer*. After a struggle of two years he took it to Fort Madison, where it was purchased by James G. Edwards, who, on March 24, 1838, converted it to a Whig sheet called *The Fort Madison Patriot*. The paper was finally moved to Burlington where it is now known as *The Hawk-Eye*. On August 4, 1838, *The Iowa Sun and Davenport and Rock Island News* appeared simultaneously at Davenport, Iowa, and at Stephenson (now Rock Island, Illinois), and was published by Andrew Logan. The fourth paper was *The Iowa Standard*, first brought out at Bloomington October 23, 1840, and a year later removed to Iowa City.

The Iowa Standard was only four days ahead of *The Bloomington Herald*, issued on October 27, 1840, with Thomas Hughes and John B. Russell as editors. This paper, after some changes, became *The Muscatine Journal*, under which name it is still published. *The Courier* was established at Fort Madison by R. Wilson Albright on July 24, 1841.

INDIAN PAPERS OF OKLAHOMA

To the Cherokees unquestionably belongs the honor of printing the first and many of the early papers in what was the Indian Territory but is now the State of Oklahoma. The first of these was *The Cherokee Messenger*, started in August, 1844, at Cherokee Baptist Mission. Edited by the Reverend Evan Jones, it was more of a religious and temperance pamphlet than a newspaper: printed at irregular intervals it might more justly be considered the precursor of journalism in the Indian Territory.

The first real newspaper was the national organ of the Cherokee Nation. Its National Council on October 25, 1843, had passed an act to establish a printing-press and to print a newspaper, and on September 26, 1844, there appeared at Tahlequah the first number of *The Cherokee Advocate*. Under the editorship of William P. Ross it was printed in both the English and Cherokee languages. The Cherokee Nation fixed the subscription price at three dollars per year "except to those persons who read only the Cherokee language and they shall pay two dollars."

The paper was discontinued in 1853, but was revived again in 1870.

Another Indian Journal, *The Vindicator*, was started by J. H. Moore at New Boggy in June, 1872, in the interest of the Choctaws and Chickasaws. It afterwards united with *The Oklahoma Star*. Still another Indian paper was *The Indian Journal*, first begun in May, 1876, at Muskogee by M. P. Roberts. It was the official organ of the Creek Nation.

The Territorial Advocate, started at Beaver by E. E. Eldridge in May, 1887, was the first real English newspaper in Oklahoma and had the distinction of being probably the only newspaper ever published in the United States outside the pale of established law of any character. The pan-handle portion of the State of Oklahoma, in which Beaver is located, was prior to 1889 known as "No Man's Land." *The Advocate* is now published under the name of *The Beaver Herald*.

The first paper after the Territory was opened was one issue of *The Guthrie Get-Up*, on April 29, 1889. It was a small sheet folded in the center and printed only on one side. Having only one issue it is not, strictly speaking, to be classed as a newspaper. Its immediate successor was *The Oklahoma State Capitol*, started in Guthrie a little later. The latter paper survived until 1911 when it was taken over by *The Guthrie Daily Leader*.

ORIGIN OF JOURNALISM IN OREGON

Oregon City, in 1844, thought it ought to have a newspaper. Accordingly, a company was formed known as the Oregon Printing Association. According to the articles of compact, the following regulation was set down for the guidance of the editor: "The press owned by, or in connection with, this Association shall never be used by any party for the purpose of propagating sectarian principles or doctrines; nor for the discussion of exclusive party politics."

As soon as a press could be secured from New York, the organization brought out the first newspaper in Oregon on Thursday, February 5, 1846. It was called *The Oregon Spectator* and had for its motto, "Westward the Star of Empire takes its Way." Its first editor was Colonel William G. T'Vault, who was then Postmaster-General of the Provisional Government, and its first printer was John Fleming, who had immigrated to Oregon in 1844. T'Vault did not sit long in the editorial chair, for on April 16, 1846, the name of Henry A. G. Lee appeared as the editor. He had been the original choice of the Oregon Printing Association, but had wanted a salary of six hundred dollars, which was considered too exorbitant. Mr. Lee, a descendant of Richard Lee, of Virginia, did not preside over the editorial columns much longer than his predecessor, for he severed his relations with the issue of August 6, 1846. For two months following, John Fleming, the printer, was the editor of the paper.

Early in October, George L. Curry, who had come to the Territory of Oregon by way of the Cow Creek Canyon, took up the editorial reins and tried to direct the editorial policies with a "firm and consistent American tone." In his attempts to put his theories into practice he was severely handicapped by the seigniorship exercised by the Oregon Printing Association. So strained became the relations between the editor and publishers of the paper that Mr. Curry resigned in 1848. After leaving *The Spectator*, Mr. Curry decided to start a rival newspaper and accordingly bought about eighty pounds of type from the Catholic Missionaries. Having no press, and being unwilling to wait until one could be secured from the East, he constructed one of a rude sort chiefly out of wood and scrap iron. The type which he had purchased from the Catholic Missionaries, and which had been used to print religious tracts in French, had but few letter "w's." This obstacle was overcome by whittling a number out of hard wood. The typographical appearance of the paper printed with an occasional handmade "w" may well be imagined.

Curry's paper was called *The Free Press* and lasted until October, 1848, when it ceased publication, largely on account of the wild rush of subscribers to the mines in the Territory. Incidentally, it may be said that Curry was appointed Governor of the Territory of Oregon in 1854 and held that office until 1859. On January 1, 1861, he joined forces with S. J. McCormick, of *The Portland Daily Advertiser*, started on May 31, 1859. The first daily, however, was *The Daily News*, begun by S. A. English and W. B. Taylor, April 18, 1859, in Portland. After Curry left *The Spectator*, Aaron E. Wait, a native of Massachusetts, became the editor and on February 10, 1848, he enlarged the paper to twenty-four columns.

On September 7 it was necessary to suspend publication because its printer, John Fleming, had left for the mines. The paper appeared again, however, on October 12, with S. Bentley as printer and with the following note of apology: —

The Spectator, after a temporary sickness, greets its patrons and hopes to serve them faithfully and, as heretofore, regularly. "That gold fever" which has swept about three thousand of the officers, lawyers, physicians, farmers, and mechanics of Oregon from the Plains of Oregon into the mines of California, took away our printer — hence the temporary non-appearance of *The Spectator*.

Mr. Wait left *The Spectator* with the issue of February 22, 1849. Soon after the paper suspended publication for a time, but on October 4, 1849, the Reverend Wilson Blain, a Presbyterian clergyman, revived the paper. On April 18, 1850, Robert Moore became the owner of *The Spectator*, but he retained Blain as its editor.

On September 12, D. J. Schnebly became the editor and about a year later, on September 9, 1851, he became the owner. *The Spectator* frequently had trouble in getting a supply of white paper on which to print the news and had to change its size. In 1852 it became a distinctly political newspaper to plead the cause of the Whig Party. It failed to receive sufficient support and was compelled to suspend on March 16, 1852. Even after it was revived in August, 1853, the paper was not well supported and finally had to be sold to C. L. Goodrich in the latter part of 1854. With the permanent suspension of *The Spectator* in March, 1855, the history of the first paper in Oregon ends.

A month later, however, W. L. Adams, one of the pioneers of 1847, used the plant, starting *The Oregon City Argus* on April 21, 1855. According to the best information obtainable, this was the first real Republican paper, not only in Oregon, but also on the Pacific Coast. Mr. Adams, needing a printer, employed David W. Craig, who had been working on *The Oregon Statesman*. Starting in as a foreman, Mr. Craig became the owner of *The Argus* on April 16, 1859, but he retained his former employer as editor until October 24, 1863. On that date *The Statesman* and *The Argus* consolidated and continued publication under the name of *The Statesman*.

The Western Star was the fourth paper published in Oregon. This paper was first published at Milwaukie, on November 21, 1850, but in May, 1851, was moved to Portland. Here the name *The Western Star* was dropped and a new one, *The Oregon Weekly Times*, was selected for the issue of June 5, 1851.

The Weekly Oregonian, the fifth paper in Oregon, was started December 4, 1850, at Portland. Its press was purchased in 1852 by T. F. McElroy and J. W. Wiley, who took it to Olympia and on it printed *The Columbian*, the first paper north of the Columbia River. The first issue was dated Saturday, September 11, 1852. Six months later the editor told of his struggles as follows: "We commenced publication without a subscriber and without a dollar. Since that time we have kept 'batch,' done our own cooking and our own washing, our own mending, cut our own wood, made our own fires, washed our own dishes, swept out our own office, made up our own bed, and composed our own editorials out of the cases — writing paper being luxuries which we have been deprived of — and done our own press work. Now we have three hundred and fifty subscribers." Under such difficulties were some of the earlier papers on the Pacific Coast produced.

CATHOLIC AND MORMON PRESSES OF CALIFORNIA

At Monterey, Robert Semple, former editor of *The Philadelphia North American*, and the Reverend Walter Colton, Chaplain of the United States Frigate Congress, brought out the first paper in California on August 15, 1846. It was most appropriately called *The Californian*. In a book which Colton later published, he described his partner at the time the paper was brought out as follows: "He is in buck-skin dress and fox-skin cap; he is true with his rifle, ready with his pen and quick at the type-case."

Colton once asserted that the materials in his office had been used by a Roman Catholic monk in printing a few sectarian tracts; that the press was old enough to preserve as a curiosity, and that the types were all in pi and were so rusty that it was only by hard scouring that the letters could be made to show their faces. There were no rules or leads, and in their absence two or three sheets of tin were cut with the help of a jack-knife for substitutes. Fortunately, there was enough ink for the press, but unfortunately no paper. A supply of paper sent to California to be used to wrap cigars was purchased from a coaster, and on these sheets, not much larger than the common-sized foolscap, was printed the first issue of *The Californian*. One half of the paper was in English, the other in Spanish, and single copies sold for twelve and one half cents — considered cheap at that. The first issue contained a declaration of war between the United States and Mexico with an account of a debate in the Senate.

The Californian after six months boasted that it had been able to meet expenses, but in spite of this assertion it was forced to move from Monterey to Yerba Buena, — now San Francisco, — where on May 22, 1847, it issued the first number of its second volume with Robert Semple as its sole publisher. Before this change of place of publication, another paper had already been started at Yerba Buena called *The California Star*, first issued on January 7, 1847. It was published by Samuel Brannan and edited by E. P. Jones. It was much better printed than *The Californian*, and in spite of the fact that its press was brought to California by the Mormons it announced that it would eschew sectarian discussions and confine itself strictly to the news. *The Star* was used extensively to boom California and extra editions were printed for circulation in other States.

The Star and *The Californian* were merged on January 4, 1849, into *The Alta California*.

PIONEERS OF MINNESOTA

The first newspaper in Minnesota was announced in its prospectus as *The Epistle of St. Paul*. When the paper appeared, however, it bore the name of *The Minnesota Pioneer*, and was published at St. Paul, April 28, 1849. It was a four-page, six-column sheet for the first few months, but in October it was enlarged to seven columns. Its editor and owner was James M. Goodhue, a native of Hebron, New Hampshire. He has been aptly described as "the James Gordon Bennett of Minnesota."

The early issues were printed under difficulties. The only available printing-office was the basement of the only public house in St. Paul. The editor in describing his early experiences said that it was as open as a corn crib, and that the pigs in seeking shelter under the floor frequently jostled the loose boards on which rested the editorial chair of *The Minnesota Pioneer*.

Such editorial assertions as, "He stole into the Territory; He stole in the Territory, and then stole out of the Territory," got Goodhue into serious difficulties — difficulties out of which he escaped only with the help of his fist and a pistol. Like James Gordon Bennett, he published full accounts in *The Pioneer*. An editorial tribute published in *The Pioneer* on September 1, 1853, says of Goodhue, "Many of his editorials would have done no discredit to *The New York Herald* in its most palmy days." Goodhue died on August 27, 1852. His successor was Joseph R. Brown.

Other early papers of Minnesota may be briefly mentioned. The second was *The Minnesota Chronicle*, first published May 31, 1849, at St. Paul, with James Hughes, a former resident of Ohio, as its editor and proprietor. It was a Whig paper of the same size of *The Minnesota Pioneer*. The third paper, *The Minnesota Register*, had its first issue in St. Paul on July 14, 1849, though an earlier number had been printed in Cincinnati, Ohio, dated Saturday, April 27, 1849, and had been sent by steamboat to St. Paul for distribution. A monthly missionary sheet was the fourth paper: printed half in English and half in the Dakota language, it was called *The Dakota Friend*. Goodhue made an interesting comment in his paper on March 6, 1851, when he said, "The little press at *The Chronicle* office has been horribly twisted and distorted by printing the crooked Sioux dialect of *The Friend*." Colonel B. A. Robertson brought out the fifth paper, *The Minnesota Democrat*. In order to give the people of the other side a newspaper, Elmer Huyler, a tailor of St. Anthony, — now Minneapolis, — issued on May 31, 1851, *The St. Anthony Express*, the sixth newspaper. Other papers, arranged in the order of their establishment, were *The Minnesotian*, first published on September 17, 1851; *The North Western Democrat*, first published on July 13, 1853; *The Minnesota Times*, first published on May 15, 1854; *The Minnesota Republican*, first published on October 5, 1854; *The St. Paul Financier and Real Estate Advertiser*, first published on November 3, 1854. The papers just mentioned make the first eleven newspapers to be published in Minnesota. Of these, only *The Minnesota Pioneer* now survives and even that paper has undergone so many changes that it now bears the title of *The Dispatch Pioneer Press*.

AN OASIS OF JOURNALISM IN UTAH

When the Mormons were expelled from Nauvoo in 1846, they gathered on the banks of the Missouri River near a point where Council Bluffs now stands. From here various bands were dispatched to the Rocky Mountains; one of the earliest of these to leave had a wagon loaded with an old Ramage press, a supply of paper, and a few fonts of type. This outfit was hauled across the plains from the Missouri River to the Salt Lake Valley, a distance of over one thousand miles, by team. Upon its arrival at Salt Lake City, preparations were made for printing *The Deseret News*, to be the official organ of the Church of Jesus Christ of Latter Day Saints — familiarly known as the Mormon Church.

Brigham Young appointed William Richards as editor, Horace K. Whitney as typesetter, and his nephew, Brigham H. Young, as pressman. The first number appeared on June 15, 1850. Its motto was, "Truth and Liberty," and its price, fifteen cents per copy. Travelers and immigrants were charged twenty-five cents per copy, but this amount included the notice of their names, place of residence, and time of arrival and leaving. The setting-up of a newspaper plant in the wilds of the Rockies, nearly a thousand miles from civilization, before Denver, Omaha, or Kansas City was on the map, and when San Francisco was only a cluster of Mexican shanties, may be taken as a splendid illustration of that spirit which animated the early Mormon pioneers.

Naturally, grave difficulties were encountered in publishing a paper under the conditions just outlined. Currency was scarce, but *The News* accepted "flour, wheat, corn meal, butter, tea, tallow, and pork" in exchange for subscriptions. For years it made its own supply of paper from rags gathered in the early settlements of Utah. Most of its foreign news was obtained from Eastern papers brought by chance visitors on their way to the California gold fields. Not infrequently it apologized for absence of such items with a note like the following: "From all the immigrants we were not able to obtain one whole paper: they were all wet, damaged or destroyed on the way." In local news it was more fortunate, for at the same time that Brigham Young established *The News* he founded a university, a theatrical association, and an instrumental and vocal society which flourished and spread and from which grew the University of Utah, the famous Salt Lake Theater, and the noted Tabernacle Choir of the present time. The doings of these enterprises filled many a column of *The News*.

The News has been continually printed at Salt Lake City, except during "The Utah War" of 1857–58 when the Governor sent an expedition to that Territory to quell the so-called "Mormon Insurrection." The Mormons moved a second time before the advance of the army, but they always took their newspaper plant with them. The press was installed in a special wagon and wherever the company camped there appeared *The News*. Its longest temporary stop was at Fillmore City, where the first issue dated at that place appeared on May 5, 1858. *The News* was printed as a weekly and later as a semi-weekly until 1867, when it came out daily. *The News* to-day presents a striking contrast to the little pamphlet sheet issued in 1850.

The Daily Telegraph was started in Salt Lake City on July 4, 1864. Five years later it was moved to Ogden, but was discontinued the same year (1869).

When the Pony Express reached Salt Lake City, journalism took a jump. *The Mountaineer* of that city on February 2, 1861, said: "We are favored by the Pony Club of this city with a copy of their telegraphic dispatches bringing dates from New York and Washington up to the 22nd ult."

A curiosity in Utah journalism was *The Manti Herald*, started on January 31, 1867, at Manti, Utah, by F. C. Robinson. This paper was printed entirely by hand and with pen and ink.

WHIG PAPERS OF WASHINGTON

The old-fashioned Ramage press, which had been used to print the first number of *The Oregonian* in Oregon and several early papers of the Pacific Coast, was the press on which was "pulled" the first newspaper in Washington — *The Columbian*. This paper appeared on September 11, 1852, at Olympia, and was edited and owned by J. W. Wiley and Thornton F. McElroy. In March of 1853, Wiley retired, but he again appeared as its editor on December 3. From the start Wiley advocated a separation from Oregon. Through the columns of his paper he arranged a meeting of the more prominent settlers to arrange for the organization of Washington as a territory. (See Oregon papers.)

The Columbian later became *The Washington Pioneer*, and with this change was made over into a radical Democratic journal. Because of its new political affiliation it became in February, 1854, *The Pioneer and Democrat*. It suspended in 1861.

The second paper, a Whig sheet, was started at Steilacoom on May 19, 1855, by William B. Affleck and E. T. Gunn. Called *The Puget Sound Courier*, it lasted about a year, but was revived however, in January, 1871, at Olympia where it became a daily in January, 1872. About two years later, December, 1874, the paper suspended for lack of support, but was revived again as *The Daily Courier* early in 1877.

These pioneer sheets of Washington frequently retailed at fabulous prices — especially when they contained information about the discovery of gold in new fields. Occasionally copies of *The Washington Pioneer* or *The Puget Sound Courier* sold in San Francisco at five to ten dollars a copy. Sometimes the demand for papers was so great that their printers reproduced items about the discovery of gold on thin strips of paper: these news-strips brought just as high prices as complete copies of the paper.

EARLY NEWSPAPERS OF NEBRASKA

The first five papers in Nebraska were printed in Iowa. The first of these, and incidentally, the first printed in Nebraska, was *The Nebraska Palladium*. Number 1 was dated July 15, 1854, and was printed at St. Mary's, a hamlet just below Bellevue on the Iowa shore of the Missouri River. The first number to be printed in Nebraska was that of November 15, 1854. For the privilege of turning off the first number, E. N. Upjohn gave one dollar. From that date on until April 11, 1855, it was a distinctly Nebraska-made publication. While Thomas Morton was its publisher, Daniel Reed & Company were set down as editors and proprietors.

The second paper in Nebraska was *The Omaha Arrow*, dated at Nebraska City, but printed at Council Bluffs, Iowa. It first appeared July 28, 1854, and was discontinued December 29 of that year. Its publishers were J. W. Pattison and J. E. Johnson. The former of these is credited with the honor of being the editor, and doubtless was the author of the following introductory remark in the first issue of the paper: "Well, strangers, friends, patrons, and the good people generally, wherever in the wide world your lot may be cast, and in whatever clime this *Arrow* may reach you, here we are, upon Nebraska soil. Seated upon the stump of an ancient oak, which serves for the editorial chair, and the top of our badly abused beaver for a table, we purpose inditing a leader for *The Omaha Arrow*."

In spite of the fact that *The Arrow* was never printed in Nebraska, it attracted much attention from a contemporary press. In its eleventh issue it published five columns of notes about itself clipped from other newspapers.

On May 5, 1858, *The Nebraska Republican*, dated at Omaha, but printed at Council Bluffs, Iowa, appeared with E. F. Shneider and H. J. Brown as editors and publishers. In 1859 its name was changed to *The Omaha Republican* and E. D. Webster became its editor. *The Nebraska News* was originally printed in Sydney, Iowa, by Dr. Henry Bradford, but on November 14, 1854, it was removed to Nebraska City and published in the second story of the Block House of old Port Kearny. It was owned by the

Nebraska City Town Site Company. Its editor was J. S. Morton, who had formerly been connected with *The Detroit Free Press*.

The Omaha Nebraskan first appeared on January 17, 1855, and was the first newspaper printed at Omaha. It was established by B. B. Chapman. The last issue was on June 15, 1865. The first regular daily was *The Telegraph*, which appeared on December 5, 1860, published simultaneously at Omaha and Council Bluffs. Its life was short, however; it did not last more than a year. On June 19, 1871, Edward Rosewater started *The Bee* at Omaha, Nebraska. *The Herald* had been begun in Omaha, October 2, 1865: it was purchased in 1888 by Gilbert M. Hitchcock.

DÉBUT IN SOUTH DAKOTA

The first newspaper published within the present boundaries of South Dakota was *The Dakota Democrat*, founded at Sioux Falls City, now Sioux Falls, September 20, 1858. Its owner and publisher was Samuel J. Albright. He published the paper, which was a four-page sheet with five columns to the page, rather irregularly until July 2, 1859. After that date he rarely skipped an issue until the autumn of 1860, when he turned the paper over to Mr. Stewart, who changed its name to *The Northwestern Democrat*. The reason for this change was that Albright took with him the original heading of the paper — *The Democrat* — and the new owner was forced to use one which had been previously employed in printing a paper at Sergeant Bluffs, Iowa. When the Indian war broke out in 1862, the settlement of Sioux Falls was abandoned. In sacking the town the Indians destroyed the printing-plant, but carried away most of the type. After peace was declared the type came back again to the whites in the shape of ornaments used to decorate the pipes which the Indians fashioned out of the red pipe stone and sold to the settlers. *The Dakota Democrat* was "the official organ" of the Legislature which first convened at Sioux Falls, 1858–59.

The second paper, *The Weekly Dakotaian*, the oldest continuous newspaper in South Dakota, was established in Yankton, June 6, 1861, by Frank M. Ziebach. In March, 1862, it was sold to J. C. Trask, the first Public Printer. The daily edition was started April 26, 1875. William Kiter started *The Pantegraph* at Sioux Falls in February, 1872. This newspaper was printed on the coöperative plan and was published at irregular intervals until October, when it went into "winter headquarters." It was revived in April, 1873, and was again published with occasional interruptions until the spring of 1877 when the plant was closed by an order of the court. Later, the material of the plant was used in starting *The Roscoe Express*. Of the other early editors of *The Pantegraph*, mention may be made of F. D. Cowles, F. E. Everett, and W. S. Guild.

Another paper in Sioux Falls was *The Independent*, which was first issued on May 15, 1875, by Charles W. McDonald; on January 6, 1881, it was merged with *The Dakota Pantegraph*. Among those who edited the newspaper before this merger were E. A. Sherman, F. E. Everett, W. A. Williams, and L. C. Hitchcock. *The Dakota Pantegraph* was started in Sioux Falls in the spring of 1877 by G. M. Smith and M. Grigsby. The press and type used to bring out this paper had been formerly employed to get out *The Era* at Swan Lake. Grigsby continued as editor until April, 1878, when *The Pantegraph* was sold to Caldwell & Stahl.

Other early papers in South Dakota were *The Dakota Union*, established at Yankton, June 21, 1864, by George W. Kingsbury; *The Press*, at Yankton, August 10, 1870, by George H. Hand; *The Dell City Journal*, established in 1871, was an interesting innovation in the journalism of South Dakota in that this newspaper was printed at Webster City, Iowa, but was issued at Dell Rapids, South Dakota, by J. C. Ervin; *The Advocate*, at Canton, April 26, 1876, by Skinner & Tallman; *The Times*, at Sioux Falls, November 15, 1878, by E. O. Kimberly and C. M. Morse; *The Exponent*, at Dell Rapids, February, 1879, by E. C. Whalen; *The Centinel*, at Madison, April, 1879, by J. H. Zane and F. L. Fifeld; *The Leader*, at Herman, June, 1879, by F. C. Stowe; *The Beadle County Sentinel*, at Huron, March 17, 1880, by John Cain.

WRITTEN NEWSPAPERS OF NEVADA

Among the prospectors who hastened to Nevada after the discovery of gold and silver in that region was Joseph Webb. He was not successful prospecting and settled for a while at the Carson River Crossing where Dayton now stands. Gold had been found there in some quantities and then it became a station for immigrants along the trail on their way to California. Webb gathered up the gossip of the trail, supplemented by what news was told him by passersby, and then with pen and ink made a written newspaper which he sold to travelers, who paid for it with gold dust taken from Carson River with milk-pans and wash-basins. He called his written newspaper *The Golden Switch*. Unfortunately, but few copies of this written newspaper have survived. It was started some time in 1854 and lasted not later than 1858. At about the same time that Webb was getting out his sheet, Stephen A. Kensey was issuing a rival written newspaper called *The Scorpion* in the little village of Genoa at the eastern foot of the Sierra Nevada Mountains.

The first printed newspaper, however, in Nevada was *The Territorial Enterprise*, issued November 18, 1858, at Genoa by Alfred Jones and W. L. Jernegan. On November 5, 1859, it was purchased by Jonathan Williams and J. B. Woolard, who took the paper to Carson City, the Capital of the Territory, and where later it was purchased by Joseph T. Goodman and Dennis E. McCarthy and again moved to Virginia City, where it became the mouthpiece for the mines of that place. Its fortune fared in direct ratio to the prosperity of the mining camps in that vicinity. *The Enterprise* lasted until May 30, 1916, when it was merged with *The Virginia City Chronicle*.

The Enterprise is best remembered as the paper on which Mark Twain worked. In response to a request to attend a reunion at Virginia City, Mr. Clemens wrote: "Those were the days — those old ones. They will come no more. Youth will come no more. They were full to the brim with the wine of life. There have been no others like them. But I cannot come out. Would you like me to come out and cry? It would not become my white head. Good-bye. I drink to you all. Have a good time, take an old man's blessing."

After *The Territorial Enterprise* was moved from Carson City to Virginia City its place was almost immediately taken by *The Silver Age*. The new venture was successful almost from the start because it was favored by the Legislature in the matter of public printing.

The third paper in Carson City was started by W. W. Ross on July 27, 1863. It was called *The Daily Independent* and expired on October 11, 1864.

H. W. Johnson & Company had started *The Daily Evening Post* of Carson City on August 27, 1864. Its appearance had undoubtedly something to do with the death of *The Daily Independent*, because when the latter paper suspended publication *The Evening Post* became a morning paper. In January, 1865, it, too, suspended publication. The following December John C. Lewis, who had been editor of the morning edition of *The Post*, took the plant to Wasshoe City, where he started *The Eastern Slope*. Unsuccessful here, he moved the plant to Reno in July, 1868, where he printed *The Crescent* until 1875. He then sold the paper to J. C. Dow, who commenced *The Daily Nevada Democrat*, which later became *The Reno Daily Record*.

ARRIVAL IN ARIZONA

The first paper in Arizona, *The Weekly Arizonian*, was started at Tubac by Sylvester Moury in all probability on or near March 3, 1859. Number 20 of Volume I, the earliest known issue of this paper, was dated July 14 of that year. The press on which the paper was printed came around the Horn in 1858 and was brought from Guaymas to Tubac by wagon. In 1860 the paper was removed to Tucson where it was published by Jack Simms and George Smithson. It suspended publication in 1861. In advertising the sale of its plant, it included among the office equipment two derringers. This mention, brief as it is, showed a necessary adjunct, along with "shooting-irons," in the office of many of the Western papers. As a matter of fact, one reason for the suspension of the paper was the fact that its publishers were charged with a stage robbery and in resisting arrest one of them was killed.

In 1867 the paper was revived under its old name by W. S.

Moury. Out of this paper grew the present *Citizen* of Tucson. Incidentally, it may be remarked that in the fall of 1879 the old press was taken to Tombstone, where it was used to print *The Nugget*, the first paper in that camp.

The second paper in Arizona was called *The Miner* and was started in Prescott on March 9, 1864, by John H. Marion. Interested in the enterprise was R. C. McCormick, the secretary of the Territory for that year. Beginning in 1866, Marion published *The Daily Arizona Miner* during the session of the Legislature.

The third paper was *The Sentinel*, started in Yuma in 1870.

Among the most interesting of the early Arizona papers was *The Epitaph*, started on May 1, 1880, at Tombstone. Its founders were John P. Clum, the mayor and also the postmaster at Tucson, Charles D. Reppy, and Thomas Sorin. The name of the paper was suggested by John Hayes Hammond, who later became distinguished as one of the foremost mining engineers. He was dining, with the gentlemen who were about to start the paper, at the Can Can Restaurant. When he asked what the name was to be he was informed that no title had as yet been selected. Hammond, recalling a rather exciting adventure which had recently happened, suggested that in view of the character of the news the paper would probably print, there could be no more fitting title than *The Epitaph*. The title was thought very appropriate and was promptly adopted.

When *The Epitaph* was founded there were but six counties in the Territory of Arizona and but ten newspapers printed in the English language. These included *The Nugget* at Tombstone, *The Record*, *The Citizen*, and *The Star* at Tucson, *The Silver Belt* at Globe, *The Salt River Herald and Territorial Expositor* at Phœnix, *The Enterprise* and *The Miner* at Prescott, and *The Sentinel* at Yuma.

ROCKY MOUNTAIN PAPERS OF COLORADO

In Denver *The Rocky Mountain News* has the distinction of being the oldest paper in Colorado. Its first issue was April 23, 1859, in a struggling, home-seekers' settlement which had not yet a definite name. The discovery of placer gold some months earlier had made a settlement at the junction of the Platte River and Cherry Creek. On each bank of the river there was a rival town site, so that William N. Byers very wisely dated his paper as published at Cherry Creek, Denver Territory. The first issue of *The Rocky Mountain News* was printed on brown wrapping-paper. At the start it was published weekly, but later it became a daily. It has been published uninterrupted since its establishment, with a single exception in the early sixties when a flood in Cherry Creek wiped its plant out of existence.

The day *The Rocky Mountain News* started was one of the most exciting in frontier journalism. When the news of the discovery of gold in the "Pike's Peak Region" had reached as far east as the Missouri, it promptly started two small newspaper plants which had for their motto, figuratively speaking, "A newspaper near Pike's Peak, or bust." One left Omaha and was owned by William N. Byers, Thomas Gibson, and John L. Bailey; the other set out from St. Joseph, Missouri, and consisted of the outfit which John L. Merrick had purchased from *The St. Joseph Gazette*. Both outfits had to cross the plains by ox teams.

Merrick was the first to arrive. Not knowing that competitors were on the way, he leisurely commenced preparing for the first issue of *The Cherry Creek Pioneer*. Ten days later the Omaha plant arrived and the competition for the honor of the first paper in Colorado began. The settlement offered a suitable prize to the winner and appointed a committee of citizens to referee the contest. Both *The Rocky Mountain News* and *The Cherry Creek Pioneer* announced their date of first publication April 23, 1859. At ten-thirty o'clock, on the evening of April 23, the first copy of *The News*, a four-page sheet, was pulled from the old Washington hand-press. Other copies soon circulated among the pioneers surrounding the log cabin print-shop. A little later *The Pioneer* also appeared on the streets. The decision of the committee, however, was that *The News* had won by twenty minutes.

Worn out by his efforts and depressed by defeat, Merrick the next morning offered to sell his plant to his rival upon terms which were later accepted. Merrick then set off for the mountains, not to hunt for news, but for gold.

As the pioneer settlement grew into a larger town, *The News* always led in a movement for law and regulation. In his attempts to clear the town of its rougher element, Editor Byers often wrote his editorials and news with a rifle across his knee while armed men guarded his printers. For nineteen years Byers conducted *The News*.

Under difficulties seldom equaled, and never surpassed, he brought out his paper. When the Indian outbreak caused an embargo on traffic over the Western plains in 1864–65, he frequently ran out of white paper, and in such emergencies he printed the news on wrapping-paper, gathered from Denver stores. That he might have the news before the mails from the East arrived in Denver, he established an overland pony express. By means of a relay of horseback riders he had brought the news from the nearest express lines with a speed which to-day almost seems incredible. Of course, it was expensive to run such a private pony express, but *The News* in those days cost forty-four dollars a year and single copies sold for one dollar and twenty-five cents apiece. In 1878 the paper was sold to the Rocky Mountain News Printing Company, with W. A. H. Loveland as editor and principal owner.

Two papers were established in Denver in 1867: the first of these was *The Daily Argus*, begun on October 25; the second, *The Rocky Mountain Star*, begun on December 8. A third attempt was made by N. A. Baker, who, after bringing out a few issues of *The Colorado Leader*, left Denver, to go to Cheyenne, where he founded the first paper in Wyoming.

INFANCY OF IDAHO JOURNALISM

While there was a paper called *The Golden Age*, published at Lewiston, by Frank Kenyon in 1862, the first paper to be published in Idaho after the Territory was created on March 3, 1863, was *The Boise News*, started on September 30, 1863, at Bannock City — now called Idaho City. It was published by T. J. and J. S. Butler. J. S. Butler had left Auburn, Oregon, in the fall of 1862 to look after a band of cattle in the Powder River Valley. Later, he organized a pack-train to take goods to Walla Walla, Washington, and still later he ran a pack-train to Bannock (now Idaho City), Idaho. At Walla Walla he met Major Reese, of *The Walla Walla Watchman*, who had just bought out a rival newspaper. The sale gave Butler an idea: realizing that a great many people were gathering in the Boise Basin, nearly three hundred miles from any newspaper, and that a great political campaign was approaching, he conceived the idea of starting a newspaper there. Purchasing the extra outfit from Major Reese, he sold his packing business and sent for his family and also his brother, T. S. Butler, who became the editor of the new paper. The outfit sold to Butler was far from being complete. He found it necessary to make composing-sticks from the tin of an old tobacco box: he improvised an imposing-stone by using a large slab split from a pine log, which he dressed off on one side, mounted on a frame, and covered with sheet iron: he chiseled a chase out of old horseshoe iron. In spite of such handicaps, however, *The Boise News* was a fairly creditable production. It was continued by the Butler brothers for about thirteen months, and often sold for two dollars and fifty cents a copy.

In addition to getting out *The Boise News*, the plant printed a campaign paper for each of the political parties. On October 29, 1864, the paper was sold to Street & Bowman, who changed the name of the paper to *The Idaho World*. Before *The Boise News* was started, Portland papers were sold extensively in Idaho by rival express companies.

The second paper in Idaho was *The Union*, edited by John Charleton, first issued in Idaho City October 8, 1863.

The third paper was *The Idaho Daily Statesman*, established on July 26, 1864, by James S. Reynolds and his brothers, T. S. and S. W. Reynolds. It has been run continuously ever since under that title.

BEGINNINGS IN MONTANA

Journalism in Montana began in the cellar of a log cabin at Virginia City on August 27, 1864, when John Buchanan brought out *The Montana Post*. He had brought a press and material from St. Louis to Fort Benton, only to locate, however, at Virginia City. After two issues of *The Post* he sold the paper to D. W. Tilton and Benjamin R. Dittes. The latter having secured complete control of the paper, took it to Helena, where in May, 1868, he again resumed publication. The reason for the change was that Virgina City was a placer camp, and after its mineral beds were exhausted the miners left the city and there was no longer need of a newspaper. On April 23, 1869, Helena was swept by fire, and from that time until June 11 of the same year *The Post* continued to appear, but was unable to make any collections either for subscriptions or advertisements on account of the paralysis of business. On the date last mentioned *The Post* was compelled to suspend publication.

The second paper was *The Montana Democrat*, established in 1865 at Virginia City by John P. Bruce. In 1857 Kirk Anderson, reporter and correspondent for *The Missouri Republican*, had established a "Gentile" newspaper in Salt Lake City. After running the sheet for about a year and a half he returned to St. Louis after he had sold his printing-plant to Bruce. With this material Bruce started *The Democrat*, which became a daily in 1868. In 1865 T. J. Favorite, having removed the worn-out type and hand-press of *The Radiator* from Lewiston, Idaho, started in Helena *The Montana Radiator* on December 17, 1865, with Bruce Smith as editor. *The Radiator* continued until November 15, 1866, when it was bought by *The Helena Herald*, the third paper in Montana. That paper continued publication until December 27, 1902, when it became *The Montana Daily Record*. *The Rocky Mountain Gazette* was first issued on August 11, 1866. It was destroyed in the conflagration of 1874 and did not resume publication.

The Independent, which had been published originally in Deer Lodge, secured John H. Rogers as editor and then moved to Helena, where it is still published.

COMMENCEMENT IN WYOMING

Wyoming Territory, organized in May, 1869, was composed of land from three other territories, namely, Idaho, Utah, and Dakota. The first newspaper published in the boundaries of Wyoming was *The Cheyenne Leader*. It first appeared September 19, 1867, with N. A. Baker as editor and proprietor, from a primitive printing-office on the east side of Eddy Street. In truly primitive style Baker thus reported a wedding in the winter of 1867-68. "On the east half of the northwest quarter of section twenty-two (22), township twenty-one (21), north of range eleven (11), in an open sleigh, and under an open and unclouded canopy, by the Rev. J. F. Mason, James B., only son of John Cox of Colorado, and Ellen C., eldest daughter of Major O. Harrington of Nebraska." Published tri-weekly, *The Leader* sold for twelve dollars a year, or fifteen cents a copy. Before coming to Cheyenne, Mr. Baker had made an unsuccessful attempt to establish *The Colorado Leader* at Denver in July, 1867.

In the spring of 1868 A. E. Slack started another Wyoming paper at South Pass under the name of *The South Pass News*, and in the fall of 1869 S. A. Bristol started *The Wyoming Weekly Tribune* at Cheyenne. The latter had a precarious life and only survived about five years.

In Laramie A. E. Slack brought out Volume I, Number 1, of *The Independent* on December 26, 1871. It continued publication in that city until March, 1876, when Mr. Slack moved his plant to Cheyenne and consolidated with *The Daily News* of that city under the name of *The Cheyenne Sun*. (*The Cheyenne News* had been started in 1874.) Later, *The Sun* united with *The Leader* and the union was known as *The Sun-Leader*. As time went on, *The Sun* set and left only *The Leader*. The paper is still published as *The Leader* at Cheyenne.

Two Wyoming papers of unusual importance must be noticed. The first was *The Boomerang* at Laramie, started on March 17, 1880, by Edgar Wilson Nye, and *Bill Barrow's Budget* at Douglas in 1886, by W. C. Barrow.

END OF BEGINNINGS

Colonel Clement A. Lounsberry was the founder of journalism in *North Dakota*, the last of the States and Territories to have a newspaper. On July 6, 1873, he established *The Bismarck Tribune*. His first issue was remarkable in that it contained an advertisement of every business establishment in Bismarck. In the fall of that year it was forced for a short time to print on wall-paper on account of a snow blockade. For the same reason the following winter the size was reduced from a seven to a four column sheet. *The Bismarck Tribune* had the usual experiences of frontier journalism, in that numerous gun and revolver shots were frequently heard in the establishment: once its local editor narrowly escaped a lynching. In 1878 Stanley Huntley and Marshall H. Jewell came from Chicago at the instance of Major Alonson W. Edwards, of *The Fargo Republican*, to establish an opposition paper to *The Bismarck Tribune* with the help of local Democrats. Dennis Hannafin, a unique local character, who was known as "the Squatter Governor," gave a bonus of one hundred dollars. Lounsberry, being financially embarrassed at the time, sold *The Tribune* to a syndicate headed by the men just mentioned and as part payment took their notes. These were not paid on maturity and he again assumed control of *The Tribune*, but sold the job office to Mr. Jewell. In 1883 he took Mr. Jewell into partnership and established *The Daily Tribune*.

The second newspaper was *The Fargo Express*, first issued on January 1, 1874. It was published by The Fargo Publishing Company, consisting of A. J. Harwood, Gordon J. Keeney, Henry S. Back, Terence Martin, Jacob Lowell, and A. H. Moore. Harwood and Keeney were the editors and managers. W. G. Fargo, of New York, for whom Fargo was named, contributed five hundred dollars toward the establishment of the paper. About 1875 *The Fargo Express* was consolidated with *The Fargo Mirror*, established by A. J. Clarke in 1874, and *The Glyndon Gazette* (Minnesota), established by E. B. Chambers in 1872. The consolidation under the management of Chambers became *The Fargo Times*. Chambers sold the paper to E. D. Barker, who consolidated it with *The Fargo Republican*, established by Major A. W. Edwards and Dr. J. B. Hall in 1878. Still later, the paper united with *The Fargo Forum*, established November 17, 1894, by Major Edwards and Horatio C. Plummery.

The third newspaper was *The Grand Forks Plaindealer*, established in 1875 by George H. Walsh. Later, it was merged with *The Grand Forks Herald*, established in 1879 by George B. Winship.

Because the dates of the first newspapers in the various States are for the first time set forth in this volume they have been brought together in the following table: —

State	Name of Paper	Place	Date
Massachusetts	The Boston News Letter	Boston	1704
Pennsylvania	The American Weekly Mercury	Philadelphia	1719
New York	The New-York Gazette	New York	1725
Maryland	The Maryland Gazette	Annapolis	1727
South Carolina	The South Carolina Gazette	Charleston	1732
Rhode Island	The Rhode Island Gazette	Newport	1732
Virginia	The Virginia Gazette	Williamsburg	1736
Connecticut	The Connecticut Gazette	New Haven	1755
North Carolina	The North Carolina Gazette	Newbern	1755
New Hampshire	The New Hampshire Gazette	Portsmouth	1756
Delaware	The Wilmington Chronicle	Wilmington	1762
Georgia	The Georgia Gazette	Savannah	1763
New Jersey	The New Jersey Gazette	Burlington	1777
Florida	The East Florida Gazette	St. Augustine	1777
Vermont	The Vermont Gazette or Green Mountain Post-Boy	Westminster	1783
Maine	The Falmouth Gazette	Falmouth	1785
Kentucky	The Kentucky Gazette	Lexington	1787
District of Col.	The Times and Potowmack Packet	Georgetown	1789
Tennessee	The Knoxville Gazette	Knoxville	1791
West Virginia	The Potomac Guardian and The Berkeley Advertiser	Martinsburg	1789
Ohio	The Centinel of the Northwestern Territory	Cincinnati	1793
Louisiana	Moniteur de la Louisiana	New Orleans	1794
Mississippi	The Mississippi Gazette	Natchez	1800
Indiana	The Indiana Gazette	Vincennes	1804
Missouri	The Missouri Gazette	St. Louis	1808
Michigan	The Michigan Essay or Impartial Observer	Detroit	1809
Alabama	The Mobile Sentinel	Ft. Stoddert	1811
Illinois	The Illinois Herald	Kaskaskia	1814
Arkansas	The Arkansas Gazette	Post of Arkansas	1819
Texas	The Texas Gazette	San Felipe	1829
Wisconsin	The Green Bay Intelligencer	Green Bay	1833
Iowa	The Dubuque Visitor	Dubuque	1836
Oklahoma	The Cherokee Advocate	Tahlequah	1843
Oregon	The Oregon Spectator	Oregon City	1846
California	The Californian	Monterey	1846
New Mexico	The Santa Fé Republican	Santa Fé	1847
Minnesota	The Minnesota Pioneer	St. Paul	1849
Utah	The Deseret News	Salt Lake	1850
Washington	The Columbian	Olympia	1852
Kansas	The Kansas Weekly Herald	Leavenworth	1854
Nebraska	The Nebraska Palladium	St. Marys	1854
South Dakota	The Dakota Democrat	Sioux Falls	1858
Nevada	The Golden Switch	Genoa	1858
Arizona	The Weekly Arizonian	Tucson	1859
Colorado	The Rocky Mountain News	Denver	1859
Idaho	The Golden Age	Lewiston	1862
Montana	The Montana Post	Virginia City	1864
Wyoming	The Cheyenne Leader	Cheyenne	1867
North Dakota	The Bismarck Tribune	Bismarck	1873

CHAPTER XV
MEXICAN WAR TO CIVIL WAR PERIOD
1846—1860

MANY of the Northern newspapers opposed the admission of Texas to the Union until all controversies with Mexico had been settled in an amicable way. Later, these papers "pointed with pride" to their editorial comment of previous years and declared that if their advice had been followed there would have been no war with Mexico and that possibly the great conflict with the South might have been avoided. *The Tribune*, of New York, was one of these papers hostile to the Mexican War, and excited the animosity not only of office-holders, but also of well-meaning patriots. Even President Polk made a very palpable allusion to *The Tribune* in one of his messages. At one of the war meetings held in City Hall Park there was some talk of mobbing the office of *The Tribune*, but the threat was not then carried out, but was reserved until during the War of the States. The Mexican War showed the value of news to get circulation, and it was this recognition that changed the character of the American press from a "feudal" to a purely democratic régime. Party papers during this transitional period became still more independent of political parties and were changed into journals of public opinion. The attitude of the Northern press was well summed up by James Russell Lowell in his contribution of "The Biglow Papers" to *The Boston Courier*. These consisted of a collection of poems in Yankee dialect, supposedly written by Hosea Biglow, and edited with pseudo-learned notes by Homer Wilbur, A.M., pastor of the First Church of Jalaam.

FAMOUS PONY EXPRESS

At the beginning of the war practically every paper received its news of the conflict through the exchanges from New Orleans.

This meant that news had lost its flavor when it finally appeared in print: the news of the battle of Vera Cruz and the battle of Buena Vista, March 7 and 9, did not reach Boston until the last day of the month, and being published on April 1, was received by most of the readers of *The Boston Journal* as an April Fool's joke. Of the Southern papers which reported rather fully the various battles of the Mexican War, *The Picayune*, of New Orleans, took the lead. The reason for this may be found in the fact that George Wilkins Kendall, the founder of the paper, reported the war himself in a series of letters which were so important that they were forwarded to the Government at Washington.

The lateness in publishing accounts of the conflicts on Mexican battlefields led to the coöperation of a number of newspapers to gather war news. Already *The Sun*, of Baltimore, had established exclusively for its own services, "without consultation or previous arrangement or agreement with any other paper," an overland express from New Orleans. This pony express was often spoken of in the press as the "sixty horse-power," because sixty blooded horses were used in forwarding the news. To reduce the tremendous expense incurred by *The Sun*, a number of northern papers — notably *The New York Herald* and *The Philadelphia Public Ledger* — coöperated in the scheme. Later, *The Crescent City*, of New Orleans, joined the combination, whose overland express, making the trip from New Orleans to Baltimore in six days, so often beat the Southern mail from New Orleans to Washington that the Post-Office authorities started an investigation, but on finding that they were fairly beaten in the game to be first with the news, they then tried to throw all sorts of obstacles in the way of their rival news-carrier. But the news from Mexico continued to reach Washington, not through the mail-bags, but through the news-columns of the various newspapers which shared in the expense of the overland express. In fact, all through the war the pony express, rather than the Government mail, brought the story of the conflict.

It was *The Sun*, of Baltimore, which told the President and his Cabinet on April 10, 1847, of "the fall and surrender and unconditioned capitulation of the City of Vera Cruz." That

paper, in telling how it got its news from the Halls of the Monte-
zumas, paid this tribute to its faithful pony express in its issue
of October 4, 1847: "Our pony team as if in anticipation of the
great excitement prevailing in the City on Saturday evening
(October 2nd), came flying up to the stopping-post with the
most thrilling and important intelligence yet received from the
seat of the war, full twenty-four hours ahead of steamboats,
railroads, and even telegraphs. The news brought by them
twenty-four hours in advance of the mail being of such exciting
and thrilling interest, we put to press at a late hour on Saturday
night an 'Extra Sun,' with full details, which were sought after
by our citizens during yesterday morning."

These editions of *The Sun* came to be known, not only in Baltimore, but also elsewhere, as *The Southern Daily Pony Express*
— and justly so.

MODERN WAR CORRESPONDENTS ARRIVE

The Mexican War not only put the news in newspapers, but
it developed war correspondents who put the heart-throb into
their stories. A typical illustration from *The Louisville Courier*
must suffice for lack of space: —

While I was stationed with our left wing in one of the forts, on the
evening of the 21st, I saw a Mexican woman busily engaged in carrying
bread and water to the wounded men of both armies. I saw this minis-
tering angel raise the head of a wounded man, give him water and food,
and then carefully bind up his wound with a handkerchief which she
took from her own head. After having exhausted her supplies, she went
back to her own house to get more bread and water for others. As she
was returning on her mission of mercy, to comfort other wounded persons, I heard the report of a gun, and saw the poor innocent creature fall
dead! I think it was an accidental shot that struck her. I would not
be willing to believe otherwise. It made me sick at heart, and, turning
from the scene, I involuntarily raised my eyes toward heaven, and
thought, great God! and *is this war?* Passing the spot next day, I saw
her body still lying there with the bread by her side, and the broken
gourd, with a few drops of water still in it — emblems of her errand. We
buried her, and while we were digging her grave cannon balls flew
around us like hail.

From 1846, when this account appeared, newspapers became
more human, not only in their subject-matter, but also in their

mode of treatment. "The feature story" began to make its appearance until it reached its highest development in the stories of the "sob sisters" of the present-day journalism.

Out of the war correspondence from Mexico grew the popularity of Jefferson Davis, who later became President of the Southern Confederacy. The correspondents of such New Orleans papers as *The Picayune, The Herald,* and *The Delta* featured in their reports the bravery of Colonel Davis, of the Mississippi Rifle Regiment, in repulsing the charge of the Mexicans in Buena Vista.

AMERICAN ARMY ORGANS

During the Mexican War an army newspaper was found in practically every camp. The army under General Scott had its own organ known as *The American Flag,* which reported the doings of the troops under "Old Rough and Ready." The army under General Taylor also had its special newspaper. Of these special army organs mention might be made of *The Sentinel,* published in Tampico, *The American Star* at Jalapo, *The Eagle* at Vera Cruz, and *The Picket Guard* at Saltillo.

POLK'S PAPER AT WASHINGTON

Polk, like the other Presidents, had to have a special organ. *The Union* at Nashville had been a strong supporter of the Polk wing of the Democracy and *The Enquirer* at Richmond had aided in the defeat of Van Buren. Polk therefore thought it a good piece of politics to bring a representative from each of these papers to Washington for a new organ, and *The Union* in making its appearance on May 1, 1845, under the editorship of John P. Heiss and Thomas Ritchie, supplanted *The Globe* as the official paper at Washington.

During the Mexican War *The Union* was brought prominently before the people through publishing an attack on Congress for not supporting the Administration in several military matters. The criticism was not allowed to pass unnoticed, for four days after its appearance in print a resolution was introduced into the Senate calling for the expulsion of the editor of *The Union* from the floor upon the ground of libel upon the Senate and for the expulsion of the reporters of *The Union* from the press gallery on the ground of a colored report of the debate of the previous Monday. The debate which followed was important because it definitely established the rights of the press at Washington. The resolution was lost by a vote of 27 to 21.

ORGAN OF TAYLOR'S ADMINISTRATION

After the battle of Buena Vista several papers, led by *The Sentinel*, of Boston, suggested the nomination of Zachary Taylor. Other papers adopted the suggestion and strongly advocated his election. When he came to the White House he found that he was without an official newspaper at the Capital, as *The National Intelligencer* was the organ of Daniel Webster. Taylor immediately prepared to establish a newspaper which he called *The Republic*. For its editors he brought Alexander Bullitt from *The New Orleans Picayune* and John O. Sargent from *The New York Courier and Enquirer*.

During Taylor's Administration *The National Era*, the recognized organ of the anti-slavery party at Washington, published "Uncle Tom's Cabin" as a serial. No romance ever printed in an American newspaper attracted so much attention in the press. Its influence was clearly recognized by Lincoln, for when he met its author, Harriet Beecher Stowe, he remarked, "So you are the little woman who caused this great war." The great influence of this tale was due not only to its newspaper publication, but also to the book and to the play. *The National Era* should not be confused with *The New Era* later edited for the colored people by Frederick Douglass.

JOURNALISM OF THE PACIFIC COAST

The discovery of gold in California, strange to say, did not attract very much attention in the press of that State. Possibly *The Californian* published in its issue for March 5, 1848, the best account under the small caption, "Gold Mine Found": "In the newly made raceway of the Saw Mill recently erected by Captain Sutter, on the American Fork, gold has been found in considerable quantities. One person brought thirty dollars worth to New Helvetia, gathered there in a short time. California, no doubt, is rich in mineral wealth; great chances here for scientific capitalists. Gold has been found in almost every part of the country." *The Californian* gave practically the same amount of space to a local horse-race. The real news of the discovery of gold was made known through the columns of the papers published on the Atlantic Coast.

Among the newspapers which made a specialty of their special California editions were *The Tribune* and *The Herald*, of New York, *The Journal* and *The Herald*, of Boston, *The Delta*, of New Orleans, etc. These special editions, printed just before San Francisco boats sailed, were shipped to the Pacific Coast dépôts for the distribution of Atlantic papers where men, frequently in the employ of local express companies, relayed these papers in large baskets to the outlying mining camps. Miners were expected to throw a dollar into the basket in exchange for a newspaper, but if a man did not have "the dirt," he could still take a copy and pay for it later when he struck a "paying streak."

After gold had been discovered in California, many of the mining camps had what might be called a spoken newspaper. The man sent back for grub usually returned with an Eastern paper for which he had paid one to five dollars. Immediately upon his arrival he would mount a stump and then read the news to a group of miners and then the paper would be passed along to an adjoining camp, where it would again be read aloud: in this way did the California miner of the fifties get his news. Frequently these special California editions of the Atlantic papers were literally worn thumb-bare by frequent readings and handlings, for the greatest luxury in a mining camp was a late newspaper.

From the time that *The Californian* was founded at Monterey, on August 15, 1846, down to the completion of the transcontinental telegraph on October 24, 1861, three hundred and seventy-seven papers had been started in California. Many of these were printed at Marysville, Placerville, Sacramento, San José, Stockton, and Yerka, and the great majority, of course, at San Francisco. Of the daily papers located in San Francisco, mention may be made of *The Daily Herald*, started on June 1, 1850; *The Evening Picayune*, on August 3, 1850;

The Morning Post, on May 24, 1851; *The San Francisco Daily Whig,* on September 27, 1852; *The Daily Sun,* on May 19, 1853; *The Evening News,* on November 1, 1853; *The Daily Globe,* on March 13, 1856; *The True Californian,* on May 26, 1856; and *The Evening Telegram,* on October 1, 1858.

JOURNALISM HISTORY REPEATED

Journalism history repeated itself on the Pacific Coast. In the East presses which printed early newspapers had often done previous service on religious tracts: especially was this true in New England and in Pennsylvania, where for the most part these tracts were put out in the interest of that earnest band seeking religious freedom in America by settling in New England, or by the Pennsylvania Quakers, who made William Bradford their official printer. On the Pacific Coast the printing-press was first brought either to promulgate the Catholic faith among the Spanish-speaking population, or to support the principles for which the Mormon Church stood. Later, these same presses were used to print the newspapers.

Just as the colonial newspaper never forgot the arrival and departure of ships, so the early press of the Pacific Coast featured marine intelligence. In its glowing accounts of achievements of clipper ships it furnished its best illustration of its news instinct. Again, just as Henry Ingraham Blake, the first star reporter in American journalism, knew the name of every vessel docking at the port of Boston, so the nautical reporter on the early San Francisco paper knew every clipper ship which passed through the Golden Gate, — a still harder task, for in 1852 seventy-two clipper ships are said to have dropped anchor in that harbor. The arrival of these fast boats in San Francisco had another news value in that they brought news from home. These clippers were met in the harbor by rowboats which took off the news, just as it had been done at an earlier period in Boston and New York, and then hastened to the port. Their budget of news was promptly seized at the dock and rushed to the newspaper offices, where the more important facts in an abbreviated form were put into type at the earliest possible moment. The next day a longer account appeared in the papers.

The early American newspapers were filled with long extracts from English newspapers because the American colonists were especially interested in what England and the Continent were doing. In the same way the early papers on the Pacific Coast contained column after column of reprint from the Eastern papers for its settlers who wanted the news from home. A most distinctive characteristic of the early Pacific press was its catholicity of taste in printing cosmopolitan news.

Pacific Coast journalism passed through the same vicious personal era as that found in the East. Quarrels between editors became frequent, and newspapers were not considered interesting unless they were lambasting some one. Often these editorial battles led to others on the field of honor, where the number of editors killed was undoubtedly larger because the Westerners shot straighter. The author of the "Annals of San Francisco," in speaking of the editors of the era, remarked: "They were particularly exposed not merely to the literary raking fire of antagonists, but to their literal fire as well." Demands for satisfaction continued to come not only from other editors, but also from subscribers, until "The Irrepressible Conflict" in which Seward forecast the War of the States turned the editorial page from a discussion of local personalities to a broader treatment of an approaching national crisis.

MEDILL AND HIS PAPER

While the people of the village of Chicago read their first newspaper on the morning of November 26, 1833, when John Calhoun brought out the first number of *The Chicago Democrat*, the journalism of that city really dates from the birth of *The Tribune* on June 10, 1847, when an edition of four hundred copies was worked off on a hand-press by Joseph Kelley and John Wheeler. The immediate source of *The Tribune* was an earlier paper published under the bucolic title of *The Gem of the Prairie*, and it later absorbed *The Chicago Democrat*. *The Tribune*, therefore, is entitled to be considered the oldest paper in Chicago (though, strictly speaking, *The Chicago Daily Journal* has been published from 1844), and no one will deny it a first place, not only among the newspapers of that city, but also among the newspapers of the country. During its early years there were various changes in ownership, and the paper was at times in dubious financial circumstances, until Joseph Medill, in 1855, purchased an interest and the paper became a member of the Associated Press. Even then, and after it had purchased *The Democrat*, *The Tribune* was occasionally in financial straits and had to refuse the payment of its obligations, not only to the Associated Press, but also to others until it was financially forced into bankruptcy. The owners of the paper, however, had faith in their enterprise, and, undiscouraged by financial difficulties, they secured a three years' extension of their debts — all of which were discharged in twenty-one months — and began anew. The fullness with which the paper reported the Lincoln-Douglas debates brought not only an increased circulation, but also relief from financial embarrassment. Its great influence, however, came from the editorials of Medill — editorials which were only surpassed by those of Horace Greeley. It was on *The Tribune* that Horace White first made a place for himself in American journalism.

RELIGIOUS DAILY NEWSPAPERS

In every period of American journalism there have been editors who laid special emphasis upon the moral character of their newspapers. Some attempted to make their sheets distinctly religious organs. Out of the latter grew the religious weeklies of the various denominations. Occasionally an editor like Arthur Tappan, of *The New York Journal of Commerce*, positively refused to gather news on Sunday and excluded all advertisements of theaters, amusements, etc. No attempt, however, was made to found a distinctly religious daily newspaper until 1839.

FIRST IN PHILADELPHIA

In that year a number of wealthy Philadelphia gentlemen possessed of high moral and religious principles set about to publish a daily commercial sheet that should be at least semi-religious in character. After advancing the necessary capital they launched on March 29, 1839, the first number of *The North American*. Religion was kept out of the news, but the editorials were largely moral essays. No notices of the theaters were admitted in the news-columns. Rigidly excluded were all advertisements of the theaters; also under the ban were the advertisements of oyster-cellars, now commonly known as saloons. After sustaining a heavy loss the promoters of the religious *North American* sold the paper for practically the value of the type, press, etc., to George R. Graham and Alexander Cummings. These men, both able writers, succeeded in introducing new life into the newspaper because of their enterprise in getting the news first. After abandoning the original design of the paper they secured as its editor Robert T. Conrad, who had already won distinction as a jurist, a poet, a dramatist, and author.

TEMPORARY ECLIPSE OF "THE NEW YORK SUN"

From August, 1860, to December, 1861, *The Sun,* of New York, was made over into a daily religious newspaper. As the story of this experiment has never been told, it might be well to record this interesting experiment in the present chapter. An able, but fanatical, newspaper man, laboring under the delusion that he acted under the direction and guidance of the Lord in answer to prayer, conceived the idea that he should publish a daily religious newspaper. Having no funds himself, he inserted in one of the daily papers an advertisement in which he sought the assistance of some one of means to assist in such a religious enterprise. The advertisement attracted the attention of the Reverend Archibald M. Morrisson, a clergyman living in Philadelphia. The latter was the son of a Reverend Dr. Stone, of the Episcopal Church, Brookline, Massachusetts. His mother before her marriage had been courted by a wealthy gentleman who lived and died a bachelor, but who later willed all his property, amounting to several hundred thousand dollars, to the son of Dr. Stone on the condition that he adopt the name of the testator.

Morrisson was a man of fine quality, but thought that the rather peculiar character in which he had received his good fortune imposed upon him an obligation to use it in some religious way. The advertisement just mentioned suggested such a religious use. He answered the advertisement and the two men after a prayer meeting decided that the Lord needed a newspaper of his own in New York City. They accordingly purchased *The New York Sun* from Moses S. Beach for one hundred thousand dollars, with the option of taking the machinery at an additional payment of twenty-five thousand. In purchasing the paper, Morrisson paid fifty thousand dollars in cash and gave notes for the other fifty thousand secured by a mortgage on *The Sun*. They secured as editor of their religious paper William Conant Church, the brother of the writer of the famous *Sun* editorial, "Is There a Santa Claus?" Church, being a practical newspaper man, was never thoroughly in accord with the idea of making *The Sun* a religious paper, but thought that he could persuade its owners to be content with the publishing of a high-grade moral newspaper. He was unsuccessful in bringing the real owners to his point of view, for they insisted that they were directed by the Lord to conduct the paper according to plans they had outlined. Finding that he could not convince the "Vice-regents of the Lord" that their plan if carried out would speedily ruin *The Sun*, he accepted a compromise proposition. He was paid a salary in full for the term of his contract and was allowed to spend the remainder of the time in traveling in Europe. While he was abroad, his prophecy about the paper came true. Morrisson practically lost every cent he had in trying to make *The Sun* "a daily lay preacher to the poorer classes of New York." Fortunately, before embarking upon the publishing of a religious daily, Morrisson had settled a considerable portion of his estate upon his wife, and she had religiously and wisely refused to yield her money to be jeopardized in the publishing of a religious sheet. In throwing out the liquor, cigar, theatrical, and other irreligious advertisements, Morrisson had greatly reduced the income from the paper; he had also increased the expenses to such an extent that the time arrived when he was unable to meet his notes. Beach still had his lien on *The Sun*, and when the notes were not paid, he sold the property at the Merchants' Exchange and "knocked it down" to himself at his own price. *The Sun* then ceased to begin the day's work with a prayer meeting in the editorial rooms. The experiment, interesting as it was, almost caused the total eclipse of *The Sun*.

RELIGIOUS BIRTH OF "THE NEW YORK WORLD"

Alexander Cummings was one of those who had purchased *The North American* in Philadelphia after its failure as a religious newspaper. Evidently he had faith in such an enterprise, for he made a second attempt to establish a newspaper of that kind, but in another city. Getting together a number of men, chiefly from Philadelphia, who held a similar view, he started in New York on June 1, 1860, *The World* as a one-cent religious daily newspaper — not a two-cent sheet as has been so commonly asserted. It was advertised extensively in the religious press and in the back part of church hymnals. Backed by sufficient capital and possessed of experience dearly bought in Philadelphia, Cummings made a heroic struggle to give the people of New York an ideal newspaper. Church notices appeared on the first page of the first issue. Supplies for Sabbath school and sermon paper at wholesale and at retail, etc., were advertised in its columns. A special rate of four dollars a year was quoted to clergymen. It refused to print the theatrical news and rigidly excluded all theatrical advertising from its columns. Whatever might be true of its editorial policy, it was not consistent in its advertising, for early issues of *The World* saw any number of quack patent medicines, such as soothing syrup, etc., extensively advertised. After being published at a heavy loss and failing to secure sufficient popular support in its religious intelligence, it merged with *The Courier and Enquirer* on July 1, 1861, and its religious aspect was dropped. Though *The Courier and Enquirer* was the more important of the two journals, *The World* by some mere coincidence was placed first in the title. For this reason the paper after the years went by came to be known as *The World*, and after a while *The Courier and Enquirer* was dropped completely from the heading. Two hundred thousand dollars were spent in this second attempt to give New York a religious daily newspaper. The paper then became a worldly *World*.

RAYMOND AND HIS PAPER

The founding of *The New York Times* really grew out of the financial success of *The New York Tribune*. A remark by Henry Jarvis Raymond that the latter paper was clearing over seventy-five thousand dollars a year, and that a new daily in New York ought to do equally as well, aroused the interest of George Jones, a banker of Albany, New York. It must be confessed, however, that the starting of a new paper in New York had often been the subject of conversation and the chief topic of a long correspondence between the two gentlemen. In 1848 Thurlow Weed, who had founded *The Albany Evening Journal* and made it one of the most influential political sheets of the Empire State, was seriously thinking of retiring from journalism. Through George Jones the editorship of the paper was offered to Raymond, whose work on *The New York Courier and Enquirer* had attracted attention even in Albany. Negotiations failed to materialize, but the establishment of a new "Whig vehicle of intelligence in New York" was repeatedly mapped out. Nothing definite was done until Raymond, leaving journalism temporarily to go into politics, had been made Speaker of the Assembly at Albany. The remark about the success of *The Tribune* was uttered as Raymond and Jones were crossing the Hudson in the winter of 1850–51. Action, which spoke louder than words, brought about the firm of Raymond, Jones & Company to start *The New York Daily Times* on September 18, 1851.

Raymond had been well trained for the task he was about to assume. While still a student at the University of Vermont he had written for Greeley's *New Yorker*. Later, he became a paid contributor to its columns, and after *The Tribune* was established he was made one of the assistant editors and the chief reporter at the magnificent salary of ten dollars per week. In the field of reporting he achieved distinct success. Even *The Boston Post*, a Democratic daily started on November 9, 1831, and *The Boston Atlas*, a Whig organ started on July 2, 1832, admitted that Raymond was about the only journalist who could faithfully reproduce the speeches of Webster whose Latin phrases were too much for the ordinary reporter. Leaving *The Tribune* in 1843, Raymond joined the editorial staff of *The Courier and Enquirer*, with which he was connected until 1850, and in which he disputed the supremacy of James Watson Webb as a writer on political topics. In addition to his regular duties he also wrote New York letters for Western papers.

When *The Tribune* learned that Raymond was going to start *The Times* to dispute the Whig field in New York, it promptly gave notice to its carriers that if any of them should get up routes for the new paper, they would forfeit all rights to carry *The Tribune*. The large blanket sheets likewise opposed a new rival, and did what they could to insinuate that the new paper was going to be a rabid abolition sheet. When Raymond wrote his prospectus he took care to outline somewhat at length just what *The Times* hoped to become. It was going to print the local news of the day, insert correspondence from European countries, give full reports of Congressional and legislative proceedings, review books, and contain criticism of music, drama, painting, and any form of art which might merit attention. His statement about the editorial policy was of course the most important. *The Times* would inculcate devotion to the Union, the Constitution, obedience to law, and a generous love of that personal and civil liberty which the Constitution and laws are made to preserve: while it would exert and exercise the right freely to discuss every subject of public interest, it would not countenance, however, any improper interference on the part of the people of one locality with the institutions, or even the prejudices, of any other; it would seek to allay, rather than to excite, agitation; it would substitute reason for prejudice and make cool and intelligent judgment take the place of passion in all discussions of public affairs.

After the first issue of *The Times* appeared on September 18, 1851, subscriptions came in rapidly and advertising soon followed. It was not so easy to start a paper, however, in 1851 as it had been in the early thirties when Bennett started *The Herald*. The Hoe press and the mechanical outfit necessary for a daily paper cost, at a low estimate, at least fifty thousand dollars. To compete with the papers already in existence Raymond was forced to hire competent editorial assistants at a much larger salary than he received when he started to work on *The Tribune*. Over one hundred thousand dollars was sunk in the enterprise before it made a profit, and it was a long time before the paper made the amount which Raymond mentioned to Jones when they crossed the frozen Hudson in 1850. In September, 1861,

The Times showed its pocket-book as follows: "Our cash receipts have been $50,000 more this year than they were last up to the same time. All through the dullest of the summer months we have had a balance of from $15,000 to $20,000 in the bank. We have no notes afloat which we are not prepared to cash on presentation."

One thing which helped *The Times*, however, was its selection by the State Banking Department at Albany as the official paper in which the metropolitan banks should publish their weekly statements as required by law. These statements, often containing the very best of financial news and often occupying two or three columns, had to be paid for by the banks at the regular advertising rate of *The Times*. As a matter of fact, practically every New York paper was glad to publish these statements, but *The Times* was the only one to receive compensation for their notice. *The Times* had secured this concession because one of its leading stockholders, D. B. St. John, was the State Superintendent of Banks, and he naturally favored the newspaper in which he had a financial interest. By withholding these bank statements from other New York papers until they had first appeared in *The Times*, Raymond was able to square matters with Greeley, who had refused to allow *Tribune* carriers to distribute copies of *The Times*. Greeley promptly took the matter up with St. John, but was unable to secure any satisfaction: in one of his letters of protest he said: "All this insolence of this little villain is founded on your injustice," and the New York press, whenever it saw fit to attack *The Times*, spoke of its editor as "the little villain."

✓ EXPOSURE OF LAND GRAB

On January 6, 1857, *The Times* published what it called a magnificent land-stealing scheme. Among the men who left *The Courier and Enquirer* in 1851 to become connected with *The Times* was James W. Simonton, who later became connected with the Associated Press. At the beginning of 1857 he was the Washington correspondent for *The Times*. He it was who exposed the scheme of land-robbery which, under the guise of granting certain public lands to the Territory of Minnesota to help build railroads, practically gave away the larger part of that Territory. When the edition of *The Times* reached Washington, it created almost as much of a stir as the edition which startled New York by the exposure of the Tweed Ring. The House promptly ordered an investigation, and on February 19 its committee reported that the charges of corruption as published in *The Times* had been proved and recommended that four members of the House be promptly expelled. This exposure was one of the most distinct services for the public good performed by the press so far in the history of American journalism.

RAYMOND VS. GREELEY

Like Greeley, Raymond was vitally interested in politics. Unlike Greeley, Raymond conceived the idea that the first business of a newspaper was to publish the news rather than to print the political views of its editor. In politics Raymond was the more successful as he held several offices under the Whigs. In a certain sense he was the Father of the Republican Party: at any rate, it was he who announced its birth in an address "To the People of the United States," delivered before the Republican Convention at Pittsburgh, February 22, 1856. *The Times*, however, reached its greatest influence under his editorship when he retired from politics and devoted all his energy to the newspaper which he had founded. Then it widened its influence through a larger circulation, while its stock rose in value from one thousand dollars to eleven thousand dollars a share, until an offer of one million dollars for the paper was refused by its owners. Unfortunately, Raymond could not make a decision "never again to be a politician" until a short time before his death. Greeley thought himself — and was — greater than *The Tribune*. Raymond thought *The Times* was greater than himself — greater than all the men then associated with him on the paper: he was the first great editor to place his newspaper before himself.

TELEGRAPH OF MORSE

The man who brought about the greatest transformation in American journalism, not only in this period, but even in any other before or after, was not a practical newspaper man, but, strange as it may seem, a college professor, Samuel Finley Breese Morse, of New York University. During 1832–36 Morse, when not busy with his academic duties, had been experimenting with an electric device to send messages over wires he had stretched in and out of the classrooms of the old University Building on Washington Square.

To many, including several of his colleagues, the instrument was only an interesting mechanical toy of no practical value. But when Horace Greeley was given a private demonstration of the magnetic telegraph, he was most enthusiastic about its possibilities, and said to Morse, "You are going to turn the newspaper office upside down with your invention." In spite of this remark and the fact that he later wrote a magazine article about the instrument, Greeley allowed his rival, Bennett, of *The Herald*, to excel in using the telegraph to supplement the news that came by mail. The telegraph did not completely supplant the mail as a carrier of news till a much later period.

New York papers, however, were not the first to use the telegraph: this honor belongs to those of Baltimore. The cities of Baltimore and Washington had no sooner been connected in 1844 by wire — largely through Government aid — than both morning and afternoon papers of the former city began to print items headed "By Morse's Magnetic Telegraph." Later, when the telegraph line reached the Jersey coast opposite New York, the proceedings of Congress and important news of Washington, Baltimore, and Philadelphia were sent by wire and relayed by boat to New York newspapers, where they were published under a head similar to that used by the Baltimore papers.

When the telegraph came to be used in newspaper offices outside the cities on the Atlantic Coast, it was employed, strange to say, not so much to give the news as to indicate where it might be found in the exchanges coming by mail. Murat Halstead has told how, when working on a Cincinnati paper in the early fifties, he would go down to the depôt at one o'clock in the morning, wait for the train, ride on the mail wagon to the post-office, snatch the copies of the newspapers from New York, Philadelphia, and Baltimore, and then rush to his newspaper office where he would slash out with the scissors the items to which his attention had been called by telegrams. As fast as he cut them out he handed them to printers, who possibly had been standing around idle for more than an hour. In those days printers were paid for the amount of copy they set and not for the amount of time they put in at the plant. Competition, however, soon forced the publishers of newspapers to pay the telegraph charges for brief bulletins of important but late news.

TAX ON VIRGINIA NEWSPAPERS

In Virginia during most of the decade from 1840 to 1850 it was the practice of the General Assembly of that State to pass annually an act "imposing taxes for the support of the Government." From 1843 to 1848, inclusive, this act contained the following provision: "Upon every printing press of newspapers taxed the amount charged per annum for a subscription to the highest priced paper that may issue from such press: Provided, however, That no press shall pay a higher tax than ten dollars." The revenue thus derived by the State from its tax on newspapers ranged from three hundred and eleven dollars for the year ending September 30, 1843, to three hundred and fifty-five dollars for the year ending September 30, 1848. The Act of 1849 did not impose any newspaper tax. So far as can be learned, Virginia was the only State to levy a tax on newspapers during the nineteenth century. In fact, the only other direct tax, either Federal or State, was that levied by the Government during the War of the States, and this exempted many newspapers and applied only to the gross receipts from advertising and was designed to provide internal revenue to "support the Government and pay interest on the public debt."

PRESS ASSOCIATIONS OF PERIOD

During the middle of the fourth decade of the eighteenth century, there were three coöperative associations to gather the marine news of New York. The first and most important of these was the one composed of the blanket sheets, *The Courier and Enquirer* and *The Journal of Commerce;* the second was composed of *The Express*, *The Mercantile Advertiser*, and *The Gazette;* the third, of *The Commercial Advertiser*, *The Evening Star*, and *The American.*

Ten years later, in October, 1856, the General News Association of the City of New York was organized with Gerard Hallock, of *The Journal of Commerce*, as its president, and Moses S. Beach, of *The New York Sun*, as secretary. The other newspapers which were charter members of the Association were *The Express*, *The Herald*, *The Tribune*, *The Courier and Enquirer*, and *The Times*. The purpose of this Association was to reduce the cost in collecting and receiving the news. Hallock remained president of the Association until 1861, when he was succeeded by D. H. Craig, who had already achieved distinction with his press pigeons first at Baltimore and then at Boston. Designed at first to gather news for its New York members, the Association gradually extended its service to take in papers in other cities. It came to be known as the Associated Press of New York, though it never organized or incorporated under any such title.

✓ EDITORIAL GIANTS

During the decade of 1850–60 the editorial policy reached its highest development in the matter of influence. True, this period was one of the most pivotal in the history of the American Republic. In it the Democratic Party began to organize. The Whig Party was wiped out, and the Republican Party was born. The newspaper, both in the North and the South, had an opportunity to discuss a question which was destined later almost to split the Republic into two Governments. In the North especially, the editorial influence was felt where there was almost universal opposition to the spread of slavery. Such a great moral issue naturally brought out editorials of unusual strength. Of these, possibly special mention should be made of those of Greeley in *The New York Tribune;* those of Webb in *The New York Courier and Enquirer;* those of Forney in *The Philadelphia Press;* those of Bowles in *The Springfield Republican;* those of Medill in *The Chicago Tribune;* those of Raymond in *The New York Times;* those of Schouler in *The Cincinnati Gazette;* those of Bryant in *The Evening Post;* and those of Weed in *The Albany Evening Journal*. In this connection a remark of Horace White, while editor of *The New York Evening Post*, should be quoted on the value of the editorial page: he once asserted that "a newspaper which merely inked over a certain amount of white paper each day might be a good collector of news, it might be successful as a business venture, but that it could leave no mark upon its time and could have no history."

✓ LABOR CONDITIONS IN BACK OFFICE

From the time of the first strike in the office of Rivington's *Gazette* during the Revolution, down to as late as 1850, labor conditions in newspaper offices were far from satisfactory. Most of the trouble between the newspaper and its employees came from the fact that the men who put the items into type were paid for the amount of work they did and not for the amount of time they spent in the composing-room. The men who worked on the morning newspapers especially complained, with considerable justification, about the irregularity of their time. Local news and items clipped from the exchanges were usually in type by midnight. There was always the possibility, however, in the case of seaboard cities that some ship bringing important intelligence from abroad might dock at a wharf late in the evening and the newspapers must be prepared to meet just such an emergency. Printers could either hang around the office or they could go home only to be aroused from their slumbers by the office devil, who came with orders to hasten to the office in order that the latest intelligence be put in the morning issue. There was no uniformity in the price which individual papers paid their printers, although the morning papers, because of night work, were compelled to pay more on the average to their printers than the evening journals. In order to remedy these conditions, unions were organized, and by the middle of the nineteenth century they did much to improve the conditions of the printers employed on city papers. Editors at the start were not debarred from membership in these unions. Horace Greeley, for example, was the first president of the New York Printers' Union, which was established in January, 1850. Greeley, in fact, used his trenchant pen in numerous editorials to improve working conditions among New York printers. When *The Journal of Commerce* and other New York papers criticized the attempt to establish a uniform scale of wages throughout the city, it was

Greeley who took up the cudgels for the printers and defended their course to obtain a "fair day's pay for a fair day's work." Newspapers which did not accept the established scale for the employment of men were called "rat papers," a term that is still applied to newspapers which have open shops.

PUTTING THE TYPE ON THE CYLINDER

The penny papers with their large editions demanded fast presses. To meet this increased requirement Robert M. Hoe, who followed his father as the head of the firm of R. Hoe & Company tried numerous schemes, but finally found that the way to print rapidly was to take the type from the flat bed and put it on the cylinder. This was done by making beds in the cylinder — one for each page of type. The column rules, which held the type in place, were shaped like the letter V, and thus acted as a wedge when the thin edge was pushed toward the axis of the cylinder. "Projecting tongues sliding in rebated grooves cut in the cylinder" held the rules in place. The type did not fall out when the page forms were locked or fastened with usual care. Around the large type cylinder were grouped four impression cylinders at which sheets were supplied to the press — usually by boys. The first press with type on its cylinder was made for *The Philadelphia Ledger* in 1846. Its capacity per hour was about eight thousand papers printed on one side only.

As newspapers increased their demands, Hoe simply added more impression cylinders until as many as ten were grouped about the type cylinder. The hourly output of the ten-cylinder rotary type-revolving press was in the neighborhood of twenty thousand copies half-printed. America had now taken the lead in the manufacture of fast presses — a lead which it has never lost. To show how far England was behind, *The London Times*, two years after a rotary press had been in successful operation in Philadelphia, said, in an article in December, 1848, "no art of packing could make the type adhere to a cylinder revolving around a horizontal axis and thereby aggravating centrifugal impulse by the intrinsic weight of the metal." Nevertheless, Hoe had already accomplished this very thing. Subsequently *The London Times* ordered from Hoe two of his ten-cylinder rotary presses. The Lords of the Privy Council, extending the patent of this press, spoke of it as one of "the greatest steps ever made in the printing art."

∨ LOSS OF CUTS IN ADVERTISEMENTS

When Hoe took the type from a flat bed and put it on a revolving cylinder, he changed completely the appearance of the advertising columns. Making the type secure in the column-wide "turtles" which curved around the cylinder had presented mechanical difficulties which were overcome. To make large cuts adhere to the cylinder during revolution was so intricate that publishers of newspapers charged prohibitive prices for such advertising. Advertisements wider than one column necessitated the breaking of the rule and when this was done an extra charge was made. The use of large type was discouraged the same as that of cuts. Advertisers, however, were allowed to use large letters made up of smaller letters of the regular type. The letters were of course identical save for the size: the large "A" consisted only of smaller "A's"; the large "B" only of smaller "B's," etc. So common did this practice become that even after forms were stereotyped and solid letters of any size could be used, manufacturers of type continued to cast the "logotypes." With the practical abolition of cuts and heavy block-face type the newspapers became much neater in typographical appearance. Occasionally advertisers using space wider than a column would allow the rules to show rather than to pay the extra charge — much to the annoyance of readers. Advertising copy received late was frequently set up in this way.

↘ SLAVERY DISCUSSION STARTED

Editorial discussion of slavery first began to appear during the Administration of Andrew Jackson, but most papers, even in the North, were inclined to leave the matter alone until discussion of some compromise at Washington brought the matter before the people. Attention has already been called to the fact that newspapers like *The New York Times* were not disposed to interfere with the peculiar institutions of other States. The few abolition journals which appeared attracted little attention until their contents were reprinted in other papers in connection with the discussion of legislative halls. A paper, however, which carried a torch was *The Telegraph* published at Washington. This journal in some way secured the reports of the Abolition Society of New York, — so small at the time that it had attracted but little attention from the New York press, — and then by publishing the most offensive passages persuaded what papers it could that the North was seeking to deprive the planters of their slaves without remuneration. It seemed to take special pride in setting fire to secession papers.

When Douglas introduced the Kansas-Nebraska Bill of 1854, which provided that the inhabitants of these States should decide whether slavery should be permitted within their boundaries, he aroused again a press discussion which to a certain extent had been quieted by the compromise of Clay and the passage of the Fugitive Slave Law. The bill was denounced by the press, not only in the South, but also in the North. *The Evening Post*, for example, asserted at the time that out of some hundred newspapers which reached the editor's desk almost all were in condemnation of the bill. After it had become a law its sponsor, Stephen A. Douglas, became the target of editorial pens all over the country: papers, regardless of party affiliations, denounced him everywhere; even in his own State of Illinois, his personal friends found it necessary to establish, at Chicago, in 1854, *The Times* as a political organ to defend the attacks brought against him.

The Kansas-Nebraska Bill, repudiating as it did the Missouri Compromise, had a national effect upon the press of the period. Its most immediate effect, however, was felt in Kansas. The Free-Soilers started bands of immigrants from New England to Kansas. Border Ruffians, determined to make it a slave State, camped temporarily in the Territory. Both sections had their papers which did much to promote trouble and to cause Kansas to lose some of its best blood.

This chapter of Kansas history may almost be read in the titles of the papers established there during the second half of the decade 1850–60. (See "Beginnings in Kansas.") At Atchison, *The Squatter Sovereign* was started on February 3, 1855; at

Topeka, *The Kansas Freeman,* on July 4, 1855; at Le Compton, *The New Era,* on September 26, 1855; at Prairie City, *The Freeman's Champion,* on June 25, 1857; at Sumner, *The Sumner Gazette,* on September 12, 1857. At Lawrence, settled for the most part by Free-Soilers from Massachusetts, four papers, every one of which had its office destroyed by Border Ruffians, were established during these fateful years. Of these papers the most important was *The Herald of Freedom,* the first issue of which, though dated at Wakarusa, Kansas, October 21, 1854, was printed in Pennsylvania: the second was published at Lawrence on January 6, 1855. Second was *The Kansas Free State,* begun in January, 1855. On May 21, 1856, when Border Ruffians attacked Lawrence, they dumped the press, type, books, papers, etc., of *The Free State* into the street and did practically the same thing for *The Herald of Freedom,* but in addition set the building on fire. This act of the Border Ruffians stirred up the press of the North so that a subscription for money with which to purchase new types and press for the owners of *The Herald* was started by the Chicago press, headed by *The Chicago Tribune, The Chicago Journal,* and *The Staats-Zeitung.* Horace Greeley, of *The New York Tribune,* also helped to raise money for the enterprise.

In the next period Lawrence had a practical repetition of this act of violence. *The Kansas Tribune,* which had been started at Lawrence on January 5, 1855, in removing to Topeka in November of that year, escaped the violence of the Border Ruffians. *The Tribune,* however, again returned to Lawrence on January 1, 1863. After the offices of *The Herald of Freedom* and *The Kansas Free State* had been mobbed, and their printing-plants destroyed, their place was taken by *The Lawrence Republican,* established on May 28, 1857. Both *The Tribune* and *The Republican* suffered a like fate on August 21, 1863, when their offices were destroyed, and the papers suspended. *The Tribune* was revived in November, 1863, and *The Republican* in February, 1868, but these revivals belong to another period.

SOUTHERN PRESS ON SECESSION

The press of the South, save a few "bitter-enders," was unusually conservative, in spite of the commonly accepted opinion, in the matter of secession. About three hundred journals were received in exchange from below the Mason and Dixon Line by *The National Intelligencer*, of Washington: of these, only fifty were for the Nashville Convention. *The New York Herald,* in commenting on this fact, remarked that some of these fifty were "backing down." Both the Whig and the Democratic press of the South were continually urging their readers to await the results of compromising measures. The Whig journals of the South, with *The Richmond Whig* as a leader, were strongly opposed to secession. *The Texas Advertiser* once recommended that the introduction of the slavery question into Congress be punished with expulsion. *The Louisiana Gazette* frequently scouted the idea of dissolution. *The Raleigh Press* begged that "if we have to fight for liberty, let us fight with the Stars and Stripes." *The New Orleans Crescent* opposed violence. *The Memphis Eagle* even went so far as to characterize the peaceful secession of a State as a most absurd vagary. *The Memphis Inquirer* urged every one "to put his foot on disunion." Such newspapers as *The Mobile Advertiser, The New Orleans Bulletin, The Nashville Banner, The Natchez Courier,* etc., warned the South of its dependence upon the North, and suggested that before any drastic action be taken the South should be made independent of "Yankee" factories for the manufacture of finished products.

On the other hand, a few papers of the South thought they saw the approaching conflict. *The Savannah Republican* again and again prophesied that civil war between the free and the slave States was inevitable. *The Abbeville Banner* asked the South to rebuke the North by refusing to read the papers of the latter even if they were cheaper. *The Natchez Free Trader* boldly recommended secession as a constitutional and safe remedy for the wrongs of the South. *The Charleston Mercury* asserted that "the tea has been thrown overboard" and that "the Revolution of 1860 has been initiated." From *The Hornet's Nest* of Charlotte, North Carolina, came many "stings" for the North. That paper

CHARLESTON

MERCURY

EXTRA:

Passed unanimously at 1.15 o'clock, P. M. December 20th, 1860.

AN ORDINANCE

To dissolve the Union between the State of South Carolina and other States united with her under the compact entitled "The Constitution of the United States of America."

We, the People of the State of South Carolina, in Convention assembled, do declare and ordain, and it is hereby declared and ordained,

That the Ordinance adopted by us in Convention, on the twenty-third day of May, in the year of our Lord one thousand seven hundred and eighty-eight, whereby the Constitution of the United States of America was. ratified, and also, all Acts and parts of Acts of the General Assembly of this State, ratifying amendments of the said Constitution, are hereby repealed; and that the union now subsisting between South Carolina and other States, under the name of "The United States of America," is hereby dissolved.

THE

UNION

IS

DISSOLVED!

THE EXTRA IN CHARLESTON WHICH ANNOUNCED
THE ORDINANCE OF SECESSION
(Reduced)

went so far as to publish a list of the business houses in the North which did not rally to the support of the South and asked editors to keep this list standing in their newspapers. The suggestion was warmly seconded in Atlanta by *The Southern Confederacy*, one of the most violent secessionist papers of the South. The secession press was strongest in South Carolina and next in Mississippi.

SEWARD AND GREELEY AGAIN

In the earlier part of another chapter mention was made of the dissension which arose between Greeley and Seward, partners in several newspaper enterprises. Greeley had another grievance against Seward: when the Whig Party was out of control Greeley was nominated as State Printer, but when at the next election the Whigs were successful the office went to his rival, Henry J. Raymond, of *The Times*. Greeley took this very much to heart, as it enabled — to quote his own words — "St. John to show his *Times* as the organ of the Whig State Administration." Later, Raymond was nominated on the Whig ticket for Lieutenant-Governor and the fight for his election was left by Seward to Greeley. There were numerous other instances where Greeley thought he was treated unjustly by Seward. The story has already been told how Seward pardoned Webb, the editor of *The Courier and Enquirer* — a paper which had continually abused Greeley.

But Greeley waited his time — as he said he would. His day came when the Republican Party met at Chicago in 1860. How Greeley defeated Seward and nominated Lincoln in that Convention has been told so often that no repetition is necessary. *Vanity Fair*, the cartoon weekly of the period, told it in wordless journalism with a picture entitled "Et Tu, Greeley?" with Seward portrayed as Cæsar, Greeley, of *The New York Tribune*, as Brutus, Raymond, of *The New York Times*, as Marc Antony, and Blair, of *The Washington Globe*, as Casca. By way of repetition, *Vanity Fair* told the same story in verse (Brutus Greeley speaking) : —

> I have nipped him at Chicago,
> I have made my Seward wail,
> I've ordained that Uncle Abram
> Shall be ridden on the rail.

The influence of *The Tribune*, with its daily and weekly editions, at this time was possibly the greatest ever wielded by an American newspaper. Upon the completion of its twentieth year (April 10, 1861), Greeley published an editorial in which he said that "our habitual readers must considerably exceed One Million." The circulation was given as 287,750, of which 101,631 was credited to New York State, but a note intimated that the last figure was too large because "newsmen" in the city bought copies to ship out of the state. The distribution among other states was indicated by the following figures: Pa. 26,091; Ohio 24,900; Ill. 16,477; Ind. 11,081; Wis. 10,965; Iowa 11,968; Mass. 9327; Mich. 9907; Me. 10,539; Conn. 10,766; Calif. 5535; Kans. 2173; Texas 35; La. 30; N.C. 52; Ala. 42; Ga. 35; S.C. 23; Miss. 21; Fla. 10; N. Mex. 5. In a second notice, the circulation of the daily alone was set down as "some 55,000 copies." An interesting comment in the first editorial was that the expenses of *The Tribune* during its first week of existence were $525 and the receipts, $92; while the weekly expenses were now something over $10,000 per week, with an income slightly in excess of this amount.

By way of contrast with *The Tribune, The New York Herald* had a daily distribution of over 75,000 copies — said to be the largest in the world at the time and 25,000 in excess of *The London Times*. The circulation of *The Sun* was about midway between *The Herald* and *The Tribune*, that of *The Times* was about 35,000, and that of *The Evening Post*, 18,000. *The Herald* could say with some justification that without New York journalism there would have been no Republican party because the New York press was probably at the height of its greatest influence in a national way. Of the New York newspapers *The Herald* said editorially:

Several of them, possessing revenues equal in amount to those of some of the sovereign States, are unapproachable by influences except those of a national policy, and they constitute a congress of intellect in permanent session assembled. The telegraph and the locomotive carry their influences to the remotest corners of the land in a constantly increasing ratio. These, then, are to be the leading powers which are to range parties, and conduct the discussions of the great questions of the generation that is before us.

CHAPTER XVI

CIVIL WAR PERIOD

1860—1865

THE nomination of Abraham Lincoln, due in part to the activities of Horace Greeley, of *The New York Tribune*, was a great surprise to the Democratic journals of the North. Amazed at the defeat of Seward, who was the logical candidate, they did all they could to belittle the ability of Lincoln, whom they repeatedly referred to in their campaign attacks as "Old Uncle Abe." The Republican papers, on the other hand, promptly came to Lincoln's support and spoke of him as "a man of the people" and gave him the name of "Honest Abe."

After the election of Lincoln, the conservative papers, regardless of their political affiliations, rallied to his support. Both *The St. Louis Democrat* and *The Missouri Republican* asked that he be given a square deal, and *The Washington Star* asserted that he had been constitutionally elected and that his elevation to office could no longer be resisted save by naked and palpable revolution.

THE COPPERHEAD PRESS

Yet in the North there were newspapers which were in favor of acceding to the demands of the South. Even *The New York Tribune* advocated letting "the erring sisters depart in peace," and another New York newspaper, during the first year that Lincoln was President, compiled a list of newspapers in the free States which were opposed to what is called the "Present Unholy War." *The New York World* went so far as to say that Lincoln's election meant that the Union neither would be restored nor would slavery be abolished. Other papers encouraged the South to persevere and condemned the North for using arms to force States to remain in the Union. Northern papers opposed to the "Unholy War" came to be known as the "Copperhead press." They were so influential that they greatly hindered the War Department in its activities and were a source of much encouragement to the South, but they possibly did the greatest amount of harm in continually opposing the issue of Treasury notes.

EDITORIAL ATTACKS OF STOREY

Especially savage in attacks upon the paper currency of the United States Government was *The Chicago Times*, one of the foremost leaders of the Copperhead press: it repeatedly spoke of such currency as the paper having the largest circulation of any in the country, and every decrease in the value was hailed as a fulfillment of its prophecy. Its editor was Wilbur D. Storey, who adopted an editorial policy that was always opposed to the Union Government and later became so seditious that General Burnside suppressed the paper for two days. When President Lincoln, always slow to wrath and tender in mercy, learned what Burnside had done, he revoked the order, enforced at the point of the bayonet, and allowed *The Times* to continue publication. The suppression, instead of acting as a restraint upon Storey, seemed to incense him all the more. His editorial comments, more seditious than ever, caused his paper to be known as "Old Storey's *Copperhead Times*" and brought frequent threats of destruction to the building and personal violence to the editor. His editorial rooms, now always prepared for a siege, were equipped with loaded muskets and hand-grenades, and had a hose so attached that the floor might instantly be flooded with the scalding steam and boiling water from the boilers of the plant. So bitter were some of Storey's editorial comments that when reports of them reached various regiments in service in Union lines, soldiers time and time again sent word that upon their return from the war they were going to destroy *The Copperhead Times* — threats, however, which were never carried out.

"TRIBUNE" DRAFT RIOTS

The plant of *The New York Tribune* also narrowly escaped destruction — but for quite a different reason. For some time before the battle of Bull Run, Horace Greeley kept the following paragraph standing on the editorial page of his *Tribune:* —

The Nation's War Cry. Forward to Richmond! Forward to Richmond! The Rebel Congress must not be allowed to meet there on the twentieth of July! By that date the place must be held by the National Army!

This call on the part of Greeley for an immediate advance on Richmond undoubtedly had something to do with the defeat at Bull Run. At the outbreak of the war *The Herald*, seeming a little too lukewarm in its allegiance to the cause of the North, had been most bitterly and incessantly criticized by *The Tribune*. After the defeat at Bull Run *The Herald* promptly denounced *The Tribune* and its editor as being one of the immediate causes of the disaster, and indicated that the time would come when the people would find it expedient to hang Greeley upon a lamp-post, because he poisoned and killed the Republic with abolition sentiment. Undoubtedly the attack of *The Herald* had something to do with the assault upon the building of *The Tribune* during the draft riots, when on Monday, July 13, 1863, a mob advanced against *The Tribune* with the cry: "Down with *The Tribune!* Down with the old white coat what thinks a nayger as good as an Irishman." In its attacks on *The Tribune* the mob succeeded in destroying the furniture on the first floor where all gas-burners were twisted off; it battered down the doors and windows after it had started a fire in the center in the hope of destroying the plant. The building, however, was saved by the arrival of one hundred policemen with orders to "Hit their temples, strike hard, take no prisoners." The instructions were followed: twenty-two were killed; scores taken away severely wounded. A heavy downpour of rain suddenly broke over the mob and scattered it even faster than the charge of the bluecoats. By the next day *The Tribune* building had been transformed into an arsenal; guns protruded from the second-story windows, a hose had been connected with the steam boiler in the basement, and arrangements had been made to drop shells on any attacking party. These preparations undoubtedly prevented a second attack, for on Wednesday morning *The*

Tribune announced editorially that it was prepared for any encounter and warned rioters of what would follow in an attack upon its building. Greeley always insisted that the attack on *The Tribune* building was the turning-point in the war and boldly asserted that if the raid had not been successfully resisted it would have swept all over the North and broken the Union into fragments.

During this same terrible riot week of July, 1863, proprietors of *The Times* in New York adopted strenuous measures that its plant might be in a prepared state for defense. They put a revolving cannon in the publication office and laid in a store of rifles with which to ward off any invasion by the mob. Thus defended, *The Times* did not hesitate to send out red-hot shots in its editorial columns headed, "Crush the Mob." It turned its editorial guns not only on the mob, but also on the other New York newspapers which sought to characterize the riots as "rebukes of the laboring men." "These are libels," said *The Times*, "that ought to have paralyzed the fingers that penned them." The conclusion of the editorial was, "Give them grape, and plenty of it." Because of its determined stand on the matter of the riot, *The Times* also came to be somewhat severely criticized.

GENERALS VS. CORRESPONDENTS

General McClellan on August 5, 1861, invited the war correspondents to meet him for consultation about handling war news. At this meeting a resolution was passed, requesting the Government "to afford the representatives of the press facilities for obtaining and immediately transmitting all information suitable for publication, particularly as touching engagements with the enemy." But correspondents in their desire to be first with the news were so careless at first that the Union generals found it necessary to place numerous restrictions upon publishing military intelligence. General Rosecrans complained that the army in occupation of Western Virginia was handicapped by having the strength and movements of his troops made public in the press so that all advantages of secrecy of concentration and surprise failed at critical moments. In contrast, he said, the newspapers of the South never betrayed the movements of the

Confederate armies. Later, General McClellan, in a dispatch to the War Department, called attention to the violation by newspapers of the agreement not to publish, "either as editorial or as correspondence, any description, from any point of view, any matter that might furnish aid or comfort to the enemy," and suggested that editors be held responsible for its infraction. Major-General Benjamin F. Butler, in a communication addressed to the newspaper correspondent connected with the Army of the James, asserted that, while he had never interfered with the quality or the quantity of the communications of the correspondents, he wanted them to speak only of acts done and not of movements in preparation or in progress, because in forty-eight hours at the farthest the enemy had such news in printed form. Offering to put at the disposal of the correspondents many public and official documents, he cautioned them especially against describing the movements of officers of high rank mentioned therein. Major-General Foster, in command of the Department of North Carolina, complained in September, 1862, that *The New York Evening Post* had betrayed the numbers and positions of his troops and asserted that "such information from our friends was more injurious than that gained by the Rebel spies."

SUSPENSION OF SOUTHERN SHEETS

Union generals did not hesitate to suppress any newspaper in the South whenever they thought such papers were guilty of treason. In New Orleans, for example, *The Bee, The Delta,* and *The Crescent* were suppressed at various times. Northern generals when they suspended a newspaper occasionally allowed a continuation of the sheet under the editorial supervision of war correspondents from the North. Such was the case when General Wallace suspended *The Daily Argus,* of Memphis, for publishing a "fake" item about the capture of Cincinnati by Confederate troops. He put the paper into the hands of A. G. Richardson, a correspondent of *The New York Tribune,* and Thomas W. Knox, a correspondent of *The New York Herald.* In other cases, where newspapers published editorials in "an incendiary or treasonable spirit," the resignation of the writer of the editorial was demanded under threat of total suspension. General Grant, incensed at an editorial entitled "Mischief-Makers," in *The Avalanche*, of Memphis, ordered that either the paper suspend or the writer of the offensive editorial resign. Jeptha Folkes accordingly withdrew from the editorial staff and *The Avalanche* continued for a short time, only to suspend a little later for other reasons until the war was over.

CONDITIONS OF REVIVAL

The following editorial notice from *The Evening Whig*, the only paper to make its appearance in Richmond after Evacuation Day, set forth the conditions under which publication of a newspaper was generally permitted by Federal authorities: —

The publication of *The Whig* is resumed this afternoon, with the consent of the military authorities. The editor, and all who heretofore controlled its columns, have taken their departure. The proprietor and one *attache* of the recent editorial corps remain. The former has had a conference with General Shepley, the Military Governor, who has assented to the publication of the paper on conditions which will be cheerfully and faithfully complied with. *The Whig* will therefore be issued hereafter as a *Union paper*. The sentiments of attachment to our "whole country," which formerly characterized it as a journal will again find expression in its columns, and whatever influence it may have for the restoration of the national authority will be exerted.

As soon as practicable a full and efficient editorial force will be organized. For the present we ask the indulgence of our readers. We will do the best we can under existing circumstances, promising a daily improvement in the variety and interest of the contents of the paper, until we shall make *The Whig* commend itself to the favor and support of all persons loyal to the Government of the United States.

The terms cannot, as yet, be definitely fixed. We shall commence with such charge, in Federal currency, as we conceive to be fair and reasonable. In a short time we will resume the issue of a double sheet.

CENSORSHIP OF THE PRESS

General Rosecrans has mentioned that the papers of the South seldom betrayed the movements of Confederate troops in such a way as to give valuable information to the North. This condition was due to the fact that most of the papers in that section of the country received their war news through an official press association. By means of this organization the Confederacy was better able to control what appeared in the newspapers than was the Government at Washington, in spite of its censorship.

During the early part of the war, Washington officials made several blunders in adopting too stringent measures to prevent the publishing of news which might help the army of the South. The papers in the larger cities were repeatedly informed by telegraph that nothing whatever in regard to military movements would be allowed to come over the wires. This threat was never fully carried out, but a censor was put in the telegraph office at Washington whose duty it was to inspect all news dispatches and to suppress any communication which he deemed inexpedient to publish. To deceive the generals of the Confederacy false reports must have been circulated: Henry J. Raymond, of *The New York Times*, complained bitterly in an editorial in his paper that when on the night of the battle of Bull Run he had placed in the telegraph office a "perfectly accurate statement of the result," derived from personal observation, the Government Agent refused to allow the account to be sent to *The Times*, and instead reported that the Union army had achieved a victory. So much dissatisfaction resulted, on account of the censorship, that a change was made, with a result that greater freedom for the expression of truth was given to the dispatches and additional facilities were provided by the War Department for the gathering of news by correspondents in the Union army.

NEWS FROM WASHINGTON

The assertion was frequently made that *The Tribune*, because of the part it had played in nominating Lincoln, was granted special privileges in the matter of publication of items, issued by various departments at Washington. The truth of this charge was never proved, except that correspondents for that paper were possibly more energetic in calling on the various members of the War Cabinet. The policy of giving items to the newspaper correspondent who had called first created so much disturbance and ill-feeling that arrangements were made whereby the news from all departments was turned over to a special newspaper repre-

sentative, who, in turn, supplied the items to all papers. The
most practical way of carrying out this scheme was to select
the official representative of the Associated Press at Washington
and he became the buffer between newspapers and Government
officials. This change in the matter of Government publicity
proved more satisfactory and seemed to please the press, save
the local representatives at Washington, who suffered some
delay and a little more expense by the new method. They
appealed to President·Lincoln, who, in turn, passed their request
along to Secretary Stanton with this note: —

Hon. Secretary of War: I am appealed to by the proprietors of papers
here because they have to get telegraphed back to them from New
York, matter which goes from the War Department. Might not this
be avoided without harm or inconvenience in any way?

This was done and the New York papers were no longer to
be the first publishers of Washington news.

TREATMENT OF NEWS

During the War of the States, the news, both in its subject-
matter and its mode of treatment, was so modern that no special
space needs to be taken for the discussion of this topic. In the
South, however, one peculiarity will be noticed. After South
Carolina seceded from the Union, the papers of that State published all items from the North under the head of "Foreign Intelligence." Secession papers in other States later followed the
example set by South Carolina. Throughout the war the most
important news, save the announcement of a victory or of a defeat, was the long list of dead or wounded soldiers which newspapers printed in small type. In the composition of headlines,
however, there was extreme modesty: seldom were they wider
than one column and frequently they were the same, day after
day. Northern papers frequently used as a standing head "The
Rebellion," or, set in smaller letters, "The Great Rebellion."
Another headline, repeated with routine monotony, was "Important From Washington." After the battle of Bull Run a
favorite was the slight variation, "Important — If True." The
assassination of Lincoln appreciably increased the length, but
not the width, of newspaper headlines.

In the matter of publishing war news, possibly the most important papers were those of New York, which still had an extensive circulation out of the city. Honors were fairly evenly divided among *The Herald*, *The Times*, and *The Tribune*. The first had already learned the value of the interview in connection with John Brown's raid at Harper's Ferry, and this innovation proved of the utmost value in getting news from those in authority. Before Sumter was fired upon, *The Herald* had sent to the various strategic points in the South correspondents with instructions to gather Southern newspapers, to collect all information possible about Confederate situations, and to forward the same at once to New York. The data thus gathered enabled *The Herald* as hostilities broke out to publish a muster roll of the Confederate army with such accuracy that a leak was suspected in the War Office at Richmond. Several times *The Herald* published items based upon such accurate information that rivals positively asserted that *The Herald* was in collusion with Confederate authorities. In the number of war correspondents possibly *The Herald* excelled. Every army of the North had its *Herald* headquarters equipped with tents, a wagon bearing the name of the paper, and several attendants. A full half-million dollars was spent by this paper on its war correspondence. *The Times* had for its representatives equally as daring men: one of them, being caught in an unavoidable delay which prevented his presence with the Union forces, deliberately surrendered himself to the Confederate army in order that he might witness the battle from the opposite side. His correspondence was unusually interesting, because, being written inside the Confederate lines, it gave a new point of view to military manœuvers. Correspondents for other papers outside of New York, however, achieved distinction because of the excellence of their reports. C. H. Ray, of *The Chicago Tribune*, attracted much attention when he exposed the fake correspondents of *The London Times*. (Incidentally, it may be said that much of the correspondence which appeared in English papers was written in London and was based upon data taken from Union and Confederate newspapers.) *The London Times* was also criticized in the American press because of the insertion of an item, sent by its New York correspondent, which asserted that "Lincoln writes English that passes muster in America, but that would not be tolerated in a British school for young men." This was taken as a direct insult to the President and numerous newspapers which had criticized his military campaigns came at once to his defense as a writer of English.

CLEVER TRICKS OF CORRESPONDENTS

Some of the tricks employed by war correspondents to get news through the lines were unusually clever. A Union soldier released from Libby Prison walked into the office of a New York newspaper, cut a button from his military coat, and handed it to the man in charge of the office. When the button was pried apart it was found to contain a letter written on thin tissue paper from a war correspondent still in prison. The notes of the letter, when expanded, made a long article. Another correspondent wrote an account on thin tissue paper which he wrapped in tin foil and put inside a quid of tobacco. This he gave to a soldier about to be exchanged. When the latter was being searched, his mouth was examined, but in preparation for such an investigation he had taken the quid from his mouth and no one thought enough of the matter to look at the tobacco. The correspondence, save for a slight yellow stain or two, reached successfully a Northern newspaper. Another common trick was to rip a pocketbook apart, insert the news-letter, and then resew the wallet. In a similar way, news items were literally carried on foot by insertion in the leather sole of a shoe of the messenger. In the attempts of various correspondents to give their papers a beat on various encounters, resort was made to all sorts of devices to hold the telegraph wire: on one occasion a correspondent instructed the operator when to add the first chapter of Genesis to the dispatch. This chapter was sufficiently long to delay other reports until his newspaper secured a lead which enabled it to be first on the street with the report of the battle.

LEADING EDITORIALS OF THE PERIOD

The most important editorial printed during the Civil War Period was probably the one from the pen of Horace Greeley.

It appeared in *The New York Tribune* on Wednesday, August 20, 1862, and was entitled, "The Prayer of Twenty Millions." In it Greeley, "sorely disappointed and deeply pained" at the conduct of the President, severely criticized Lincoln for not enforcing the laws of Congress and for not doing enough for the negro. The editorial drew from Lincoln a characteristic reply which was given to the press the following Saturday. The note stated Lincoln's position on the slavery question so clearly and so succinctly that in the North there was hardly a newspaper of any importance which did not make some editorial comment. It changed completely the attitude of many papers which had been previously opposed to the policies of the Administration. Because of its influence on the journalism of the period the note, as given to the press, is reprinted in full: —

Dear Sir: I have just read yours of the 19th, addressed to myself through *The New York Tribune.* If there be in it any statements or assumptions of fact which I know to be erroneous, I do not now and here controvert them. If there be in it any inferences which I may believe to be falsely drawn, I do not now and here argue against them. If there be perceptible in it an impatient and dictatorial tone, I waive it in deference to an old friend whose heart I have always supposed to be right.

As to the policy I "seem to be pursuing," as you say, I have not meant to leave any one in doubt.

I would save the Union. I would save it the shortest way under the Constitution. The sooner the national authority can be restored the nearer the Union will be "the Union as it was." If there be those who could not save the Union unless they could at the same time save Slavery, I do not agree with them. If there be those who would some time *destroy* Slavery, I do not argue with them. My paramount object in this struggle is to save the Union and is not either to save or destroy Slavery. If I could save the Union without freeing any slave, I would do it, and if I could save it by freeing all the slaves, I would do it, and if I could save it by freeing some and leaving others alone I would also do that. What I do about Slavery and the colored race, I do because I believe it helps to save the Union, and what I forbear, I forbear because I do not believe it would help to save the Union. I shall do less whenever I shall believe what I am doing hurts the cause, and I shall do more whenever I shall believe doing more will help the cause. I shall try to correct errors when shown to be errors; and I shall adopt new views as fast as they shall appear to be true views. I have here stated my purpose according to my view of official duty, and I intend no modification of my oft-expressed personal wish that all men, everywhere, could be free.

The publication of Lincoln's reply was accompanied by other comment in the more important papers in which rebuke to Greeley was freely expressed. *The National Intelligencer*, of Washington, for example, hoped that now Lincoln had stated his position Greeley would be "less arrogant, dictatorial, and acrimonious." It added: "Twenty millions of Greeley's countrymen have a right to claim this at his hands in deference to the high office whose incumbent he ventures to arraign before the bar of public opinion in their name."

Lincoln was delighted with the response from the press to his note. He found that the better understanding between himself and the newspapers paved the way, to a certain extent, for the Emancipation Proclamation issued on the 22d of the following month. When that appeared, Greeley wrote another famous editorial which concluded, in capital letters, "GOD BLESS ABRAHAM LINCOLN."

In the South the curtailed newspapers had, on the whole, but little room for editorials. Most of their space was given to the news of campaigns, with here and there an injection of comment by the editor. Southern newspapers of the War Period have not been so extensively preserved as in the North: consequently, the problem is harder to pick the most influential editorial. Possibly none attracted greater attention, not only in the South, but also in the North, than the one which early appeared in *The Courier*, of Charleston, South Carolina, when it indited the following: —

The sword must cut asunder the last tie that bound us to a people, whom, in spite of wrongs and injustice wantonly inflicted through a long series of years, we had not yet utterly hated and despised. The last expiring spark of affection must be quenched in blood. Some of the most splendid pages in our glorious history must be blurred. A blow must be struck that would make the ears of every Republican fanatic tingle, and whose dreadful effects will be felt by generations yet to come. We must transmit a heritage of rankling and undying hate to our children.

This editorial from *The Courier* must be judged by the standards of the period and not by those of to-day. It was no worse than some of the treasonable doctrine advanced by the Copperhead press of the North.

BUTLER'S FAMOUS OR INFAMOUS ORDER

General Butler's Order Number 28 was a common topic for editorial discussion and divided the press into two camps regardless of section. This much-discussed order directed that any female who should annoy or insult a Union soldier on the streets of New Orleans should be arrested at once and treated like any bold woman of the town plying her trade. Whatever may have been the necessity for such an edict, it aroused press rebukes from feminine pens. A Southern woman, writing to the editor of *The Savannah Republican*, urged "every woman in our Confederacy" to contribute "her mite to the ripe sum" of ten thousand dollars offered in a paper of the South for "the infamous Butler's head."

PUBLICATION OF FORGED PROCLAMATION

A forged proclamation, reported to have come from the pen of President Lincoln, was published in May, 1864, by two New York newspapers, *The World* and *The Journal of Commerce*. The proclamation was designed by those interested in the forgery to promote financial disturbance in the stock market which could be taken advantage of by the promoters. It called for four thousand citizens between the ages of eighteen and forty-five, either by volunteer or by draft, to take up arms for the preservation of the Union and in addition appointed a day of fasting and prayer. The forged proclamation was received by *The World* and by *The Journal of Commerce* on thin manifold sheets exactly like those received regularly from the Associated Press, and the time of its delivery was so arranged that the late arrival did not permit extensive investigation before publishing.

Both *The World* and *The Journal of Commerce* were deceived. After their discovery of the imposition, they did all in their power to rectify the wrong. The sale of papers by newsboys and over the counters was stopped at once. Where it was possible, papers which had already been mailed to distant points were recalled. Rewards were offered for the discovery of the forger. The Associated Press was requested to notify every newspaper in its service that the proclamation was a forgery. In spite of all that was done, however, a guard on May 18 was thrown around the offices of *The World* and *The Journal of Commerce* and for four days the publication of these papers was suspended and their editors and owners arrested and imprisoned in Fort Lafayette, but were soon released. As *The World* was the official spokesman of the Copperhead press of New York, and as it was a bitter opponent of Lincoln's war policies, Secretary Stanton may have been misled in issuing the order of suspension, but that he committed a tactical blunder cannot be questioned. Manton Marble, the editor of *The World*, drew up a long statement about the forgery, and after printing it in *The World* forwarded it with other documents to President Lincoln. The suspension caused a great sensation at the time and was looked upon as an attempt on the part of Stanton to get even with the Copperhead press which had so bitterly criticized his acts.

Other New York papers, including *The Tribune* and *The Times*, narrowly escaped being fooled by the same bogus proclamation. Copies were sent to all morning papers of the city, but the boy to whom they were given delivered the copy for *The Tribune* at the wrong door of the building and aroused so much suspicion that *The Tribune* called up *The Times* to see whether the proclamation was a genuine dispatch from the Associated Press. *The Times*, which had accepted the message in good faith, was in turn aroused, and, finding that the copy did not come from the Associated Press, suppressed the document. *The Sun*, on account of its large circulation, already had gone to press when its copy arrived. *The Herald*, before its suspicions were aroused, had actually printed over twenty thousand copies of the paper with the bogus proclamation, but when it found that neither *The Times* nor *The Tribune* was printing the document, it immediately substituted something else and recalled the copies already printed, save a few which had already been mailed to points outside the city.

The author of the forgery, Joseph Howard, was arrested and upon his full confession was also sent to Fort Lafayette. The bogus proclamation caused trouble for other papers which reprinted it in good faith. *The Picayune*, in New Orleans, for example, reprinted it, and General Banks, on discovering the hoax, ordered the plant of the newspaper to be seized and the newspaper suppressed from May 23 to July 9, 1864. Other papers of the South, when they learned of the suppression of *The World* and *The Journal of Commerce* in New York, enlarged on the fact and declared that it was Lincoln's policy to suspend other newspapers "until freedom of speech was effectually suppressed and crossed out in the North."

PERIPATETIC PAPERS

Of all the peripatetic papers published in the South, during the War of the States, possibly *The Memphis Appeal* had the most interesting history. This newspaper, the mouthpiece of the Southern soldier, for it spoke for the Confederate army in general and for the Army of Tennessee in particular, was forced time and time again to move its type, presses, etc., from place to place in order to keep in advance of the invading army. The first of these migrations was on Friday, June 6, 1862, during the "sea" fight in front of Memphis, when *The Appeal* retreated in a box car to Grenada, Mississippi. The following Monday, June 9, it appeared as an afternoon paper, and was published under difficulties because the exchanges and mail from which it got most of its news continued to be delivered at Memphis. When the Federals crowded down toward Grenada, *The Appeal* went farther back to Jackson, Mississippi: from November 29, the date of the last issue at Grenada, there was no issue until December 13, when *The Appeal* made its bow at Jackson as follows: "Though driven from home, we are not among strangers." Here again the paper had its same troubles with the exchange list and the scarcity of paper, and for over six weeks it appeared with its news set in nonpareil type on paper of varying shape, color, and size. Shelled out of Jackson on May 14, *The Appeal*, taking its presses and its type, retreated by way of the Southern Railroad to Meridian, only to find a more permanent place at Atlanta, where it was located between Whitehall Street and the Atlanta and Westpoint Railroad, but it left a few cases of type and an old proof-press, with which to get out small extras daily, at Meridian. From Atlanta the press and type were shipped to Montgomery, but part of the staff continued to issue extra

news-slips from a proof-press. Again the paper, finding it necessary to make a change, went to Macon, but made a stop at
Columbus on the way. At Macon the press, hid in a safe place,
was not discovered until after General Sherman had issued an
order that the destruction of both public and private property
must cease, but the proof-press, and the few cases of type which
had been left behind in Columbus were, after being pied, destroyed by the order of Major-General Wilson. Thus for three
years *The Memphis Appeal* was printed away from its home
city, but immediately after Appomattox the paper returned
to Memphis, where it brought out its first issue November 5,
1865.

Another peripatetic newspaper of the South was *The Chattanooga Rebel*, often spoken of as the organ of the Army of Tennessee. A link in Southern Journalism between the *ante-bellum*
papers and those of the period devoted to the reconstruction,
it made its first appearance in August, 1862, being published
by F. M. Paul, with the assistance of John C. Burch. An early
editor was Henry Watterson, who later achieved still greater
fame as the editor of *The Louisville Courier-Journal*. After the
First Manassas, Watterson, giving up his Washington correspondence, came to Nashville, where he joined the staff of *The
Republican Banner*. Upon the suspension of that newspaper and
the fall of the city, Watterson joined the Confederate army as a
voluntary aide. It was while serving in this capacity that he met
the publisher of *The Rebel*, who persuaded him that he could serve
the South better with his pen than in any other way. Neither
Paul nor Watterson approved of the conduct of Bragg, who was
in control of the army. The publisher, however, thought that
Bragg's official position entitled him to editorial immunity from
The Rebel. Watterson, however, thought otherwise, and later,
during the absence of the publisher in North Carolina, wrote one
of his typical editorials in which he attacked the commander.
For this "mutiny" the punishment was prompt; the next day
General Bragg issued an official order forbidding the circulation
of *The Rebel* within the Confederate lines. Associated with Watterson on *The Rebel* was Albert Roberts, who had worked with
the former on *The Republican Banner*. After the suspension both

went to Atlanta where they became associated with *The Constitution* of that city. *The Rebel* was permitted to appear once again and did excellent service, always keeping just a little in advance of the Federals, until it was finally forced to surrender at Selma in April, 1865.

ARMY ORGANS

During the War of the States the Federal troops frequently found newspapers in towns taken by Union arms. Often they used the printing-press of such a paper to issue an army organ. When the Third Iowa Regiment, for example, passed through Macon, Missouri, some of the members of the regiment who were printers seized a press and some type belonging to *The Register* of that place and published an army paper called *The Union*. When General Banks received the surrender of Port Hudson, Louisiana, on January 8, 1863, some of the printers in the army seized a local newspaper and got out one issue of *The Port Hudson Freeman* on July 15, 1863, to tell the other soldiers, with large display heads, about the Union victories. The editor of *The Port Hudson Freeman* was Charles A. Ackert. One of the best of these army organs was *The Weekly Junior Register*, issued after the capture of Franklin, Louisiana, by General Banks: its issue for April 25, 1863, was printed on the blank side of wallpaper. Especially interesting was *The Kettle-Drum*, the small official organ of a Pennsylvania regiment.

Confederate forces were not without their own newspapers. *The Missouri Army Organ* was a four-page sheet published in the interest of the Confederate army of that State. It was edited by Joseph W. Tucker, a Methodist preacher, who had been editor of *The Missouri State Journal* at St. Louis. It was first published on October 28, 1861, when the army was in camp at Neosh. An editorial note asserted that "this little newspaper is paid for by the State, expressly for the use of the army." The last number was issued at Camp Churchill Clark, near Corinth, Arkansas. *The Rebel and Copperhead Ventilator* at Edina, Missouri, was also in a certain sense an army sheet.

EDITORS AS GENERALS

If the newspapers of the North seemed too willing, without sufficient military preparation, to tell the Government how the war should be conducted, they were but doing what thousands of others were doing, from the select coterie who dropped into a metropolitan club for a little chat down to the farmers who gathered around the stove beside the cracker barrel in the country grocery store. Much criticism has been made of these editors who told McClellan how to take Richmond and advised Farragut how to capture New Orleans, but the fact must not be lost sight of that the close relation which existed between the press and politics was not to be severed suddenly even by the outbreak of a great war. Very often the suggestion of military criticism had come from some official in Washington too petty to forget political aspirations even at such a time as the Civil War.

Much of this criticism of newspaper generals was directed toward New York editors in general and toward Horace Greeley, of *The Tribune*, in particular. The latter, it must be remembered, had been the semi-official adviser of party officials and had been instrumental in nominating Lincoln at Chicago, and naturally thought it was his duty to advise the President, whom he considered rather inexperienced for such great problems as now presented themselves for solution. Secretary of State Seward had been a partner of Greeley in party organs, and again it was perfectly natural for the editor of *The Tribune* to think himself equally, or even better, informed about international relations. Some of the carping criticism which Greeley bestowed upon Lincoln may have been due to the fact that the latter had elevated to the highest office within his power a man whom Greeley had "nipped at Chicago" for reasons already given in a preceding chapter.

The New York newspaper generals were favorite topics for the pens of the cartoonists of the period. One of the best products of their pen was a cartoon which caricatured Greeley, of *The Tribune*, Raymond, of *The Times*, and Bennett, of *The Herald*, as "The Three Bedlams" who were continually stirring the pot of "Governmental Botheration." Another cartoon was

GREELEY'S EDITORIAL ATTACK

"On to Richmond" as seen by a contemporary

a picture of the newspaper offices on Park Row: it showed *The Tribune* building transformed into a military school which advertised itself as having "no connection with the shop [*New York Times*] over the way." Unusually popular at the time was one which, entitled, "Assault by the Press Gang," featured Bryant, of *The Evening Post*, and Greeley, of *The Tribune*, attacking Secretary Stanton and General McClellan: in the cartoon Greeley was holding under McClellan's nose a copy of his editorial, "On to Richmond." This advice by Greeley, "On to Richmond," kept standing so long at the top of his editorial columns, appealed to the pen of cartoonists — especially after the failure of the attack, doubtless hastened by Greeley's command. A careful survey of the cartoons published during the Civil War Period disclosed the interesting fact that Greeley was caricatured more often than any other man, not excluding Abraham Lincoln.

ABSENCE OF CARTOONS

For some reason the daily papers of the Civil War Period published no cartoons. They did circulate, however, through such media as envelopes, broadsides, colored lithographs, etc. And the artists connected with *Vanity Fair*, a comic weekly published in New York in the early sixties, drew most of their inspiration from the stirring events of the period. The chief cartoonist of *Vanity Fair* was H. L. Stephens: it was he who pictured New York editors as he saw them in their paper military campaign. In the absence of cartoons, however, the press lacked a great weapon to supplement the power of its editorials. Possibly the absence of cartoons in daily papers may be explained by the fact that when Hoe put the type on the cylinder, he made illustrations extremely difficult and costly. But, it must be confessed, the leading metropolitan dailies had, even in the early days of the war, begun to stereotype their pages and to use war maps extensively. The explanation, therefore, may be the one most often given: there was no one connected with the newspapers of sufficient artistic ability to do the work. Until *The World* revived cartoons in the eighties the illustrated weeklies had the field of wordless journalism to themselves.

CIRCULATION CONTEST CARICATURED

Something resembling a cartoon, however, did appear on the first page of *The New York Times* on the morning of December 11, 1861. Bennett, having won a wager that his *Herald* had a larger circulation than that of Greeley's *Tribune*, began blowing a bag of braggadocio that *The Tribune* and *The Times* together did not "have one half as many subscribers as *The Herald*, which sells from one hundred and five thousand to one hundred and thirty-five thousand of its daily issue." Raymond accepted the challenge and *The Times* offered the following wagers: —

$2500 that *The Herald* daily issue is Not..........	135,000
$2500 that it is not.............................	105,000
$2500 that it is not.............................	100,000
$2500 that it is not.............................	75,000
$2500 that *The Times* average daily issue is over ...	25,000
$2500 that it is over...........................	30,000
$2500 that it is over...........................	40,000
$2500 that it is over...........................	50,000
$2500 that it is over...........................	75,000

On the morning mentioned, *The Times* published two caricatures of Bennett. The first pictured him, in Scotch costume, inflating the wind-bag of *The Herald*. Under it *The Times* reprinted numerous extracts from *The Herald* about the latter's boasted circulation and again repeated the wagers offered. The second and lower caricatures showed Bennett in a recumbent position with pins puncturing the bag, from which all the wind had escaped. Under it *The Times* reprinted from *The Herald* the following extracts which had appeared after the wagers were first offered: —

BROTHER BENNETT RESORTS TO THE CONSOLATIONS OF RELIGION

From *The Herald*, Dec. 5.

Betting, even when fair, is AGAINST OUR RELIGION, and we cannot consent to let him have the information he seeks in that way.

From *The Herald*, Dec. 7.

Mr. Mephistopheles GREELEY and that little villain RAYMOND are greatly moved upon the subject of the relative circulation of *The*

Herald and their own petty papers, and are affected to tears about the matter. We are sorry for them, — but *their attempts to inveigle us into a silly bet are absolutely in vain.* THE PRACTICE OF BETTING IS IMMORAL. *We cannot approve of it.* It may suit GREELEY and RAYMOND, who have exhibited very little morality in the conduct of their journals, *but it will not do for us.*

According to the terms one half of the wager was to be deposited immediately in the bank and the whole was to be devoted by the winner to the relief of families of Civil War volunteers. If reproduced, this page would show, not only both caricatures, but also a typical war map so frequently inserted during the Civil War Period, not merely in *The Times*, but also in many other papers.

For the bet Bennett suggested as substitute that *The Times* and *The Tribune* try to get the post-office printing of advertised letters awarded to the local paper with the largest circulation. Raymond's rejoinder was that the post-office offered rates too far below the established charges of *The Times* to make the job profitable. Bennett never explained why it was morally right to bet with *The Tribune* and morally wrong to bet with *The Times*. On the other hand, Raymond, who had started with determination to keep personalities out of his paper, regretted that he had inserted the caricatures which had only advertised *The Herald* in the columns of *The Times*.

SOUTHERN SCARCITY OF PAPER

Southern newspapers were warned by *The New Orleans Bulletin* that they ought to say less about secession until they ceased to use Northern type, Northern presses, Northern ink, and Northern paper in bringing out their sheets. The assertion has been made that the tone of many papers in the South was tempered by a realization of their dependence upon the North for printing supplies, but the election returns of 1860 showed that the voters of the South, while opposed to putting Lincoln in the White House, were not in favor of secession, for the total vote of the various tickets opposed to secession was larger than that of the candidate favoring a separation. Hence this charge of an ulterior motive influencing editorial expression has no more foundation than a similar charge brought against the voters of the South.

The threat implied in the assertion of *The New Orleans Bulletin* proved only too true during the war. The supply of paper soon became so inadequate to the demand that practically every paper at strategic points in the South was forced to reduce its size. *The Charleston Courier*, for example, was compelled several times to make such reductions: the first was on September 1, 1861, when it reduced its pages to 18 x 26; the second on January 1, 1862, when the pages were reduced to 15 x 24; the third on April 1, 1862, when the pages were made 13 x 20, with only five columns to the page; later it appeared on a single printed sheet, until by February 13, 1865, it was a small sheet, 10 x 15, with only four columns to the page. In numerous instances papers of the South did away with headlines, and simply issued small news-sheets about the size of handbills in which the news was printed on the smallest type with which the office was equipped. On account of the scarcity of paper some of the leading newspapers began a systematic gathering of "cotton or linen rags, white or colored," for which the highest market price was paid either in money or in subscriptions to the newspapers themselves. Many of the papers were forced to suspend publication entirely: others, not knowing how long they might continue publication, published notices limiting the period for which they would receive subscriptions. *The Memphis Daily Appeal* did not take subscriptions for a period longer than two months and *The Macon Daily Confederate* refused all orders for more than three months.

EDITIONS ON WALL-PAPER

Before entirely ceasing publication many newspapers availed themselves of such materials as common wrapping-paper, writing paper, and paper bags: a few actually printed the news on the blank side of wall-paper. Among the latter with wall-paper editions were the following: *The Pictorial Democrat*, of Alexandria, Louisiana; *The Daily Citizen*, of Vicksburg, Mississippi; *The Courier*, of Opelousas, Louisiana; *The Southern Sentinel*, of Alexandria, Louisiana; *The Courier*, of St. Martinsville, Louisiana; *The Stars and Stripes*, of Thibodaux, Louisiana; etc.

SUBSCRIPTION RATES RAISED

The scarcity of paper greatly increased subscription rates. The prices asked by a few sheets may be mentioned by way of illustration. During 1864 the subscription price of *The Macon Daily Telegraph*, published by Joseph Clisby, was forty-eight dollars a year; in October, 1864, it raised its subscription price to sixty dollars a year; in December, 1864, it went to seventy-two dollars a year; in January, 1865, it again advanced the price to ninety-six dollars a year; in March, 1865, it boosted the price to one hundred and twenty dollars a year. In view of the fact that *The Macon Daily Telegraph* was often a small one-page sheet, such a subscription price seems unusually high. *The Memphis Appeal*, though it continued to be sold at half-price to Confederate soldiers, advanced its regular subscription price in June, 1863, to two dollars and a half per month; again in July to three dollars a month; still again in January of the next year to four dollars a month; and once again in March to five dollars a month — these prices were for coin currency and not for paper money. The daily edition of *The Georgia Journal and Messenger*, published at Macon by Knowles & Rose, charged seventy-two dollars a year at the beginning of the war, and later advanced its rate as paper became more scarce.

Evidently the high prices charged for single copies of newspapers must have aroused numerous protests. In one of its wall-paper editions, June 18, 1863, *The Citizen*, of Vicksburg, printed an item on "The Price of Our Paper and the News Boys," in which the following explanation was given: "The price of our paper at the office is twenty-five cents. Newsboys who charge fifty cents on the streets are not authorized by us to sell at that price; and those who object to the extortion should call at the office and get their papers at first cost. We cannot control the trade nor the prices of newsboys and can only sell our papers to them at the same prices that we get from those who call at the office."

Some of the papers in the South avoided total suspension by leading a peripatetic career. Box cars were transformed into printing-offices and taken from place to place with each advance of the Federal forces. Occasionally papers temporarily suspended for the same reason as that given by *The Daily Confederate*, of Macon, Georgia: "There was no paper issued from *The Confederate* office on Sunday morning. Every man in the establishment was in the field on Saturday. We hope our subscribers will consider this a sufficient excuse. Two of our employees, we believe, were 'shot in the neck.'"

INKS AND NEAR-INKS

The scarcity of ink caused the publishers of newspapers in the South almost as much annoyance as the scarcity of paper. The poor typographical appearance of some papers was not the fault of the printer, but of the materials with which he had to work. Home-made inks, though often so poorly mixed that they did not spread evenly over the rollers, nevertheless gave a far better impression than did some of the substitutes or "near inks." The extremity to which certain publishers were put when printing-ink could no longer be bought from the North was illustrated rather forcibly when they were compelled to print their sheets with ordinary shoe-blacking. *The Memphis Appeal* was one of these papers which had to employ such a substitute for ink.

NEWSPAPER TICKETS

When federal troops occupied Southern cities and permitted the publication of its newspapers, under certain restrictions, some difficulty was experienced in arranging payment for subscriptions. Usually this difficulty was met by selling tickets in amounts ranging from two to five dollars in Federal currency. Each ticket thus sold was good for one copy of the paper daily during the time for which the subscription had been paid. Occasionally notes for amounts mentioned, payable in thirty days, were taken from responsible parties. In other instances all copies were sold over the newspaper counter and only coin was accepted in payment. Resentment was felt by the local citizens because Confederate bills were refused as of no value whatever.

CONDITIONS IN THE NORTH

In the North the daily paper suffered no such difficulties as found in the South in the matter of securing the raw product on which to print the news. The larger dailies, however, were forced to carry the additionally heavy burdens of war correspondents. In the general advance in prices on all merchandise the newspaper was no exception. Printers shared in the increase in wages and this added a considerable amount to the cost of production. Printing-paper doubled in cost the first year and again the second until it brought thirty cents a pound. After the first year of the war most of the leading dailies advanced their prices about one cent every twelve months until they were selling at four and five cents a copy. There were, however, a number of noticeable exceptions to this advance in price. *The Sun,* of New York, which had been founded as a penny paper and had taken great pride in its price, held off for a long time before increasing its rate: even then it found a subterfuge by advertising, "Price one cent in gold, two cents otherwise." Part of this increase in price was due to the fact that newspapers increased their size, not by enlarging the sheet as in the case of the old six-penny blanket papers, but by increasing the number of pages, now possible through the invention of Hoe. Other papers partially met the increased cost by increasing the charges for advertising and by still keeping their old size.

The war, especially in the North, made many additional newspaper readers. Papers were eagerly purchased in order to learn whether relatives or friends were among those wounded or lost in battle. The desire to know the news gave a great impetus to the Sunday newspaper, which, until the Civil War, had attracted but little attention. For the Sunday edition, though no larger than regular issues, an increase of one cent was generally asked. This additional charge was justified on the ground that the distribution of papers cost more on Sundays. Gradually the papers began to add, by way of good measure, a few additional features, chiefly semi-news in value, to the Sunday editions. In this way began the differentiation between the daily paper and the Sunday.

CONDITIONS IN THE WEST

In the West different conditions obtained. Here the scarcity of paper was especially felt. *The Rocky Mountain News*, of Denver, frequently found itself in the same position as that of many of the Southern papers and made its regular appearances only with the help of wrapping-paper, tissue paper, and even writing-paper. The towns of the West and those in some of the Border States were compelled, when martial law was declared, to reduce their size and print little else than military orders and official notices. On the Pacific Coast there was no increase in subscription rates. The price of "one bit" (12½ cents) was still sufficient to meet the increased cost of white paper, as the newspapers did not increase their size, but met the situation by a more careful pruning of the news items. The California papers became masters of the art of boiling down the news in small space.

STATE EXEMPTIONS FOR WORKERS

Many of the States in the Confederacy provided for the exemption of newspaper men from military duty in order that the public might not be deprived of newspapers. Some restrictions were, of course, imposed. In South Carolina, for example, provision was made that the number thus excused should not exceed seven for a daily in Charleston, five for a daily in Columbia, and two for a country paper. In Virginia the law exempted "one editor of each newspaper now being published in the state, and such employés as the editor or proprietor may certify on honor to be indispensable for conducting the publication of the newspaper, so long as the same is regularly published at least once a week."

The Northern States during the war were not so generous in excusing editors and printers from military service. The result was that numerous country weeklies found themselves severely handicapped in getting out their issues. The difficulty was met by sending to a newspaper in a near-by city and having the latter paper print one half of the sheet with the latest available war news. The other half was printed in the country town and filled with local news and local advertising. From this scheme of coöperation grew the present plan of getting out newspapers with the help of patent "insides," or "outsides," as the case may be. In this way the cost of production for country weeklies was greatly reduced. Often the half-printed sheets were sold for the cost of white paper. The profit of the producing company was made from general advertising.

IMPROVEMENTS IN STEREOTYPING

Though *The London Times* in 1856 had adopted a modern *papier-maché* process of stereotyping, it used the process, not for pages, but only for columns, which were fastened on the type-revolving cylinder of Hoe's press by means of V-shaped rules. In the same year a proposition was made to *The New York Tribune* by English stereotypers to establish a plant in New York and to stereotype *The New York Tribune* at so much per column. Nothing, however, came from these negotiations. Newspapers in New York and in other large cities continued to buy new outfits of type practically every three months.

When the War of the States broke out, circulation had increased so rapidly that it was impossible for either *The New York Tribune* or *The New York Herald* to meet the demand for papers and Richard Hoe was negotiating with Greeley and Bennett for the construction of twenty-cylinder type-revolving presses to meet the situation. Meanwhile, Charles Craske, a stereotyper by the clay process, had been experimenting with the *papier-maché* process in an attempt to apply it to newspaper pages. His experiments were carried on in rooms provided by *The New York Tribune*, which had reached the point where it must have the faster presses already mentioned or set its pages in duplicate, as had been the practice of *The London Times* before it adopted the *papier-maché* process. His idea was to cast the whole page after the manner now employed, but in his experiments, covering over two years, he failed to make satisfactory progress because he attempted to cast the plates type-high. It was only when he reached the conclusion to cast a thin plate and then to compel press-builders to change the cylinder that he succeeded in overcoming his difficulty. In August, 1861, *The Tribune* commenced to print from curved stereotyped plates of whole pages.

An unfortunate though humorous incident delayed the success of Craske for several months. His room in the building of *The Tribune* was directly over the editorial sanctum of Horace Greeley. In the course of one of his experiments some hot and exceedingly dirty water from the steam heaters was spilled upon the floor: it leaked through the boards and dropped directly upon Greeley's bald head. Some of the hot water which carried chemicals in solution actually stained the halo of whiskers under Greeley's chin. The accident so incensed the editor of *The Tribune* that he went upstairs and threw the stereotyping outfit from the building.

There has been little change in stereotyping newspaper pages since August, 1861, when *The Tribune* adopted the *papier-maché* process. *The New York Times* soon adopted the new process, as did *The New York Herald*. Because of this process it was no longer necessary to add additional cylinders to the press. Pages could be duplicated to the number desired and several presses could be employed at the same time to print the same edition of the newspaper. Craske not only revolutionized newspaper stereotyping in America, but he also changed completely the construction of American printing-presses. By 1880 forty-five daily newspapers in the United States were printing with plates made by this *papier-maché* process: they were distributed among the following States — Pennsylvania, 10; New York, 9; Ohio, 6; Illinois, 6; Massachusetts, 2; Maryland, 2; California, 2; Missouri, 2; Wisconsin, 1; Minnesota, 1; New Jersey, 1; Kentucky, 1; Indiana, 1; Michigan, 1.

ADVERTISING OF THE PERIOD

Newspaper advertising, not only in the South, but also in the North, reflected the spirit of the great conflict of the period. Both Governments used the advertising columns extensively to make known their various needs for army supplies. Other advertisements for some unaccountable reason escaped the watchful eye of the censor, even in the South, where the censorship was more strict than in the North. The following advertisement, printed in *The Charleston Mercury* early in 1861, "boiled down" an important news item: —

Wanted — A first class strongly built clipper. She must be fast, light draft, and capable of being fitted out as a privateer. Address *Sumter* through the post-office.

In the North newspaper pages fairly bristled with advertisements like the following: —

An officer of the First Division proposes to raise a Regiment to Volunteer its services to the State in support of the Federal Union. Persons desirous of uniting in such a movement are requested to address, post-paid, Union Volunteers, N.Y., Post Office Station D.

Attention! — Persons desirous of joining a Military Organization for the purpose of Defending the Union, and to uphold the laws at all hazards, will please address Volunteer, *Tribune* Office.

The advertisements in the newspapers of the Secession States continually indicated the tremendous fluctuation in the value of the paper currency of the Confederacy. In the North a similar condition obtained even though the fluctuation was not so marked. A clothing store, for example, published an announcement that, owing to the victory of the Union army and the fall in gold, it was offering its stock of gentlemen's furnishings at greatly reduced prices. Other advertisements were linked with war news in similar ways: a Chicago bookstore advertised seasonable books, in treasonable times, at reasonable prices. Whatever was the product offered for sale, its advertisement often had a distinctly war-time flavor. The conditions were identical so far as mode of treatment of advertisements was concerned with those which obtained when the United States united with the Allies in 1917, save that heavy advertisers did not give up their space for the insertion of notices urging citizens to buy Government bonds.

In the most exciting places of publication, newspapers did not neglect their attention to advertising even where the supply of paper was only sufficient to print single sheets. *The Evening Whig*, for example, in its first issue after Richmond had been evacuated, told its readers: —

Several days will elapse, we suppose, before business is actively resumed. Still, there are stocks of goods in the city, and others will be rapidly introduced by loyal persons who may be authorized to carry on trade in Richmond. We suggest that parties having anything for sale in Richmond, especially the necessaries of life, will make the fact known through the advertising columns of *The Whig*.

POSTAL REGULATIONS

Changes in the postal laws affecting newspapers were so slight after 1825 that they have not been noticed under the various periods. Always, however, there was some discussion by Postmaster-Generals, in their reports to Congress, about the advisability of charging for newspapers by weight rather than by piece. Attention was repeatedly called to the fact that small, struggling sheets paid the same postage as the mammoth blanket sheets of New York and elsewhere, which were, on the average, six feet square. On March 3, 1845, a new act, while changing letter postage, allowed the old newspaper rates to stand, except that all papers were granted free postage for not exceeding thirty miles from place of publication, provided that they were "of no greater size or superficies than 1900 square inches." In 1847 newspaper postage to California and Oregon was fixed at four and one half cents. In 1851 the free limit of thirty miles was abolished, but free circulation within the county of publication was granted. Under the same Act of 1851 quarterly rates were established. Weeklies, for example, paid five cents a quarter for all distances, under fifty miles and out of the county; ten cents for over fifty and under three hundred miles; fifteen cents for over three hundred and under one thousand miles; twenty cents for over one thousand and under two thousand miles; thirty cents for over two thousand and under four thousand. For semi-weeklies it was double, for tri-weeklies treble, and for dailies five times these rates. A distinction was made for newspapers under three hundred square inches: they were charged only one quarter of the rates just given.

These changes affected in no way the Act of 1825 which granted to every printer of a newspaper permission to send one paper free of charge to each and every other printer of a newspaper in the United States. This special privilege, undoubtedly abused by the printers, imposed heavy burdens upon the Postal Department, for Postmaster-Generals were continually discussing the so-called "unjustifiable discrimination in favor of editors." During the first year of the period, Postmaster-General Holt published a report for 1859. His comment was typical of the attitude of the Postal Department: —

The newspapers received by the journalist is, in American parlance, his stock in trade. From their columns he gathers materials for his own, and thus makes the same business use of them as does the merchant of his goods or the manufacturer of the raw material which he proposes to manufacture into fabric. But as the government transports nothing free of charge to the farmer, merchant, or mechanic to enable them to prosecute successfully and economically their different pursuits, why should it do so for the journalist? If the latter can rightfully claim that his newspaper shall thus be delivered to him at the public expense, why may he not also claim that his stationery and type, and indeed everything which enters into the preparation of the sheet he issues as his means of living, be delivered to him on the same terms? It has been alleged, I am aware, that postage on newspaper exchanges would be a tax on the dissemination of knowledge. But so is the postage which the farmer, mechanic and merchant pay on the newspaper for which they subscribe; yet it is paid by them uncomplainingly. If it should be insisted that the publishers of newspapers, as a class, are in such a condition as to entitle them to demand the aid of the public funds, it may be safely answered that such an assumption is wholly unwarranted. Journalism in the United States rests upon the deepest and broadest foundation, and has here won a career far more brilliant and prosperous than in any other nation in the world. The exceedingly reduced rates at which its issues pass through the mails secure to it advantages enjoyed under no other government.

The newspapers fought bitterly any attempt to abolish this special privilege by which they secured the news. Already, however, the larger dailies had united to form press associations to share the financial burdens of gathering the news. The smaller papers then began to condense from their daily contemporaries so that there was no longer any necessity for this wholesale exchange. By the time all newspapers were charged by weight the exchange privilege had adjusted itself to such reasonable limits that it no longer warranted any special attention from the Postal Department.

Before the War of the States the local postmaster was very lax in collecting postage on newspapers. To a certain extent they had been corrupted by publishers who were unusually generous in supplying free copies to postmasters, postal clerks on trains, stage-drivers, etc. This petty graft often gave the provincial newspaper free circulation even outside the county of publication. Or, at best, it reduced appreciably the revenue due the Government. The large increase in newspaper production during the war brought about a radical change due to the activities of the Postal Department. New stamps in denominations of five, ten, and twenty-five cents were prepared for the defraying of postage of newspaper packages and more careful postal inspection prevented any loss in revenue to which the Government was entitled.

The Post-Office Department did not hesitate to deny Northern newspapers the use of the mails when they published matter adjudged to be treasonable. One illustration must suffice. On August 16, 1861, the Grand Jury of New York City "presented" *The Journal of Commerce*, *The Daily News*, *The Day Book*, *The Freeman's Journal*, and *The Brooklyn Eagle* to the Circuit Court of the United States on the charge that these papers contained treasonable utterances "calculated to aid and comfort the enemy," and added to its presentment the following conclusion: "The conduct of these disloyal presses is of course condemned and abhorred by all loyal men, but the grand jury will be glad to learn from the Court that it is also subject to indictment and condign punishment." Thereupon the Post-Office Department at Washington sent the following notice to the Postmaster of New York: —

Sir: The Postmaster-General directs that from and after your receipt of this letter none of the newspapers published in New York City which were lately presented by the grand jury as dangerous, from their disloyalty, shall be forwarded in the mails.

At other times the Post-Office Department denied the mails to Northern papers which expressed dissatisfaction with the use of force to overcome the States then in secession.

CHAPTER XVII

RECONSTRUCTION PERIOD

1865—1880

THE period after the War of the States was one of reconstruction, not only in the world of politics, but also in that of journalism. Many changes had been wrought in the mechanical production of papers. Hoe, in order to get speed out of the press, had taken the type from a flat bed and put it on a revolving cylinder: Craske had stereotyped the page of type so that pages could be duplicated for as many presses as the plant possessed: Bullock had begun to feed paper to the press from a huge roll: Morse, to help gather the news, had stretched from Dan to Beersheba an electric wire which ran direct to the newspaper office. Other changes were soon to come. Mergenthaler told the compositor to stop distributing type into cases after the paper had been printed and to cast a line-of-type at a time, to be thrown back, when used, into the melting-pot; another inventor found a cheap method of manufacturing paper from wood pulp; still another, in order that the paper might have a late entry, put a "fudge" attachment upon the press so that even after the cylinders had started revolving, a bulletin of the latest item might be printed on the front page — in a colored ink if desired. The Government agreed to carry papers by weight regardless of distance to all points of the United States for two cents a pound and free of charge to places in the county of publication, save where delivery was made to homes by mail-carriers, for which an extra fee was charged.

A city news association collected the local items in every field of industry. A press association, composed of newspapers scattered over the continent, sent in the happenings of national importance. An international bureau of the four great news-gathering organizations literally watched the four corners of the

world. In addition, a special corps of reporters and correspondents at strategic points not only at home, but also abroad, supplemented, but did not supplant, the coöperative agencies. The
one-man commentator on the news became an editorial staff of
several members. Their daily conferences made the editorial
"we" a truth and a reality. But they still left a column or two
for the letters of "Pro Bono Publico" and "Veritas," and let the
cartoon, in a wordless editorial, state the policy of the paper.
Pegs were driven in the walls of the sanctum for the hats of the
city editor, the sporting editor, the dramatic editor, the literary
editor, the Sunday editor, the financial editor, etc.

But this is going too fast with the story. During the war the
people demanded the latest news, and in their efforts to supply
this demand the newspapers had put forth every energy, regardless of the cost. After the war the press realized that the reading
public which had been accustomed to startling events would be
no longer willing to go back to the newspapers of slavery days,
and it continued the custom of seeking the news which interested
the people. The chief contribution of the War of the States to
American journalism, save for the mechanical improvements in
production already listed in the preceding paragraphs, was the
willingness of newspapers to spend money for news-gathering.

REACTIONS OF THE WAR

The war reacted in another way on the American newspaper:
it put the editorial in the background. During the stirring days
of 1860–65, readers began to care less for editorial opinions and
more for the news. They came to speak no longer of *The Herald*
as Bennett's paper, of *The Times* as Raymond's paper, or of
The Tribune as Greeley's paper. Amid the gigantic struggle for
the preservation of the Union they lost much of their interest
in personalities. The newspapers, however, especially in the
North, continued to have their party affiliations and were seldom
free from a biased point of view. In New York, for example,
The World continued to print items to show that the South was
still disloyal; *The Tribune*, on the other hand, took quite the
opposite point of view from that of its neighbor; midway between the two was *The Times*, which in its neutral position

devoted itself to a definite policy of reconstruction; to get all the news, readers were forced to take more than one paper. Toward the close of the period newspapers, in spite of party affiliations, had partially ceased bitter attacks which had formerly been made because of the demands of party rivalry. They had even begun to print items which reflected upon their party; they had banished the former policy of coloring reports lest the truth hurt their candidates: most important of all, they had learned the folly of printing slander against rivals. The evolution of independent journalism has ever been slow, but it made a most appreciable advance during the Period of the Reconstruction.

STANDARD SET BY BOWLES

Prominent among the leaders of this new journalism was Samuel Bowles, of *The Springfield Republican*. It was his aim to create a newspaper "that should stand firmly in the possession of powers of its own; that should be concerned with the passing and not with the past; that should perfectly reflect its age, and yet should be itself no mere reflection; that should control what it seemed only to transcribe and narrate; that should teach without assuming the manners of an instructor, and should command the coming times with a voice that had still no sound but its echo of the present." *The Republican* had been started by his father, who, having learned his trade in Hartford, Connecticut, put a small hand-press and a little type on board a flatboat and went with his wife to Springfield, Massachusetts, where he issued the first number on September 8, 1824. About twenty years later, March 27, 1844, it had commenced daily publication and even before the war it had become one of the most influential papers of the provincial press.

PICRIC JOURNALISM

The political upheavals of the early Reconstruction Period, however, brought a temporary relapse of the bitter personal journalism. Its picric qualities, on the other hand, may have hastened the purification process. New York was no worse than other cities in this respect, but it attracted more attention be-

cause of the prominence of its editors. One of the worst offenders was Horace Greeley, of *The Tribune*. For his special benefit
Raymond, of *The Times*, on one occasion — April 15, 1868 —
published a "Lesson on Good Manners in Journalism" of which
the following was a part: —

The Tribune headed a leading editorial article a day or two ago,
"Governor Seymour as a Liar," and proceeded to vindicate the epi-
thet by showing that, in a political speech in Connecticut, Governor
Seymour had largely overstated the annual expenses of the government. *The World* came to the Governor's defense, and tried to show
that the statements he had made were substantially correct; whereupon *The Tribune* replies statistically, and then adds that the editor
of *The World* is a liar as well as the Governor. And in yesterday's issue
The Tribune undertakes to vindicate not only the truth of its statement,
but the gentlemanly character and perfect propriety of its language,
"taking issue," as it says, with the code that assumes that it is "rude
and ungentlemanly" to call a man a liar, and insisting that "it is only
the liar who proves himself to be no gentleman."

We do not propose to discuss the morality of lying, or the manners
of men guilty of it. But as the editor of *The Tribune* is to preside at the
dinner to be given to Mr. Dickens on behalf of the Press of the United
States, and thus becomes in a certain sense a representative of American newspapers, we deem it worth while to dissent from his theory
of journalistic manners. We do not think it either "gentlemanly" or
proper for a newspaper to call Governor Seymour or any other man a
"liar," because we do not think the use of such epithets proper any
where. Mr. Greeley would not use them in conversation. He would not
use them in personal intercourse, nor would he invite a man who did
use them to social relations with himself or his family.

In a reply Greeley said in *The Tribune:* —

The New York Times favored us with a column lecture on manners and
professional courtesies *apropos* of *The Tribune* and Governor Seymour,
wherein it compared the matter at issue between us to the diversity
of taste between two gentlemen, one of whom should prefer to eat his
beef with mustard, the other without. We received the rebuke with
due meekness, and only ventured, at its close, to propound the question, "Is it true or is it false that our government is now spending
$300,000,000 per annum, apart from payments on account of the
national debt, and that $150,000,000 of this is the cost of holding the
South in subjugation by means of a great standing army?" Hereupon
The Times favors us with another column of moralities and courtesies,
but never a word of answer to our questions. It appears to have no

choice between beef *with* mustard and beef without. . . . We would have *The Times* use such terms as most forcibly express its ideas. We especially beg it not to be "mealy-mouthed" in speaking of *The Tribune.*

On another occasion Greeley, through the columns of *The Tribune,* said to William Cullen Bryant, of *The New York Evening Post,* "You lie, you villain, you sinfully, wickedly, basely lie." This time *Punchinello,* the leading cartoon weekly of the period, rebuked on May 28, 1870, not only Greeley, but also other editors by a cartoon entitled, "Editorial Washing-Day in New York." It showed the editors at their editorial tubs with Greeley's celebrated "U-Lye-Soap," "guaranteed to remove all stains, impurities, etc.," on the wash-boards. In connection with its cartoon *Punchinello* also published this letter-press: —

Observe *Punchinello's* Cartoon, in which you shall behold the editorial laundresses of New York City having a washy time of it all around. There is a shriek of objurgation in the air, and a flutter of soiled linen on the breeze. Granny Marble, of *The World,* to the extreme left of the picture, clenches her fists over the pungent suds, and looks fight at Granny Jones of *The Times.* The beaming phiz of Granny Greeley of *The Tribune* looms up between the two, like the sun in a fog. But the real *Sun* in a fog is to be seen to the extreme right. There you behold Granny Dana of *The Sun,* shaking her brawny bunch of fives in the face of Granny Young of *The Standard,* whose manner of wringing out the linen, you will observe, is up to the highest *Standard* of that branch of art. Further away, Granny Tilton of *The Independent* flutters her linen with spiteful flourish, nettled by the vituperation of Granny Hastings of *The Commercial Advertiser* who hangs up her *Commercial* clothes on the line. The tableau is an instructive one; and it is to be hoped that all the U-Lye soaps used by the washerwomen is used up by this time, and that they will replace it with some having a sweeter perfume.

In this remark *Punchinello* was speaking one word for the paper and two for the people, who had grown tired of the bitter personal quarrels of editors who were continually hurling the lie with or without adjectives at each other.

PICRIC JOURNALISM IN THE WEST

Picric journalism, however, died slowly. In the West it survived after it had become a thing of the past in the East. In

October, 1871, it was vigorously defended at the Annual Convention of the Kansas Editors' and Publishers' Association by Captain Henry King, who later achieved such distinction while editor of *The St. Louis Globe-Democrat*. Captain King believed in personalities and thought the journalist was never so powerful as when he was personal. By way of proof he cited the case of Nathan, who first preached general principles, in the form of a parable, to David, but who was unable to move the guilty monarch until he pointed a finger of scorn and asserted, "Thou Art The Man." The most influential editors, according to Captain King, had been exceedingly and often offensively personal in their criticism and to take it out of journalism would mean descent into bankruptcy. "Banish the words blackguard, liar, and villain from our newspapers and even the 'good and useful' Greeley would quit the business in disgust," was the way he put it. Personal journalism to Captain King meant the application of such words only to scoundrels and rascals who could be effectively denounced in no other way. In its modified form personal journalism survived in the West until a much later period.

Evidently certain members of the first Kansas Legislature did not hold the views advocated by Captain King, for one member, a Mr. McMeekin, moved that if any reporter of a Kansas newspaper vilified any member of the Legislature, the member so vilified should be authorized and expected to thrash the representative of the press who made the attack. Captain King, however, thought that by such a scheme aggrieved parties could obtain satisfaction more surely and promptly than by libel suits and that offending editors could escape the expense and annoyance of court attendance. The resolution proposed by Mr. McMeekin, however, did not pass the Legislature, owing to the opposition of the Kansas press.

PRESS ON WHEELS

No history of American journalism would be complete without some mention of *The Frontier Index* which, true to its name, was published on the frontier and was literally a press on wheels. Though published at twenty-five different places along the line of the Western advance, it was founded at Old Kearny City, Nebraska Territory, in May, 1866, by F. K. and L. R. Freeman, two brothers who had come West from Culpeper County, Virginia. It was printed on an old-time hand-roller press which had been abandoned by General Joseph E. Johnston, who prior to 1861 had been in command of the United States troops in the Far Western territories.

The Frontier Index in the fall of 1866 was taken by three ox teams driven by Mexican greasers to a temporary terminus of the Union Pacific Construction Company at North Platte. As soon as the site was laid out for this mushroom terminal station, some four thousand adventurers flocked there to live in tents and portable houses, and *The Index* did a "land office" business in printing small circulars for which it charged twenty dollars for one hundred words. The next move was to Julesberg in January, 1867. In forty-eight hours North Platte was depopulated after the inhabitants moved to the new terminus which *The Index* was the first enterprise to reach. Another place of publication was Laramie City, one hundred and five miles west of Cheyenne. While published at this place *The Index* received a large subscription list and an extensive advertising contract from Brigham Young, of Salt Lake City. To continue the trail followed by *The Frontier Index* would be to publish a list of the temporary terminals of the Pacific railroad. On one or two occasions when *The Frontier Index* was being moved its wagon train was held up by Indians, who took no pains to conceal their disgust when they found that the ox carts contained nothing except the printing outfit. The trail ended for *The Frontier Index* at North Yakima, Washington.

MISFORTUNES OF GREELEY

The acceptance by Horace Greeley of the presidential nomination in 1872 to run against Grant, the regular candidate of the Republican Party, was most unfortunate. He resigned the editorship of *The Tribune* and was never again in supreme control. He was caricatured with all the picric qualities of the period. The opposition press was filled with burlesques of "The Liberal Candidate," in which his familiar white hat and linen duster were prominently portrayed. The people refused to take his nomination seriously, for since the foundation of *The Tribune* he had opposed the party whose standard-bearer he became. Because of the caricatures spread over the country Greeley was forced to take the stump, "not to advocate political claims, but to show that he retained some semblance of the human form." The illness of his wife later demanded his constant presence at her bedside, day and night, until her death just seven days before his crushing defeat at the ballot box. On November 7, 1872, Greeley published a note under his own signature "that the undersigned resumed the editorship of *The Tribune* which he relinquished on embarking on another business six months ago." That Greeley assumed the editorship only in name was shown by the insertion of another editorial — not from Greeley's pen — entitled "Crumbs of Comfort." In the second editorial mention was made that "every red-nosed politician who had cheated the caucus and fought at the polls looked to the editor of *The Tribune* to secure an appointment as a gauger, or as an army chaplain, or as Minister to France"; and that in frequent instances the editor of *The Tribune* was telegraphed in frantic haste to come to the Capitol to "save this bill, to crush that one, to promote one project and to stop another." A crumb of comfort was that office-seekers would now keep aloof from the defeated candidate who had not influence enough to get any one appointed as "a deputy sub-assistant temporary clerk in the pastepot section of the folding-room at Washington."

Greeley's amazement at reading the second editorial must have been greater than that of any of the subscribers. In vain did he try to secure the insertion of the following note of correction: —

By some unaccountable fatality, an article entitled "Crumbs of Comfort" crept into our last, unseen by the editor, which does him the grossest wrong. It is true that office seekers used to pester him for recommendations when his friends controlled the custom house, though the "red nosed" variety was seldom found among them; it is not true that he ever obeyed a summons to Washington in order that he might there promote or oppose this or that private scheme. In short, the article is a monstrous fable, based on some other experience than that of any editor of this journal.

In justice to those in control of *The Tribune* at the time, it must be confessed that the newspaper was in an extremely embarrassing position because of its relations to the two political parties: founded to support one, it had for some months past been ardently supporting the other. But for its great vitality and this public announcement of its position, it doubtless would have succumbed with its founder, who, after his mind had given way, died on November 29, 1872.

DANA'S ATTACKS ON GRANT

Of all the newspaper critics of Grant's Administration, the most bitter was unquestionably *The New York Sun*, which was under the editorship of Charles Anderson Dana. Forced from the position as managing editor of *The Tribune* by Greeley, Dana had gone to Washington in November, 1862, as Second Assistant Secretary of War. Resigning this position on July 1, 1865, he returned to journalism as editor of *The Daily Republican*, which had just been started in Chicago, and which undoubtedly would have been successful had it not been so severely handicapped for lack of funds and by political dissention among its owners. After a vain struggle of about a year, Dana became so discouraged that he resolved to leave and go to New York, expecting either to buy or to start a newspaper. His previous connection with *The New York Tribune* had brought him in contact with several men of wealth, so that he had little difficulty in raising the necessary capital to commence a new paper when he was offered *The Sun* for $175,000. He accepted the offer and on January 25, 1868, announced his policies as follows: —

The Sun will continue to be an independent newspaper, wearing the livery of no party and discussing public questions and the acts of public men on their merits alone. It will be guided, as it has been hitherto, by uncompromising loyalty to the Union, and will resist every attempt to weaken the bonds that unite the American people into one nation.

Of the acts of public men those of Grant received the most attention. Henry Watterson summed up the situation in the following editorial, headed, "One Who Hates The *Sunlight*": —

There is only one man that objects to *The Sun* violently, and that is Grant. He sees nothing but spots on it. The very sound of the word is so hateful to him that he loathes the whole solar system.

In the platform of *The Sun* for 1872 Dana advocated numerous reforms. Among them were that both Grantism and Tweedism be abolished by laws for the summary punishment of present-taking and bribe-taking as well as of public robbery; that political rights be restored to all persons concerned in the late rebellion; that the civil service be so reformed that appointments to office no longer depend on party patronage; and that the President cannot appoint his own relatives or those of his wife to office. When, however, *The Sun* linked together the names of Grant and John Barleycorn the reading public of New York resented this *Sun*stroke. It cancelled its subscription, but *The Sun* shone on. *The Sun* was but a typical representative of a portion of the press which was most bitter in attacking this weakness of Grant. David Dudley Field said in a magazine article in 1876 that the following item was a fair sample in the press opposed to the Administration: —

"Periodical Neuralgia" is what they call it in Washington now. Grant has it, and has not been able to see visitors for several days. Parson Newman prayed for him on yesterday, and the parson's intimate relations with Divine Providence, backed by continued liberal doses of hydrate of chloral, justify the hope that the patient will get his nerves steadied in a day or two.

"THE BITER BIT"

Other newspapers were just as bitter toward Grant, and *The Sun* has been selected for illustration simply because of its greater prominence. The assertion has been frequently made that the hostility of *The Sun* to the Grant Administration was due to the fact that its editor had not been appointed to the Collectorship of the Port of New York. Those who knew Dana best denied most emphatically the truth of such an assertion, and pointed out that the editor of *The Sun* never criticized the military tactics of Grant, but only those acts of his Administration which demanded condemnation. The enemies of Dana, however, inspired the publication of a pamphlet entitled "The Biter

Bit," which was supposed to be "a narrative of some of the blackmailing operations of Charles A. Dana's *Sun*." "The Biter Bit," however, did not shake the confidence of the friends or acquaintances of Dana in his integrity as a journalist, nor did it affect Dana's own confidence in Amos Cummings or Isaac Ingland or any of the other subordinates who came over to *The Sun* from *The Tribune* and were incidentally assailed in this scurrilous pamphlet.

TOMBSTONE CARTOON PUBLISHED

The most biting rays which *The Sun* shed on Grant appeared on November 30, 1876, when *The Sun* published in its columns a picture of a tombstone with the following inscription: —

Sacred
To the Memory of
American Liberty
Born
July 4, 1776
Died
At Columbia, S.C.
By Order of
Ulysses I
November 28, 1876
Age 100 yrs., 4 mo., 24 days

DANA'S ATTACK ON HAYES

After the great political conflict of 1876, which declared that Hayes had been elected, *The Sun* turned its rays from Grant to the new President. On Saturday, March 3, 1877, when Hayes was about to take office, *The Sun* came out with inverted column rules, thus giving the paper the appearance of mourning. Upon his first visit after the election to New York, *The Sun* found a spot on May 14, 1877, for his picture with the word "Fraud" printed across his forehead. Under the picture it published this quotation from Charles Francis Adams: "A person who must forever carry upon his brow the stamp of fraud first triumphant in American history. No subsequent action can wash away the letters of that record." It again reprinted the picture on May 15, when Hayes was still in the city.

DANA AND HIS PAPER

Nothing under the sun could make Dana move his paper from the orbit he had once outlined and he was most fertile in thinking up something new for his paper. It was, however, his mode of treatment rather than his news that made *The Sun* so distinctly a newspaper-man's paper. After assuming the editorship of *The Sun*, Dana outlined in his first issue how the news would be treated in the future: "It will study condensation, clearness, point, and will endeavor to present its daily photograph of the world's doings in the most luminous and lively manner." This determination to tell the news "in the most luminous and lively manner" gave such a peculiar style to items in *The Sun* that it became possible to distinguish a story handled in Dana's way, whether it appeared in his own newspaper or in *The Tombstone Epitaph*. Dana applied the same mode of treatment to his editorials. In 1880 he referred to General Hancock, then a presidential candidate, as "a good man, weighing two hundred and forty pounds." It was Dana, and the men whom he trained, who gave the editorial essays of *The Sun* that distinctly literary charm which did much to soothe the anger aroused by the vituperative political squibs in neighboring columns. For the struggling poet of merit Dana always found a place in *The Sun*. No finer tribute was ever paid Dana in this connection than the one which came from the pen of Eugene Field.

FRANCO–PRUSSIAN WAR

During the Franco-Prussian War, *The New York Tribune* spent unusually large sums in reporting that conflict. Practically no attention was paid to the cable tolls. Short as was this war, *The Tribune* paid for its telegraphic news $83,303.51; its additional bill for this correspondence — also paid in gold — was $42,263.46. Such lavish expenditure was then unknown in journalism, in spite of the expense to which papers had been put for correspondence during the War of the States. *The Tribune* rapidly achieved such a reputation for being first in war news that it disputed this field with *The Herald*. For the sake of comparison Whitelaw Reid furnished the following figures for *The Times* and *The Tribune* during the year 1863 of the Civil War: —

Expense	Tribune	Times
Editors and correspondence, not war..............	$49,228	$45,660
War Correspondence...........................	25,706	14,040
Compositors..................................	49,547	45,741
Special telegraphing..........................	12,623	7,817
Supplements, *Tribune*, 21, *Times*, 11..............	9,000	4,730

At just about the time that *The Tribune* would have reaped the benefits of its Franco-Prussian enterprise, it was overshadowed by the activities of *The New York Times* in exposing the famous Tweed Ring.

EXPOSURE OF TWEED RING

After the death of Raymond, Lewis J. Jennings became the editor of *The New York Times*. How Boss Tweed and his Ring had secured control of New York at a loss to the city of millions of dollars is a story, too long to be told in this book. Attacks on their graft appeared in *The Times* long before that paper had absolute proof of the facts, though of the frauds of the Ring there could be no question. On July 28, 1871, *The Times* came out with a special supplement in which it exposed the gigantic frauds of the Ring, and published the astounding bills of furniture dealers, carpenters, plasterers, and plumbers — in other words, $9,789,482.16 had been signed away without question for repairs and furniture for the new Court-House, etc. This issue of *The Times* sold by hundreds of thousands. Even the Mayor of New York was forced to admit that the bills were perhaps exorbitant. But Tweed only asked the cynical question — "What are you going to do about it?" The accounts of the swindle in *The Times*, aided by the cartoons of Nast in *Harper's Weekly*, so aroused the people that they overthrew the Tweed Ring and sent many of its members to jail. All of this is, of course, an old story, but it permitted *The Times* to say with Othello, to quote a quotation of the present editor of that paper, "I have done the State some service."

ATTITUDE OF TWEED TOWARD NEW YORK PRESS

During the days when Tweed controlled New York, it is asserted that eighty-nine newspapers were on his pay-roll and that after the exposure of the Ring by *The New York Times*, twenty-seven of these papers, which had depended upon city plunder for existence, were compelled to suspend. The records showed that messages of the Mayor which the reading public accepted as news were really paid advertisements charged to the city at the rate of one dollar a line. During the Tweed régime some of the smaller evening papers received an annual subsidy of one thousand dollars a month. Unsettled newspaper claims from various papers totaled over two millions. A remarkable thing connected with the Tweed control was the fact that two hundred dollars a year was voted by the Aldermen to reporters for omitting to report the activities of the Aldermen.

The attitude of Tweed toward the New York press *Punchinello* portrayed in a cartoon of contentment: it showed Tweed smoking his Tammany peace pipe while on the bowl sat a reporter to represent the newspapers of the city. To the latter Tweed said, according to the cartoon: "Say, young man, ain't you afraid you'll burn your breeches?" This remark was but a repetition of a better-known Tweed twitter, "Well, what are you going to do about it?" What the people did about it was to tan thoroughly the hide of the Tammany Tiger.

SIMILAR EXPOSURE OF WHISKEY RING

Somewhat similar to the exposure of the Tweed Ring by *The New York Times* was the exposure of the Whiskey Ring by *The St. Louis Democrat*. This Ring was organized in St. Louis to defraud the Government of the revenue tax from the distillers. A large fund was raised to bribe the Government officials and "to put the soft pedal" on St. Louis papers.

The exposure of this Ring was due to the activity of George Fishback, editor of *The St. Louis Democrat*, who secured the appointment of Myron Colony, the financial editor of *The Democrat*, as a special agent to expose the frauds. Colony was supposedly gathering commercial statistics for *The Democrat,* and obtained bills of lading of all shipments out of St. Louis. He paid no attention to any save those of distilled liquors. The discrepancies between these bills of lading and the records furnished the internal revenue office gave him the material for his great exposure. After *The St. Louis Democrat* had once started the work, it was materially aided by many newspapers in other cities. Yet so powerful was the Ring that a congressional amendment in the matter of libel, called by the newspapers the "Press Gag Law," was passed. Just as the Sedition Law, mentioned in an earlier chapter, aided in the defeat of the Federal Party, so the Press Gag Law undoubtedly had much to do with the Democratic victories which followed in 1874 in many of the States. Several men whom Grant had appointed to public office were involved in these whiskey scandals.

REVIVAL OF RELIGIOUS JOURNALISM

At the time of the relapse into bitter personal journalism, there was in the East a revival of religious journalism. Among the few daily newspapers with religious leanings started during this time was *The Boston Daily News* which began publication "every forenoon and afternoon" on July 19, 1869. Its editor, E. P. Marvin, asked his subscribers, on October 11, 1869, to wait a day for the marriage of *The Boston Daily News* with *The Boston Daily Tribune*, as the object of the union was to "increase the strength and permanency of the advocacy of the great moral questions of the day of which temperance is prominent."

With the issue of December 24, 1869, the Reverend E. D. Winslow, who had had practical experience with church weeklies, became associated with *The Daily News*. In 1870 *The Boston Daily News* boasted of being "a moral, religious daily." It called attention to the fact that it gave "all the news for a penny a day." In May, 1875, the Reverend Winslow bought *The Boston Post*, but in completing the transaction he made the "trifling" mistake of committing forgery, which was not discovered, however, until several months later. When the facts of the case were made public, Winslow fled to Holland and *The News* continued publication for a short time, but on February 11, 1876, it announced its last edition with that issue because the affairs of the newspaper were so involved with those of Mr. Winslow that legal obstacles made the suspension necessary. The stigma which was attached to *The Boston Daily News* did much to dampen the religious ardor of those who had planned to establish daily religious newspapers in other cities, for *The Boston Daily News* had not practiced what it preached.

A decade after the attempt in New York City to found *The World* as a daily religious newspaper, *The New York Daily Witness*, "a Christian, one-cent, afternoon newspaper," appeared. It started on July 1, 1871, and aimed not only to be religious in character, but also "to give the news of the day and much excellent family reading besides." It inserted no advertisements of "liquors, theaters, lotteries, or anything inconsistent with its character." It failed to receive the financial support it expected and was fittingly interred in the newspaper graveyard alongside of its more secular companions. No attempt to found a daily religious newspaper was successful until Mary Baker Eddy started *The Christian Science Monitor* in Boston on Wednesday, November 25, 1908.

RECONSTRUCTION OF SOUTHERN PRESS

During the Reconstruction Period, *The Charleston Mercury* was revived in 1867 under Colonel R. Barnwell Rhett, Jr. At about this time South Carolina was holding its Reconstruction Convention which was spoken of in Charleston as "the ring-streaked and striped convention." A secret editorial conference of *The Mercury* was held, and in spite of some objection it was decided "to make any attempt to establish a mongrel government in South Carolina a stench in the nostrils of the public and to make the odium of it too great for white men to bear." *The Mercury* then proceeded to publish the careers of all the "carpet-baggers and scallywags" then running for office. The articles were illustrated with numerous cartoons showing the carpet-baggers and the negro delegates to the Reconstruction Convention in the most ridiculous juxtapositions. So well did *The Mercury* carry out its purpose that to this day the stigma of "Republicanism and Mongrelism" remain odious in South Carolina.

But *The Charleston Mercury*, which before the war had been the chief organ of the secession press of South Carolina, suspended publication in November, 1868. Its suspension was the more remarkable because *The Mercury* as late as August, 1868, had the largest circulation of any newspaper in the State. The reason given by its editor, R. B. Rhett, Jr., was that he desired to "take his place among the ruined children of the South — better so than to be the proudest and most honored of her successful enemies — and to wait, hoping, praying, expecting the bright coming of a final deliverance, the independence and prosperity of the South."

CARPET-BAGGERS AND THEIR ORGANS

To offset the political influence of the older Democratic sheets, numerous papers were started in the South as Republican organs to promote political schemes of Northern carpet-baggers. Again, South Carolina may be taken by way of illustration. Most of its new papers were published in the interest of what the old Southern press called "Thad Stevens's Ring-streaked Rule and Negro Misrule." *The South Carolina Ledger*, edited by Allen Coffin at Charleston, had as its motto, "Free Labor and General Reforms." The local press revised this motto to read, "Free Lunch and General Graft." Lieutenant-Governor A. J. Ransier, of South Carolina, had his special organ to which he gave the rather sanctimonious name of *The Missionary Record*, but which the regular established press of Charleston looked upon as an incendiary newspaper, as it appealed to the passions of the negro. *The South Carolina Republican* was another carpet-bag newspaper printed in the interest of Northern political control. *The Columbia Union* was also a radical paper edited by a carpet-bagger afterwards convicted of forgery.

The various methods resorted to by Congress to reconstruct the South brought about many unfortunate evils which were continually placed before the people by the press. Naturally, the Force Bill of 1870–71, by which the Federal judges tried those indicted for depriving a man of his privileges under the Constitution, were criticized by the press of the South, especially where Federal arms were used to enforce the law.

Such acts of the Northern carpet-baggers frequently drew forth the ire of Southern editors. Particularly was this true in New Orleans, where *The Bulletin* in 1874 attacked so bitterly the Reconstruction Government in a series of articles that a pitched battle finally resulted on Canal Street with a comparatively heavy loss of life. *The Bulletin,* in apologizing to its subscribers for its meager report of the battle, offered by way of explanation the excuse that the whole staff of the paper was in the fight and consequently could do no reporting. At Columbia, South Carolina, John T. Sloan was expelled by the House on January 15, 1869, for denouncing in his correspondence to *The Charleston Courier* the attempt to turn out the white professors and to substitute negroes at the State University.

In Memphis, Tennessee, *The Appeal* had two or three fights with the Reconstructionists before it accepted the results of the war and began its great work of rebuilding Tennessee in general and Memphis in particular.

The Southern press was practically unanimous in its support of the movement to disfranchise the negro. But almost without exception it insisted that nothing should be done that would in any way violate the Constitution of the United States. Some of the newspapers were very frank in acknowledging that the new constitutional conventions were designed to overthrow negro control, provided nothing be done to conflict with the laws of the United States. In this movement to avoid negro suffrage the South was seldom condemned by the press of the North. Even Republican organs, in confessing that such suffrage as had been tried was a failure, admitted that the movement to get rid of ignorance and superstition at the ballot-box was pardonable.

ORGANS OF KU-KLUX KLAN

One of the methods employed to keep colored voters from the polls of the South was the organization in Tennessee of a secret society called the Ku-Klux Klan. It was really a revival of the night patrol of slavery days when a negro was not allowed to be away from home without a pass from his owner. The chief purpose of this organization seemed to be to prey upon the superstitions of the negro. Some method of restraining the negro was undoubtedly necessary, but no excuse existed for the severities which the Ku-Klux Klan later adopted in other States. In fact, its extreme violence was deprecated even in the South. The organization had its special organs which wielded at one time much influence. Of these, *The Independent Monitor* at Tuskaloosa, Alabama, was a typical illustration.

NEW PAPERS AND OTHERS

During the period of the Reconstruction, many of the papers of the South, which had suspended on account of the war, were revived. In addition, many other papers were born both in the North and South. Lack of space — no editorial fib — permits only the briefest mention of some of the more important. In Nashville *The Republican Banner* resumed publication on September 27, 1865, and was followed by *The Union and American* on December 5, 1865. The following year the latter absorbed *The Dispatch*, a paper born during the war, and in the beginning used the type of the old *Republican Banner*. Subscribers to each of these revived papers received from carriers on September 1, 1875, a united sheet called *The American* — a most appropriate title for the new era dawning in the South. Under this title it continued publication until September 26, 1910, when it absorbed *The Nashville Tennessean*. *The Courier* of Louisville, Kentucky, which had died at Nashville in the winter of 1861–62, was revived at its old home by its founder and owner, Walter N. Haldeman. In Charleston, South Carolina, several papers appeared to divide the field with *The Courier*. Among these were *The Charleston Daily News*, started on August 14, 1865; *The Journal of Commerce*, edited by Colonel R. B. Rhett, Jr., formerly the editor of *The Charleston Mercury* and later editor of *The New Orleans Picayune; The Sun; The World; The Budget; The Evening Post; The Charleston Review*, etc. In New Orleans, *The Times*, which had started on September 20, 1863, united on December 4, 1881, with *The Democrat* which had started on December 18, 1875. The first of these two papers had been the leading force in the settlement of the political differences of the period and in reporting the revival of the progress in Louisiana.

It was *The Times* which bitterly denounced the Republican Returning Board which gave the election to Hayes. *The Daily States*, established January 3, 1880, used as its motive power to turn its press an "old and blind but willing and muscular darky." In Boston *The Journal*, founded February 5, 1833, grew so prosperous from the start given it during the Civil War by the correspondence of Charles Charleton Coffin that *The Globe* was established in that city on March 4, 1872, with an evening edition on March 7, 1878. At Chicago *The Republican* appeared on May 30, 1865; *The Evening Post* on September 4, 1865; *The Evening Mail*, on October 18, 1870; *The Interocean* on March 25, 1872; *The Daily News*, on December 26, 1875. In Philadelphia *The Record* was launched on June 1, 1877, as a one-cent newspaper, the first after the Civil War; it was the outgrowth of *The Public Record*, a paper founded on May 10, 1870, which had no influence and was a losing venture until William M. Singerly bought its Associated Press franchise for his new paper, that was most successful from the beginning. *The Evening Bulletin*, which had been founded in 1847 by Alexander Cummings under the title *Cummings's Evening Telegraphic Bulletin*, was in 1865 sold at auction for eighty-nine thousand dollars and passed through various hands until it finally, after its circulation had dwindled to less than five thousand, became the property of William L. McLean. *The Press*, founded in August, 1857, by John W. Forney and one of the most influential newspapers during the Civil War Period, passed into the control of Calvin Wells in 1879. *The Pennsylvania Inquirer* changed its name to *The Philadelphia Inquirer* and became one of the most influential Republican newspapers of the State. The first number of *The News* appeared in Indianapolis on December 7, 1869; a few subsequent issues were called *The Evening News*, but after a few months it became *The Indianapolis News*, under which title it is still published. In Washington, D. C., *The Evening Star*, which had been founded December 16, 1852, became after the war a newspaper whose growth has been contemporaneous with the development of Washington. After the war, John W. Forney devoted most of his time to *The Press* of Philadelphia and allowed his Washington organ, *The Chronicle*, to die. The latter's place was, to a certain extent, taken by *The Post*, which Stilson Hutchins established in Washington, December 6, 1877.

In San Francisco *The Examiner* was started as a successor of *The Democratic Press*, whose office had been mobbed on the assassination of Lincoln by a crowd provoked to violence by its previous attacks on the martyred President. In October, 1880, *The Examiner* became a morning paper and shortly after passed into the control of George Hearst, who wanted to further his aspirations to the United States Senate. On taking a seat in that body on March 4, 1887, he turned the paper over to his son, William Randolph Hearst, who used it as a starter for the chain of Hearst newspapers. In 1869 *The Daily Alta California*, the successor of *The Yerba Buena Star*, and the first daily paper in the State, absorbed *The Times* and enjoyed a period of prosperity until it was acquired by James G. Fair, who used the sheet to promote his personal interests and his political aspirations. In spite of the wealth of its owner, *The Alta California* gradually lost circulation and finally disappeared completely in 1891. *The Bulletin*, which had been started in San Francisco on October 8, 1855, six years after the famous gold rush, by James King, of William, who lost his life in May, 1855, for his attack upon James Casey, accused of stuffing ballot-boxes, had been a Democratic paper until 1861, but at the outbreak of the Civil War it changed to a Republican and did much to keep California loyal to the Union cause. Unlike many other editors of the *post-bellum* period, its editor, Loring Pickering, never forced his personality upon his readers, but he gave his paper a state-wide reputation for incorruptible honesty. For a number of years he was also a part owner of *The San Francisco Call*, then a morning newspaper, and took an active interest in the editorial management. *The San Francisco Post* was started in 1871.

Two papers, started like theater programmes during this period, later became influential newspapers. The first of these was *The Bee*, a small two-page evening paper founded in Omaha on June 19, 1871, by Edward Rosewater. The second was *The Dramatic Chronicle* established in San Francisco on June 16, 1865, by Charles de Young. Its initial numbers had the appearance of play-bills and were distributed free in theaters and other places. After each performance at San Francisco theaters copies of *The Dramatic Chronicle* were gathered from the floors and elsewhere, smoothed out by an old-fashioned kitchen iron, and then sent to points outside the city. In this way the paper became a very valuable advertising medium. Enterprising from the start, *The Chronicle* reached an important prestige during the Modoc War when it distanced all other San Francisco dailies in publishing the news. The distinctly dramatic character of the paper was abandoned on September 1, 1878, when it became a regular daily newspaper. Shortly after the paper was started, M. H. de Young joined his brother in the editorship and management of *The Dramatic Chronicle*.

OTHER NEWSPAPER CHANGES

In Cleveland William W. Armstrong, a prominent newspaperman, assumed charge of *The Plaindealer* which J. W. and A. N. Gray, two school-teachers, had founded in 1841 upon the remains of *The Cleveland Advertiser*, a Democratic daily started in 1832. In Columbus *The Ohio State Journal*, with which William Dean Howells had been actively connected as a sub-editor, became one of the most important Republican organs of the State; the paper had been started in 1811 in the little village of Worthington as *The Western Intelligencer* by James Kilbourne, but in 1814, in moving to Columbus, it added *Gazette* to its name and in 1825 it took into partnership State Printer Nashee, of Chillicothe, — famous in Ohio journalism, — who insisted that *Ohio State Journal* be put first in the title. In Detroit, *The Evening News*, started in August, 1873, by James E. Scripps and sold on the streets at two cents a copy, became a rival of *The Free Press* and *The Detroit Tribune*. In Milwaukee *The Sentinel*, established on June 27, 1837, and *The Evening Wisconsin*, established on June 8, 1847, became leaders of Wisconsin journalism. In St. Louis *The Republic*, which changed its name from *The Republican* because its editor, Charles H. Jones, found it impossible to convince his friends that he was running a Democratic and not a Republican newspaper, became, under the editorship of William Hyde, a paper with no straddling or wabbling editorial policies. In Pittsburgh *The Gazette* acquired in

1877 the controlling interest in *The Commercial*, a paper established in 1864 by C. D. Bingham: this consolidation, called *The Commercial Gazette*, was edited by Russell Errett.

PULITZER IN ST. LOUIS

One newspaper change can be recorded in a sentence. Toward the close of the period, Joseph Pulitzer purchased *The Post-Dispatch* of St. Louis. "The penniless son of a Jewish father and a Catholic mother," Pulitzer left Hungary in 1864 to come to America. After various precarious attempts to earn his living, he became at twenty-one a reporter on *The St. Louis Westliche-Post*, then under the management of Carl Schurz. By strange coincidence he was the secretary of the Cincinnati Liberal Republican Convention which nominated Horace Greeley, of *The New York Tribune*, for President. After securing control of *The Post-Dispatch*, Pulitzer made the paper a power for good by attacking the corrupt interests which had again become intrenched following their exposure by *The Democrat* during Grant's Administration. It was in St. Louis that Pulitzer first tried out many of his theories about the editing and making of a newspaper which he later developed and perfected after he purchased *The New York World* from Jay Gould in May, 1883.

FIRST COÖPERATIVE PAPERS

During the War Colonel A. H. Belo was a soldier in the Confederate Army, but after the surrender at Appomattox he went on horseback to Galveston, where he arrived in June, 1865. Becoming associated with *The News* he made it one of the most successful papers in the State. In 1881, in reorganizing a company to publish *The News*, he drew its charter in such a way that it might publish papers not only in Galveston, but also in other cities in Texas and became the first successful publisher of coöperative newspapers. With the privilege granted by the new charter, he established in Dallas a second daily also called *The News*. He made no mistake in trying to make the latter paper a minor publication. For all practical purposes *The News* in Dallas was quite independent of its older relative in Galveston and had its own newspaper plant, its own staff of editors, and its own corps of reporters. To Texas, therefore, belongs the honor of being the first in coöperative journalism in America.

PASSING OF PRENTICE

In Louisville, Kentucky, there came a most remarkable journalism change brought about by the new conditions which had arisen in that city, where for more than thirty years George Denison Prentice had been not only the foremost journalist of Kentucky and the entire South, but also one of the greatest editors of the middle nineteenth century. His journalistic career began in 1828 on *The New England Review*, as an associate of John Greenleaf Whittier, who, though a Quaker, was a most intense fighter for the freedom of the negro. Induced by Connecticut Whigs at Hartford to prepare a campaign life of Henry Clay, Prentice went to Kentucky to gather data. At that time the Democrats were determined to defeat Clay in his own State and Prentice was persuaded to start a paper to attack the Jackson Democracy. Accordingly *The Louisville Journal* appeared on November 24, 1830. From the start the paper had attracted national attention by its clever satirical epigrammatic paragraphs, which William Cullen Bryant of *The New York Evening Post* called "the stinging, hissing bolts of scorn." Many of these satiric arrows from his editorial quiver were aimed at Andrew Jackson. When it was announced that General Jackson had become a member of the Presbyterian Church, subscribers of *The Journal* wondered what Prentice, who had been educated in a Presbyterian school, would say: following his bare announcement of Jackson's decision were two lines to which no Presbyterian could object, for they were taken from a hymn by Dr. Watts: —

While the lamp holds out to burn
The vilest sinner may return.

The mention of sinners recalls another flip from Prentice's pen, "A well-known writer says that a fine coat covers a multitude of sins, but it is still truer that such coats cover a multitude of sinners." Many of these squibs were later collected in a book entitled "Prenticeana, or Wit and Humour in Paragraphs."

Prentice was ever prepared to fight, not only with his pen, but also with his pistol. So frequent were the attacks upon him that he was commonly caricatured by cartoonists with a pistol in one hand and a pen in the other. Possibly the nearest that he ever came to losing his life was when he was fired upon by George J. Trotter, editor of *The Kentucky Gazette*. At the beginning of the war, he espoused the cause of the Union and put into his column all the ardent enthusiasm of his nature in spite of the threats of his enemies and the enlistment of his two sons, whom he loved devotedly, in the Southern Army. An old-time Whig, he could not become either an out-and-out Republican or an out-and-out Democrat. This indecision during the Reconstruction Period proved a handicap to *The Journal*, which was not heeding the new voice of the South. Henry Watterson, however, in reviving an old suspended newspaper in Nashville, was attracting a great deal of attention with his editorials. It was to him that Prentice, in retiring, turned to find a successor for the editorial chair of *The Journal*. Later, Walter N. Haldeman, who had revived *The Courier*, made even a more attractive offer to Watterson. The offer was refused, and for a while the papers continued a separate publication, though always on friendly terms. On Sunday, November 8, 1868, however, subscribers were surprised to find on their doorsteps a united sheet, *The Courier-Journal*. At the start, Watterson had found himself at a disadvantage following the steps of Prentice. Gradually he impressed upon his subscribers his own remarkable abilities as an editor. During the Hayes-Tilden fight, "Marse Henry," a sobriquet bestowed upon him by the press, announced that he was prepared to lead one hundred thousand Democrats to Washington for no other purpose than to put Samuel J. Tilden in the White House. On the other hand, Watterson did much to disseminate broadcast a better feeling between the North and South.

EVENING PAPERS OF NEW YORK

Augustus Maverick, writing in 1870 about the New York press in general and *The New York Times* in particular, expressed surprise at the alarming growth of New York evening papers during recent years and asserted that it was a mystery which no writer on the subject of journalism could explain. Speaking specifically of some of these papers, he said: —

> The youngest of these sheets, *The Republic*, died suddenly at the end of 1869; yet nine survive. The prices at which these nine are sold range from one cent to five cents each. The oldest is *The Commercial Advertiser*, which has been in existence since 1794. The next in age is *The Evening Post*, established in 1801. The third in order is *The Express*, first issued as a morning paper, but changed into an evening sheet several years ago. Then were born *The Evening Mail, The News, The Commonwealth, The Telegram, The Democrat,* and *The Press and Globe.* Some of these have gained a daily circulation of ten thousand copies; others, seven to eight thousand; others, a few hundreds only. No one of them can ever reach the circulation which is regarded as essential to the existence of a morning paper; for the latter is never accounted a success until it is delivered daily to at least twenty thousand readers; but the advertising patronage of the business houses in the city is fairly apportioned among all, in great part through the skilful manipulation of Advertising Agencies; and thus a respectable support is secured.

The evening paper had not yet come into its own as a daily bulletin board of the news, to which might be added illustrated and special features designed primarily to appeal to the women.

CHICAGO FIRE AND LOCAL PRESS

The great fire which occurred in Chicago in October, 1871, showed the ingenuity of the newspaper publishers of that city. Within forty-eight hours after the fire had been stopped, *The Journal, The Republican, The Mail, The Times, The Tribune,* and *The Post* were again reappearing. To be sure, they were printed on smaller sheets, but they gave the news of the city. Within two months, the Chicago papers were back again to their original size. To their help came the other newspapers of the country with offers of type, presses, etc. For example, *The Tribune* of New York offered to ship its entire auxiliary plant to its namesake in Chicago. This offer was brought about by John Hay, who was reporting the conflagration for *The New York Tribune* — no easy task, for pitted against him were three representatives of *The New York Herald.* The offer, however, was seed sown on good ground, for later, when Hay was acting as editor of *The New York Tribune* in the absence of Whitelaw Reid, a paragrapher of the editorial staff of *The Chicago Tribune* began a somewhat savage, though disguised as humorous, attack on New York papers, whereupon Hay reminded Medill, editor of *The Chicago Tribune*, of the services offered at the time of the fire and asked that the picric squibs be stopped. It was done.

ATTACK ON ASSOCIATED PRESS

How James W. Simonton, when Washington correspondent of *The New York Times*, had exposed the "land graft" has been recorded in another chapter. During Grant's Administration, Simonton was the general manager of the Associated Press and undoubtedly had much to do with the publicity given to the chicanery of many of the appointees of the Administration. Their exposure led to an attempt to depose Simonton as the "sole telegraphic historian of the country." They drew up an indictment of the Associated Press in which they tried to cast reflections upon its manager. Their attack upon the organization, forming a basis of others which followed later, may be quoted as the attitude of its opponents not only in this period, but in the others which followed: —

The Associated Press is engaged ostensibly in the collection, sale, and distribution of news dispatches for such of the newspaper press of the country as find favor in its sight. It has numerous agents in the towns and cities of the United States, employed to send dispatches to its headquarters at New York. It makes special and exclusive contracts with combinations of favorite newspapers, and within their charmed circles no other papers are admitted. Being favored by the Western Union Telegraph Company with terms and conditions as to cost and precedence of business much more favorable than any rival concern can secure, the Associated Press has become a power in the land, amounting to a *censorship of the press;* for as it virtually monopolizes the only telegraphic system which extends generally throughout the United States, of course no papers can compete with the Associated Press "ring" newspapers in the completeness of news by telegraph. The *manager* of this overshadowing power has the appointment and removal of all its agents, and his good will being the tenure of their employment, it is in his power to give color and tone to all press dispatches.

Were the manager a man devoted to giving legitimate information concerning passing events, and above all temptation to spread false information, either for gain or to gratify personal feeling, still it would seem hard that he should have the power to dictate which of the papers of the land should be forced upon people who must have the news even though they have to patronize papers not in accord with their sentiments. But if the manager should be an unscrupulous man, devoid of all regard for truth and justice, filled with prejudice and hatred growing out of punishment inflicted upon him, and bent upon building up or tearing down the reputation of individuals by reckless misstatements scattered broadcast throughout the land, he would be able to play the tyrant and assassin, and would possess a power which ought to be unknown among a free people.

This résumé was followed by an attempt to show that Simonton, "at whose bidding the so-called news dispatches of the day are concocted, is a man of the class last described." Simonton, however, had simply published the facts as he found them in Washington. While Grant may be justly blamed for the selection of the men he put in office, he was not, according to the records, directly implicated in the questionable deals put through at Washington.

The Associated Press during the Period of Reconstruction was not an incorporated body, being simply a combination of smaller associations loosely held together through a written agreement for the exchange of news. The New York City Association, as during the Civil War Period, was the clearing-house for the smaller branches. These branch associations were determined by a community of interest due, for the most part, to geographical situation. The parent association at New York attended to the exchange with European agencies and stationed agents in the sparsely settled sections of the great plains West of the Mississippi. The telegraph company during the period permitted its operators to act as agents and to forward news by wire: in fact, they were expected to add to the revenue of the company by such service. Distributing stations were also established at Chicago, Cincinnati, Detroit, Memphis, Milwaukee, and St. Louis; from these cities abbreviated accounts — technically known as "pony reports" — were distributed along circuits to the dailies in the smaller cities. The exclusive features of the Associated Press led to the organization of a rival company, the American Press Association, which sold its news to any newspaper on payment of stated weekly charges. A distinct reorganization of the Associated Press occurred in the next era.

GRANT'S POSTMASTERS

There was much complaint on the part of the Democratic press that Grant's postmasters showed partiality in distributing newspapers to the advantage of the Republican editors. The charge brought by *The Syracuse Courier* was typical of what was said to be a general condition in many sections. The postmaster at Baldwinsville, according to *The Courier*, "kept back Democratic papers and to some of the subscribers he delivered the copies a week after arrival and to others he did not deliver the papers at all but when a package of loyal newspapers reached him, the alacrity with which he flew around and put them in boxes was beautiful to behold." Such a condition has obtained, however, during the administrations of presidents other than Grant — especially in the rural sections.

NO THIRD TERM FOR GRANT

In 1874 the editorial pages of American newspapers bristled with items about the possibility of a third term for Grant. The commotion, which is said to have been started by *The New York Herald*, announced that Grant was willing to set aside the precedent established by Washington and to accept a third term. If *The New York Herald* really started the matter, it threw a firebrand among the Democratic sheets, which with surprising alacrity proceeded to denounce Grantism and "Third Termism." The Republican press was not so prompt to consider the question, but was later forced to take sides. Urged by friendly newspapers, Grant finally made known his position in which he said, "I do not want it any more than I did the first," but he added that the Constitution did not expressly restrict a president to two terms and that conditions might be such as to make it an imperative duty to accept. The reply so divided the Republican press that many warm supporters of Grant in previous campaigns came out boldly and asserted that any departure from the custom set by Washington would be unwise and fraught with great peril to the American Republic. This revolt, aided by the Democratic journals, undoubtedly defeated the third nomination for Grant.

TAX ON ADVERTISING REMOVED

During the Reconstruction Period all acts which had imposed a tax upon newspaper advertisements during the war were repealed. On July 1, 1862, an act was passed which provided that after August 1, 1862, all newspapers and other periodicals should pay a tax of three per cent on the gross receipts for all advertisements and for all other items for which pay was received. On June 30, 1864, another act provided that in cases where the rate on the price of advertising was fixed by law of the United States, of the State or Territory, it was lawful for the newspapers publishing such advertisements to add the tax to the price of the advertisements, "any law to the contrary notwithstanding," because of the burden that the tax imposed upon the smaller newspapers. The act of 1864 provided for the exemption of taxes on newspaper advertisements to the amount of six hundred dollars annually: it also provided that all newspapers whose average circulation did not exceed two thousand copies should be exempted from all taxes for advertisements. Because of continued opposition on the part of newspapers, these various acts relating to a tax on advertisements were repealed on March 2, 1867.

PAPER MADE FROM WOOD PULP

While paper made from the fiber of soft wood began to be fed to the printing-press as early as 1867, it did not come into extensive use until later, for at the start it cost too much money to manufacture in proportion to the cost of raw material. For the years covered in the period of Reconstruction the contract price of news print paper delivered in New York were as follows: —

Year	Cents	Year	Cents
1865	12.6	1873	11.2
1866	17.2	1874	8.6
1867	15.	1875	8.5
1868	14.6	1876	8.2
1869	12.5	1877	8.2
1870	12.3	1878	6.46
1871	12.1	1879	6.
1872	12.	1880	6.9

Whitelaw Reid, of *The New York Tribune*, in addressing the New York Editorial Association on June 17, 1879, said: —

I look forward to the day when printing paper will sell far below its present price; and I rest this faith on the simple supposition that a manufactured article, the process of manufacture of which is easy and comparatively cheap, cannot long be continuing to be sold at six cents a pound, when the bulk of the raw material entering into it grows in the forests on every hillside and can be bought at two dollars a cord. The disproportion between the cost of the raw material and the cost of the manufactured article is too great to be permanently maintained. It is true enough that paper-makers have only the narrowest margin of profit now; but better processes for making wood pulp and improved machinery for converting into paper must surely come.

It did come. During the decade between 1880 and 1890 the price of wood-pulp paper dropped from six cents to four cents. During the next decade it touched the remarkable low price of one and six tenths cents per pound for the larger cities, where it was purchased in rolls. From that time it gradually advanced fraction by fraction until the problem of white paper became most acute, during the great European War.

POSTAL REGULATIONS OF PERIOD

After years of unsuccessful agitation, the Postal Department finally secured from Congress an act, approved June 23, 1874, by which postage on newspapers was paid by weight and without reference to distance carried. The rate provided by this act was two cents per pound for papers issued weekly or oftener and three cents per pound for those published less frequently than once a week. Newspapers for subscribers living outside of the county of publication were made up in bulk, carted to the post-office, where they were weighed. The postage for the proper amount was given to the postmaster in stamps instead of being adjusted to the papers or packages sent through the mail. The newspaper stamps, now a rarity, ranged in denomination from two cents to sixty dollars. The new system of collecting postage at the office of publication, rather than at the offices of destinations, returned the Postal Department additional revenue, for postmasters had been most lax in collecting postage due. The act of June 23, 1874, provided this exception: "That newspapers, one copy to each actual subscriber residing within the county where the same are printed, in whole or in part, and published, shall go free through the mails; but the same shall not be delivered at letter-carrier offices or distributed by carriers unless postage is paid thereon as by law provided." An act of March 3, 1879, fixed the uniform rate of two cents a pound for postage on second-class matter to which newspapers belonged. All publications now paid the same rate. The two-cent rate prevailed until March 3, 1885, when it was reduced to one cent a pound.

STATISTICAL RÉSUMÉ OF PAPERS

Statistics as to the number of newspapers in the United States until after the Census of 1880 were most unreliable, especially as to the number of papers in the newly settled States and Territories. The reports of the census for 1850, 1860, 1870, and 1880 being, however, the most authoritative statements as to the increase in number of newspapers, should be quoted in a comparative table. According to this table, there were in the United States 254 dailies in 1850, 387 in 1860, 574 in 1870, 971 in 1880; 115 tri-weeklies in 1850, 86 in 1860, 107 in 1870, 73 in 1880; 31 semi-weeklies in 1850, 79 in 1860, 115 in 1870, 133 in 1880; 1902 weeklies in 1850, 3173 in 1860, 4295 in 1870, 8633 in 1880. Of all these classes, there were in 1850, 2526; in 1860, 4051; in 1870, 5871; in 1880, 11,314. The accompanying table, on pages 349, 350, shows the distribution of these classes for the various census years.

LOCATION OF DAILY PAPERS

S. N. B. North made for the Government in 1880 a special investigation of the newspaper and periodical press in America. In his report he published an interesting observation about the location of the daily papers. Nine hundred and seventy-one daily newspapers of the census year were published in three hundred and eighty-nine towns or cities — an average of two and one-half to each place. The strange anomaly was discovered of towns, with less than four thousand in population, having two and sometimes three daily papers. The smallest town in 1880 which had a daily was Elko, Nevada, with a population of seven hundred and fifty-two. The smallest town in which two daily papers were published was Tombstone, Arizona, with a popula-

State	1850 Dailies	1850 Tri-Weeklies	1850 Semi-Weeklies	1850 Weeklies	1860 Dailies	1860 Tri-Weeklies	1860 Semi-Weeklies	1860 Weeklies	1870 Dailies	1870 Tri-Weeklies	1870 Semi-Weeklies	1870 Weeklies	1880 Dailies	1880 Tri-Weeklies	1880 Semi-Weeklies	1880 Weeklies
Alabama	6	5	—	48	9	6	1	77	9	2	2	76	6	1	—	109
Arizona	—	—	—	—	—	—	—	—	—	—	—	1	6	—	—	11
Arkansas	—	—	—	9	22	2	3	37	3	1	4	48	6	—	1	104
California	4	4	—	3	14	—	—	89	33	4	—	140	58	2	1	250
Colorado	—	—	—	—	—	—	1	—	4	—	1	9	19	—	11	63
Connecticut	7	—	—	30	5	—	1	37	16	—	3	43	17	—	2	99
Dakota	—	—	—	7	—	—	1	—	—	—	—	3	9	—	1	57
Delaware	1	—	—	8	12	1	4	10	1	—	1	12	5	—	—	20
District of Columbia	5	1	—	9	—	2	2	4	3	1	9	12	5	—	2	23
Florida	1	—	—	37	—	5	1	19	—	2	4	20	3	—	3	40
Georgia	5	5	—	84	23	1	1	73	15	5	1	73	16	4	2	163
Idaho	—	—	—	—	—	—	—	—	—	1	—	4	—	1	17	7
Illinois	8	1	—	95	13	6	2	238	39	—	1	364	74	6	1	758
Indiana	9	3	—	25	9	1	5	160	20	10	4	233	40	3	—	390
Indian Territory	—	—	—	—	—	—	1	—	—	3	8	—	—	—	3	3
Iowa	1	4	—	38	3	2	2	112	22	—	—	196	30	1	3	500
Kansas	—	—	—	37	4	1	1	24	12	1	2	78	20	—	1	310
Kentucky	9	2	—	39	8	3	3	64	6	3	16	68	11	2	7	160
Louisiana	11	2	—	54	8	1	1	70	7	4	—	75	13	1	1	94
Maine	4	1	—	126	6	4	—	52	7	4	1	47	12	—	—	90
Maryland	6	2	11	47	17	2	4	49	8	1	3	69	15	1	13	111
Massachusetts	22	7	3	46	8	3	3	145	21	1	—	153	39	3	3	279
Michigan	3	6	—	45	4	1	1	103	16	3	2	174	33	1	—	397
Minnesota	—	5	—	35	5	2	—	45	6	5	16	79	10	5	2	205
Mississippi	1	4	—	43	16	3	—	65	3	6	—	92	5	8	—	109
Missouri	5	4	—	1	—	—	1	143	21	5	3	225	43	—	1	415
Montana	—	2	—	—	—	—	—	—	3	1	—	—	4	—	—	14
Nebraska	—	1	—	—	—	—	1	12	7	1	—	30	15	—	1	165
Nevada	—	4	—	—	—	—	—	—	5	1	2	5	14	—	—	22
New Hampshire	6	4	—	35	15	—	—	20	7	—	1	37	10	1	6	66
New Jersey	—	—	—	43	—	—	1	70	20	—	1	95	27	—	—	163
New Mexico	—	—	—	1	—	—	—	2	1	—	—	4	3	—	—	15

	1850				1860				1870				1880			
	Dailies	Tri-Weeklies	Semi-Weeklies	Weeklies	Dailies	Tri-Weeklies	Semi-Weeklies	Weeklies	Dailies	Tri-Weeklies	Semi-Weeklies	Weeklies	Dailies	Tri-Weeklies	Semi-Weeklies	Weeklies
New York	51	8	13	308	74	7	10	366	87	5	22	518	115	5	24	892
North Carolina	—	5	—	40	8	1	4	57	8	3	5	44	13	2	3	113
Ohio	26	10	—	201	24	8	4	260	26	8	3	299	56	8	4	584
Oregon	—	—	1	2	2	—	—	12	4	—	—	26	7	—	—	59
Pennsylvania	24	2	—	261	29	1	3	297	55	3	2	385	98	4	3	674
Rhode Island	5	—	2	12	5	—	1	19	6	—	1	19	8	—	1	31
South Carolina	7	5	1	27	2	4	—	35	5	4	—	42	4	3	—	69
Tennessee	8	2	—	36	8	7	—	61	13	2	1	65	12	1	2	154
Texas	—	5	1	29	3	3	—	79	12	5	5	89	30	—	2	231
Utah	—	—	—	—	—	—	—	—	3	1	3	3	5	—	4	8
Vermont	2	1	—	30	2	—	—	28	3	—	1	43	5	—	—	72
Virginia	15	12	1	55	15	5	11	103	16	7	8	69	20	5	6	124
Washington	—	—	—	—	—	—	—	4	1	1	—	10	4	1	—	23
West Virginia	—	—	—	—	—	—	—	—	4	2	—	48	2	—	2	96
Wisconsin	6	4	—	35	14	8	—	130	14	2	3	160	21	3	2	283
Wyoming	—	—	—	—	—	—	—	—	2	1	—	4	3	—	—	8

tion of nine hundred and seventy-three. In California the town of Eureka, with a population of twenty-six hundred and thirty-nine, had three daily papers, and the town of Red Bluff, population of twenty-one hundred and six, two daily papers. Galena, Kansas, had one daily for a population of fourteen hundred and sixty-three; Greenville, Michigan, two dailies for a population of thirty-one hundred and forty-four; Olean, New York, one daily for a population of three thousand and thirty-six; Winnemucca, Nevada, one daily for a population of seven hundred and sixty-three; and Milton, Pennsylvania, one daily for a population of twenty-one hundred and two.

END OF PERIOD

The period practically began with an impeachment of a President of the United States and closed with a contest of one whose very election to the White House was most seriously questioned and had to be determined by an unconstitutional Electoral Commission distinctly partisan in bias. Under such conditions it was but natural that a somewhat inflammable press should mirror the times often at white-heat with political passion. From material of unrefined ore the editors fashioned their papers under a forced draft that left no time for the cooling process. Yet the centrifugal force threw out much of the slag and left the newspaper nearer the pattern given by Samuel Bowles, of *The Springfield Republican*.

E. L. Godkin, of *The New York Evening Post*, had a vision of a new type of journalism, when, at the death of Raymond, he said editorially:

The Times under his management came nearer the newspaper of the good time coming than any other in existence; in this, that it encouraged truthfulness — the reproduction of the facts uncolored by the necessities of a "cause" or the editor's personal feelings — among reporters; that it carried decency, temperance, and moderation into discussion, and banished personality from it; and thus not only supplied the only means by which rational beings can get at the truth, but helped to abate the greatest nuisance of the age, the coarseness, violence, calumny, which does so much to drive sensible and high-minded men out of public life or keep them from entering it.

CHAPTER XVIII

PERIOD OF FINANCIAL READJUSTMENT

1880 — 1900

MANTON MARBLE, one of the ablest of the early editors of *The New York World*, claimed in a published lecture on journalism two things for the maker of newspapers: —

A. That he is a merchant of news. He buys it everywhere — he sells it in any market not stocked with his commodity. Enterprise and industry get him, and other merchants, success and honor, and of like kind. Probity has the same reward in public confidence. Shrewd and far-sighted combinations bring to the merchant of news — or of flour, or of pork — profit and credit.

B. That he has it in trust and stewardship to be the organ and mould of public opinion, to express and guide it, and to seek, through all conflicting private interests, solely the public general good. Herein his work is allied to the statesman's, the politician's, and takes rank as it takes tribute of letters, science and the law.

COMMERCIAL JOURNALISM

The financial readjustment under which the larger daily newspaper went during the last two decades of the nineteenth century brought many changes in journalism. There was a time when the subscriber paid his money primarily to see what Horace Greeley had to say in *The New York Tribune* or to read what Joseph Medill wrote for *The Chicago Tribune:* even after Greeley's death the upstate farmer renewed his subscription for *The New York Tribune* because he thought Horace still prepared its contents. But the impersonal and commercial journalism changed completely conditions and customs. Formerly, the editor was practically supreme in control: he was the employer of the publisher, of the advertising manager, of the circulation agent, etc. After he ceased to have the controlling interest, it passed into other hands represented at official councils by the business manager: only occasionally, the exception which proved the rule, did the editor have sufficient wealth or its equivalent in credit at the bank to buy or to start a daily in any one of the larger cities. The dividing line between the A and the B of Manton Marble's claims grew very distinct: the former became the downstairs office devoted to the business; the latter, the upstairs office devoted to the profession. Here and there, more frequently in the West than in the East, arose a man who was both a good business executive and an able editor.

The metropolitan daily represented too heavy a financial investment to be organized on any save a sound business basis. The telegraph and the cable made news a most perishable commodity because of the rapidity with which it could be placed before the public. Shop-worn goods the merchant can sell at a special sale to bring at least the cost of production, but stale news the publisher cannot market at any price. The franchise in a press association became harder to get and at the same time carried with it a constantly increasing charge for better service. Presses jumped from hundreds to tens of thousands in cost of manufacture. Extra ones were purchased for emergency cases so that if one press broke down the plates of the paper could be shifted to another without danger of missing the mails. Typographical unions kept pushing the wages of printers and pressmen higher and higher up the scale. Competition reduced the selling price, but increased the cost of distribution. The return privilege by which newsdealers did not pay for unsold papers kept the "profit and loss" entry on the ledger first in red and then in black ink according to sales. Additions to the editorial staff increased the number of employees while "bids" from rivals raised the salaries of other members. More and more the revenue came from advertising and less and less from circulation. Such conditions demanded a business pilot at the wheel to steer the newspaper craft sailing over seas uncharted by editors of previous periods.

VIEWS OF CHARLES DUDLEY WARNER

Charles Dudley Warner, long associated with *The Courant*, of Hartford, Connecticut, thus explained clearly and succinctly journalism conditions obtaining at the beginning of the Period of Financial Readjustment in a lecture on "The American News-paper" before the Social Science Association on September 6, 1881: —

The recognition of the fact that the newspaper is a private and purely business enterprise will help to define the mutual relations of the editor and the public. His claim upon the public is exactly that of any man-ufacturer or dealer. It is that of the man who makes cloth, or the grocer who opens a shop: neither has a right to complain if the public does not buy of him. If the buyer does not like a cloth half shoddy, or coffee half chicory, he will go elsewhere. If the subscriber does not like one news-paper, he takes another, or none. The appeal for newspaper support on the ground that such a journal ought to be sustained by an enlightened community, or on any ground than that it is a good article that people want, — or would want if they knew its value, — is purely childish in this age of the world. If any person wants to start a periodical devoted to decorated teapots, with the noble view of inducing the people to live up to his idea of a teapot, very good; but he has no right to complain if he fails.

On the other hand, the public has no rights in the newspaper except what it pays for; even the "old subscriber" has none, except to drop the paper if it ceases to please him. The notion that the subscriber has a right to interfere in the conduct of the paper, or the reader to direct its opinions, is based on a misconception of what the newspaper is. The claim of the public to have its communications printed in the paper is equally baseless. Whether they shall be printed or not rests in the dis-cretion of the editor, having reference to his own private interest, and to his apprehension of the public good. Nor is he bound to give any rea-son for his refusal. It is purely in his discretion whether he will admit a reply to any thing that has appeared in his columns. No one has a right to demand it. Courtesy and policy may grant it; but the right to it does not exist. If any one is injured, he may seek his remedy at law; and I should like to see the law of libel such and so administered that any per-son injured by a libel in the newspaper, as well as by slander out of it, could be sure of prompt redress. While the subscriber acquires no right to dictate to the newspaper, we can imagine an extreme case when he should have his money back which had been paid in advance, if the newspaper totally changed its character. If he had contracted with a dealer to supply him with hard coal during the winter, he might have a remedy if the dealer delivered only charcoal in the coldest weather; and so if he paid for a Roman-Catholic journal which suddenly became an organ of the spiritists.

The advertiser acquires no more rights in the newspaper than the subscriber. He is entitled to use the space for which he pays by the in-sertion of such material as is approved by the editor. He gains no interest in any other part of the paper, and has no more claim to any space in the editorial columns, than any other one of the public. To give him such space would be unbusiness-like, and the extension of a preference which would be unjust to the rest of the public. Nothing more quickly destroys the character of a journal, begets distrust of it, and so reduces its value, than the well-founded suspicion that its editorial columns are the property of advertisers. Even a religious journal will, after a while, be injured by this.

To be just to Mr. Warner, and to inform the reader that in this "commercialization of the press" the second claim of Manton Marble, of *The New York World*, was not completely overlooked, a comment from "The American Newspaper" should be given in this connection: —

It is scarcely necessary to say, except to prevent a possible misapprehension, that the editor who has no high ideals, no intention of benefiting his fellow-men by his newspaper, and uses it unscrupulously as a means of money-making only, sinks to the level of the physician and the lawyer who have no higher conception of their callings than that they offer opportunities for getting money by appeals to credulity, and by assisting in evasions of the law.

Before taking up the changes and historical developments of the period, it should be said that *The Hartford Courant* practiced what Mr. Warner preached in "The American Newspaper" at Saratoga Springs in September, 1881.

INCREASE OF ADVERTISING

The Period of Financial Readjustment was marked by a tremendous increase in the amount of advertising printed in the newspapers. During this period came the development of the great department stores in the large cities. Their increase in size may be traced almost invariably by the increase in the amount of space they used to advertise their wares in the newspapers. Stores which inserted advertisements of a half a column at the beginning of the period were using a full page at the close of the century, when individual stores were paying as high as fifty thousand dollars a year to one newspaper in order to market their merchandise to readers. Railroads, instead of inserting a time-table occupying two squares of the old blanket sheet, became heavy purchasers of space to advertise the scenic beauty of the various roads and to attract settlers to the new territory opened up along their lines. Manufacturers of patent medicines seemingly entered upon competition to see which one could use the most printer's ink in American newspapers. New advertisers appeared with announcements of breakfast foods, laundry soaps, baking powders, — in fact everything used in modern American homes. Local gas companies urged women to "cook with gas"; electric light and power companies pointed out how easy it was to attach the sewing machine to the current from the incandescent light; telephone companies started campaigns to get housewives to "shop by wire"; book publishers, usually the most conservative advertisers, caught the advertising fever and by the close of the period were, in exceptional cases, using a whole page in certain newspapers to advertise a popular novel; etc. Classified advertising grew from a column or two of "Help Wanted" and "Houses to Let" to several pages. The worst feature of this tremendous increase in the amount of advertising was the fact that it was possible to insert at a higher cost almost any advertisement disguised as a bit of news. Sometimes these paid reading notices of advertisers were distinguished by star or dagger, but more frequently there was no sign to indicate to the reader that the account had been bought and paid for and was not a regular news item.

JOURNALISM THAT MAKES NEWS

Though the journalism that makes news really started when *The New York Herald* sent Henry Morton Stanley to find David Livingstone, the English missionary who was lost "somewhere in Africa," the newspapers were somewhat slow in sowing seed in a field so long fallow. *The Herald* on July 2, 1872, startled the world with its exclusive announcement that Stanley had found Livingstone at Ujiji and that the latter had discovered the source of the Nile. At the time this remarkable piece of news was looked upon as a piece of good fortune on the part of an American war correspondent who had been sent to witness the opening of the Suez Canal, to report the results of Baker's Expedition up the Nile, to learn the truth about the Russian Expedition bound for Khiva, and to write interesting letters from Bagdad, Persepolis, etc. Stanley's achievement possibly caused a greater sensation in England than in America. The London papers promptly acknowledged the achievement of *The New York Herald*. *The London Post* went so far as to say that the expedition surpassed everything which had hitherto been achieved by journalistic enterprises.

EXTRAMURAL ACTIVITIES

The example set by *The Herald* later led other American newspapers to undertake humanitarian enterprises which had not been formerly associated with the editing and making of a newspaper. Such enterprises became more distinctly local, but the sum total of good accomplished was greater than the more sensational finding of a man lost in the wilds of Africa. Among these humanitarian enterprises was the establishment of a Free-Ice Fund by *The New York Herald*. On May 29, 1892, the paper that had sent Stanley to find Livingstone laid before its readers a proposal to furnish free ice for the relief of mothers and babies in the tenement-house districts of New York. The fund, started with a donation of five hundred dollars by *The Herald*, met with the enthusiastic encouragement of charity organizations, welfare workers, physicians, and others, who longed to do something to relieve the distress which the extreme heat produced in tenement districts. On July 2 of that year *The Herald* distributed sixteen thousand pounds of ice from seven different stations with the result that over one hundred families were benefited. When the season closed on September 15, over forty thousand pounds of ice were being distributed daily from fifteen stations in the poorer sections of the city for the benefit of about twelve thousand, five hundred men, women, and children. During the extreme hot summer of 1914 a daily average of seven hundred thousand pounds were distributed among twenty-two thousand families. The ice was distributed upon presentation of tickets secured on the recommendation of social workers, physicians, ministers, and others who were familiar with the needs of the people living in the district of the station.

Somewhat similar to the Free-Ice Fund was the Fresh-Air Fund originally associated with *The New York Evening Post*, but taken over by *The New York Tribune* in 1881. This movement was a practical application of the text from which the Reverend Willard Parsons, a young clergyman, preached at Sherman, Pennsylvania, on June 3, 1877: "Inasmuch as you have done it unto the least of these, my brethren, you have done it unto me." In the course of his sermon he outlined the distress which prevailed in that section of New York where he once had a mission church and urged that his parishioners alleviate such suffering by taking into their homes for brief periods during the summer some of the children from the tenements. From the time that *The Tribune* became interested, it worked along two lines: first, it provided outings for children in private families in the country; second, it provided outings for children in so-called fresh-air homes and camps maintained by the Fund annually raised by the paper. Except in rare instances no organization except *The Tribune* has attempted to provide outings in the first of these two ways. Later, many organizations started sending children to institutional homes and camps for brief rests during the summer. *The Tribune*, in connection with this Fund, now maintains some ten homes and camps. It utilizes these primarily for special classes of children for whom it is either unwise or impossible to secure the hospitality of private families such as negro children, under-nourished children, tubercular children, etc. In 1881 *The Tribune* sent thirty-two hundred to the country for two weeks, and in 1900, the year in which the period closed, it sent seven thousand, four hundred and thirty-one. The maximum number was in 1892, when fifteen thousand, two hundred and sixty-seven were sent. The price of board in the country, the amount of annual subscriptions, etc., are factors which determine the number which can be helped. *The Tribune* has aided in establishing a similar movement in other countries: in England it is known as "The Country Fortnight" and in France, as "Les Œuvres du Grand Air."

Special attention has been given the enterprises just mentioned because they were pioneer humanitarian enterprises of the press. Other papers, however, have attended to other things than putting ink on paper. *The Press*, of Pittsburgh, Pennsylvania, started a subscription which raised forty thousand dollars to build a home for the newsboys of that city. It raised a fund to erect a monument to the memory of Steven C. Foster, a native of Pittsburgh, who wrote "The Old Folks at Home"; it started a young folks league, a baseball club, a brass band and drum corps, two clubs for girls, an athletic league, etc. *The Times*, of Troy, New York, following the example set by *The New York Tribune*, started its Fresh-Air Fund by which hundreds of children could get the benefits of a two weeks' vacation at the fresh-air home erected by *The Times* in the mountains of Rensselaer County. *The Tribune*, of Chicago, Illinois, initiated two reforms which developed into a national movement, that of a "Sane Fourth of July" and the "Good Fellow Club," the object of which was to make the children of the poor acquainted with Santa Claus. *The News* of Indianapolis, Indiana, built a fresh-air village for sick women and children, in addition to building several public monuments. But in doing this *The News* did not forget that such humanitarian enterprises could begin closer at home. It established a sub-station system of delivering papers to boys in the neighborhood where they lived and appointed a district man to look over them, to keep in touch with their parents, and to guard them as jealously as a school teacher, and above all to teach them business thrift. In this way *The News* eliminated the old-style newsboy with dirty face and worn shoes. *The Press*, of Grand Rapids, Michigan, was one of the pioneer papers to carry on all-round welfare work for its newsboys. Knowing that boys like a noise, it started two bands, a senior and a junior, the latter to teach the rudiments of music to beginners. It went into the business of education to start a day school for the lads handling the noon editions and the extras: to be sure, the school was ungraded, but the teacher, always a high-grade woman with a good salary, has taught the boys from the poorer families so well that the movement has the endorsement of public school officials. To its Hoe press it added the strange equipment of baths and a swimming-pool for the use of its boys. It put in a lunch counter where the carriers could get sandwiches, milk, buns, etc., for less than cost. The crowning feature of the welfare work of *The Press* has been the "Happy Hour" held in its own halls every Sunday afternoon. Here the programme begins with a flag service full of thrillers and closes with motion pictures. *The Journal*, of Milwaukee, Wisconsin, early started a similar welfare movement for its carriers. *The Nashville Tennessean*, at Nashville, Tennessee, soon devoted its attentions to the school children of the city and at its own expense it provided public lectures to amuse, entertain, and instruct the children. Its manager recently said: "It is far from the province of the daily press to print only the news — a newspaper should be a community and section builder." *The Chronicle*, of San Francisco, California, was instrumental in establishing the zoölogical gardens in 1880; it started the movement for the Golden Gate Park Museum in 1885. *The Examiner*, of the same city, erected the Little Jim Hospital for Incurables and the Free Eye and Ear Infirmary for the treatment of unfortunate children of the poorer classes. If space permitted, many other humanitarian newspaper enterprises could be mentioned, but the beginnings of the movement distinctly belong to the Period of Financial Readjustment.

PRESS AS DETECTIVE

With the financial readjustment many newspapers not only undertook humanitarian enterprises, but also assumed other extramural activities. Not content with mere publicity for crime, the press in numerous cities undertook active detective work in locating criminals. Mention might be made of how *The Daily News*, of Chicago, Illinois, followed D. D. Spencer, president of the State Savings Institution, who had absconded with something like half a million dollars from the vaults of the Bank of Chicago, step by step across Canada, over the Atlantic and thence through Europe until it finally located him at Stuttgart; or how *The Argus*, of Albany, New York, after the police of that city were completely baffled in an attempt to locate a kidnapper, not only found the child, but also captured the criminal.

The most remarkable instance, however, was possibly the identification by *The World*, of New York, of the man who made an attempt upon the life of Russell Sage. Isaac D. White, then a reporter on *The World* and now head of its Bureau of Accuracy and Fair Play, secured a button from the trousers and a piece of cloth from the clothing of the would-be murderer. The button was stamped "Brooks, Boston." Going to that city White found that there was only one tailor by the name of Brooks and that he still had his roll of cloth like the sample cut from the trousers. Investigation of the order books proved that material for only one pair of trousers had been cut from it. It was comparatively easy to find, by means of the tag number of the roll, the name and address of the man for whom the trousers had been made: the address was the business office of Norcross at Boston. White, on going to this office, learned that Norcross had been away for several days. He then went to the home of Norcross in Somerville, where he found that the man had been missing for several days and that his disappearance had greatly worried the family. The parents of Norcross recognized the sample of clothing and came to New York with White, where they identified the head of their son.

Many other illustrations might be given of the excellent work that the press has done in the field of detection of criminals. Every police commissioner in the city of New York who has proved himself competent to hold that office has frankly admitted the great assistance of the press. In every great city there is only one thing members of the police department fear, that is, the exposure of their incompetence by the daily press. Publicity for the defenders of the law has accomplished almost as much good as publicity for the offenders of the law.

PRESS VS. PRESIDENTS

The question of a presidential third term again came up for discussion in the press in 1880. Grant had returned from a most spectacular trip around the world and his friends again started a movement in the newspapers for a third-term nomination. There is every reason to believe that Grant in this instance did not desire such an honor, but was used simply as a tool by Roscoe Conkling, the senior Senator from New York, to prevent the nomination of James G. Blaine, who had become such an important Republican leader that he was disputing the field with Conkling. The struggle was even more bitter than in a former contest. Editorial pages in the opposition press fairly bristled with almost a standing caption over the leading article, "Anything to Beat Grant." The result, as every student knows, was that both Grant and Blaine were defeated and the nomination went to James A. Garfield.

CARTOON REVIVED

To *The New York World* belongs the honor of reviving the cartoon, the wordless editorial of American journalism. From the time that Franklin had cut a snake into eight parts, each part representing a section of the country, and published the same in his *Gazette* under the caption "Join or Die," cartoons had appeared spasmodically in the American press — usually at times of great political or national excitement. *The New York World*, however, was the first newspaper to make the cartoon a regular feature. Its first cartoon, printed on August 10, 1884, was entitled "The Difference Between Two Knights," and was a contrast of Blaine and Cleveland. This cartoon was not signed. In August, 1884, *The World* began in its Sunday issue a series of political cartoons which attracted a great deal of attention and so increased its circulation that new presses had to be ordered. So popular, indeed, were these cartoons that they were introduced into the daily edition. Of these early cartoons none was more popular than that entitled "Belshazzar's Feast," which appeared on August 30 and dealt with the coming presidential election of the Cleveland-Blaine Campaign. It occupied half of the first page and showed the Republican chiefs in the robes of Babylonian revelers at the Belshazzar banquet of Special Privilege. Though the cartoon was crudely drawn, it had a certain strength which caused it to be remembered long after Cleveland was elected to the Presidency.

FIGHT OF TYPOGRAPHICAL UNION

In 1884 *The New York Tribune* possibly aided the election of Grover Cleveland — though not through the support of its editorial page. This assistance, such as it was, grew out of a strike which started in December of 1883 when the Typographical Union decided upon a boycott of the paper because of some disagreement about wages of printers. A circular was sent to labor organizations throughout the United States to announce the boycott and to ask the withdrawal of all support from *The Tribune*. Pressure was brought to bear to get advertisers to withdraw from the columns of *The Tribune* and a weekly paper, *The Boycotter*, was started to induce other trade unions to take up the fight. As the strike at the start proved unsuccessful, the Union decided to enter politics, for *The Tribune* was considered at that time the leading exponent of the principles of the Republican Party. A committee was sent to the Republican National Convention, when it met in Chicago on June 3 of the following year, to inform the delegates that the policy of *The Tribune* was hostile to organized labor and to request the convention to repudiate that paper as a Republican organ. When no satisfaction was received, the Union in August passed a resolution that "until the Republican National Committee give us written assurance that they will repudiate *The Tribune* the future policy of *The Boycotter* shall be to boycott *The Tribune* and James G. Blaine." In spite of the activity of political leaders to adjust the dispute, *The Tribune* was not repudiated and many of the Union printers decided to vote against Blaine. As Cleveland carried New York State by a plurality of only 1144 votes, and as the Union numbered over 3500 printers, the assertion has been made that, New York being the pivotal State in the election, Blaine was defeated because *The Tribune* refused to come to terms. A year later the Republican State Committee took the matter up with *The Tribune* in order to bring about a settlement of the controversy, and a satisfactory agreement was finally reached so that by 1892 the Union announced its willingness to send a committee to the National Republican Convention at Minneapolis to declare that all hostilities against *The Tribune* and against the Republican Party had ceased.

BRYAN AND PARTY PRESS

When William Jennings Bryan was nominated for the Presidency at the Democratic Convention held in Chicago in 1896, many of the Democratic papers refused to support the party ticket because of the stand taken by the nominee on the question of free silver. Colonel A. K. McClure, editor of *The Philadelphia*

Times, thus summed up the remarkable editorial change in policy of these papers: —

A number of the leading newspapers of the country which had supported Cleveland in his three contests repudiated the Chicago platform and its candidate, and they stood in the forefront of American journalism. Not one of them ever had conference or communication with the McKinley leaders, or received or proposed any terms for their support, or ever sought, accepted, or desired favors from the McKinley administration. Some of them suffered pecuniary sacrifice, but they performed a heroic duty, and it was the inspiration they gave to the conservative Democratic sentiment of the country that made McKinley President by an overwhelming majority.

This opposition of the press undoubtedly explains the criticism which Mr. Bryan later showered upon newspapers in general and those of New York State in particular. *The New York World* in explaining its own course said, "Never before in a Presidential campaign had the leading newspaper of either party declined to support the ticket and platform presented by the politicians, not only without loss of power and prestige, but actually with a gain in both."

Yet it was to this New York newspaper that Grover Cleveland once said he owed his election to the Presidency.

JOURNALISM DURING WAR WITH SPAIN

In the war with Spain, the American war correspondent reached his highest development. Arthur Brisbane has told what it meant to report that conflict in the American press. It meant, to quote his own words: —

To cover the field of possible action in advance from Manila to Porto Rico; to place the right man in the right place, select the man through intuition; to secure boats and arrange telegraphic facilities; to get the news into the office first, into the newspaper first, on the street and all over the country first; to sift the kernel of fact from the mass of rumors; to exercise discretion and reasonable conservatism without falling behind in the great fight for news priority and supremacy; to meet the problems of circulation grown suddenly to be vastly in excess of the mechanical facilities; and — with the weaker papers — to meet with limited capital the problem of expense unlimited, to make mental resource replace the hard money sinews of the newspaper war reporter.

The explosion which sank the Maine occurred on Friday evening, February 15, 1898, at 9.40 o'clock. The first reports from Havana, however, did not reach the New York papers until about half-past two the following morning. Yet before noon of that day a tug chartered by *The New York World* left Key West with three divers on board. The correspondent of *The World* at Havana received the following instructions by cable: —

Have sent divers from Key West to get actual truth, whether favorable or unfavorable. First investigation by divers with authentic results worth one thousand dollars, extra expense, to-morrow alone.

When the boat chartered by *The World* reached the Maine its divers were not allowed to make any investigation and the only direct result to *The World* from this expedition was an expense amounting to one thousand dollars. Yet this incident was fairly typical of the enormous expense to which American newspapers were put in reporting the war. One New York newspaper reported that it spent on the average of three thousand dollars a day during the entire war.

Immediately after the sinking of the Maine, correspondents from all the leading papers hastened to Havana. From the start they met continued opposition from the Spanish censor, who sometimes let what they wrote go through, but who just about as often threw their communications into the waste-basket. To overcome this difficulty several of the more influential American newspapers chartered special boats to ply between Havana and Key West. Their cargo consisted, as one war correspondent put it, "of a little package of copy which a man might carry in the vest pocket of his coat." After the blockade was established the newspapers had to increase the number of boats, which patroled the waters of the West Indies. All this, of course, meant a tremendous expense for getting the news from Cuba.

After the correspondents were compelled to leave Havana and the blockade was firmly established, it became still more difficult to get news through the lines. Some of the newspapers, which up to that time had been gathering news separately, now pooled their interests in self-preservation.

As the war progressed, newspapers had additional difficulties to meet. There were only two cables between Key West and the mainland of Florida. Because the official Government dispatches took precedence over everything else, correspondents found that the cables were soon overloaded and they had to wait the pleasure of the Government. Some of the newspapers then made arrangements to run their dispatch boats to Miami on the main coast of Florida. This trip took longer, but it got the messages through.

After the American correspondents left Havana, several of them joined the insurgents and thus kept in touch with what was going on. Every so often they returned to some point on the coast where they were met by dispatch boats which forwarded their copy to their newspapers.

When Sampson sailed for Porto Rico, correspondents stationed at Key West found that the censor had placed an embargo on any word relating to the departure for San Juan. One correspondent, in spite of this censorship, managed to get the information, as he thought, to his managing editor in New York. The latter, with a stupidity unusual in newspaper work, failed to interpret the news in the personal message, "Tell father to send my valise to San Juan," and cabled the reply, "Can't find father, send better address." By this time the Key West censor, who was Lieutenant-Colonel Allen, of the Signal Corps, had read between the lines and refused to allow the correspondent to send any more personal messages. The correspondents, however, were poorly prepared to report the sea fight outside of Santiago. Of all the dispatch boats on the south side of the island only two were present at the time Cervera's fleet was destroyed. The explanation was that none of the newspaper correspondents thought that Cervera would come out and were devoting all their attention to the exciting events on the island.

Correspondents located in Madrid had their problems almost as difficult as those of their brethren in Havana. The cable companies took their messages, but neglected to forward the same to New York. In vain did the correspondents protest that either the messages should be sent or the money returned. The American newspapers spent thousands of dollars for which they never received a single word of news. Later, the American correspondents in Madrid sent their news by special couriers to France, thence the messages were sent without censorship, and without other molestation from authorities. Such messages had to be paid for in gold and in advance and the expense for this service for one New York newspaper totaled over two thousand dollars a week. After the Manila cable was cut, a certain newspaper in order to be first with the news chartered a special dispatch boat to run to Hong Kong and thereafter sent its war news by cable from that place at $1.80 a word.

At home the American newspapers were put to great expense in being forced to get out extra editions. *The New York Evening Journal*, for example, printed as many as forty editions in a single day, and *The Evening World* nearly, if not quite, as many. The size of editions reached startling figures: one New York newspaper, for example, frequently printed over one million copies a day and failed even with such an output, to meet the demand.

APPEARANCE OF BIG HEADLINES

The immediate effect of the war with Spain upon American journalism was the large streamer headline. During the war the headline of the most important item, or news story, stretched itself across the page. It not only increased in width, but also in length, until some of the more sensational newspapers used one which occupied fully one half of the first page, except a little corner where the name of the newspaper appeared in small type. In the absence of exciting news, certain newspapers adopted rather questionable methods in the composition of headlines. A half-page would be given to the two words "BIG BATTLE," in large black letters. Underneath these two words and directly under the fold of the page would be some qualifying expression, in small type, such as "Expected To-morrow." When the paper was on the stand or when it was held aloft by the newsboy, all the passer-by could see was "BIG BATTLE." Such questionable tactics brought certain papers into bad repute with their readers. While the newspapers of the better class never practiced such deceptions, they did increase the size of their headlines. Even the World War did not produce any such flaring headlines in American newspapers as appeared during the time the United

States was fighting Spain. The flaring streamer headline is not in itself open to such hostile criticism as it has received: the American people, with their hustle and bustle, seem to take kindly to a paper which gives them the latest news of the hour in a headline which can be read by those who run to catch trains, and they do not consider it a piece of extravagance to pay one cent or more for a newspaper which is prodigal in its use of space. But when these sensational headlines are absolutely misleading, or feature something that is silly or that has no permanent news interest, they are open to just criticism.

NEWSPAPER STRIKE IN NEW YORK

One of the most important newspaper strikes, at least in New York City, was the one that commenced on August 5, 1899, in the plant of *The Sun*. Until July of that year *The Sun* had put its news into type by hand composition, — chiefly because Dana thought such composition gave a neater typographical appearance to the page, — but it then determined to adopt machines to do the work. As the old hand compositors, not being familiar with the mechanism of the machines, were unable to set matter by this process, *The Sun* was forced to employ a number of expert machinists. According to a statement issued by *The Sun*, the old compositors simply "stood by, looked on, and drew their salaries." The Typographical Union, on the other hand, insisted that the strike grew out of an attempt to make *The Sun* an open shop, and pointed by way of proof to an advertisement inserted in a Philadelphia newspaper asking for compositors to work on a newspaper a short distance from Philadelphia. After the strike had been declared, some of the men hired in Philadelphia came to New York and worked on *The Sun*. With the assistance of *The Evening Post*, *The Sun* was able to get out its regular issues, but in reduced size. The strike was bitterly fought on both sides. *The Sun*, under Dana, had passed from a newspaper of the masses to one of the upper classes. For this reason it was better prepared to stand a strike than other morning papers of the city with larger circulation among the laboring people. Pressure was brought to bear upon advertisers to withdraw from the columns and the reading public was asked in various ways to boycott the paper. Relief was sought in the courts, and injunctions, forbidding the boycott, were issued. Posters and circulars were then printed after the style of the Brisbane headline — only reversed: —

It is illegal to

BOYCOTT THE SUN
BOYCOTT THE SUN

Hostilities did not cease until March 12, 1902, when a mutual agreement was reached, the strike declared off, and the Union refrained from "further action repugnant or injurious to the paper."

CHANGES OF OWNERSHIP

During the Period of Financial Readjustment there were many changes of ownership in newspapers. Of these only a few may be noticed without expanding beyond the legitimate limits of this volume. On July 1, 1881, *The Evening Post* in New York City passed into the control of Henry Villard who had achieved distinction as a great railroad builder in the West. He was a man of the highest patriotic motives, and he early declared his intention to make *The Evening Post* " independent of himself, independent of its counting-room, and independent of party." This intention he carried out by putting all his shares in trust and turning them over to trustees with full power to act. Upon his death the control of *The Evening Post* passed to his wife, but his son Oswald Garrison Villard became the president of the company which published the paper. He, too, has kept *The Post* as independent as it was in the days when it was conducted by William Leggett.

Two activities of *The Post* during this period deserve more than passing mention. In 1885–86 *The Evening Post* rendered a distinct service to the country in general and to the South in particular when it opposed the Blair Educational Bill which proposed to appropriate one hundred million dollars from the National Treasury to promote negro education below the Mason and Dixon Line. The opposition of *The Post* to this measure was based upon the fact that its passage fostered a distinct loss to the South, not only in self-reliance, but also in self-respect. During 1890 *The Post* fell upon Tammany Hall, which it nearly destroyed by means of a series of biographical sketches of the leaders and numerous editorials about the work of the organization. While numerous warrants were issued for the arrest of its editor on the complaint of the various politicians whose biographies appeared in *The Post*, none of these cases actually came to trial.

ARRIVAL OF PULITZER IN NEW YORK

The newspapers of New York printed an advertisement on October 31, 1876, that the "Hon. Joseph Pulitzer of Missouri at eight o'clock at Cooper Union speaks for Tilden, Hendricks, and Reform." The next morning *The World* had at the top of its fifth column on its last page the name of Joseph Pulitzer in black letters and under it the words, "His Stirring Speech at Cooper Union Last Night." This was probably the first time that Mr. Pulitzer's name ever appeared at the top of a column in *The New York World*. The next evening he was one of the Democratic speakers at Tammany Hall. Among the others was Manton Marble, who, as editor and publisher of *The World*, had been successful in the first rôle, but a failure in the second. After the speeches were over the two gentlemen had a long conversation about the possibilities of making *The World* successful financially in New York City. Nothing definite came out of the conference at the time and *The World* passed into the control of Thomas A. Scott, president of the Pennsylvania Railroad, who made William Henry Hurlburt its editor. Money to meet the weekly deficit came regularly from an unknown source by express.

Of *The World* under Hurlburt's régime, St. Clair McKelway, long editor of *The Brooklyn Eagle*, has left the following account:

It upheld Horatio Seymour when he insisted on the gold standard for New York State in a time of irredeemable paper currency. It warred on William M. Tweed's criminal alteration of the city charter from behind which he practiced highway robbery to the tune of millions in the name of the law. It made now and then a stand for better municipal results by informal fusion of parties. But it never sought the art of commanding a living by the approbation and confidence of the masses, for the tendency of its management inclined to the satisfaction of the capitalists with its steadiness, and to the applause of the carping, the cynical, the sciolistic, and the pessimistic by its selection and treatment of topics. Its mistaken sense of humor comprised the discussion of serious matters from a comedy side and the discussion of trivial matters from a serious side.

Upon the death of Scott, *The World* passed into the control of other capitalists. During all this time the paper steadily lost in circulation until it had less than ten thousand in New York City, due doubtless to the reasons already outlined by Mr. McKelway.

Ever since his talk with Manton Marble, after both had spoken at Tammany Hall, Pulitzer had watched the movements of *The World* on the chance that he might sometime become its owner. Finding that its proprietors were willing to be relieved of an unprofitable burden, he purchased the newspaper in May, 1883. On the eleventh of that month he published over his own signature the following editorial: —

The entire *World* newspaper property has been purchased by the undersigned, and will, from this day on, be under different management — different in men, measures and methods — different in purpose, policy and principle — different in objects and interests — different in sympathies and convictions — different in head and heart.

Performance is better than promise. Exuberant assurances are cheap. I make none. I simply refer the public to the new *World* itself, which henceforth shall be the daily evidence of its own growing improvement, with forty-eight daily witnesses in its forty-eight columns.

There is room in this great and growing city for a journal that is not only cheap, but bright, not only bright but large, not only large but truly democratic — dedicated to the cause of the people rather than that of purse-potentates — devoted more to the news of the New than the Old World — that will expose all fraud and sham, fight all public evils and abuses — that will serve and battle for the people with earnest sincerity.

In that cause and for that end solely the new *World* is hereby enlisted and committed to the attention of the intelligent public.

Sidney Brooks, a distinguished London journalist, in discussing "The American Yellow Press" in one of the great English reviews, asserted that Joseph Pulitzer would probably be best remembered as the founder of the yellow press in America. Yet Mr. Brooks admitted in the same article that Mr. Pulitzer conducted one of the most independent and most fearless newspapers in the United States. Now that the hysteria about yellow journalism has passed, Mr. Pulitzer will probably be remembered as the editor of the paper which tried to, and in many respects did, live up to the doctrines he set forth in making his bow as a newspaper publisher in New York. Once forced by competition to adopt questionable methods to secure a circulation, he later saw whither such a course led and ordered a "right about face."

It was to the editorial page that Mr. Pulitzer paid most of his attention. He cared little to be a great merchant of news, and in the words of one of his associates "the details of business management never engaged his attention longer than was necessary." He agreed with his editorial predecessor on *The World*, Manton Marble, that "the journalist has it in trust and stewardship to be the organ and mould of public opinion, to express and guide it, and to seek, through all conflicting private interests, solely the public general good."

Pulitzer died on board his private yacht in the harbor of Charleston, South Carolina, after having guided the editorial policies of *The World* for not quite thirty years. Toward the close of his career he was totally blind, but he never let this affliction interfere with his interest in *The World*, which he continued to direct through the liberal use of the telegraph and the cable while traveling in the pursuit of health, lost through too constant devotion to his paper.

"QUIET" ENTRANCE OF HEARST

William Randolph Hearst, whose newspaper activities in California have already been noticed, came to New York in 1896, where he purchased *The New York Journal*, founded by Albert Pulitzer, a brother of Joseph Pulitzer, of *The World*. Before coming East Hearst is said to have added together the circulation of all the New York dailies and, after comparing the total with the population of the city, declared that there was room for a daily which met the needs of those who were not subscribing for any newspaper. According to the gossip of Park

Row, Hearst "broke into New York with all the discreet secrecy of a wooden-legged burglar having a fit on a tin roof": according to a member of the staff of *The New York American*, Hearst, when he first came to New York, was compelled to "blow his horn unusually loud to attract the crowd, but once he secured his audience he became more dignified." He brought with him all the circulation schemes which he had successfully used in San Francisco to increase the sale of his *Examiner*, and in addition tried many others such as sending New Yorkers each a card to which a penny had been attached with the instructions to buy a copy of *The Morning Journal*. He secured many of the men whom Pulitzer had trained and at once began to toot his newspaper horn so loudly that even those who ran were forced to hear that *The Journal* had made a new entry. Separating the paper into two editions, he later called the morning one *The New York American* while the evening still retained the old name of *The Journal*. In charge of the latter he placed Arthur Brisbane, son of Albert Brisbane, who had worked with Greeley on *The Tribune*. Brisbane by still more sensational methods advanced the circulation by leaps and bounds until *The New York Evening Journal* led all other American newspapers in number of copies printed. Not until the next period did Hearst enter the newspaper field in Boston, Chicago, Los Angeles, etc.

FIRST APPEARANCE OF MUNSEY

In 1891 Frank A. Munsey purchased *The Star*, a daily which had been established on September 22, 1885. On February 1, 1891, he changed its name to *The Daily Continent*. A distinguishing feature of *The Continent* was its small size, for it presented the news in tabloid form. Mr. Munsey had the idea that a smaller sheet with the news presented concisely would be more convenient than the conventional blanket-size newspaper. His venture, though it attracted considerable favorable attention at the start and carried a good deal of advertising, was not successful and was discontinued on June 30, 1891. No other attempt has been made in New York to give the people of that city a daily tabloid newspaper.

DEATH OF DANA

Charles Anderson Dana, so long editor of *The New York Sun*, died on October 17, 1897. The paper which he had guided for nearly thirty years told of the occurrence in these two lines: —

Charles Anderson Dana, editor of *The Sun*,
died yesterday afternoon.

There were no inverted column rules, there was no long article in praise of the deceased editor. The announcement in fact was typical of the editor whose death it recorded. For a short time after his death, *The Sun* was edited by his son, Paul Dana. Later, E. P. — initials which in *The Sun* office stand for Editorial Page — Mitchell became its editor.

Mention has already been made how, in the handling of news, Dana wielded a tremendous influence, for he made *The Sun* a sort of school of journalism in which he trained bright young college men who had the itch, or, to use a more academic word, the urge to write. Dana saw no reason why the news column should not be as well written as any piece of literature, for to him reporting was an art. He also insisted that the headlines of the newspaper should have some sort of literary form, so that *The Sun* in time shone not only with a literary finish in its news columns, but also in its still larger rays in the headlines. Dana liked to quote Dickens as being a great police-court reporter; and pointed to the Bible as a place where stories were boiled down, the story of the Crucifixion, for example, being told in six hundred words. The making of a newspaper in all its phases required, so he asserted, the skill of an artist in every department, and when he came to put into a book his ideals about the editing and publishing of a paper, he called it "The Art of Newspaper Making."

CHANGES IN CHICAGO

The Herald has been unusually popular as a name for a newspaper. On March 11, 1881, *The Herald* appeared in Chicago. It had obtained the Associated Press franchise of *The Telegraph*, an old organ of the Greenback-Labor Party, and had no connection with two other papers of the same name which had been established in Chicago. Under James W. Scott, one of the chief owners of the United Press, the paper was Democratic, but when *The Herald* passed into the control of H. H. Kohlsaat one year before the historic campaign of 1896, it became a Republican paper. *The Record* later united with *The Herald* which was started almost at the same time. It first appeared on March 31, 1881, as the morning edition of *The Chicago Daily News* and was known as *The Morning News* until January 11, 1892, when it became *The Record*. In March, 1901, Frank B. Noyes, who had been associated with his father on *The Washington Star*, became the publisher on the 28th of that month of the united papers known as *The Record-Herald*, the name under which it was published until May, 1914, when James Keeley, in consolidating *The Record-Herald* and *The Interocean*, called the new enterprise simply *The Herald*. *The Interocean*, started in 1872 as the political organ of the "Stalwart" Ring of the Republican Party of the West, was built upon the ruins of *The Chicago Republican* once edited by Charles Anderson Dana. *The Chicago Daily News*, a one-cent evening paper which first appeared on December 20, 1875, was started by Melville E. Stone with a capital stock of something like five hundred dollars and with its entire plant purchased on time. Within eighteen months it purchased *The Chicago Post* and *Mail* and in this way secured an Associated Press franchise. From the beginning *The Daily News* aimed to make the first page worth the price of the paper. It was one of the first papers to believe that women readers were more valuable than men. It published mystery stories and offered cash prizes to women readers for the best solution of the mystery.

The City Press Association of Chicago was founded about 1885. At that time the Chicago newspapers paid a great deal of attention to suburban news, printing a page or two of personals or small society happenings in the Chicago suburbs. Minor weddings and club functions in Chicago were also given much space. J. T. Sutor conceived the idea of covering these events in a syndicate way for the Chicago papers. Sutor started with two men to help him. The work was acceptable to the papers and the organization, as time passed, gradually took over more and more territory for the newspapers. Various reorganizations and changes in management have occurred since then and the news-gathering organization, now known as the City News Bureau of Chicago, employs over fifty men, serves all the English papers, and covers all avenues of news in Cook County with the exception of finance, labor, and politics.

NELSON OF KANSAS CITY

One of the most picturesque figures among makers of American newspapers was William Rockhill Nelson, editor and publisher of *The Star*, of Kansas City, Missouri, from the date of its establishment, September 18, 1880, until his death, April 13, 1915. When *The Star*, called by the local press "The Twilight Twinkler," first began to shine, it was a small four-page paper and "twinkled" for two cents a day or ten cents per week: when its owner died it equaled in size any of the metropolitan dailies and shone morning and evening and Sunday for the same rate of ten cents per week. At the start pennies were scarce in Kansas City, where papers sold for five cents per copy, and Mr. Nelson was forced to import them by the keg from the United States Mint in order that newsboys might have the change for customers. By the end of the first month *The Star* published a little note that it had more readers than any other newspaper published there. The purchase of *The Mail* in 1882 gave the paper an Associated Press franchise, which in turn furnished the telegraph news so much needed at the time. When *The Times* was bought in 1901 it was made the morning edition of *The Star* with the issue of November 18. The Sunday edition of *The Star* was begun on April 29, 1894. The delivery of thirteen papers by carriers morning, evening, and Sunday for ten cents per week has never been duplicated by any other newspaper publisher in America and practically stifled competition in Kansas City.

Two incidents in the history of *The Star* will illustrate the personality of its founder. An early issue called attention to the fact that the town opera house, owned by Colonel Kersey Coates, was poorly constructed and sadly in need of proper exits. Coates denied the danger from fire and denounced the editor as a blackmailer, but later went to Nelson and, after remarking that he was going to reconstruct the opera house, he added, "The town needs such a newspaper as yours, and if you ever need help, come to me." It was the same Coates who helped Nelson raise the funds to purchase the first web perfecting press used by *The Star*. Years later a manager of a local theater complained about the treatment given him by *The Star* and threatened to withdraw his advertising unless a change was made. Nelson gave the change when he replied, "Out you go and out you stay!" — a decision he never reversed.

These two incidents, selected from many much more spectacular, explain what *Collier's Weekly* meant when it said in an obituary notice, "The founder and editor of *The Kansas City Star* took his place in journalism's Hall of Fame by kicking in the door with hobnailed boots." Nelson, himself, expressed the same idea, but more moderately, when he asserted, "I've tried to be gentle and diplomatic, but I've never done well in my stocking feet." He was one of those men to whom reference has already been made in this chapter as being great editors and good business executives. By means of *The Star* he pulled Kansas City out of the mud, — for there were "no pavements and only a few plank sidewalks" when he arrived, — and made it a city of parks and boulevards.

The Star, it may be remarked in passing, secured the interview with General Nelson A. Miles which led to the condemnation of the army supplies used in Cuba in the war with Spain. *The Star*, through the liberality of its readers, did much to relieve the starving people of Matanzas, Cuba.

OTIS OF LOS ANGELES

Harrison Gray Otis became editor and owner of *The Los Angeles Times*, Los Angeles, California, on August 1, 1882. The paper had been started on December 4, 1881, and grew out of a weekly which bore quite a different name — *The Mirror*. The latter paper had been started in 1873 as a little "thumb-nail journal" by the owners of a second-hand job plant in the hopes that the sheet might bring business to the office.

On August 5, 1890, there began in the office of *The Times*, between its owner and the local typographical union, a struggle which stretched over a period of nearly two decades. The strike started in the offices of the four Los Angeles newspapers, but finally concentrated on *The Times*. On October 1, 1910, occurred the widely known disaster which resulted in the destruction of the building of *The Times* and the loss of the lives of twenty members of its force when the plant was dynamited by lawless labor unions. While the attitude of the owner of *The Times* toward organized labor would not be within the scope of this book, the following official résumé of the publisher of the paper may be quoted: —

The Times has never objected to lawful and legitimate organizations formed and maintained by laborers in any branch of industry. The paper does not do foolish things, but what it objects to is the tyrannical management of labor unions by the generally irresponsible, always ignorant, and frequently vicious leaders of these organizations. There has never been a word printed in *The Times* objecting to lawful organizations of working people *per se*. All the fault ever found in the columns of the paper with these organizations has been leveled at some gross and mischievous abuse in the management of the organizations by the leaders of them. It has been a fight made for legitimate labor more than for any other interest in the country.

Mr. Otis, before his death, denounced the destruction of his building as "the crime of the century." His side of the controversy has been described in a small brochure entitled "The Story of a Sixteen Years' Battle."

OTHER LEADERS OF THE WEST

While the newspapers — especially in the East — were becoming more distinctly impersonal in character, there were in the West numerous editors who, during the decade of 1880–1890, impressed their personalities upon their newspapers. Among these leaders of Western journalism were Murat Halstead, of *The Commerial Gazette*, John R. McLean, of *The Inquirer*, and Charles P. Taft, of *The Times-Star*, in Cincinnati, Ohio; Edwin Cowles, of *The Leader*, William W. Armstrong and L. E. Holden, of *The Plaindealer*, in Cleveland, Ohio; General J. M. Comley, of *The Commercial Telegram*, in Toledo, Ohio; W. D. Bickham, of *The Journal*, in Dayton, Ohio; J. S. Clarkson, of *The Register*, and John Watts, of *The Leader*, in Des Moines, Iowa; John Arkins, of *The Rocky Mountain News*, in Denver, Colorado; John Atkinson, of *The Tribune*, W. E. Quinby, of *The Free Press*, and James E. Scripps, of *The Evening News*, in Detroit, Michigan; A. H. Belo, of *The News*, in Galveston, Texas; John H. Holliday, of *The News*, John C. New, of *The Journal*, and W. J. Craig, of *The Sentinel*, in Indianapolis, Indiana; Henry Watterson, of *The Courier-Journal*, in Louisville, Kentucky; J. M. Keating, of *The Appeal*, in Memphis, Tennessee; Horace Rublee, of *The Sentinel*, and William E. Cramer, of *The Evening Wisconsin*, in Milwaukee, Wisconsin; W. E. Haskell, of *The Tribune*, and J. S. McLain, of *The Journal*, in Minneapolis, Minnesota; A. S. Colyar, of *The American*, in Nashville, Tennessee; H. L. Pittock, of *The Oregonian*, in Portland, Oregon; O. H. Rothaker, of *The Republican*, in Omaha, Nebraska; George K. Fitch, of *The Bulletin*, M. H. de Young, of *The Chronicle*, and John P. Irish, of *The Daily Alta California*, in San Francisco, California; William Hyde, of *The Republican*, and Joseph B. McCullagh, of *The Globe-Democrat*, in St. Louis, Missouri; J. A. Wheelock, of *The Pioneer Press*, and Lewis Baker, of *The Globe*, in St. Paul, Minnesota.

SUNDAY PAPERS

After the War of the States was over some of the newspapers which had been printing an edition on Sunday suspended publication on that day. Others, especially in the South, continued their edition on Sunday, but omitted the issue on Monday. But the reading public demanded the news daily. How *The New York Tribune*, which had discontinued its Sunday edition, discovered this fact has been described by Whitelaw Reid in an address delivered on the Bromley Foundation at Yale University: —

For a long time I resisted the general tendency to extend the daily publication over into Sunday. Nearly every man I knew approved of this refusal to print a Sunday paper. Old friends went out of their way to congratulate me on thus setting my face against the pernicious habit of Sunday publication. They hoped I would never yield it; it was a noble stand and gave them yet greater confidence in my paper. Finally, as they kept introducing the subject, I took to explaining to these excellent and well-meaning men that my noble stand seemed to result merely in sending all my regular readers, when Sunday came, over to one or another of my competitors; and next, turning suddenly on each, I would ask, "By the way, what paper do *you* read on Sunday?" Then came stammering and hesitation, to be sure; but not once, during the years this went on, did I fail to find that, with the single exception of some of the clergy, the men who were exhorting me to continue setting a noble example for Sabbath observance by not publishing on Sunday, were themselves quietly gratifying their own craving to know what was going on by reading some Sunday paper!

Other papers by costly experience learned the same facts and then resumed their Sunday issues. The Sunday paper, as it is understood to-day, did not appear until the early eighties. Its development and enlargement were due to several causes. The department stores, finding the Sunday edition an especially valuable advertising medium, increased their space to set forth the bargain attractions of the coming week. The auxiliary presses purchased by papers for use in cases of emergency were utilized for the Sunday edition to print additional supplements in which were portrayed numerous interesting phases of city life. At about this time, S. S. McClure, founder of the magazine which bears his name and later editor of *The Evening Mail*, of New York City, began to retail to the newspapers, for simultaneous publication on Sunday, novels and short stories by writers who had previously sold their manuscripts only to the better-class magazines. In addition to fiction, special articles about men and matters of moment were similarly syndicated for use in the Sunday papers. While McClure was developing his syndicate service, Morrill Goddard, whom Pulitzer had placed in charge of the Sunday edition of *The New York World*, was applying psychology to newspaper-making. Goddard, knowing the value of the optical center, began at once to develop the illustrated features and to enlarge the size of the pictures until they spread all over the pages. From his knowledge of psychology, he knew what features would give readers a thrill, and he emphasized such articles so much that people came to buy the paper on Sunday not so much for its news as for its special articles. Thus was the pace set for the feature editors who followed in Goddard's footsteps.

Sunday journalism was strangely influenced by a Puritan

strain in the matter of presentation of the special features. By chance two early products of American printing came to the notice of a Sunday editor. The first, published in Boston in 1656, was entitled, "Spiritual Milk for Boston Babes in either England. Drawn out of the Breasts of both Testaments for their souls nourishment But may be of like use to any Children. By John Cotton, B.D., late Teacher to the Church of Boston in New England"; the second, published in Cambridge in 1657, was entitled, "The Watering of the Olive Plant in Christs Garden. Or a Short Catechism For the first Entrance of our Chelmesford Children: Enlarged by A three-fold Appendix. By John Fisk, Pastour of the Church of Christ at Chelmesford in New-England."

"That's the way to write captions for our special features" was his exclamation. From that time dramatization of fact became the popular mode of treatment. Did a special article tell how Constantinople was freed from its plague of dogs? It bore the caption, "Constantinople No Longer a Dog Kennel." Not only were the headlines treated this way, but the practice crept into the text columns. The old essay was dramatized and made to live. "Don't preach, write a parable," was the advice given to copy-writers. Contents of the Sunday supplements became not a story that was told, but a drama that was enacted before readers. So popular was the new mode of treatment that even magazines adopted it.

Though *The New York World* had installed in 1893 a press capable of printing in colors and later added a larger press of the same type, both were allowed to lie idle except to put a tint now and then on a supplement page. When Don C. Seitz came to *The World* he urged that the color presses be used to print a comic section and Pulitzer cabled instructions of one word, "Experiment." Seitz "experimented." The yellow comic came when the pressman complained that "wishy-washy" tints gave no results and asked for more solid colors. R. F. Outcault had just submitted to the Sunday editor, Arthur Brisbane, who followed Goddard in that capacity, a series of "black-and-whites" which portrayed life in "Hogan's Alley." By way of experiment the "kid" in the pictures was given a robe of solid yellow. With the arrival of the "yellow kid," the success of the comic supplement was assured as a circulation-getter. The circulation of *The World* on Sunday jumped from a quarter to a half million. Other papers, following the example set by *The World*, issued a colored comic section on Sunday.

The addition of a section printed on coated, or glossy, paper permitted the insertion of advertisements which had previously appeared only in the magazines. Other features and other sections were added until by the close of the period the Sunday paper became a "journalism department store" wherein every reader could find something for his amusement and entertainment. No other country has anything like the American Sunday newspaper.

EVENING PAPERS

Many evening papers borrowed some of the Sunday "stuff" and became feature papers. Daily beauty hints, the bedtime story for the "kiddies," the comic "colyum," the woman's page, etc., crowded the space devoted to the news. Extensive use of the telephone by evening papers made the news more scrappy and bulletin-like in form. Even the editorial page was "popularized" in form. The growth of interest in baseball, "the great American game," was mirrored in the "sporting extra" in the publication of which *The Evening Sun*, of New York, and *The Press*, of Pittsburgh, were leaders. Enlarged size came when department stores and other advertisers learned that the evening paper went to the home and was extensively read by women. The change in the character of afternoon papers was most noticeable in the Period of Financial Readjustment.

WILD-WEST WEEKLIES

Journalism, in what was popularly called "the wild and woolly West," if told in detail would make a most interesting chapter. When a Colt revolver and a pen lay side by side on an editor's desk it was but natural that the contents of his newspaper should have a tang of the desert, a flavor of the sagebrush. The editor of a great metropolitan daily never had "anything on" these editors in the matter of excitement. Chief among these fighting editors was Alvin S. Peek, who once boasted that he "had run newspapers in nine different states and territories, had shot eleven men who took exception to his editorial opinions, but had never been compelled to swallow a single opinion which he had uttered in his newspaper — thanks to his ever-loaded pistol." He finally died "with his boots on" at the age of fifty-one. Another such editor was Albert Tyson, of _The Rising Star X-Ray_, of Texas, who announced himself in print "Lying and Fighting Editor." At the top of his editorial column he printed his motto, "Do Unto Others as You Would Have Them Do Unto You, and Do It Fust."

These weeklies were what might primarily be called one-man sheets. One of them, _The Yampa Leader_, of Oregon, enlarged upon this fact in the following editorial notice: —

The great city papers think they are smart in having a large staff, and, although we have not published ours before, we shall do so to take some of the conceit out of the city brethren. The editorial staff of _The Leader_ is composed of: Managing editor, V. S. Wilson; city editor, Vic Wilson; news editor, V. Wilson; editorial writer, Hon. Mr. Wilson; exchange editor, Wilson; pressman, the same Wilson; foreman, more of the same Wilson; devil, a picture of the same Wilson; fighting editor, Mrs. Wilson.

In the struggle for existence these pioneer editors duplicated the experiences of the colonial printer. The editor of _The Gem_, of Flagstaff, Arizona, printed an editorial notice very similar in subject-matter to what Peter Zenger once published in _The New York Journal_. Though slightly different in its phraseology it read: —

Have you paid your subscription yet? Remember even an editor must live. If the _hard times_ have struck your shebang, don't forget turnips, potatoes, and corn in the shock are most as welcome as hard cash at the _Gem_ office. Also hard wood. Our latch-string is always out, or same (i.e., the turnips, etc.) can be delivered to our wife, who will give receipt in our absence.

The society news was found in such Western journals and was just as interesting as the "tommy-rot" of metropolitan dailies. The following is taken from an account of a wedding printed in _The Fairplay Flume_, of Colorado: —

The groom wore a long pair of overalls and a cutaway coat. The bride wore a calico dress and apron. They both looked the picture of health, and were ably assisted — the groom by the bride's sister and the bride by Mr. Sam Meadows, a particular friend of the groom's.

The titles of these Western papers make interesting reading. For example, there was *The Hannibal Hornet,* of Hannibal, Missouri; *The Bliss Breeze,* of Dallas, Texas; *The Arizona Arrow,* of Arizona; *The Mustang Mail,* of Oklahoma; *The Mother Lode Magnet,* of California; *The Rifle Reville,* of Colorado; *The Javelin,* of Texas; *The Oasis,* of Arizona; *The Creede Candle,* of Colorado.

These weekly papers of the West were nothing if not original. One, for example, published notices of births, marriages, and deaths under the following respective headlines: "Hatched," "Matched," and "Dispatched." Inducements to subscribers were often unique: it was not at all uncommon for such a paper to publish a notice like the following: "All subscribers paying in advance will be entitled to a first-class obituary notice in case of death." By way of illustration the following obituary notice may be quoted as typical: —

☞ JAKE MOFFATT GONE SKYWARD! ☜

As we feared on hearing that two doctors had been called in, the life of our esteemed fellow-citizen Jake Moffatt ebbed out on Wednesday last, just after we had gone to press. Jake was every inch a scholar and a gentleman, upright in all his dealings, unimpeachable in character, and ran the Front Street Saloon in the very toniest style consistent with order. Jake never fully recovered from the year he spent in the county jail at the time of the Ryan-Sternberg fracas. His health was shattered, and he leaves a sorrowing widow and nary an enemy.

Many of these papers were published in mining camps and led peripatetic lives. The few of them which have survived to the present time, while having the same name, have lost their individuality with the advance of the telegraph and the railroad.

PRESS ASSOCIATIONS

How the Associated Press in 1880 was composed of smaller organizations scattered over the country has been outlined in the preceding chapter. At various times discrepancies arose between a local branch and the general association. On one occasion the Western Associated Press withdrew from the general association and tried to maintain an independent and rival news-gathering organization. After a short period of competition, however, the differences were compromised and the Western Associated Press came back into the fold. With a development of new telegraph companies, and with the foundation of new newspapers unable to secure the news service of the Associated Press, came a more formidable competitor known as the United Press. Competition between these two organizations became extremely keen until an agreement was reached by which they worked in harmony and refrained from competing with one another in gathering and distributing the news. In 1892 the Western Associated Press again withdrew from the organization with headquarters at New York and the New York Associated Press was absorbed by the United Press. In the period of rivalry which followed, both associations had the co-operation of the Reuter News Agency of Europe. In their services they divided the United States along geographical lines. The United Press furnished news to practically all of the leading daily papers east of the Alleghany Mountains, the newspapers of the South, and a few newspapers in the West. But in the section last mentioned the Western Associated Press supplied most of the newspapers. Later, the Western Associated Press succeeded in obtaining the exclusive use of the news gathered by the Reuter Association and the United Press was put under a severe handicap in the gathering of European news: so much so that several of the New York, Philadelphia, and certain New England newspapers left the United Press to join the Western Associated Press. The depletion was so great that on April 8, 1897, the United Press was forced to discontinue its services and between two hundred and three hundred of its members joined the Western Associated Press. Other members formed a bureau, headed by *The New York Sun*, which practically supplanted the old United Press. The Western Associated Press was incorporated under the laws of Illinois and had its headquarters at Chicago. Its general manager was Melville E. Stone. In 1900 the present Associated Press was organized out of the old West-ern Associated Press.

AMERICAN NEWSPAPER PUBLISHERS' ASSOCIATION

That the period was one in which the emphasis, on the whole, was placed upon the marketing of news, was shown by the forma-tion of the American Newspaper Publishers' Association, which, after preliminary steps had been taken at Detroit, Michigan, on November 17, 1886, was organized at Rochester, New York, February 16, 1887, to provide a clearing-house for the business departments of its members and to protect them in case of labor difficulties. From the start, it devoted most of its attention to a study of paper conditions, a supervision of advertising agencies in an attempt to weed out the undesirable, a campaign against the imposition of press agents who tried to secure the insertion of advertising as pure reading matter, etc. The association came to be a great force in American journalism, as its membership included the most influential newspapers in the country. The need of such an organization early became patent when legis-lators at Washington began to take steps looking toward the regulation of the press.

PRINTING-PRESSES OF PERIOD

The two decades from 1880 to 1900 saw the printing-press of the newspaper develop into the greatest mechanical achieve-ment of the human mind. Hoe had produced a press which would print on both sides of a continuous roll of paper, but there were several minor difficulties to overcome. Among these were the unequal distribution of ink and a frequent tearing of the paper web. Hoe took these matters up with the leading manufacturers and insisted that the ink-makers produce a product which would spread evenly from the ink fountain of his press; he next turned his attention to the paper manufacturers and demanded that they produce a paper of even thickness and uniform quality, while he in turn experimented with presses where the paper pressure would be uniform. Other inventors perfected the me-chanical arrangement of the press by means of adjustments too complicated to describe in a book of this character. Tucker and

Campbell produced the rotary folder which made possible the great speed in creasing the web sheets transversely. The latter also gave the stationary longitudinal folder and perfected the rotary delivery of the printed sheets. Another inventor added the sheet-turning bar by which two parts of different webs were brought together. Later, Hoe produced the mechanical marvel which gathered together several streams of paper and united them into one printed product. Mergenthaler so improved his linotype that newspaper publishers were forced by the saving in cost of composition to adopt his machine.

BY WAY OF CRITICISM

The journalism of the period had as its most severe critic the editor of *The New York Evening Post,*

> Godkin the righteous, known of old,
> Priest of the Nation's moral health,
> Within whose *Post* we daily read
> The gospel of the rights of wealth.

Early in the period he was attacking Dana's policy that what the Lord let happen was all right to print; in the middle he was regretting the country-wide reduction in price of newspapers; at the close he let his *Post* fall full weight upon the sensational press. That some of his picric criticism was justified is shown by the ethical advance recorded in the next chapter. When Adolph S. Ochs, after buying *The New York Times* in 1896, announced his motto "All The News That's Fit To Print," much sport was made of this slogan in certain newspaper circles.

Godkin, in turn, did not escape criticism. He was said to have approved of nothing since the birth of Christ. When *The Post* doubled its size in 1887, Dana remarked that it would now be dull in sixteen pages instead of eight. Later as a test for a bridge across the East River, he suggested that a truck containing a copy of *The Evening Post* be carried over. The situation in New York was summed up by Mrs. F. P. Bellamy, "What can you expect of a city in which every morning *The Sun* makes vice attractive, and every night *The Post* makes virtue odious." Opinions differ widely as to the ability of Godkin as an editor, but he rendered excellent service as a critic of the press. He retired as editor of *The Post* on January 1, 1900.

CHAPTER XIX

PERIOD OF SOCIAL READJUSTMENT

1900—

WITH what is said to be characteristic candor, Henry Watterson, the veteran editor of *The Louisville Courier-Journal*, thus summed up the conditions obtaining at the opening of the Period of Social Readjustment: —

Journalism is without any code of ethics or system of self-restraint and self-respect. It has no sure standards of either work or duty. Its intellectual landscapes are anonymous, its moral destination confused. The country doctor, the village lawyer, knows his place and keeps it, having the consciousness of superiority. The journalist has few, if any, mental perspectives to fix his horizon; neither chart of precedent nor map of discovery upon which his sailing lines and travel lines have been marked.

NEWSPAPER ETHICS CODIFIED

Practically every newspaper before 1900 had been, as Mr. Watterson asserted, a law unto itself, without standards of either work or duty: its code of ethics, not yet codified like those of medicine and of law, had been, like its stylebook, individualistic in character. The most important change to leave its mark upon the journalism of the period was not in the gathering of news, not in the speed with which it could be placed before the public, not in the ownership and control of the journal from the individual to the incorporated company, but in the ethical advance made in all departments of the newspaper. New standards of ethics were established, not only for the editorial, but also for the advertising and circulation departments. Yet the press but reflected again the trend of the times, for it was an era of moral awakening. *Collier's Weekly* in "taking stock" asserted: —

Fifty years from now, when some writer brings Woodrow Wilson's "History of the American People" up to date, we think he will say that the ten years ending about January 1, 1914, was the period of the greatest ethical advance made by this nation in any decade.

FEMINIZING THE NEWSPAPER

Another change was what might be called feminizing the newspaper. To a certain extent it was doubtless the reaction of the suffrage movement, or, to be more exact, the movement whereby women widened their activities, social, commercial, and political. The time came when every page, possibly with the exception of that devoted to sports, had to be written so that the intelligent woman could understand it. Even the advertising columns were prepared to appeal to women as merchants learned that the housewife made the purchases for the home. Dorothy Dix in a journalism lecture at New York University emphasized this point when she said: —

Women spend the money of the world. Except for his vices and his outside clothes, the average man does not handle a penny of the money he earns. His wife spends it. She buys the groceries, the furniture, the piano, the jewelry, — everything that is advertised in the newspapers, and the advertisers, of course, support the paper. Therefore, surprising as it may seem to the uninitiated, it is the women readers and not the men who are considered first in the make-up of a paper.

GOVERNMENT REGULATIONS

The period also saw numerous regulations of the press by both state and national legislation. While most of the bills presented, and a great majority of those passed by legislators, related to advertising, some were aimed at the reportorial and editorial columns, especially in handling the news about crime and in the attacks on personal character. More drastic libel laws were passed by numerous States. In several instances, the courts held that newspapers, in printing privileged matter such as the reports of divorce and criminal cases, must not overemphasize such accounts either by sensational headlines or by emphasis upon sordid details in order to increase street sales, and construed such action as constructive malice. Most of the regulations, however, affecting the newspapers came from the Postal Department.

These three changes were so closely interwoven, both objectively and subjectively, that it is almost impossible to separate them. Every one, however, was so important that each deserves discussion somewhat more in detail.

ADVERTISING ETHICS ADVANCED

The first advertising advance was made when the immoral personal advertisement was thrown into the hellbox — the technical name in the newspaper office for the receptacle in which rubbish and other waste matter is deposited. Previously such advertisements formed practically a directory of the houses of ill-fame to be found in the red-lighted streets of the city tenderloin. In 1907 the United States District Attorney forced one newspaper to pay a fine of about $30,000 for publishing such obscene matter in its advertising columns devoted to "personals." *The Daily News* and *The Tribune*, of Chicago, were among the leaders to exclude such advertising, which in that city had been so cunningly designed that it deceived many readers as to its true character. The stylebook of several newspapers now contains paragraphs about classified advertisements which are based upon regulations adopted by *The Chicago Daily News* and which specify kinds of advertising which under no condition may be accepted for publication and about others which must be rejected unless O.K.'d by a responsible member of the advertising staff who has made a personal investigation of the advertiser. Another ethical advance was the exclusion from the newspapers of what *The Journal*, of Minneapolis, called "the filthy, dangerous, fraudulent medicinal, and near-medicinal advertising." A few newspapers have gone so far as to exclude all medicinal advertising. Others, like *The North American*, of Philadelphia, accept no medicinal advertising which would promote a drug-forming habit, or which guarantees to cure an incurable disease, such as cancer, etc. Many conflicting opinions exist about the advertising of patent medicines. The code of ethics of the better newspapers on this point suggests that the newspaper may insert the advertising of any patent medicine which the publisher of the paper is willing to use in his own home. The suggestion of medical societies, that the press should exclude all patent medicine advertising, is not well accepted. A newspaper is inclined to believe that physicians are not entirely unselfish in such a desire and suggests that the doctor pay more attention to the ethics of his own profession and less to that of the press. The manufacturers of medicines of merit maintain that it is just as honorable to advertise a product which will relieve a stomach of an ache as it is to advertise a mincemeat that puts an ache in the stomach: that it is as ethical to describe the merits of a corn plaster to take corns away as it is to sell shoes which make corns. Whatever opinion may be held about these matters, there can be no question that the American newspaper is no longer a directory of patent medicine manufacturers.

GOOD ADVERTISING DRIVES OUT THE BAD

While it took newspaper publishers some time to learn that the reverse of Gresham's law, of bad money driving out the good, applied to advertising, they had no trouble in reading the handwriting when it appeared on the walls of the counting-room. Especially was this true of financial advertising. The advertisement of the swindler was weighed in the balance and found wanting and the press refused to be a partner in selling a hole in the ground for a gold mine or a swamp-lake for real estate. The modern code of ethics demands that any financial advertising which promises an unusually high rate of interest should be carefully investigated before appearing in print. It also demands the exclusion of the announcement of that advertiser who, dealing previously in gilt-edged securities, "changes his line" and seeks to insert the announcement of "gold brick mining schemes." *The Tribune*, of Chicago, once set a very good precedent: it received by telegraph an order for the insertion of a page advertisement which in flamboyant words predicted immediate wealth through the purchase of stocks advertised, but instead of publishing the advertisement, *The Tribune* gave a whole page with something like the following printed in the center: "Mr. Blank telegraphed last night that he wished a page in *The Tribune* in which to print an advertisement of the So-and-So mines. *The Tribune* is through with Mr. Blank. It will print no more of his advertising and takes this method of announcing its position to its readers."

The ethical advance extended to other advertising columns. The copy for fire and bankruptcy sales were among those to be revised. Even department stores were urged to do away with the evils of comparative prices. At about the time the editorial columns were conducting a national campaign of "Swat the Fly!" advertising clubs all over the country were demanding that the newspapers "Swat the Lie!" whenever it occurred in any form of advertisement. A few newspapers positively guaranteed the reliability of assertions in the advertising columns. *The Tribune*, of New York, went so far as to offer to refund to its readers in case of dissatisfaction whatever had been paid for purchase of products advertised in its columns. It did so whether the purchase was of a pair of stockings or of an automobile. The amount that it had to refund, however, was very small when compared with the total amount of purchases made.

DEPARTMENTS FOR THE HOUSEHOLD

Whether the efforts on the part of newspapers to reach women readers were due to commercial reasons or to a sincere desire to be of social service, may be a debatable question about which to make a specific generalization. *The Tribune*, of Chicago, accepted the view that the modern newspaper "must not only help in the fight for a clean city, but must aid the clergy and others to fight for a clean home, and in entering the everyday life of its readers, it must, like the parish priest, be guide, counselor, and friend." It was while speaking on this point that the general manager of *The Tribune* said: "I have often thought that a newspaper can most closely realize its real mission the nearer it comes to attaining the ideals of the parish priest and the clergyman in his ministrations to his flock. And the newspaper's flock is often numbered in the hundreds of thousands."

Academic and pedantic critics have made no end of fun of newspaper departments conducted under such headlines as "Advice to the Lovelorn" or "First Aid to Wounded Hearts." Positive proof exists, however, that such departments conducted by Dorothy Dix, Laura Jean Libbey, etc., in spite of protests over the modern desecration and decadence of the American newspaper, have played no mean part in the social service of the press. James Keeley, when general manager of *The Tribune,* of Chicago, left this testimonial to the value of such departments: —

In a little over two years Miss Libbey has received fifty thousand letters asking advice, and if you could have read the letters, as I did, not all, but hundreds, you would have felt as I did, that she was, to use that trite saying, "filling a long-felt want." They were from lonely human beings with human problems. Over two hundred girls and young women have written and acknowledged that her words of warning saved them from taking the irretrievable false step which often confronts the friendless girl in a large city. Almost as many have testified that she has prevented the wrecking of homes in a divorce court. Several hundreds of her readers have written her that she saved them from the folly of an elopement which would have been accursed. Other hundreds have written that she straightened out the kinks in their affairs, and sent wedding invitations or announcements with thanks to her that they are established happily. Probably the most interesting thing revealed in Miss Libbey's journalistic career is that it has brought to light so many persons hopping heedlessly in the direction of a bad finish, when a sharp word from a woman professionally engaged in giving advice would bring them to their senses.

Of the department, "Marion Harland's Helping Hand," Mr. Keeley said: —

It is a department through which a great exchange is conducted reaching from coast to coast. Actually hundreds of old trusses, abdominal belts, invalid chairs, and crutches, as well as other articles discarded by those who no longer need them, have been sent to those who do, and not only have a dozen encyclopædias been given to those who need them, but half a dozen typewriters and one piano have found places where they would be of real value. Over a dozen orphans have found homes through her efforts. Mrs. Harland has three secretaries, and together they sort the applications from those who want and the offers from those who have and use their best efforts that the helping hand shall be extended to those deserving. Queer work, the old-time editor would think. But it is real work.

SOCIAL SERVICE WORK

The social service work of *The Tribune,* of Chicago, has been selected for illustration chiefly because that newspaper was a pioneer in the field and blazed a trail along which many other papers followed. An examination of the dailies in the larger cities, especially of the evening papers, will show that almost every edition has numerous departments which aim to make bad homes good and good homes better. There can be no question that the introduction of such features has made the newspapers better advertising mediums and doubtless numerous newspapers adopted them for that reason. The late Mayor Gaynor, of New York, knew whereof he spoke when he said to a gathering of Gotham newspaper men, "A paper going into the home is worth a hundred littering the streets or clogging the sewers of the city." Advertisers also know this fact. In addition, a newspaper which goes into the home must have the ethics of a gentleman or the good American housewife puts the sheet into the kitchen range.

POSTAL REGULATIONS

When the Postal Department first began to enforce the sections of the Revised Statutes which forbid the delivery of mail and the payment of money orders to concerns which advertise fraudulent schemes to obtain money under false pretenses and promises, there was a distinct lack of coöperation in work on the part of many newspapers. The reason was undoubtedly the enormous amount such concerns paid for newspaper advertising — which was often their greatest item of expense. In commenting on this fact an official report of the Solicitor of the Postal Department asserted: —

In one case the evidence showed that several hundred thousand dollars had been paid for advertising during a period of eighteen months, as high as fifty thousand dollars having been paid in a single month; and it was developed in a number of cases that fabulous amounts have been spent for this purpose. It will be readily seen, therefore, that the financial interests of some publications will be seriously affected by the loss of this class of advertising if the loss is not made up in another way; and it is not expected that hearty coöperation can be enlisted at once from all publishers.

This lack of coöperation was shown in the suppression of news relating to the issuance of fraud orders by the Postal Department. On this point the report to which reference has just been made said: —

The reasons assigned for this course by some of such newspapers is that they fear libel suits; but it is difficult to understand wherein the liability for the publication of such news differs from the liability, if any, for the publication of the action of public officers in other classes of cases or of court proceedings, which are generally published and frequently command front-page space. As a matter of fact, a number of newspapers do give the greatest publicity to these fraud orders, and I have yet to hear of any civil or criminal action being attempted against them for the publication of such news.

Yet such conditions did not obtain long, for the ethics of newspaper-making demanded a new standard. With the higher standard and the broader vision the old common-law doctrine of "let the buyer beware" (*caveat emptor*) was discarded by many of the better newspapers. A report of the Solicitor to the Postal Department recorded the movement to free newspapers from fraudulent advertising as follows: —

Another and very striking effect of the policy of this administration with respect to fraudulent operations through the mails is that the leading organizations of advertising men and newspaper proprietors throughout the country have inaugurated and are now actively carrying out plans to "clean up" all false and fraudulent advertising. It is strongly urged by those behind this movement that the public will have more faith in advertising matter generally and that it will patronize the advertising columns to a greater extent when advertisements are uniformly honest, and that the standing of the newspapers themselves will soon be rated by the character of the advertisements they carry. Many newspapers now make it a rule to accept none but absolutely clean and true advertisements, and some papers even go so far as to guarantee the truth of the representations contained in their advertisements and to offer to reimburse any one defrauded by having placed reliance upon them.

COÖPERATION OF NEWSPAPERS

Then came the coöperation recorded a year later (1916): —

The movement for truthful advertising among publishers of newspapers and advertising clubs and associations, to which reference was made in my last annual report, has continued with undiminished vigor. This office has lent every proper assistance to the movement by keeping in touch with its leaders, supplying them with information with reference to fraud orders and acting upon complaints filed by them. The movement has been encouraged from its inception by this office in the realization that practically every fraudulent scheme depends upon false advertisements and that the withdrawal of such means of reaching the public would greatly handicap their operation. This campaign for truthful advertising is resulting in a great change in the nature of advertisements carried by many newspapers and in the conservative tone which is becoming more and more a characteristic of the advertising of legitimate business. Its effect is also to be seen in the fraudulent advertising laws which have recently been passed by many State legislatures and by Congress in legislating for the District of Columbia. It may be stated in this connection that widespread public interest has been aroused in this fraud-order work which has formed a subject for numerous syndicated articles of a highly commendatory character published throughout the country, as well as many favorable editorials, some by the leading daily metropolitan papers of all shades of political opinion. There have been no adverse newspaper comments so far as I have observed.

For the passage of the honest advertising laws mentioned in the paragraph just quoted especial credit should be given to *Printer's Ink*, a weekly journal published in the interest of advertising, and to the Associated Advertising Clubs of the World.

STATEMENT OF OWNERSHIP AND CIRCULATION

By an act of August 24, 1912, it was provided: —

It shall be the duty of the editor, publisher, business manager, or owner of every newspaper, magazine, periodical, or other publication to file with the Postmaster-General and the postmaster at the office at which said publication is entered, not later than the first day of April and the first day of October of each year, on blanks furnished by the Post-Office Department, a sworn statement setting forth the names and post-office addresses of the editor and managing editor, publisher, business managers, and owners, and, in addition, the stockholders, if the publication be owned by a corporation; and also the names of known bondholders, mortgagees, or other security-holders; and also, in the case of daily newspapers, there shall be included in such statement the average of the number of copies of each issue of such publication sold or distributed to paid subscribers during the preceding six months. Any such publication shall be denied the privileges of the mail if it shall fail to comply with the provisions of this paragraph within ten days after notice by registered letter of such failure.

This regulation was somewhat bitterly attacked on the part of both rural and metropolitan journalism. There appeared shortly after it went into effect numerous editorials similar in vein to the following quoted from *The Record*, of Bushnell, Illinois: —

Uncle Samuel is keeping a fatherly and watchful eye on the newspaper boys. Just why the old gentleman has any more right to poke his venerable nose into the private affairs of a man who runs a newspaper than he has to interfere with a grocer, a butcher, a dry-goods man, or a manufacturer has not yet been explained. As will be noted by the statement published this week, a paternal government has been given some weighty and important information about *The Record* — and it is hoped the country has thereby been saved.

While Uncle Sam is prying into private affairs that are none of his business, perhaps it might be in order to inform him that *The Record* man is a brunette and a Republican; he has a pretty bad corn on his left foot and his hair shows signs of falling out; he has only one good eye and walks a little splay-footed; he has a wife, a daughter, a couple of grandchildren, an alleged automobile, a horse, a Jersey calf, and a peg-legged cat. He thought he was running for the Legislature last fall, but he found out he wasn't even walking. He hopes to be able to keep on making an honest living without having to stop every little while and answer impertinent questions, as he is neither a criminal nor a dependent.

Metropolitan papers questioned the legality of the act and took the matter to the Supreme Court of the United States. The latter declared that no act had been enacted to abridge the freedom of the press, as newspapers might still continue to print editions if so desired, and were simply deprived of the use of the mails for distribution of copies if they did not obey the regulation. Later publishers came to accept the regulation as guaranteeing "full-weight" circulation just as the Government had insisted upon "full-weight" packages.

LABEL FOR ADVERTISEMENTS

Another act of August 24, 1912, was still more revolutionary, for it provided: —

All editorial or other reading matter published in any such newspaper, magazine, or periodical for the publication of which money or other valuable consideration is paid, accepted, or promised shall be plainly marked "advertisement." Any editor or publisher printing editorial or other reading matter for which compensation is paid, accepted, or promised, without so marking the same, shall, upon conviction in any court having jurisdiction, be fined not less than fifty dollars ($50) nor more than five hundred dollars ($500).

This second regulation was also assailed on the ground that if the letter of the law was enforced book reviews and dramatic criticisms would have to bear an advertising label. *The Evening Post*, of New York, was somewhat facetious in its comment: —

When book reviews and dramatic criticisms are duly labeled "Advertisement," as the Post-Office authorities would have it, H. Sillingsbee Jones, author of the original novel, "Heartache," may find notices of the following nature in his weekly envelope from the clipping bureau: —

"Heartache" is a fairly appropriate title for this latest story from the pen of Mr. H. Sillingsbee Jones, but "Headache" would have been better. There may have been a reason why this book should have been inflicted on a long-suffering public, but the reason, like the author's grammar, is not obvious. If the possession of nothing to say, and an utter inability to say it, constitute a call to authorship, then Mr. Jones is divinely inspired. There may be worse books than this in print, but we do not know where they are to be found. In all seriousness, why should labor and money be wasted on stuff like this? *Advertisement.*

Such a postal regulation, however, did much to help codify the code of ethics for newspapers, — a code which, at the beginning of the period, was without form, — and imposed by law a self-restraint and self-respect upon newspapers outside the straight and narrow way. No attempt has been made to make it apply either to literary or to dramatic criticism.

"DRY" JOURNALISM

The Prohibition movement found a prompt reaction in the press. As time went on, one newspaper after another began to exclude advertisements of spirituous liquors. As one section after another became dry, numerous complaints were made that distillers and brewers were using the columns of the newspapers to market liquors in sections where their sale was prohibited by law. Protests were so numerous that Congress passed a law — approved March 3, 1917, and effective July 1, 1917 — which, according to Liquor Bulletin No. 1, issued by the Postal Department and mailed to publishers and news agents, provided: —

No letter, postal card, circular, newspaper, pamphlet, or publication of any kind containing any advertisement of spirituous, vinous, malted, fermented, or other intoxicating liquors of any kind, or containing a solicitation of an order or orders for said liquors, or any of them, shall be deposited in or carried by the mails of the United States, or be delivered by any postmaster or letter-carrier, when addressed or directed to any person, firm, corporation, or association, or other addressee, at any place or point in any State or Territory of the United States at which it is, by the law in force in the State or Territory at that time, unlawful to advertise or solicit orders for such liquors, or any of them, respectively.

If the publisher of any newspaper or other publication or the agent of such publisher, or if any dealer in such liquors or his agent, shall knowingly deposit or cause to be deposited, or shall knowingly send or cause to be sent, anything to be conveyed or delivered by mail in violation of the provisions of this section, or shall knowingly deliver or cause to be delivered by mail anything herein forbidden to be carried by mail, shall be fined not more than one thousand dollars or imprisoned not more than six months, or both; and for any subsequent offense shall be imprisoned not more than one year. Any person violating any provision of this section may be tried and punished, either in the district in which the unlawful matter or publication was mailed or to which it was carried by mail for delivery, according to direction thereon, or in which it was caused to be delivered by mail to the person to whom it was addressed.

Before the passage of the national legislation, regulation in some of the States had been very strict about the insertion of advertisements of liquors. In Texas, for example, there appeared under every advertisement of whiskey, beer, wine, etc., a notice to the effect: "No orders solicited in, filled in, or shipped into prohibited territory in violation of the Texas laws." In "wet" territory, the exclusion of liquor advertising by newspapers was usually due to agitation started by women who somehow knew how to establish a boycott without breaking the state law. Other papers voluntarily excluded liquor advertising because they thought that newer standards demanded that the paper going into the home should be without the odor, or, to be more exact, the suggestion, of the alcoholic beverage. Unquestionably the decision of magazine publishers, who were the first to exclude liquor advertising, had much to do with the policies adopted by the newspapers. The change in editorial attitude of magazines and newspapers on the temperance question was one of the most remarkable total reversions of policy in journalism history.

INFLUENCE OF CIVIC SOCIETIES

That the period was one devoted to social readjustment may be seen by the attention which civic leagues paid to local newspapers. From these leagues came a constant demand for improvement in the advertising and news columns. In Denver, for example, was organized the Citizens' Protective League with purposes thus outlined by one of the Colorado papers published outside that city: —

One hundred leading citizens of Denver have organized the Citizens' Protective League, which has for its only purpose the squelching of the knocking and blackmailing newspaper. The most remarkable feature of this action is the length of time it required to awaken Denver's substantial citizenry to a realization that the newspaper condition was the heaviest millstone that beautiful but benighted city has been carrying for a dozen years.

It is common knowledge that certain newspapers there have had the business men of Denver — and there is no more abject coward on earth than the average business man — at their mercy through fear of attack, and even blackmail. This situation is incomprehensible when one stops to think that a combined stand against any newspaper by its patrons could put it out of business in six months.

Citizens of Denver, you have it in your power to make good Indians of the Denver newspapers, and if it is necessary to adopt the measures used to make good Indians of the aborigines, you are justified in the light of past experience. There is no newspaper published in Denver that is so absolutely necessary to your existence that you must stand for everything. And an occasional penance is not enough. Make them behave, as decent citizens are expected to do, all the time.

The press and the people of the interior are with you.

The official platform of the Citizens' Protective League was thus stated in advertisements published in Denver newspapers: —

1. That no news story, editorial, or advertisement be published which is unfit for a fifteen-year-old boy or girl to read.

2. That fake stories, misrepresentations, and exaggerations of all kinds be eliminated.

3. That stories of divorce, murder, suicide, and other forms of crime and immorality be kept in the background.

4. That the petty quarrels and constant warfare between the newspapers be permanently discontinued.

5. That stories which, though having some basis of fact, might be hurtful to Colorado or to any city in Colorado, should not be exploited in a sensational manner.

6. That malicious or unwarranted statements injurious to Colorado, or to any city or citizen of Colorado, or to any legitimate industry of Colorado be barred from publication.

Similar organizations in other cities did much to help codify that code of ethics the absence of which Henry Watterson so much regretted.

FOR ACCURACY AND FAIR PLAY

In 1908 William Bayard Hale sold to *The Century Magazine*, of New York, an article which contained an interview with the German Kaiser. After the article had been put into type and was actually on the press, the German Foreign Office requested its suppression — a request which the publishers of *The Century* granted, even though the act necessitated a stopping of the presses and the substitution of another article and a delay in the publication of the number. When the news of its suppression leaked out, the public became very much interested in the suppression and was unusually anxious to know what the Kaiser had said. *The World*, of New York, gave a wild guess which it published on November 21, 1908. Immediately upon the appearance of what purported to be a synopsis of *The Century* article, Mr. Hale gave to the press the following statement: —

I repudiate absolutely the story which *The New York World* this morning published purporting to tell what passed at my audience with the German Emperor. It is pure falsification from beginning to end and I so declared to *The World* reporter who showed it to me before publication.

The World was then forced to admit that it had imposed upon its readers in the publication of the article. The reaction which followed undoubtedly had something to do with the establishment by *The World* of its Bureau of Accuracy and Fair Play, the object of which was thus stated by Ralph Pulitzer, who succeeded his father on *The World* : —

To promote accuracy and fair play, to correct carelessness, and to stamp out fakes and fakers.

Isaac Deforest White, head of the Legal Department of *The World*, was placed in charge of the Bureau. He then sent to the various correspondents of *The World* the following declaration of policy: —

The World aims to be accurate. It aims to be fair and just to every person who reads it and to every person whose name it prints.

Accuracy and fair play are inseparable in journalism. Inaccuracy often means injury to innocent persons. A newspaper's influence is measured by the number of people who read it AND BELIEVE IN IT.

The words "accuracy and fair play" sum up the law of libel. If what is published is true and fair, the writer need not worry about the libel law, civil or criminal.

All complaints about inaccuracy of news items or about unjust treatment of persons mentioned in the columns are promptly turned over to this Bureau, which makes a careful investigation to determine whether there is any foundation for the complaint, and if so, where the responsibility lies. During the first year of its establishment, two hundred and sixty-two complaints were sustained and one hundred and sixty-four corrections were published in the newspaper.

A more liberal policy in the matter of making corrections or offering apologies, adopted by newspapers all over the country, marked the passing of the so-called infallibility of the press. Even such a conscientious editor as Samuel Bowles, of *The Republican*, of Springfield, Massachusetts, always hesitated to make corrections in his paper. The story is told that a man whose death had been recorded in *The Republican* appeared before the editor and demanded a correction. Upon being told the policy of the paper, he exclaimed, "But I am not dead, as you can see." To this the editor replied, "We cannot print a correction, but as your case demands some attention, we will bring you back to life by putting your name in the birth column." Whether this story be fact or fiction, it recorded an attitude taken by many newspaper publishers before the Period of Social Readjustment.

Not only did many papers establish complaint departments, but a number adopted the policy of submitting, before publication, any item reflecting on a man's character to the man himself, that false or incorrect statements might be corrected. It is but justice to *The Evening Post*, of New York, to say that that paper was among the first thus to safeguard the accuracy of its news of this character. With the movement "Safety First!" in railroading came that of "Accuracy First!" in newspaper-making.

DANGERS OF UNLICENSED JOURNALISM

With the "purified publicity" there came occasionally a discussion of the advisability of licensing newspaper men. Attention was called to the fact that before a man could practice at the bar, enter the pulpit, teach in the schools, run an automobile, etc., he must take out a license to demonstrate his ability and proficiency, but that any one might start a newspaper — if possessed of the necessary capital. Lieutenant-Governor Barratt O'Hara introduced into the Illinois Legislature a bill which provided for the licensing of journalists. Though it failed to pass and become a law, its introduction drew forth much comment in the press. The ablest presentation, however, of the dangers of a free press and unlicensed printing came, not from the pen of an American, but from that of the Russian publicist, Pobiedenostseff: —

Any vagabond babbler or unacknowledged genius, any enterprising tradesman, with his own money, or with the money of others, may found a newspaper, even a great newspaper. He may attract a host of writers and *feuilletonists*, ready to deliver judgment on any subject at a moment's notice; he may hire illiterate reporters to keep him supplied with rumors and scandals. His staff is then complete. From that day he sits in judgment on all the world, on ministers and administrators, on literature and art, on finance and industry. It is true that the new journal becomes a power only when it is sold on the market — that is, when it circulates among the public. For this talent is needed and the matter published must be attractive and congenial for the readers. Here, we might think, was some guarantee of the moral value of the undertaking — men of talent will not serve a feeble or contemptible editor or publisher; the public will not support a newspaper which is not a faithful echo of public opinion.

This guarantee is fictitious. Experience proves that money will attract talent under any conditions, and that talent is ready to write as its paymaster requires. Experience proves that the most contemptible persons — retired money-lenders, Jewish factors, news-venders, and bankrupt gamblers — may found newspapers, secure the services of talented writers and place their editions on the market as organs of public opinion. The healthy taste of the public is not to be relied upon. The great mass of readers, idlers for the most part, is ruled less by a few healthy instincts than by a base and despicable hankering for idle amusement, and the support of the people may be secured by any editor who provides for the satisfaction of these hankerings, for the love of scandal, and for intellectual pruriency of the basest kind. Of this we meet with evidence daily; even in our capital no search is necessary to find it; it is enough to note the supply and demand of the newsvenders' shops and at the railway stations.

Such a paper may flourish, attain consideration as an organ of public opinion, and be immensely remunerative to its owners, while no paper conducted upon firm moral principles or founded to meet the healthier instincts of the people could compete with it for a moment.

The full text of this criticism of journalism by Pobiedenostseff will be found in the appendix of Albert J. Beveridge's book entitled "Russian Advance."

RURAL JOURNALISM

Preceding chapters have recorded the relationship which Horace Greeley, of *The New York Tribune*, bore to his daily contemporaries. Yet Greeley exerted such a tremendous influence over the country weekly that it still bears his imprint. The latchstring of his editorial sanctum in New York was ever out for the country editor who cared to call, no matter whether he wanted to talk about the present coming presidential election or to discuss the squash or pumpkin crop in his own county; for Greeley was always prepared to give advice on either topic. Of all the New York editors of his time, Greeley was the most willing to send his paper to, or to exchange with, country publishers, and no matter how busy he might be he always found time to give advice about country weeklies. One such letter, which was extensively published, so influenced the making of the country weekly that it ought, in spite of its length, to be reproduced in this chapter. On April 3, 1860, Greeley penned the following letter: —

FRIEND FLETCHER: — I have a line from you, informing me that you are about to start a paper at Sparta, and hinting that a line from me for its first issue would be acceptable. Allow me, then, as one who spent his most hopeful and observant years in a country printing-office, and who sincerely believes that the art of conducting country (or city) newspapers has not yet obtained its ultimate perfection, to set before you a few hints on making up an interesting and popular gazette for a rural district like yours.

I. Begin with a clear conception that the subject of deepest interest to an average human being is himself; next to that, he is most concerned about his neighbors. Asia and the Tongo Islands stand a long way after these in his regard. It does seem to me that most country journals are oblivious as to these vital truths. If you will, so soon as may be, secure a wide-awake, judicious correspondent in each village and township of your county, — some young lawyer, doctor, clerk in a store, or assistant in a post-office, — who will promptly send you whatever of moment occurs in his vicinity, and will make up at least half your journal of local matter thus collected, nobody in the county can long do without it. Do not let a new church be organized, or new members be added to one already existing, a farm be sold, a new house be raised, a mill be set in motion, a store be opened, nor anything of interest to a dozen families occur, without having the fact duly though briefly chronicled in your columns. If a farmer cuts a big tree, or grows a mammoth beet, or harvests a bounteous yield of wheat or corn, set forth the fact as concisely and unexceptionably as possible. In due time, obtain and print a brief historical and statistical account of each township, — who first settled in it, who have been its prominent citizens, who attained advanced years therein, &c. Record every birth as well as every marriage and death. In short, make your paper a perfect mirror of everything done in your county that its citizens ought to know; and whenever a farm is sold, try to ascertain what it brought at previous sales, and how it has been managed meantime. One year of this, faithfully followed up, will fix the value of each farm in the county, and render it as easily determined as that of a bushel of corn.

II. Take an earnest and active, if not a leading, part in the advancement of home industry. Do your utmost to promote not only an annual county Fair, but town Fairs as well. Persuade each farmer and mechanic to send something to such Fairs, though it be a pair of well-made shoes from the one or a good ear of corn from the other. If any one undertakes a new branch of industry in the county, especially if it be a manufacture, do not wait to be solicited, but hasten to give him a helping hand. Ask the people to buy his flour, or starch, or woollens, or boots, or whatever may be his product, if it be good, in preference to any that may be brought into the county to compete with him. Encourage and aid him to the best of your ability. By persevering in this course a few years, you will largely increase the population of your county and the value of every acre of its soil.

III. Don't let the politicians and aspirants of the county own you. They may be clever fellows, as they often are; but, if you keep your eyes open, you will see something that they seem blind to, and must speak out accordingly. Do your best to keep the number of public trusts, the amount of official emoluments, and the consequent rate of taxation other than for common schools as low as may be. Remember that — in addition to the radical righteousness of the thing — the tax-payers take many more papers than the tax-consumers.

I would like to say more, but am busied excessively. That you may deserve and achieve success is the earnest prayer of

Yours truly,

HORACE GREELEY.

In view of Greeley's prominence in the journalism world, this letter was taken as a guidebook by the country publisher, who ever since has tried to follow all the advice given save that mentioned in the last paragraph. For some reason, the country weekly could not break away from partisan bias — something that Greeley himself was unable to do. The party "pap" which politicians handed out to local papers undoubtedly had something to do with this allegiance of party and country press. The printing of the session laws of the State, the insertion of announcements about sales by the sheriff, the publishing of the calendar of the county court, etc., were too profitable to the country publisher to make him independent of party allegiance. In addition, the printing of the campaign literature always went to a party publisher in spite of the fact that the independent printer would do the job cheaper. Only in recent years has the country publisher learned that "the taxpayers take more papers than the tax consumers," and the lesson has not been very well learned yet, as any newspaper directory will show.

Country weeklies of which there are now more than twenty thousand, have on the whole been closer to readers than the daily papers. The suggestion given by Greeley and followed by rural editors partly explains the fact, for the weekly became the printed diary of the home town. No finer tribute has been paid to rural journalism than that which came from the pen of William Allen White, editor of *The Gazette*, of Emporia, Kansas: —

Our papers, our little country papers, seem drab and miserably provincial to strangers; yet we who read them read in their lines the sweet, intimate story of life. And all these touches of nature make us wondrous kind. It is the country newspaper, bringing together daily the threads of the town's life, weaving them into something rich and strange, and setting the pattern as it weaves, directing the loom, and giving the cloth its color by mixing the lives of all the people in its color-pot — it is this country newspaper that reveals us to ourselves, that keeps our country hearts quick and our country minds open and our country faith strong.

The country press has not been without its influence. *The Independent* of New York City once offered a prize for the most meritorious essay describing "The Best Thing in Our Town." It was awarded to a preacher in a Missouri town who told about the local weekly of his parish. The country weekly often is just that — the best thing in our town.

FAMOUS LIBEL SUIT

A libel suit brought by the United States Government against *The World* of New York and against *The News* of Indianapolis attracted much attention. On December 15, 1908, President Roosevelt sent to Congress a special message upon the purchase of the Panama Canal Right for forty million dollars in which he asserted that the Government authorities should bring suit for libel for the intimation that the money was not paid to the French Government, but to an American syndicate, which had purchased the effects of the Panama Canal Company. President Taft, who went into office on March 4, 1909, kept aloof from the matter, but the Government continued its prosecution of the two papers on the grounds that it was their purpose to "stir up disorder among the people." The charge against *The World* was that it circulated twenty-nine copies containing the item "within the fort and military reservation of West Point." *The World* fought the suit on technical grounds, for reasons best known to itself, and resisted the pretense of the Federal authorities that they had a coördinate jurisdiction with the State authorities in prosecuting libel. No action was taken by the Government to bring the suit to the District of Columbia. The matter came up for trial in the United States Circuit Court of New York City on July 25, 1910, and the Court ordered that a judgment be entered quashing the indictment because it was not authorized by the statute upon which it rested. *The World* then urged that the matter be taken to the Supreme Court, which the Department of Justice did on January 3, 1911. Judge Hough handed down an opinion in which he quashed the indictment on the ground that the Federal Government had no jurisdiction. On January 4, 1911, *The World* thus summed up the results: —

The unanimous decision handed down by the United States Supreme Court yesterday in the Roosevelt-Panama libel case against *The World* is the most sweeping victory won for freedom of speech and of the press in this country since the American people destroyed the Federalist Party more than a century ago for enacting the infamous Sedition Law.

EXPERIMENTS IN JOURNALISM

The Period of Social Readjustment saw many experiments in journalism. When the United States undertook to dig a canal across the Isthmus of Panama, it later found itself also engaged in quite a different thing — that of publishing a newspaper. Employees who worked on "the big ditch" had to have news printed in English. There was nothing else for the Government to do but to establish *The Canal Record*. This paper, practically a country weekly for the Isthmus, was a letter from home and a diary of local events. It was distributed without charge to all the Government employees engaged in any sort of work on the Canal. Other new ventures in the field of journalism are outlined somewhat more in detail in the paragraphs which follow.

THE ADLESS DAILY PAPER

The endowed newspaper and the "adless" newspaper have frequently been the subject of academic discussion. No attempt has been made to establish the former and but one of the latter. On September 28, 1911, *The Day Book*, an adless daily newspaper, appeared in Chicago. Several issues were published before it was placed on sale and the circulation was kept to two hundred divided between two routes of one hundred each. With the carrier on Saturday went a personal representative of the paper to talk with the subscribers. Its object was to secure all its revenue from its readers in order that the paper might be under no obligation to anybody save to them. In December, 1912, *The Day Book* was gradually put on the newsstands with a corresponding increase in circulation which was as follows: 1912, 3446; 1913, 7886; 1914, 15,762; 1915, 19,562; for the six months ending September 30, 1916, 20,742. The daily average for October of that year was 22,938, but when on November 20 the retail price was raised from one to two cents there was a falling-off in circulation. At the higher rate *The Day Book* might possibly have been successful had there not been the very rapid increase in the cost of white paper due to the Great European War. With the increased cost of production, the paper, however, was forced either to raise its rates again or to suspend publication. The latter course was adopted. *The Day Book* did not prove very popular with the women, chiefly because it did not advertise the bargains of the department stores. How necessary store news is to the modern newspaper, Samuel Hopkins Adams has outlined in his novel, "The Clarion." The only substitute for such store advertising seems to be to hire a special reporter to report the news of shopping centers. The adless newspaper may possibly be a part of the journalism of to-morrow, if fifty thousand people will be willing to pay ten cents per copy for their daily paper and will agree not to cancel their subscription orders even though displeased with the presentation of the news or offended at the editorial policy adopted by the editors.

THE ENDOWED NEWSPAPER

The endowed newspaper has often been advocated. Hamilton Holt, editor of *The Independent*, of New York City, once outlined, before a National Newspaper Conference held under the auspices of the University of Wisconsin at Madison, Wisconsin, somewhat in detail just how an endowed newspaper should be conducted.

However ideal the endowed newspaper may be in theory, practical newspaper men like Don C. Seitz, business manager of *The New York World*, and James Keeley, editor and publisher of *The Chicago Herald*, do not think the scheme practical. Mr. Keeley once expressed himself as follows: —

An ideal paper, broadly speaking, is impractical. The people can endow a newspaper. No one else can. There are too many men of many minds in this as in every other land to make an ideal paper possible. Oatmeal may be the ideal breakfast food from a dietetic point of view, but it never has been universally adopted and never will be until all palates are set in the same gustatory key. So what might be the ideal mental oatmeal to some would prove caviar to the general multitude. Even class and technical papers, which one would think should speak with unanimity and authority, do not long remain as oracles in sole possession of their fields. Opposition develops and competitors appear expressing divergent views. One man's physical food is another man's poison, and until all think alike the ideal paper cannot come into being. And may it never come, for when all men think alike the spice of life will be gone, initiative will be smothered, and the world will be reduced to a dull level of mediocrity.

The nearest that the endowed newspaper has come to a realization in America was the partial promise of Andrew Carnegie to be one of ten men to finance such a venture. It would take just about ten men of Mr. Carnegie's wealth to establish successfully an endowed daily newspaper.

THE MUNICIPAL NEWSPAPER

The most pretentious attempt to publish a municipal newspaper was tried in Los Angeles, California, in 1912, when *The Municipal News* was started to publish the facts concerning the city's business and to give fully and accurately the arguments of contending sides. It was published weekly and circulated sixty thousand copies which were distributed by newsboys every Wednesday afternoon absolutely free throughout the residence sections of the city. One copy was left at every house regardless of whether the resident desired the paper or not. The paper was under the control of the Municipal Newspaper Commission, composed of three citizens who served without pay, and who were appointed by the mayor subject to confirmation by the city council. Each commissioner held office for four years, subject to recall by the voters at any time and to removal at any time by the mayor, subject to the referendum. Special columns were set aside solely for the use of political parties which furnished the items for insertion. Financial support came from two sources; first, there was the appropriation of $36,000 set aside by the city of Los Angeles; second, there was the revenue derived from advertising, for which the rates were one dollar an inch for one insertion. In addition to the municipal news, there was a page intended primarily to interest pupils attending city schools. The weekly expenses for publishing *The News* amounted to a little over a thousand dollars a week. The remarkable fact about *The Municipal News* was that in spite of the fact that it went into the home with its free distribution, it carried no department store advertising, except for four weeks when one proprietor, against the wish of his advertising manager, announced the special bargains offered at his store. A referendum vote, a vote by which the paper was established, later ordered the discontinuance of the sheet, chiefly on account of the financial cost.

The Municipal News did not compete with the daily papers of Los Angeles, California, because it printed no telegraphic intelligence. It was restricted by the ordinance which created the paper from printing any editorial opinion or argument about a religious question or any political question which pertained to National or State politics. A political party polling three per cent of the vote of Los Angeles had the right without charge to one column each issue in which it might set forth its views on public questions. The local committee of each party selected its own editor to edit its own column, which was free from censorship by the editor of the paper on the condition that matter submitted must be lawful for publication. The mayor or any member of the city council could have half a column in any issue of the paper.

In discussing the possibilities of a daily newspaper publicly owned, George H. Dunlop, manager of *The Municipal News*, once expressed his views as follows: —

The publicly owned daily newspaper, covering the entire field of journalism, must be a very high grade paper if it is to be of value. Its news must be accurate, its arguments fair, and its style interesting. It must not present the weaknesses of mankind as worthy, nor the vices of mankind as amusing, nor the virtues of mankind as stupid. It must not rely on scandal and vice, the improprieties of the stage and pictures of perfect women, as the means for interesting its readers. It will not seek to ingratiate itself with the childhood of the community with comic pictures whose humor is in inverse proportion to their general "smart-aleckness" and downright depravity. Above all, it must not preach the gospel of hate and try to make each half of the community believe the other half is the bitter foe of all progress and of their fellow-men. No one can say when we shall see a publicly owned daily newspaper of this kind, but I venture to say that the necessity for such a publicly owned newspaper lies in the very nature of things, and that in the inevitable course of events, it is on its way. The day is coming when it will arrive.

"TRADING STAMPS GIVEN"

In December, 1904, an interesting journalism experiment was started in Detroit, Michigan. S. P. Hutchinson, who had already attracted notice through trading stamps which bore his name, along with that of his partner, conceived the idea that a newspaper which gave premiums for coupons cut out of the sheet would be very successful. Accordingly he had special presses constructed which could print in the upper right-hand corner of each newspaper a little tri-cornered red coupon and started *The United States Daily*. These little coupons could be exchanged for premiums which ranged all the way from oak rockers and marble clocks to bicycles and automobiles. In charge of *The United States Daily* was the well-known journalist, Willis J. Abbot, who had been chairman of the National Democratic Press Bureau. He secured many of the features which had proved successful in New York in attracting circulation. In addition, he surrounded himself with an exceptionally able editorial and art staff and produced a paper which would seemingly compare very favorably with the popular newspapers of the Atlantic Coast. But the venture did not prove successful; even the coupons failed to bring a circulation, and after a spectacular career of sixty-eight days *The United States Daily* was interred in the journalism graveyard at Detroit on February 22, 1905. Brief as was its career, it aroused the bitter opposition of the other newspapers in Detroit, especially that of *The Journal, The Free Press*, and *The News*, and it failed to secure the coöperation of local department stores which had previously taken kindly to the trading stamp idea.

NEW TESTAMENT JOURNALISM

Shortly before the period opened, the Reverend Charles Sheldon had published a book which had a nation-wide sale under the title of "In His Steps, or What Would Jesus Do?" The suggestion was made to *The Daily Capital*, of Topeka, Kansas, that it would be a good idea to turn the paper over to the Reverend Dr. Sheldon for a week to be conducted as he thought Jesus Christ would have edited it. The offer when made to Dr. Sheldon was accepted and the experiment began on March 13, 1900, and continued for a week. Dr. Sheldon had long held the view that the daily newspaper was as much bound to give readers the things they needed instead of what they wanted as was the pulpit to give what was needed instead of what was wanted. He once asserted, "I have as much right to go into my pulpit next Sunday and preach to my people the things they want in theology or moral living as editors have to print in their papers anything below the high standards that govern human beings, for the rules of moral conduct are the same for an editor as for a minister." The edition during the week of Mr. Sheldon's editorship of *The Capital*, of Topeka, was sold on the newsstands all over the country. The immediate result was that several editors offered to preach the Gospel as Christ would have preached it, if pulpits were provided. The latter offers, however, were not accepted by the clergy. Fourteen years later a number of distinguished Kansan editors occupied pulpits and preached lay sermons on journalism the Sunday preceding the meeting of a National Newspaper Conference held under the auspices of the University of Kansas, at Lawrence, Kansas. For that conference Melville E. Stone, general manager of the Associated Press, prepared a lay sermon, using for his text, "For unto whomsoever much is given, of him shall be much required; and to whom men have committed much, of him they will ask the more." (St. Luke, XII, 48.) The conclusion of the sermon thus summed up the text, as applied to the Associated Press: —

Obviously then, the very magnitude of the Associated Press work tends to make truthfulness and impartiality in the service imperative. It cannot be used for private aims, to serve any special interest, or to help any political party or faction or propaganda. I am not laying

claim to any great virtue. I am saying that, under its system of operation and in view of the millions of critics passing upon its work, the
Associated Press is automatically truthful and fair. If you hear a man
whining that the Associated Press is run in the interest of this party or
that you may put it down that what he wants is not fair play, but a leaning his way. As one evidence of the truthfulness of our reports, I direct
your attention to the fact that during the life of the present organization we have never paid a dollar of damages in an action for libel, nor
have we compromised any case. Thus do we aim to keep in mind our
obligation, "Unto whomsoever much is given, of him shall be much required."

CHRISTIAN SCIENCE DAILY PAPER

In spite of unsuccessful attempts in Boston, New York,
Philadelphia, etc., to establish daily religious newspapers, Mary
Baker Eddy, the founder of Christian Science, made up her mind
that she would start a daily paper modeled along lines which had
been suggesting themselves to her for a long time in connection
with her work. Taking as her motto a Scriptural phrase about
lifting up a standard which should be a light unto the people,
she resolved that her newspaper, instead of being a mirror for
reflecting destructive agencies, should be a journal to record
achievements in every useful field of human endeavor. She accordingly started *The Christian Science Monitor* in Boston, November 25, 1908. From the start the paper was more international in scope than most rivals in the secular field. Special
attention was paid to commercial conditions in foreign lands in
general, and in South America in particular. Art and education
were given prominent positions in the paper; its religious propaganda was limited to a daily article on one of the back pages.
From the first issue the paper was successful, due largely to the
wonderful coöperation of the church of which Mrs. Eddy was the
visible head. It is but justice to *The Monitor* to say that no paper
has a higher standard of ethics. Its circulation has not been confined by any means to members of the Christian Science Church.
Even a distinguished Chicago journalist once remarked, "I
have n't any more use for Christian Science than Hetty Green
had for a poorhouse, but I consider *The Christian Science Monitor* one of the greatest dailies in America and I read it religiously,
not for its propaganda, but for its secular news."

ASSOCIATED PRESS

On May 23, 1900, the State of New York issued a charter to a corporation known as the Associated Press. The new organization was virtually a continuance of the Western Associated Press which had had its headquarters at Chicago. This change was doubtless made because the Supreme Court of Illinois, after a suit had been brought against the Associated Press by *The Chicago Interocean* to secure the news service of the Association, had handed down the following decision: —

The Associated Press from the time of its organization and establishment in business sold the news reports to various newspapers who became members, and the publication of that news became of vast importance to the public so that public interest is attached to the dissemination of that news. The manner in which that corporation has used its franchise has charged its business with a public interest. It has devoted its property to a public use, and has, in effect, granted to the public such an interest in its use that it must submit to be controlled by the public, for the common good, to the extent of the interest it has thus created in the public in its private property. The sole purpose for which news was gathered was that the same should be sold, and all newspaper publishers desiring to purchase such news for publication are entitled to purchase the same without discrimination against them. . . . The appellee corporation being engaged in a business upon which a public interest is engrafted, upon principles of justice it can make no distinction with respect to persons who wish to purchase information and news, for purposes of publication, which it was created to furnish. . . . The legal character of the corporation and its duties cannot be disregarded because of any stipulation incorporated in a contract that it should not be liable to discharge a public duty. Its obligation to serve the public is not one resting on contract, but grows out of the fact that it is in the discharge of a public duty, or a private duty which has been so conducted that a public interest has attached thereto.

The position taken by the Associated Press is that it has no monopoly of the news. Its general manager, Melville E. Stone, has explained the situation as follows: —

The output of the Associated Press is not the news; it is its own story of the news. There can be no monopoly in news. At the point of origin, Havana, the destruction of the Maine was known by every man, woman, and child. Any one could have written a story of it. The Associated Press men did. It was their own story. Who shall say that they, or those who employed them, were not entitled to its exclusive use? And is this not equally true, whether the employer be one man, or ten men, or nine hundred men acting in coöperation?

Charges of unfair play have on several occasions been brought against the Associated Press. Oswald Garrison Villard, president of *The New York Evening Post*, has drawn the following conclusion about these charges: —

I personally have examined one mare's nest after another, only to find that each was due to ignorance of the technique of the profession or of the facts. Most of them would never have been heard of had the suspicious ones gone to headquarters to inspect the records. It is only in the tenth or one hundredth case that I have found that there was a genuine error. And it goes without saying that I have yet to learn of a constructive suggestion as to something better to take the place of the Associated Press.

The Associated Press secured in 1917 a court decision which established the legality of its claims to ownership of its own story of the news. The comparison was made that the product of the organization was like ore which had been mined and refined. To make claims still stronger newspapers which were members of the Associated Press posted a notice on editorial pages to the effect: —

The Associated Press is exclusively entitled to the use for republication of all news dispatches credited to it or not otherwise credited in this paper and also the local news of spontaneous origin published herein. All rights of republication of all other matter herein are also reserved.

UNITED PRESS

While the present United Press was organized in June, 1907, it really dates back to the breaking up of the old United Press in 1897, though between the two organizations there is no direct connection. At the time, however, that the discontinuance of the service of the old United Press was announced, several of its members were unable to join the Associated Press and others refused to do so. Among the latter was E. W. Scripps, one of the owners of the Scripps-McRae string of newspapers, pub-

The Call=Chronicle=Examiner

SAN FRANCISCO, THURSDAY, APRIL 19, 1906.

EARTHQUAKE AND FIRE:
SAN FRANCISCO IN RUINS

DEATH AND DESTRUCTION HAVE BEEN THE FATE OF SAN FRANCISCO. SHAKEN BY A TEMBLOR AT 5.13 O'CLOCK YESTERDAY MORNING, THE SHOCK LASTING 48 SECONDS, AND SCOURGED BY FLAMES THAT RAGED DIAMETRICALLY IN ALL DIRECTIONS, THE CITY IS A MASS OF SMOULDERING RUINS. AT SIX O'CLOCK LAST EVENING THE FLAMES SEEMINGLY PLAYING WITH INCREASED VIGOR, THREATENED TO DESTROY SUCH SECTIONS AS THEIR FURY HAD SPARED DURING THE EARLIER PORTION OF THE DAY. BUILDING THEIR PATH IN A TRIANGULAR CIRCUIT FROM THE START IN THE EARLY MORNING, THEY JOCKEYED AS THE DAY WANED, LEFT THE BUSINESS SECTION, WHICH THEY HAD ENTIRELY DEVASTATED, AND SKIPPED IN A DOZEN DIRECTIONS TO THE RESIDENCE PORTIONS. AS NIGHT FELL THEY HAD MADE THEIR WAY OVER INTO THE NORTH BEACH SECTION AND SPRINGING ANEW TO THE SOUTH THEY REACHED OUT ALONG THE SHIPPING SECTION DOWN THE BAY SHORE, OVER THE HILLS AND ACROSS TOWARD THIRD AND TOWNSEND STREETS. WAREHOUSES, WHOLESALE HOUSES AND MANUFACTURING CONCERNS FELL IN THEIR PATH. THIS COMPLETED THE DESTRUCTION OF THE ENTIRE DISTRICT, KNOWN AS THE "SOUTH OF MARKET STREET." HOW FAR THEY ARE REACHING TO THE SOUTH ACROSS THE CHANNEL CANNOT BE TOLD AS THIS PART OF THE CITY IS SHUT OFF FROM SAN FRANCISCO PAPERS.

AFTER DARKNESS THOUSANDS OF THE HOMELESS WERE MAKING THEIR WAY WITH THEIR BLANKETS AND SCANT PROVISIONS TO GOLDEN GATE PARK AND THE BEACH TO FIND SHELTER. THOSE IN THE HOMES ON THE HILLS JUST NORTH OF THE HAYES VALLEY WRECKED SECTION PILED THEIR BELONGINGS IN THE STREETS AND EXPRESS WAGONS AND AUTOMOBILES WERE HAULING THE THINGS AWAY TO THE SPARSELY SETTLED REGIONS. EVERYBODY IN SAN FRANCISCO IS PREPARED TO LEAVE THE CITY, FOR THE BELIEF IS FIRM THAT SAN FRANCISCO WILL BE TOTALLY DESTROYED.

DOWNTOWN EVERYTHING IS RUIN. NOT A BUSINESS HOUSE STANDS. THEATRES ARE CRUMBLED INTO HEAPS. FACTORIES AND COMMISSION HOUSES LIE SMOULDERING ON THEIR FORMER SITES. ALL OF THE NEWSPAPER PLANTS HAVE BEEN RENDERED USELESS. THE "CALL" AND THE "EXAMINER" BUILDINGS, EXCLUDING THE "CALL'S" EDITORIAL ROOMS ON STEVENSON STREET BEING ENTIRELY DESTROYED.

IT IS ESTIMATED THAT THE LOSS IN SAN FRANCISCO WILL REACH FROM $150,000,000 TO $300,000,000. THESE FIGURES ARE IN THE ROUGH AND NOTHING CAN BE TOLD UNTIL PARTIAL ACCOUNTING IS TAKEN.

ON EVERY SIDE THERE WAS DEATH AND SUFFERING YESTERDAY. HUNDREDS WERE INJURED, EITHER BURNED, CRUSHED OR STRUCK BY FALLING PIECES FROM THE BUILDINGS, AND ONE AND ALL SEN WERE WORKING AT THE OPERATING TABLE AT MECHANICS PAVILION IMPROVISED AS A HOSPITAL FOR THE COMFORT AND CARE OF 300 OF THE INJURED. THE NUMBER OF DEAD IS NOT KNOWN BUT IT IS ESTIMATED THAT AT LEAST 500 MET THEIR DEATH IN THE HORROR.

AT NINE O'CLOCK, UNDER A SPECIAL MESSAGE FROM PRESIDENT ROOSEVELT, THE CITY WAS PLACED UNDER MARTIAL LAW. HUNDREDS OF TROOPS PATROLLED THE STREETS AND DROVE THE CROWDS BACK, WHILE HUNDREDS MORE WERE SET AT WORK ASSISTING THE FIRE AND POLICE DEPARTMENTS. THE STRICTEST ORDERS WERE ISSUED, AND IN TRUE MILITARY SPIRIT THE SOLDIERS OBEYED. DURING THE AFTERNOON THREE THIEVES MET THEIR DEATH BY RIFLE BULLETS WHILE AT WORK IN THE RUINS. THE CURIOUS WERE DRIVEN BACK AT THE BREASTS OF THE HORSES THAT THE CAVALRYMEN RODE AND ALL THE CROWDS WERE FORCED FROM THE LEVEL DISTRICT TO THE HILLY SECTION BEYOND TO THE NORTH.

THE WATER SUPPLY WAS ENTIRELY CUT OFF AND MAY BE IT WAS JUST AS WELL, FOR THE LINES OF FIRE DEPARTMENT WOULD HAVE BEEN ABSOLUTELY USELESS AT ANY STAGE. ASSISTANT CHIEF DOUGHERTY SUPERVISED THE WORK OF HIS MEN AND EARLY IN THE MORNING IT WAS SEEN THAT THE ONLY POSSIBLE CHANCE TO SAVE THE CITY LAY IN EFFORT TO CHECK THE FLAMES BY THE USE OF DYNAMITE. DURING THE DAY A BLAST COULD BE HEARD IN ANY SECTION AT INTERVALS OF ONLY A FEW MINUTES, AND BUILDINGS NOT DESTROYED BY FIRE WERE BLOWN TO ATOMS. BUT THROUGH THE GAPS MADE THE FLAMES JUMPED AND ALTHOUGH THE FAILURES OF THE HEROIC EFFORTS OF THE POLICE, FIREMEN AND SOLDIERS WERE AT TIMES SICKENING, THE WORK WAS CONTINUED WITH A DESPERATION THAT WILL LIVE AS ONE OF THE FEATURES OF THE TERRIBLE DISASTER. MEN WORKED LIKE FIENDS TO COMBAT THE LAUGHING, ROARING, ONRUSHING FIRE DEMON.

NO HOPE LEFT FOR SAFETY OF ANY BUILDINGS

San Francisco seems doomed to entire destruction. With a lapse in the raging of the flames just before dark, the hope was raised that with the use of the was of dynamite the course of the fire might be checked and confined to the triangular sections it had cut out for its path. But ere the Barbary Coast the fire broke out anew and as night closed in the flames were eating their way into parts untouched in their ravages during the day. To the south and the north they spread, down to the docks and out into the resident section. In and to the north of Hayes Valley by the o'clock practically all of St. Ignatius' great buildings were as ruins. They had been leveled to the heap that marked what was once the metropolis of the West.

The first of the big structures to go to ruin was the Call Building, the famous skyscraper. At eleven o'clock the big 18 story building was a furnace. Flames leaned from every window and shot skyward from the circular windows in the dome. In less than two hours nothing remained but the tall skeleton.

By five o'clock the Palace Hotel was in ruins. The old industry famous the world over, withstood the seige until the last and although dynamite was used in frequent blasts to drive

Continued on Page Two

BLOW BUILDINGS UP TO CHECK FLAMES

The dynamiting of buildings in the track of the fire, to stay the progress of the flames, was in charge of John Bermingham, Jr., superintendent of the California Powder Works. Several experienced men from the powder works, assisted by policemen and members of the fire department, did the heaviest work of blowing up the buildings. They were razed in acts of three, but the open spaces where the destroyed buildings fell were quickly turned into holocausts of flame. The work was most effective in the downtown section back of Kearny street.

WHOLE CITY IS ABLAZE

At 9 o'clock last night the fire demon still was destroyed by the flames which swept unchecked across the city from Montgomery street, east and Kearny. The fire then ran down Kearny towards Post and it seemed as if the whole of business section was to be destroyed. Shortly after 10 o'clock the fire had eaten its way southward from Post towards Market and the hills north of the city. There seemed no hope to stay the course of the flames then, and all the buildings in that district were doomed. The men fighting the fire were plainly disheartened. There seemed no way to stay the progress of the flames.

CHURCH OF SAINT IGNATIUS IS DESTROYED

The magnificent church and College of St. Ignatius, on the northwest corner of Van Ness avenue and Hayes street represents in its destruction a material loss of over $1,500,000. The initial cost of the great building was over $800,000, but during the years which have elapsed since its erection the church has been enriched by paintings and frescoes, which were priceless. Some of these were works of art which can never be replaced, however striking man lamented is the church sought to as may be at present in the effort.

MAYOR CONFERS WITH MILITARY AND CITIZENS

At 1 o'clock yesterday afternoon 50 representative citizens of San Francisco met the Mayor, the Chief of Police and the United States Military authorities in the police office in the basement of the Hall of Justice. They had been summoned thither by Mayor Schmitz early in the forenoon, the fearful possibilities of the situation having forced themselves upon him immediately after the shock of earthquake in the morning and the news which at once reached him of the completeness of the disaster. He lost no time in making out a list of citizens from whom to seek advice and assistance and in summoning them to the conference. It was called at the Hall of Justice as virtually the first news which reached the Mayor regarding the extent of the disaster was that of the ruin of the City Hall. He did not realize that even while the conference was to be going on citizens would be crawling down and windows being fragments as the Hall of Justice also, and that before a short daperate of one would be made to have the structure up in the vast endeavor by the secret to check the advance of the flames in the southern section of the town district.

All, or nearly all, of the citizens summoned by the conference

Continued on Page Two

JOINT ISSUE OF SAN FRANCISCO MORNING PAPERS THE DAY
AFTER THE EARTHQUAKE
(Reduced)

lished in the Middle West, which had been organized around a nucleus of *The Cincinnati Post, The Cleveland Press,* and *The St. Louis Chronicle.* Probably the reason that Scripps did not care to join the Associated Press was the fact that he thought that any papers which his company was planning to establish in other cities would be unable to secure franchises. So he started his own news-gathering organization at about the same time that the newspapers in the East, who were not members of the Associated Press, organized the Publishers' Press, with headquarters in New York. The latter organization was prepared to furnish its service to both morning and evening papers while the former limited its field to the evening dailies. A little later another organization came into existence which furnished a brief or "pony" report of the news to a string of small dailies stretching from Chicago to San Francisco. The three organizations after about ten years saw that strength was in union and organized the present United Press with John Vandercock as president and general news manager. Upon his death, shortly after the union, Roy Howard succeeded him as manager. Whenever the Associated Press is attacked on the ground of having a monopoly of the news, it points to the claims of the United Press to show that it has a formidable rival in the field.

The United Press differs from the Associated Press in that its services are available to any newspaper which can pay the necessary charges for a leased wire, etc. There is no "power of protest" such as belongs to the Associated Press.

PAPERS OF SCRIPPS

E. W. Scripps is the Benjamin Franklin of modern journalism. Just as Franklin used to furnish an apprentice with a printing outfit and send him to a newly settled section to start a paper, so Scripps puts out a bright young journalist and furnishes him the funds with which to establish under a partnership agreement a new paper in another field. There are some thirty-odd newspapers, large and small, in his string of papers, the distinguishing characteristic of which is said to be that they address themselves primarily to the interests of the working class.

STATISTICAL RÉSUMÉ

During the first decade of the twentieth century, the number of daily newspapers increased 16.8 per cent: in every geographic division of the United States there was an increase, except in New England, but the greatest increase both relative and absolute was in the Pacific and the West South Central divisions. In every State of New England there was a loss in the number of dailies during the first decade except in Rhode Island where conditions remained stationary.

According to the same statistics gathered for the Thirteenth Census of the United States, New York led among the individual States with a total daily circulation of over one fifth of that for the entire country. Pennsylvania came second with a little more than one eighth and Illinois third with about one tenth. The only other States which had over three per cent of the total daily circulation were California, Massachusetts, Missouri, and Ohio. New York reported the largest absolute increase in circulation and Louisiana the least; the highest per cent of gain was in Oklahoma, and the lowest in Louisiana.

By 1909 the circulation of the evening dailies exceeded that of the morning in eight of the nine main geographic divisions of the United States. The Mountain division was the only one where the morning circulation was greater than the evening.

The total circulation of the daily newspapers in the ten leading cities of the United States showed a decrease from 50.5 per cent in 1904 to forty-seven per cent in 1909, in comparison with that for the entire country. This fact proved that the circulation of dailies published outside the metropolitan centers increased the more rapidly. In 1909 the circulation of the daily papers of New York City was 16.9 per cent of that of all the dailies in the country; in 1904 it was 18.3 per cent. The census of 1910 showed that the preponderance of the evening circulation increased in Boston, Chicago, Cleveland, New York, and Philadelphia, and that the morning circulation increased, but in decreasing proportion, in Baltimore and San Francisco. In St. Louis the evening papers had a larger circulation than the morning in 1909 — a condition quite the reverse of that in 1904; the same condition obtained in Pittsburgh.

In the matter of Sunday newspapers there was an increase of twenty-nine for the five-year period 1904–09; though there was a decrease in number in the West North Central and the South Atlantic divisions there was an increase in the total circulation of the Sunday newspapers published therein. With the exception of the Middle Atlantic and the East North Central divisions there were increases both in number and in total circulation. The aggregate number of copies reported for 1909 was sufficient to furnish one copy for every fifth person who was ten years of age or over, and was able to read. The growth in circulation of the Sunday newspaper in the metropolitan cities was checked by the establishment of Sunday editions in smaller places. In only two of the ten leading cities, however, was there a distinct loss in circulation on Sunday — Baltimore and San Francisco.

EFFECTS OF EUROPEAN WAR

Press dispatches told the American reading public of the effect of the war on European newspapers. The great struggle had scarcely begun when the French papers began either to suspend publication or to reduce their size, and those which continued publication for the most part confined themselves to a single edition a day and abolished all headline display. Americans who subscribe for London dailies noticed an immediate reduction in size as soon as war had been declared. A cablegram from Amsterdam announced that over eight hundred and fifty German newspapers, according to statistics gathered by the Postal Department, had suspended the first year of the war. Belgian journalism soon became a thing of the past, save that conducted under German supervision.

The effect of the war on American journalism has been even more pronounced, though along different lines. Size and circulation of papers in this country were not at first curtailed, but the amount spent by the American press to gather the news, even when all was quiet near Ypres, would, it is said on good authority, have bankrupted the journalism of Continental Europe. The increased sales of both regular and extra editions put additional financial burdens on the leading dailies. Those who think that the advertisers footed the bills could not be more mistaken

in their deduction. While advertising rates were computed on
the basis of circulation, no newspaper could advance its charge
for advertisements on short notice, as contracts, often covering
a term of months and in some cases years, prevented a sudden
increase in rates. Advertisers, not the newspapers, profited by
the increased circulation.

The most immediate effect of the war was noticed in the rapid
advance in cable tolls, which, not only the news-gathering organization, but also the newspapers themselves, were forced to
pay for the special war dispatches. So high were these tolls that
newspapers pooled their interests. In New York City, for example, *The World*, *The Times*, and *The Tribune* used a joint
cable service which reduced the tolls to one third for each newspaper. As the London newspapers sold their news service to anybody, the three papers just mentioned had been getting practically the same special war dispatches at three times the cost they
later had to pay. In the beginning the British censors, however,
were a source of much annoyance to American newspapers, for
every one seemed a law unto himself. The proof-sheets of *The
London Daily Mail*, for example, filed for transmission to American newspapers, would be blue-penciled one way by one censor
and another by a second. Such irregularities in censorship did
much to promote the newspaper combination just mentioned.

In spite of such combinations to improve the service and to
reduce the cost in cabling, the newspapers found it impossible
to print both the war news and the other routine news without
increasing the size of the regular issues to such an extent that
financial returns would not pay for the cost of production. Both
local and national news was therefore reduced in quantity. Such
reductions in the amount of local news printed released newspaper workers from many offices. The condition at Chicago,
typical of that in metropolitan cities, was thus set forth in *The
Scoop*, the official publication of the Chicago Press Club: —

The European War has created a condition in Chicago which has
seriously affected the working newspapermen of the city. The great
expense to which the newspapers are being subjected in heavy cable
tolls, and the largely increased circulation without an adequate enlarged advertising revenue, have forced the newspapers to curtail costs,

and a number of good men find themselves without employment, with winter staring them in the face. Some of the hustlers are willing to go out and create work for themselves in various ways. They will require printing, and may require credit from printing firms. *The Scoop* suggests to our printer members that in all such cases they apply the golden rule rather than the strict rule of commerce. Look up the record and personal standing of an applicant for credit, and if he be found worthy, extend a helping hand.

After the outbreak of the war the evening papers assumed a position never before held in the history of American journalism. Many of the papers of this class consisted in the past of a few pages which closely resembled in contents a bulletin board, a number of pages of special features which had no more news value than last year's almanac, and an editorial page of the human interest type. The war made a decided change by putting more news into the pages of the evening editions. The difference in time between America and Europe often gave the evening paper almost a monopoly of the war news: the late editions had not yet gone to press when the European armies bivouacked for the night. Consequently there was time — if the censor did not keep union hours — to get a report of the day's activities.

The war also produced a change in the routine handling of news. Previously newspapers had put first in the item either the most important or the most startling fact and had then hidden the source of the information in the middle of the first paragraph. After the war began the press was frequently criticized for printing misleading information. Such charges, however, were usually unfounded, as a careful perusal of the item would show some such assertion as "according to a bulletin issued yesterday." The bulletin may have contained assertions which were not true, but the press told the truth when it asserted that the bulletin contained such and such statements. Because responsibility was placed upon the newspaper rather than upon those who issued the bulletins and statements, the press usually protected itself by emphasizing in the opening sentence its source of information. Military necessity may have demanded the publication of misleading items, but military necessity must be willing to accept the responsibility for such publicity.

REVIVAL OF EDITORIAL PAGE

The war from the start did much to revive the interest in the editorial page the influence of which had declined very much in the Period of Financial Readjustment. Unfamiliar with European geography, unacquainted with the economic and political situations in the warring countries, readers found they must have the news interpreted through the editorial. The war made readers more thoughtful and the thoughtful reader has always been a reader of the editorial page. Once again American journalism found itself divided into two groups, one of which was pro-Ally, the other, pro-German, in its editorial sympathies. The editorial battles between the two developed military critics in the editorial sanctum. The entrance of America into the Great European War brought these two factors together into practically a harmonious press, with only here and there an exception to prove the general rule.

The attempt of certain newspapers, early in the war, to be strictly neutral in the publishing of the news, was rather amusing. The eighth edition of a metropolitan daily on a certain day stretched this streamer headline across the page: —

Germans Fall Like Leaves at the Battle of Ypres.

The ninth edition of the same paper on the same day bore this headline: —

Allies Fall Like Leaves at the Battle of Ypres.

Could any newspaper be more neutral?

PAPER SITUATION

The increase in the cost of white paper later made space more valuable. The result was that there was a noticeable condensation of news in all departments. Special features, instead of being set in rather large type, were made to occupy a rather smaller space through a change of font, or by the omission of leads between the lines. Headlines were reduced in size; though they often stretched across the page, they were in much smaller type than during the days of the American war with Spain when, as has already been mentioned, they sometimes, in extreme cases, practically filled half of the front page.

The increased cost of production raised the subscription rates of many daily newspapers all over the country — especially was this true of those selling at one cent. Even in the few cities where rates were not raised for local subscribers, rates were raised for those living outside the first zone: the farther zones were from the place of publication, the larger the price. Early in 1917, when the shortage of wood pulp paper was most acute, the papers not only limited the size of their editions, but frequently in so doing reduced the number. Notices similar to the following appeared:

Owing to the shortage of paper, the circulation of the morning edition of *The World* will be reduced to 350,000 copies daily. Beginning February 1st, until further notice, the paper will be absolutely nonreturnable.

When wood chips, which had been previously useful only as fuel or had been totally discarded, came also to be used to manufacture wood pulp paper, as the result of study made in the Forests Products Laboratory at Washington, and after numerous economies had been made in newspaper plants to utilize paper which had been previously thrown away, newspapers were able to print announcements similar to the following: —

The World having purchased the High Falls Pulp and Paper Company, and improved the conditions of its newsprint supply, is now able to more nearly approach meeting the demands of its readers by increasing the daily circulation on the morning edition to 375,000, but cannot exceed that figure, except on a day when news of extraordinary importance may justify a departure from this rule.

PRESS CENSORSHIP

Shortly after the entrance of America into the war, President Wilson appointed a Committee on Public Information, the purposes of which were twofold: first, to be a clearing-house for the news of the various departments at Washington; second, to act as censors for war intelligence received from other sources. The committee consisted of the Secretary of State, the Secretary of War, the Secretary of the Navy, and one civilian, George Creel. Owing to practically the united opposition of the press, Congress deprived the committee of its second function and limited it to the dissemination of information. The committee, however, did issue a pamphlet, based largely upon a similar publication put out by the Press Censor of Canada, which offered suggestions for voluntary censorship. The attitude of the press, *The Tribune*, of New York, expressed in the following editorial: —

Must every censor or would-be censor put on the clown's livery? Must he lose all sense of restraint and judgment, all touch with actualities? Certainly there seems to be something in this perilous office which goes to a man's brains and makes him the easy victim of his own fatuity.

Mr. George Creel's latest promulgation is a case in point. He has just issued a new series of "voluntary" censorship regulations and declared them in effect from yesterday. They are "voluntary" regulations only in the sense that they have no warrant of law behind them. The newspapers have not volunteered to respect them. Nor could they consent to respect all of them without at the same time submitting to a dictatorship more fantastic and oppressive than exists in any other nation now at war. Even in Turkey, we fancy, newspapers may still do what Mr. Creel wants to prohibit American newspapers from doing.

The American press was doubtless influenced by the results of censorship in England, where papers like *The London Times* and *The London Daily Mail* had asserted that press censorship was pernicious and had been used solely to protect office-holders and blunderers from the penalties of their own stupidity and inefficiency. "Secrecy helps these men," said Lord Northcliffe, owner of the two papers just mentioned, "to protect their false positions and to do damage to the nation. Publicity pricks the bubble; that is why so many of them hate publicity when it begins to be critical."

The Committee on Public Information, though deprived of all censorship save where newspapers voluntarily chose to submit news items for inspection, did excellent work in the matter of publicity for different branches of the Government. Had not the two functions, censorship and publicity, been joined at the start, the coöperation of the press would have been more complete.

When Congress passed in September, 1917, the Trading with the Enemy Act, it gave the Postmaster-General power not only to refuse the second-class entry privilege to newspapers publish-

ing treasonable or seditious matter, but also to penalize papers reprinting articles from publications declared unmailable. The Postmaster-General thus outlined how he planned to administer the act which gave him so much power over the press: —

This legislation is not to prevent criticism of the Government or the Administration or the Post-Office Department. It is not aimed against Socialist publications or any other kind of publications as a class. The newspapers can denounce the Postmaster-General or the Administration all they like, and they can have such criticism circulated through the mails. But if we find newspapers preaching disloyalty, newspapers that are really German at heart and in secret sympathy with the German Government which we are fighting, newspapers which are trying to make the masses in this country believe that this is a capitalists' war and that the Government therefore ought not to be supported — those publications we intend to suppress with a firm hand, because we are at war with the Imperial German Government. The country has declared war. Any one who deliberately sets afoot a propaganda to discourage support to the Government as against its enemies is doing a treasonable thing. We must win the war, and we cannot brook disloyalty at home.

One incident attracted considerable attention at the time. Melville E. Stone has provided this introduction: —

A great many complications resulted from the appointment of Creel. On the 3d of July, 1917, he gave out a story of two battles between our first transport fleet under Admiral Gleaves and German submarines. The statement said the attack by the submarines "was made in force, although the night made impossible any exact count of the U-boats gathered for what they deemed a slaughter."

Since U-boats are blind when submerged it was necessary that they travel alone, lest they collide and injure each other. They do not attack "in force." But this fact was no deterrent for Creel.

Trouble came when the Associated Press released this cable dispatch from London after an account of the "two battles" reached England: —

Thursday confidential following America's naval base *passed for publication U.S.A. only* quote private attitude official circles here that Daniels story made out of whole cloth there no submarine attack whatever no torpedoes seen no gunfire from destroyers stop our destroyers dropped explosive charge as precaution but no submarine or wreckage seen stop explained destroyers frequently fire at logs or anything which might prove periscope stop officials therefore decline permit aftermath story from this end.

This confidential dispatch was made public to the press because of the words "*passed for publication U.S.A. only.*" (This phrase was the rubber-stamp of the English censor and was by mistake incorporated in the message.) Secretary of Navy Daniels requested suppression, but it was too late. President Wilson took serious offence at the matter and said that he would never again speak to the General Manager of the Associated Press — an assertion which he later regretted and forgot to keep.

FIRST ARMY EDITION

The first American newspaper which had an army edition was *The Tribune*, of Chicago. On July 4, 1917, in spite of the paper scarcity, it started publishing a daily paper in Paris for the American soldiers "somewhere in France." As no young printers were available, most of the work was done by French women who did not understand English. In spite of this handicap, editions were fairly free from typographical errors. As there are few "*y*'s" and "*w*'s" in the French language, the supply was soon exhausted and editorial writers and reporters were forced to use English words which did not have these letters in their spelling. While the paper had many features of its namesake in Chicago, it gave most of its space to news of America. It sold for ten centimes or two cents per copy and its yearly rate was fixed at thirty francs, or six dollars. Though designed primarily for circulation among the American soldiers quartered in France, the army edition of *The Tribune* built up a substantial circulation among the English and American residents in Paris. Joseph B. Pierson was its first editor.

ARMY AND CAMP ORGANS

In September, 1917, arrangements were made for the publication of a soldiers' weekly newspaper in most National Army and National Guard camps. The paper to a certain extent was coöperative in that four of its pages were compiled and supplied by the central New York office. These four pages were then sent to the coöperating publisher in the local field. He added the news of the local camp and finished printing the sheet. Distribution was secured through Y.M.C.A. headquarters.

Coöperation was secured from local newspapers because the

soldiers' weekly did not carry advertising and was not sold and there could be no competition with other newspapers. To the credit of the South it should be said that its newspapers were among the first to coöperate in the plan. Early coöperation was secured from *The News-Leader*, of Richmond, Virginia; *The News*, of Birmingham, Alabama; *The Advertiser*, of Montgomery, Alabama; *The Constitution*, of Atlanta, Georgia; *The Telegraph*, of Macon, Georgia; *The Courier-Journal*, of Louisville, Kentucky.

REPRESENTED "SOMEWHERE IN FRANCE"

Represented directly with the First Expeditionary Force to France were the following newspapers and associations: —

The Associated Press.
The United Press.
The International News Service.
The Associated Papers.
The Newspaper Enterprise Association.
The Philadelphia Ledger Syndicate.
The Munsey group of newspapers.
The New York Times and group of newspapers.
The New York Herald Syndicate.
The Chicago Tribune and group of newspapers.
The New York World and group of newspapers.
The New York Tribune.
The Philadelphia North American and group of newspapers.
The Denver Post.
Collier's Weekly.

In addition to these accredited correspondents in the field, a number were permitted to go to Paris with letters to the Maison de la Presse, commending them to the French Government and opening numerous news channels of considerable breadth for them. Included in this second category were numerous magazine writers, as well as newspaper correspondents.

The official army organ overseas was *The Stars and Stripes*. It was self-supporting during the war and at the end had a large surplus, *mirabile dictu*.

OCHS AND HIS "TIMES"

In reporting the World War, *The New York Times* earned an enviable place. It pursued a fearless, aggressive, and constructive campaign from the very beginning of hostilities. It exhibited the greatest ingenuity in securing official documents. Opinions, interviews, speeches of the European statesmen which were of vital import to the news of the day found their way into *The Times* without delay, and without color or fabrication. It maintained an exceptionally able corps of authorities and correspondents at the front to supplement the service of the Associated Press. *The New York Times*, in many ways, did the most distinctive journalistic work of the War. In a time of impersonal journalism, this credit goes naturally to every man who contributed his bit to the success of this truly great newspaper, but it would not be quite fair to omit some special reference to the hand of Adolph S. Ochs, the publisher and owner.

The growth and development of *The Times* under Mr. Ochs has marked an outstanding chapter in the annals of American journalism. The War policy was simply the culmination of a far-seeing campaign which had been progressing with steady momentum and courage since August 18, 1896, when Mr. Ochs bought *The Times*. During the course of those years, Mr. Ochs has not always escaped censure for policies and journalistic ideals. And, here and there, this criticism has been justified, but it does not materially detract from an accomplishment which will come manfully through most of the tests which the discriminating might apply.

This chapter must conclude with the unprinted line which appears in the last column of the last page of the daily newspaper: —

To be continued to-morrow.

Though stopping at a time when the American newspaper is undergoing many changes, it must of necessity be an unfinished chapter — to be edited and revised later. Of nothing can it more truthfully be said, that "no man knoweth what the day or hour may bring forth," than of the newspaper.

CHAPTER XX

JOURNALISM OF TO-DAY

VIEWS AND INTERVIEWS

ATTENTION has been repeatedly called to the fact that journalism is a mirror of the times. It is a mirror of the people in general, and the individual paper is a mirror of its subscribers. Arthur Brisbane in discussing newspaper work once remarked:—

The newspaper is not, as Schopenhauer says, "a shadow on the wall," although many a newspaper is a mere shadow of what a newspaper should be. A newspaper is a mirror reflecting the public, a mirror more or less defective, but still a mirror. And the paper that the individual holds in his hand reflects that individual more or less accurately.

On this point the late Whitelaw Reid, when editor of *The New York Tribune*, said:—

The thing always forgotten by the closest critic of the newspapers is that they must be immeasurably what their audiences make them; what their constituencies call for and sustain. The newspaper cannot uniformly resist the popular sentiment any more than the stream can flow above its fountain. To say that the newspapers are getting worse is to say that the people are getting worse. They may work more evil now than they have ever wrought before, because the influence is more widespread; but they also work more good, and the habitual attitude of the newspaper is one of effort toward the best its audiences will tolerate.

Arthur Twining Hadley, president of Yale University, practically concurred in the opinions just noted when he wrote:—

If we are to have responsible newspapers, the reform must begin with the readers themselves. Most of the men who edit newspapers will give the people the kind of newspapers they want. There will, of course, be exceptionally good editors who will make their papers better than their readers demand, and try to educate the people up to a higher level; just as there will be exceptionally bad editors, who will make papers worse than the readers want, and be the instruments, whether they try to or not, of educating the public down to a lower level. But the average editor will work for the average reader. He cannot be any more independent of the man who buys his goods than the manufacturer or merchant can be. A manufacturer who refuses to produce things that the people want, because he thinks they ought to want something better, will be driven out of business, and so will a newspaper editor. People sometimes talk of "yellow journalism" as if the editors of the yellow journals were solely responsible for their existence. They are responsible to some degree; but to a still larger degree the responsibility lies with the public that will buy and read their news.

Other college presidents share this same view. While president of the University of Minnesota, George Edward Vincent declared: —

The press is more than a business. It is a social service fundamental to the national life, exerting profound influence upon it. The men of the press must recognize the social nature of their task. If the press be a corporation, it is a public service corporation with all of the social responsibility that this implies. The American press reflects the life of all of us, and it affects the life of all of us. We must all share the common task of raising slowly, steadily, courageously this life to a higher level of truth, of justice, of good will. We, the people, make the press what it is. The press can help us to make it and all our national institutions more nearly what they should be.

Those who maintain that the newspaper has outgrown the looking-glass stage, and should be developed along lines of community interest, overlook the fact that the paper which devotes its energies to community welfare is but reflecting the trend of the times. The old-fashioned church, open only on Sunday, has in many communities become the institutional church which not only preaches, but also practices the ideals of its Founder. The American university is taking the torch of learning from its academic seal and using it to light its halls at night for the instruction of those unable either on account of the time or money to take the regular course.

SUPPRESSION OF NEWS

The charge most often brought against the newspaper to-day is that it suppresses news because it fears certain powerful advertisers. This charge is quite different from that of giving free publicity to advertisers in the news columns. Oswald Garrison

Villard, of *The New York Evening Post,* has testified that the newspaper upon which he worked in Philadelphia used to send him to its large advertisers with the statement that "they could have as much space in news columns at any time as they wanted." Undoubtedly, such a condition too often existed during the Period of Financial Readjustment. No such condition, however, obtains to-day. On the other hand, the first charge deserves careful consideration. There has been in a few cities a suppression of news because of fear of advertisers, but it has always been fraught with great danger to the local press. Mr. Villard has admitted that the press of Philadelphia "has never recovered from the blow to its prestige when it actually refused to tell the story of a crime of the member of one of the large drygoods houses." Yet this omission proved the impossibility of suppressing news, for the story appeared in New York papers which sold rapidly in the streets of Philadelphia. The story was taken up and told all over the country through the pages of the monthly magazines and the literary weeklies. The suppression of the news did more harm to innocent members of the firm than had the Philadelphia papers given a whole edition to the story of the crime. The publicity given this incident would indicate that such suppressions are rare.

A controversy arose later between this same mercantile establishment and the city of Philadelphia over the question of fire prevention appliances, etc., required by city ordinances: it came from a movement started by the Alumnæ Committee of Bryn Mawr College which was studying fire prevention in factories, shops, and stores where women and girls were employed. The Bryn Mawr Committee once complained that it had wrestled in vain with the Philadelphia papers to take the matter up and that the local press had refused to mention the store save in the way of kindness. The press of Philadelphia again received rebuke at the hands of publications of national circulation. In commenting on the incident, *The Outlook,* of New York City, called attention to the serious social danger from the muzzling of the newspaper by powerful advertisers.

A letter from the manager of the Philadelphia store to the present writer said: —

Do you mind if we say we feel the condition to which you allude has been represented, we think, in an unfair way?

Unquestionably, the firm was treated unfairly by local papers which suppressed news to which the public was legitimately entitled. In justice to the firm it must be admitted that there were extenuating circumstances which if the Philadelphia papers had recorded would have put the firm before its patrons in quite a different light for the Bryn Mawr Alumnæ knew how to bring pressure upon charge customers.

Another paragraph of the letter from the manager of the store ought to be quoted: —

The matter has been settled amiably and completely by the city authorities of Philadelphia and ourselves, as you, doubtless, observed from the reports of the papers.

The present writer did observe those reports, not merely in papers published outside of Philadelphia, but also in those of that city.

Yet Philadelphia, strange as it may seem, furnishes the honest and conscientious editor with positive proof that readers will not stand any interference on the part of the advertiser in an attempt to control editorial policies. During the heat of the Presidential Campaign of 1912, the page advertisement of a department store, a rival of the one to which reference has just been made, was withdrawn one Friday night from a Philadelphia newspaper. No intimation had previously reached its editor that such a step was contemplated and the action was unaccompanied either by word or letter to throw light upon the subject. Advertising solicitors were instructed to make no inquiry as to the cause of the discontinuance of the advertisement. The editor instructed the staff to make no explanations or comments about the matter. He then left for his old home to visit his mother. He was absent about a week. Upon his return he was notified that the page advertisement would be resumed the following Monday.

The absence of the page for a whole week not only attracted much attention, but caused much comment. Readers of the paper thought that they saw in the absence of the advertisement an act of reprisal against the paper on account of its editorial attitude on national politics. Subscribers put their own interpretation on the disappearance of the advertising and inferred that the paper had been threatened with a loss of advertising unless its editorial policy on politics was modified. Letters and telegrams of protest in large numbers poured in upon the owner of the department store. Their writers threatened to refuse to trade at the store unless the advertising was returned to the newspaper. The advertising was sent back without any condition suggested or implied. The editorial policy of the paper was not changed one iota, although it may have seemed to the public that it was a little more vigorous than ever before.

In passing from Philadelphia to New York, the two stores just mentioned, for branches of them are in both cities, may again be used for purposes of illustration. When the first store opened in New York it wanted to give its name to the thoroughfare upon which its building was located. In spite of the thousands of dollars which it was spending for advertising the press of New York fought the change, although the store was only attempting what it might perfectly legitimately try to do. Later, the store attempted to free the sidewalks in front of its store from "cadets," "mashers," and all other groups of young men who follow the swish of a silken petticoat, as patrons of the store had been annoyed by the insults of these good-for-nothing chaps. It was a fine thing to do. But some one blundered in making a request that any account of this activity of the store be suppressed in the local press. The request simply sent the account of the affair to the first page and put the firm's name in the headline. Otherwise, there probably would have been just passing mention. The store was again badly treated by the newspapers for it obtained undesirable publicity about a condition which undoubtedly existed around other stores whose owners lacked the courage to take up the matter.

When the Bryn Mawr Fire Prevention study was seemingly lacking the coöperation of the Philadelphia papers, a New York evening paper — *The Evening Post*, to render unto Cæsar the things that are Cæsar's — sent a man to Philadelphia to make a quiet investigation and to discuss the situation with the Philadelphia store.   A conference with the store was sufficient without publication to bring about nearly all the changes originally desired. To the unbiased critic it may seem as though the newspaper went out of its own local news field in going to Philadelphia to make the investigation, but *The Evening Post* has ever had a high standard regarding its duty to the public.

George Creel, who was appointed by President Wilson chairman of the Committee on Public Information, in a magazine article published in January, 1917, brought against the press of New York the serious and specific charge that the department stores "can exercise an absolute censorship whenevei they choose to do so." His general conclusion — "The same condition exists in every city large enough to have department stores" — may be dismissed without further discussion because made without any proof to substantiate the generalization. His charge against the newspapers of New York, however, deserves careful consideration because it seemed to be supported by evidence based on the fact that New York papers refused to insert a political advertisement attacking the owner of the second store used for illustration. The article clearly implied that the rejection of the advertisement was due to a fear that the owner of the store might withdraw his advertising. Mr. Creel, however, failed to explain why *The New York Times* rejected the advertisement in view of the fact that the store did not advertise in *The Times* and was therefore without a club to swing at the paper. The insertion of the rejected advertisement — a copy of which lies before the present writer — would make any newspaper subject to a suit for libel. Any man running for public office must assume that his life is going to be open to attack from all points, in order that voters may be properly informed to pass upon his qualifications for office. Quite a different condition obtains in attacks made upon a man not before people for election to office. The New York papers in general and *The New York Times* in particular have refused thousands of dollars worth of advertising where the copy consisted of scurrilous attacks upon character.

For years critics asserted that the most positive proof that the department stores controlled the policies of New York papers was found in the fact that the greatest news story lying around loose was the fire hazard in these stores and that no newspaper had the courage to describe the conditions. Yet when conditions attending employment in the large department stores in New York were publicly taken up at a hearing of the Federal Commission on Industrial Relations, the New York papers printed without suppression the facts brought out at the inquiry, not only about the two stores to which reference has been made, but also about all the larger stores of the city. [For some reason, doubtless best known to city editors, the following assertion by former Chief Guerin of the Bureau of Fire Prevention was omitted: "I must say that the department store managers are fair and ready to do anything within reason to correct existing imperfect conditions." City editors have seen no reason why they should attack fire hazards in department stores when worse conditions existed in many manufacturing plants. They were unable, in spite of several attempts, to arouse the people to the necessity of better working conditions and regretted that it would take a great holocaust like the fire in the Triangle Shirt-waist Factory to arouse the public conscience.

Not long ago the owner of a large department store failed in business. There was a pretty well founded rumor that conditions had not been just right at his store for some time. Because the New York papers did not give any publicity to the matter till the failure was a legal fact, they were accused of suppressing the news because of the advertising revenue derived from the store. Such critics overlooked the fact that such publication might have made the newspapers financially responsible for the failure. During the Panic of 1907 a New York newspaper printed a story that a certain business establishment was on the verge of bankruptcy. It was, and later failed. The owners brought suit against the newspapers and collected heavy damages on the ground that the failure had been caused by the publication of the item. Courts, as Whitelaw Reid, of *The New York Tribune*, pointed out in his lecture on "Journalism" at Yale University, have been rather harsh on newspapers for publishing items of this character and newspapers cannot be blamed for the use of ordinary common sense in such matters.

One incident, unfortunate and distressing, has been tossed

about all over the country to show the control of Boston journalism by the department stores. A woman who was shortly to become a mother was arrested at one of the stores on the charge of shoplifting: she was supposed to have secreted on her person goods taken from counters of the store. While being subjected to a search she was taken ill and serious consequences followed. Her husband, after the loss of the child, sued the store for damages — as he should — and was awarded a verdict rather substantial in amount. The Boston papers, possibly with a single exception, did not — as they should not — print the story even though the testimony was somewhat sensational. For some reason the wishes of the family have been overlooked in a discussion of the incident. If ever there was a just cause for requesting a suppression of news it was here. Such incidents do not concern public welfare and ought to be omitted from the columns of American newspapers. Had there been any miscarriage of justice, there would be some justification for printing the item, but no such condition obtained.

In another city conditions were quite like those in Boston, only there had been several similar incidents, though less disastrous in results. A large store had moved farther uptown and with its larger quarters it had been forced to employ green detectives who frequently made errors. In fact, they made so many blunders that managers of other department stores went to the press with the request for publicity in order that the evil might be corrected. One newspaper publisher told the representatives from the stores, "You can't get publicity for such stuff in my paper, even if all of you withdraw your advertising." He was quite right. Such an incident does not properly belong in a book of this character, but has been inserted because of the prominence it has been given by critics of journalism.

Another Boston incident has attracted much attention. A certain department store in that city desired to unite its two buildings by a covered passageway across a city street. As certain legal technicalities interfered with the construction, the attorney-general of the State rendered an opinion that a municipal permit was not sufficient and that special action of the State Legislature was necessary. *The Evening Transcript* in

Boston printed the opinion of the attorney-general and the advertising of the department store was temporarily suspended in the columns of *The Transcript*. Newspaper critics at once jumped to the conclusion that the store withdrew its advertising in an attempt to dictate policies to *The Transcript* or to punish *The Transcript* for not being more thoughtful of department stores. To these critics the thought never occurred that there might be other reasons for withdrawal of advertising. But even if the critics were right, the incident shows the independence of *The Transcript* and may have impressed the department store with its dependence on newspaper advertising, for it is now one of the most liberal users of space in that publication. Department stores simply cannot get along without the newspapers. The great newspaper strike in Chicago showed the dependence of department stores upon newspapers — a dependence forcibly impressed by the loss of trade through inability to tell patrons about store bargains. Not until the newspapers with their store advertising appeared again on Chicago streets did business become normal.

OPINIONS OF ADVERTISERS

For some reason critics have not gone to department stores for information. A little investigation shows that department stores feel that they have not been treated squarely by newspapers. They assert that a man cannot have a harmless fit in their buildings without some account getting into the newspapers, while he may have as many fits as he chooses in a smaller store without a single line in the newspapers to record the fact. Department stores maintain that every time their delivery wagons have an accident the fact is made known in the press with the name of the store to which the wagon belonged printed conspicuously in the account, while horses attached to wagons of smaller stores may run away and do considerable damage with newspaper readers none the wiser about the event. Department stores feel that the newspapers might render a little editorial assistance in matters of public convenience and public safety such as a bridge joining two buildings occupied by the same store: they assert that the newspapers are unwilling to endorse such enterprises lest the charge be brought against them of being influenced by advertising. Almost every department store has its tale of woe about the lack of coöperation from newspapers in announcing the welfare movements started among employees. On the whole, department stores present just as strong a case against the newspapers as do the critics. Did not this condition obtain, there would be more reason to suspect truth in the charge that advertising possibly influences the news and editorial columns.

OPINIONS OF BUSINESS MANAGERS

Don C. Seitz, business manager of *The New York World*, has testified as follows about the charge that advertisers run the policy of the newspapers: —

I have been for twenty years in the business office of *The New York World* and I do not recall a half-dozen attempts on the part of advertisers to influence it, and of these attempts only one was a matter of public concern about which there were two very fair opinions. We did not accept the advertiser's view. It is some five years since I have had an advertiser ask me to do anything, even in his personal interests, unless perhaps to print a wedding notice, or the mention of some social affair, and in this I rather think the editors treated him more shabbily than if it had been some one else. Good editors are not interfered with on great newspapers. If they were, there would be neither good editors nor great newspapers.

Louis Wiley, business manager of *The New York Times*, in his address on "The Newspaper of To-day" has a long list of items which were published in *The Times* and which mention specifically department stores where omission might have been desired. *The Times* on several occasions has been absolutely fearless in printing such news. On a few occasions it avoided even the appearance of evil. For example, it refused to sell a political party several thousand copies of a certain issue containing an editorial desired for circulation among voters in an approaching election because it feared that readers might think that the editorial was inspired by party allegiance.

On this matter of outside dictation, General Charles H. Taylor, of *The Boston Globe*, once said: —

I can assure those of our friends who are filled with the fear that advertisers and the interests will control the movements, opinions, and news of the prosperous and independent press, that they need not lose any more sleep over *The Globe*. Advertisers and readers alike know that they will be treated with absolute fairness by *The Globe*, because that is the bed-rock basis on which this newspaper has been conducted for forty years and it is the rule which will guide it in the years to come.

In the few instances where powerful interests, whether through ownership or otherwise, have dictated policies which were against the interests of the common welfare, the newspapers thus controlled have lost steadily in circulation and become useless even to their dictators because of lack of influence.

DICTATION OF EDITORIAL POLICY

Another charge frequently brought against the press, somewhat similar to the one just discussed, is that outside financial interests frequently dictate the editorial policy. When Bryan was nominated for President on the Democratic ticket in 1896, there was great consternation among bankers lest his election should disrupt existing monetary standards and ruin the country. While there was no concerted action, independent bankers holding notes of newspapers did have several heart to heart talks with editors and proprietors and threatened to demand immediate payment of financial obligations if Bryan was supported. Be it said to the credit of editors who conscientiously believed in the silver standard that they told bankers "where to get off," that editorial policies were not subject to mortgage or demand notes and that they would welcome the issue if it were presented. They said that they would publish the facts in the case for their readers and were positive that they could raise enough money through popular subscription to continue publication. In other instances editors informed bankers that a suit to collect notes might cause a reduction in the size of their newspapers, but they still had funds enough to print handbills stating the reason for change in form. No such drastic action, however, was necessary, as bankers soon saw that the chief asset of a newspaper was its independence. The newspapers which did change, to a certain extent, their party affiliations did so of their own free will because they believed, as did the majority of the voters of the country, that debased currency was wrong both in theory and in practice. Numerous editors stood by this principle in spite of the opposition of wealthy owners of the silver mines who likewise tried to dictate editorial policies. In a few cases, where bankers did insist that the amount of indebtedness of newspapers to them should be reduced, on account of business conditions, they were but doing what they were requiring of all borrowers — the reduction in loans.

A large advertiser in a certain metropolitan daily did withdraw his advertising because the paper supported Bryan in his presidential aspirations, but later, on finding that he was losing business on account of the absence of this advertising, he tried to have it inserted again. The newspaper informed him very plainly in words to the following effect: "You have tried to dictate to this paper through a threat of withdrawal of advertising. You need to be taught a lesson. You are now out, and out you stay for one year, that the lesson may be forcibly impressed upon your memory." Not until the year was up was he allowed to resume advertising.

PITILESS PUBLICITY

Whether newspapers should give full publicity to crime has been a frequent subject of discussion in periodical literature. No conclusive evidence has ever been brought forth to prove that such accounts increase the amount of crime. On the other hand, only the astigmatic or myopic person fails to see that publicity is a most decided deterrent of crime. E. W. Howe, when editor of The Globe, of Atchison, Kansas, expressed this idea very epi·· grammatically, "The wages of sin is publicity"; Ralph Waldo Emerson knew whereof he spoke when he asserted, "Light is the great policeman." Unquestionably, great sorrow is brought to wives, children, and other relatives by the newspaper accounts of the acts of criminals. The duty of the newspaper, however, is plain: it must protect other wives, children, and relatives who will be brought to grief unless all forms of rascality are exposed and perpetrators of crime brought to justice. Pitiless publicity it must often be, but it is never heartless.

But for the newspaper, crime and corruption would often ex-¦ ist unmolested. A newspaper is a megaphone through which reformers call a city to arms and improve conditions. Just as the physician seeks out a diseased organ, even though he has to cut through pus and false flesh, so the newspaper which lives up to its duty must lay bare the cankered spots of the body politic. There can be no question that the public should know about the vice and corruption in order to combat the evil. J. St. Loe Strachey, editor of *The London Spectator*, thus emphasized this point in his address on "Ethics of Journalism": —

It is good to know, within reasonable limits, the evil that is being done in order that we may lay our plans and bring up our forces to check that evil.

When the Reverend C. M. Sheldon was editing *The Capital* at Topeka, Kansas, for a week in 1900 as Christ would have conducted a newspaper, he defined news as "anything in the way of daily events that the public ought to know for its development and power in a life of righteousness" and therefore excluded details of crime from the columns. In commenting on Dr. Sheldon's attitude toward stories of crime *The World* of New York City went even farther than Mr. Strachey in the matter of such publicity: —

It is painful, but it is a fact that this world is a vast battlefield between good and evil. This being the case it is of the very highest importance that the armies of the good should have the completest, the most accurate and the quickest information as to what the armies of evil are about. The journalist is an officer in the Department of Intelligence of the Armies of the Good. And whether he is working for his pay or for a principle or for both or without any conscious motive whatever, or even with a bad motive, so long as he remains true to the fundamental canon of his creed — "Publicity! Publicity! Publicity!" he is serving the cause of the good. Whenever from any motive, good or bad, he violates that canon he is a traitor to that cause, a giver of aid and comfort to the enemy.

LEGITIMATE SUPPRESSION

The "reasonable limits" mentioned by Mr. Strachey impose an obligation upon the press not to fill its columns with filth and fraud for which there is no justification. In this respect American papers are far more conservative than the English: not a single American newspaper begins to print with such fullness of detail the accounts of certain crimes and divorce trials as are found in the great London papers. Mr. Strachey commended very highly in his address the motto of *The New York Times*, "All the news that's fit to print."

Contrary to the generally accepted opinion, newspapers, even the most sensational, suppress much more than they print in the matter of criminal news. If suppression would serve the people as a whole better, the story of crime is omitted. One illustration, taken from an address by the city editor of a great metropolitan daily before a state city editors' association, will show how conscientious is the city editor worthy of that title: —

Since I have been in —— [1] there was a minister in one of the larger churches there, a high-salaried man, looked up to by his congregation and the city at large and regarded as one of the brightest men in his denomination in the world. It was brought to the ears of a certain city editor — not myself — that this man had been guilty of immoral practices, and men were put to work to run the stories to earth. Those stories were proved, and if they had been printed they would have been the sensation of the nation for a few days. But they never got beyond the city editor, and for this reason — he knew that to print them would disrupt that church, break up several families, and bring sorrow to hundreds of homes. So this is what he did. The minister in question was called in: the facts were shown him and a typewritten agreement handed him. This agreement provided that he was to resign his pulpit, quit the ministry and the city forever, and never again write or speak a word in public. The minister did all that. There was no publicity, and the church was saved, although shocked by the minister's sudden retirement. To-day he is living on a farm, a quiet, studious man.

Had this city editor suppressed the news, without the infliction of the penalty given, he would have been false to his trust. On several occasions where irregularities of conduct in priest and rabbi have been simply suppressed, offenders have gone to other parishes only to disgrace the cloth again. Had full publicity been given in the first instance, results would have been different and certain newspapers could have had a clearer conscience.

[1] I have suppressed the name of the city for the same reason the city editor suppressed the story. — J. M. L.

A paper full of the items suppressed for the good of the community would cause a greater sensation than any which has yet been printed. Even the most sensational newspapers suppress many stories of crime in the interest of the public welfare. News thus suppressed is that to which the community is not legitimately entitled and shows not the weakness, but the strength, of the American press. Newspapers occasionally make mistakes, they are but human institutions, but on the whole, they serve the community well.

PRESENT-DAY ETHICS

In the opinion of the writer the ethics of journalism of to-day are higher than those of any other profession. What the press does is known and read by all men. It does not print one edition for one class of subscribers and another for another. The only exception to this rule was an editor in a Western city who published a somewhat sensational sheet. After the regular edition was run off, he used to "lift" the stories of crime and fill the spaces with reports of acts of kindness, sermons, etc. The second edition consisted of but one copy — the copy which the editor took home to his aged mother. With this single exception, which really amounts to nothing except as an interesting incident, every reader knows exactly where the paper stands. It may be on the wrong side, but it is publicly labeled so that no one is deceived. What other profession can say as much?

How *The Bulletin*, of San Francisco, California, practically unsupported, aroused that city to a realization of the corruption of the Ruef-Schmitz machine is a story too widely known to be retold here. But as *The Bulletin* had sent Abraham Ruef to jail and then asked for his parole, its readers could not understand the attitude of the paper toward the convicted grafter: to them it seemed paradoxical. In answer to a correspondent who was indignant that *The Bulletin* should ask that Ruef be set free, Frémont Older, the editor of *The Bulletin*, explained his change in view as follows: —

I have asked mercy for Ruef because I feel that I did most to bring about his downfall. *The Bulletin* fought Ruef long before the rest of San Francisco woke up. I attacked him with all the invective I could command and all that I could hire. I cartooned him in stripes. I described him on the way to the penitentiary at San Quentin.

I was vindictive, unscrupulous, savage. I went to Washington and enlisted Heney in the fight. William J. Burns came and I persuaded Spreckles to help us. At last, after years of a man-hunting and man-hating debauch, Ruef became what I had longed and dreamed that he might become — a convict.

Then I said to myself: "You've got him. He's in stripes. He is helpless, beaten, chained. You've won. How do you like your victory? How do you enjoy the picture you have painted? Every savage instinct in your nature is expressed in the canvas."

Well, my soul revolted. I thought over my own life, the many unworthy things I have done to others, the injustice, the wrongs, I have been guilty of, the human hearts I have wantonly hurt, the sorrow I have caused, the half truths I have told, the mitigating truths I have withheld, the lies I have allowed to go undenied. I see myself now stripped of all sham and pretense and self-righteousness, holding the key to another man's cell. If society will let me, I want to unlock that barred door and for the rest of my life try to get nearer the spirit of Christ.

In a letter to the writer of this book, Mr. Older enlarged still further upon this change: —

I thought when I wrote the letter, and I think now, that we all approached the graft situation in the wrong spirit. We believed that there was only one way to put an end to municipal corruption and that was by discovering legal evidence against the grafters, indict them, try them in the courts, convict them and send them to the penitentiary. We did not know we were dealing with a disease and that there was no more occasion for hatred and denunciation than there would have been if the city had become infected with a contagious malady, and we had led a crusade to eliminate it. But in those days none of us had any doubt that the jail was the only cure. That was because we had no background of human experience. We believed that men were either definitely good or definitely bad, and that men deliberately decided to be either good or bad, just as a young man would choose a career. So we proceeded on that theory and expended vast sums of money, time, and energy in trying to put the grafters in prison. It happened that the men who had been buying privileges of Schmitz and Ruef were wealthy, and being wealthy were influential, highly respected, and belonged to our most exclusive social circles. Naturally, they did n't relish the idea of wearing stripes in a penitentiary. So they fought back hard and the conflict developed into a bitter war which lasted several years.

If we had used the money, time, and energy in making a quiet investigation of the graft in our city, and had not stopped as soon as we thought we had sufficient evidence to convict, the work would have been more valuable. I think we could have secured more complete confessions from those implicated if we had given them to understand that prison punishment would only be resorted to in the event of their withholding any part of their corrupt activities. We could then have made a complete exposé which would have been educational, and would have had tremendous value to those who are interested in making our civic life cleaner and our methods more efficient. But we did the best we knew at the time. It was certainly a liberal education for me. Some of the others still fail to see it as I do. They cling doggedly to the jail and the prison as the only cure for evil.

UNFAIRNESS OF PAPERS

Still another charge brought against the American newspaper is that it seldom, if ever, prints a speech of any length unless delivered by the President of the United States or some other very distinguished official. Attention is called to the fact that the report often contains nothing except the startling, foolish, or inflammatory utterances of the speaker. A contrast is drawn between the newspapers of to-day and those of Greeley's time when speeches were often reported at length. Such critics, however, fail to make a comparison of the sizes of the newspapers printed during these periods. The average New York newspaper is not much larger to-day than it was then, except for advertising columns — often it has fewer columns devoted to the news. Yet the number of men who make speeches in that city has multiplied to such an extent that a detailed report is now quite an impossibility. Very often, the words quoted of the speaker constitute the only new thing given in the speech, devoted for the most part to generalizations often much better expressed by others. The reading public, like the men of Athens, in Paul's time, is chiefly interested in the new thing and unless the new thing be said, readers prefer newspaper stories of deeds rather than those of speech.

In discussing a complaint of Professor Scott Nearing that he had not been treated fairly by the newspapers, *The World*, of New York, spoke as follows in an editorial: —

It is always a pleasure to discuss journalism with an honest man who knows nothing about it. Professor Scott Nearing, for example, believes that most newspapers are biased or corrupt because they are not disposed to embellish their pages with his long and not very convincing arguments against measures for national defense.

Nothing in this world is easier than for an excited individual to imagine that his failure to make a profound impression is due to somebody's prejudice or dishonesty. Many a humbug gets great space in newspapers — for a season. Many a man of one idea figures briefly in the big headlines. But many a person profoundly in earnest is taken up and quickly set down again because it is found that, after all, he has no true message.

There is hardly a day that does not develop in some line of thought a man or woman, generally young, who has discovered that the inherited experience of the human race in its social and political relations is worthless. If the humdrum newspapers which deal in their ignorant way with life as it is and has been were to accept all these prophets at their self-valuations, this world would be more of a bedlam than it is.

Truth sometimes has to fight for a hearing, but never hopelessly. Folly and presumption are much more likely to receive hasty attention. In most cases it is when folly and presumption have been found out and dropped that we hear of the unfriendliness of the press. Truth recognized and established presents no resolutions of thanks and throws no bouquets. Truth is the great silencer.

Professor Nearing speaks of journalism as a game, which it is not. Journalism is about as serious a profession as sober men ever engaged in. It has its eye upon the past for instruction and upon the future for inspiration guided by that instruction. We wish that Professor Nearing and all other reformers who are in a hurry could be similarly actuated.

POLITICAL ADVERTISING

A criticism brought against the newspaper is that it ought not to allow the insertion of advertisements which advocate policies directly opposed to those stated in the editorial columns. Especially is this true of political advertising inserted by the party whose principles are not advocated by the paper. The justice of this charge is without foundation. It is a good thing for a Republican to read in his party paper the advertisements of the Democratic Party. The advertisement, being officially prepared, is positive assurance to him that its contents have not been colored or warped by the editorial policies of the paper: it is a yardstick by which he may measure the accuracy of the news reports of the rival party. On the basis of sound advertising theory, political advertising should be given, not to papers of like policy, but to opposition papers; the advertising manager of a paper with Republican leanings presented the case squarely when he said to the manager of a Democratic press bureau who objected to the editorial policies of the paper in question: "Whom are you trying to reach, through your political advertising, those who are going to vote for Wilson, or those who are now thinking of voting against him? When you have reached your decision, remember this fact, our paper guarantees a larger circulation among those who are now opposing Wilson than any other paper in the city." To the credit of this Democratic press bureau, be it said that it used large space in the Republican sheet. Political advertising should be inserted not solely to reward papers for party allegiance, but to spread partisan doctrine where it will do the most good; it is for this purpose that people contribute funds to the campaign expenses of the great parties. It must be confessed that in the past much of this political advertising has been too personal and too bitter to be effective among intelligent newspaper readers. More and more, however, political advertising is being prepared on the same sound principles as those which govern general advertising.

EDITORIAL PROSTITUTION

Another so-called weakness of modern journalism is that editorial writers must on special occasions write opinions not believed to be just and right because the chief-of-staff insists that these policies are those of the newspaper. Tiffany Blake, chief editorial writer of *The Chicago Tribune*, put the case in its proper light when he gave this justification of such work. He thought, when a writer was, on the whole, in sympathy with the editorial policies, he might, in minor cases, support certain measures with which he did not agree. Such conduct, Mr. Blake pointed out, was in keeping with the religious and political life of any individual; a man in joining a political party does not necessarily imply that he supports every plank of the platform, but that he thinks that this party comes the nearest to agreeing with his views about the questions of the day; a man joining a church or religious sect may not agree with every article of the creed, but he chooses to become a member because this religious denomination in its larger doctrines favors his views on matters of ethics and spiritual welfare. As a matter of practice, however, an editorial writer on the larger dailies seldom has the disagreeable task of writing what he does not believe. A question is thrashed out at the editorial council and after a decision has been reached as to where the paper shall stand, the writing of the editorial is given to the man to whom the subject most appeals because experience has shown that he can generally produce the most forcible and convincing appeal on the subject.

SIGNED EDITORIALS

This practice in editorial offices shows how impossible are the recommendations of William Jennings Bryan and others that editorial articles should be signed by the names of their writers. In thrashing out a problem at the editorial council different phases of a subject are presented by various members of the staff. The man who writes the editorial frequently accepts ideas from every member of the staff in his presentation of the subject, and he would be guilty of plagiarism if he should attach his name to the editorial. The editorial "we" is the real author of the editorial: the staff, through an individual writer, has spoken for the paper. Only where the editorial staff consists of a single member would there be justification for using Mr. Bryan's suggestion of signed editorials.

CHARTING THE NEWS

A distinguished educator went over a certain New York paper systematically for three months during which time he charted the news as follows: demoralizing, 2295 items; unwholesome, 1684; trivial, 2100; worth-while, 3900 — or thirty-nine per cent. of the total. *The New York World* thought that the educator made out a fairly good case for the newspapers; that thirty-nine per cent. of worth-while news was up to the average quality of achievement in most human activities such as the preaching of sermons, painting of pictures, writing of novels, or what-not.

Other newspapers thought that the newspaper average of worth-while items was higher than thirty-nine per cent. *The Evening Tribune* of Providence, Rhode Island, expressed its views as follows: —

Nobody familiar with the legitimate objects of a newspaper, the ends which it very properly endeavors to serve, would argue that all items that are demoralizing or unwholesome in the sense that they have to do with the misconduct of human beings, with murder or robbery or arson or with worse, if possible, should be entirely ignored. It has been asserted, and with truth, surely, that it will be a sorry day for this or any other country when newspapers are forced to regard what is unwholesome or demoralizing as so commonplace, so much a matter of course, as to be undeserving of treatment as a matter of news, happenings not only of interest, but doings with which all adult persons should be made acquainted. There would speedily be formed a very false and wholly misleading conception of actual conditions of society and the state of the body politic as it is, were all reference to what is demoralizing or unwholesome suppressed. Comparisons by which progress in civilization and moral advance could be measured would be out of the question, of course. Such an ostrich-like procedure or departure would leave us in utter ignorance of existence and its environments; of the life that is being lived; it would tempt us to plume ourselves on virtues that we do not possess; on civic righteousness which is wanting. As for the trivial things of life, who shall draw the line between the important and the unimportant? A very wise philosopher has declared that "under God's mysterious dispensation there are no trifles."

LOCAL INFLUENCE OF READERS

Several writers on journalism have pointed to Charleston, South Carolina, as an example of where newspapers were virtually owned and controlled by a powerful social organization. Attention has been repeatedly called to how the newspapers of that city never report the balls and social activities of the St. Cecilia Society. Critics have overlooked the important fact that newspaper readers have moulded journalism in that city where there is a resentment against publicity, not only about the balls of the St. Cecilia Society, but also about weddings and other social events. Charleston newspaper readers have spoken in no uncertain terms about these matters. No evidence has yet been produced that the newspapers of Charleston have suppressed news to which the public was legitimately entitled and for which there could be any difference of opinion about its affecting the welfare of the city.

VIEWS ON ASSOCIATED PRESS

Answers to certain charges brought against the Associated Press have been made by two men officially connected with that organization. At a luncheon given to Melville E. Stone upon the completion of his twenty-five years of service as general manager, Adolph S. Ochs, publisher of *The New York Times* and an influential director of the organization, said among other things: —

There is a popular superstition that the Associated Press is a monopoly. Yes, it is in the sense that a family monopolizes its personal possessions and its coördination; that is, if it coördinates. I wish to remind you that the Associated Press is, in fact, a family, a club, for it is incorporated as a social club under the State laws of New York. The primary purpose of a social club is to bring into association congenial persons. It is their personality that constitutes all that makes a club congenial. To force an objectionable member into such a club impairs its purpose. So with the Associated Press.

To the charge that the Associated Press has a religious bias, Mr. Stone has replied: —

When we reported the death of Pope Leo XIII in a manner befitting his exalted station, a number of Methodist newspapers gravely asserted that I was a Catholic, or controlled by Vatican influences, although, as a matter of fact, my father was a Methodist clergyman and my mother, as I have said, was the grandniece of a coadjutor of John Wesley. On the other hand, when the Associated Press reported the Marquise de Monstier's renunciation of the Catholic faith, certain Catholic newspapers flew into a rage and asserted that I was an anti-Catholic bigot.

INFLUENCE OF THE PRESS

Ex-President Charles William Eliot of Harvard University believes that an effective bulwark of state may be found in the publicity with which American newspapers are carried on, even though there are many exaggerations, perversions, and inaccuracies in the public press, and that publicity is a new agency for the promotion of the public welfare, especially in industrial grievances and in secret combinations of either capitalists or laborers. Being a constructive critic and seeing American life in all its ramifications, he may well be quoted on the influence of the press: —

The newspapers, which are the ordinary instruments of this publicity, are as yet very imperfect instruments, much of their work being done so hastily and so cheaply as to preclude accuracy; but as a means of publicity they visibly improve from decade to decade and, taken together with the magazines and the controversial pamphlet, they shed more light on the social, industrial, and political life of the people of the United States than was ever shed before on the doings and ways of any people. This force is distinctly new within the century, and it affords a new and strong guarantee for the American Republic.

PRESENT-DAY TENDENCIES

In the larger cities the tendency is toward consolidation of newspapers. The extension of the string of newspapers controlled by William Randolph Hearst and the establishment by *The Chicago Tribune* of *The Illustrated Daily News* in New York City are the exceptions which attract attention to this tendency. Even in New York City, Frank A. Munsey first purchased *The New York Press*, and then, coming into the control of *The New York Sun*, he merged *The Press* with it. Still later, after he had purchased *The New York Herald*, he united it with *The Sun*. He later called the new combination *The Herald* and gave the title *The Sun* to what had been *The Evening Sun*. In Boston, *The Traveler* and *The Evening Herald* have been consolidated and *The Journal* has been merged with *The Boston Herald*. In Chicago, *The Herald* has been combined with *The Examiner*. In Cleveland, *The Plain Dealer* has absorbed *The Leader*. In St. Louis, *The Globe-Democrat* has absorbed *The Republic*.

Similar consolidations may be found in the smaller cities throughout the country. Such consolidations are, of course, welcomed by advertisers, who thereby profit financially. The danger lies in the fact that it becomes more and more difficult for a new paper to establish itself. More and more in the larger cities journalism becomes a fenced field on which appears the sign "No Trespassing." But this tendency to consolidation is not limited to journalism but will be found in all industrial fields.

FUDGE POSTSCRIPT

A history of journalism may well follow in the steps of the newspaper and save till the last a little space into which it may throw the latest items by a "fudge" paragraph. Rollo Ogden, editor of *The New York Evening Post* since 1903, resigned in 1920 to become associate editor of *The New York Times*, of which on the death of Charles R. Miller in 1922 he became editor-in-ohief. *The New York Evening Post* has passed out of the control of the Villard family and is now owned by a syndicate headed by Edwin F. Gay, who was formerly Dean of the School of Business at Harvard University. Willis J. Abbot, who made an interesting experiment with *The United States Daily* in Detroit, is now editor of *The Christian Science Monitor* in Boston. Robert Lincoln O'Brien, who was for many years editor of *The Boston Evening Transcript*, has put *The Herald* on the newspaper map in Boston. Cyrus H. K. Curtis, publisher of *The Saturday Evening Post*, is now publisher of *The Philadelphia Public Ledger*, which was edited, 1864–1894, by George W. Childs. Melville E. Stone has retired as general manager of the Associated Press and has been succeeded by Frederick Roy Martin. Under Mr. Stone's management that Association grew from sixty-three members in 1893 to thirteen hundred members at the present writing, when its annual budget amounts to nearly six million dollars. H. J. Wright as editor and Jason Rogers as publisher have made *The New York Globe* one of the most independent papers in New York City. Victor F. Lawson deserves great credit for the way in which his newspaper *The Chicago Daily News* "covered" the war. A New York newspaper publicly boasted in car-cards that it had the local rights to the war dispatches of *The Chicago Daily News*. Elbert H. Baker has made *The Cleveland Plain Dealer* one of the leading newspapers in the United States. The editor of *The Atlantic Monthly* gives first place as an editorial writer to Frank I. Cobb, the editor of *The New York World*. Walter S. Dickey is now editor and owner of *The Kansas City Journal* and *The Kansas City Post*. *The Hartford Courant* under the editorial control of Charles Hopkins Clark has become a paper of great influence, not only in Connecticut but also in New England.

THE END

INDEX